RTI in Literacy—
Responsive and Comprehensive

Peter H. Johnston, Editor

INTERNATIONAL
 Reading Association
800 BARKSDALE ROAD, PO BOX 8139
NEWARK, DE 19714-8139, USA
www.reading.org

The International Reading Association attempts, through its publications, to provide a forum for a wide spectrum of opinions on reading. This policy permits divergent viewpoints without implying the endorsement of the Association.

Executive Editor, Books   Corinne M. Mooney
Developmental Editor   Charlene M. Nichols
Developmental Editor   Tori Mello Bachman
Developmental Editor   Stacey L. Reid
Editorial Production Manager   Shannon T. Fortner
Design and Composition Manager   Anette Schuetz

Project Editor   Stacey L. Reid

Cover   Design, Adam Bohannon; Photographs (clockwise from top left), ©iStockphoto.com/ Leontura, ©iStockphoto.com/SteveStone, ©iStockphoto.com/peepo, ©Veer Incorporated

The publisher would appreciate notification where errors occur so that they may be corrected in subsequent printings and/or editions.

Library of Congress Cataloging-in-Publication Data

RTI in literacy : responsive and comprehensive / Peter H. Johnston, editor.
    p. cm.
 Includes bibliographical references.
 ISBN 978-0-87207-836-9
 1. Reading--Remedial teaching. 2. School failure--Prevention. I. Johnston, Peter H.
 LB1050.5.R75 2010
 372.43--dc22

                                                        2010007853

This book is dedicated to Marie Clay, who started the concept of RTI, and to my many other intellectual mentors, particularly Terry Crooks, Don Holdaway, David Pearson, George McConkie, and Dick Allington. It is also dedicated to all the teachers who refuse to view children through a narrow, fixed lens and who are prepared to critically examine with colleagues data on their own teaching practices.

CONTENTS

 **Peter H. Johnston** is a Professor at the University at Albany–SUNY where he chairs the Reading Department. He chaired the International Reading Association (IRA) and National Council of Teachers of English Joint Task Force on Assessment Standards and is a member of IRA's Response to Intervention Commission. He has served on the Board of Directors of the National Reading Conference and is currently on the editorial boards of *Reading Research Quarterly, The Elementary School Journal*, and *Literacy Teaching and Learning*, and he reviews for several other scholarly journals.

Peter's research and writing spring from his fascination with children's learning and, no less, teachers' teaching and learning. He believes that education is not simply about delivering information to children or getting them to read faster. Rather, he thinks it is about building a just, caring, democratic society and that doing so will not detract from more obviously practical educational goals such as ensuring that all children acquire productive literacies. As a result, Peter studies the consequences of our teaching and assessment practices for the lives of children and teachers and for the kinds of literacies children acquire.

His most recent books are *Choice Words: How Our Language Affects Children's Learning* (Stenhouse, 2004), *Knowing Literacy: Constructive Literacy Assessment* (Stenhouse, 1997), *Critical Literacy/Critical Teaching: Tools for Preparing Responsive Teachers* (Teachers College Press, 2005, with Cheryl Dozier and Rebecca Rogers), and *Reading to Learn: Lessons From Exemplary Fourth-Grade Classrooms* (Guilford, 2002, with Richard Allington). Peter is the assessment section editor for the *Handbook of Reading Disability Research* (Routledge, 2008). His writing is also published in a wide range of journals including *Harvard Educational Review, Reading Research Quarterly, Literacy Teaching and Learning, Journal of Educational Psychology, Contemporary Educational Psychology, Teachers College Record, The Elementary School Journal, Language Arts, The Reading Teacher*, and *Research Communications in Psychology, Psychiatry and Behavior.*

Peter completed his bachelor's and master's degrees and teacher training in his native New Zealand, which is where he began his teaching career. His master's degree is from the University of Otago in Dunedin and his doctoral degree from the University of Illinois at Urbana-Champaign, which recognized him in 2008 with a Distinguished Alumni Award. Other recognitions include an IRA

Outstanding Dissertation of the Year Award and an Albert J. Harris Award for contributions to research on reading disability, and in 2005, his election to the Reading Hall of Fame. In 2007, his book *Choice Words* topped *Instructor* magazine's list of 12 books every teacher should read.

CONTRIBUTORS

Authors of New Chapters

Sharon A. Craig
Associate Professor, Education
    Department
McDaniel College
Westminster, Maryland, USA

Danielle V. Dennis
Assistant Professor, Literacy Studies
College of Education
University of South Florida
Tampa, Florida, USA

Linda J. Dorn
Professor and Director
Center for Literacy
University of Arkansas at Little Rock
Little Rock, Arkansas, USA

Shannon Coman Henderson
Assistant Professor, Reading
    and Literacy Education
University of Arkansas at Little Rock
Little Rock, Arkansas, USA

Mei Kuin Lai
Professor and Associate Director
Woolf Fisher Research Centre
Faculty of Education
The University of Auckland
Auckland, New Zealand

Anne McGill-Franzen
Professor and Director
Reading Center
University of Tennessee
Knoxville, Tennessee, USA

Stuart McNaughton
Professor and Director
Woolf Fisher Research Centre
Faculty of Education
The University of Auckland
Auckland, New Zealand

Scott G. Paris
Head, Centre for Research
    in Pedagogy and Practice
National Institute of Education
Singapore

Rebecca L. Payne
Assistant Professor, Literacy
    Education
University of Alabama
Tuscaloosa, Alabama, USA

Donna M. Scanlon
Professor of Teacher Education
College of Education
Michigan State University
East Lansing, Michigan, USA

Joan M. Sweeney
Reading Teacher
North Colonie Central Schools
Latham, New York, USA

Authors of Reprints

Richard L. Allington

Doris Alvarez

Bobbie Burnham

Linda J. Dorn

Salli Forbes

Lynn M. Gelzheiser

Mary K. Lose

Carol A. Lyons

Anne McGill-Franzen

Hugh Mehan

P. David Pearson

Tonya Person

Debra S. Peterson

Gwenneth Phillips

Jolene Reed

Michael C. Rodriguez

Donna M. Scanlon

Christopher Schatschneider

Rynell Schock

Barbara Schubert

Robert M. Schwartz

Pauline Smith

Joan M. Sweeney

Beth Swenson

Barbara M. Taylor

Frank R. Vellutino

ACKNOWLEDGMENTS

Sometime in 2006, I was introduced to the Response to Intervention (RTI) provision of the Individuals with Disabilities Education Act. I can't remember who introduced me to it, but I quickly saw its significance. Initially I applauded its potential for improving the lives of many children by reducing the likelihood that they would become learning disabled. In schools, however, I was forced to recognize its potential for doing violence to the learning lives of even more children and their teachers if taken in the wrong direction.

At the time I was caught up in other work that was closer to my heart, and I would have left this problem to others. However, I made the mistake of pointing out the problem to Kathy Champeau of the Wisconsin Reading Association. Her determination to ensure that, for children's sake, we should take the right path on RTI led her to badger me into helping her try to influence the implementation of RTI. Because nobody works harder for children than she does, it is not possible to decline her requests, so I took up the contentious matter of RTI implementation. Besides getting me going on RTI, Kathy helped by asking difficult questions, making helpful observations, and contributing ideas, making important contributions to the discussion guide for the book.

Over the years, conversations with my colleague Donna Scanlon about literacy teaching and learning, interventions, and RTI have helped my understanding enormously, as have my conversations with Frank Vellutino and Dick Allington.

When Karen Wixson and Marge Lipson, chairs of the International Reading Association's (IRA) RTI Commission and editors of the recent book *Successful Approaches to RTI: Collaborative Practices for Improving K–12 Literacy* (IRA, 2010), suggested a book of readings about RTI, they did not flinch when I proposed that I take on the project. I took this as a vote of confidence.

The publications staff at IRA deserves my thanks, particularly Anne Fullerton, who listened to my carping and whining about the state of RTI and put the book on a very fast track. It was Stacey Reid and Shannon Fortner who pushed it along that fast track and who also deserve considerable thanks.

I am also grateful to the authors of the chapters in the book, particularly those who wrote new pieces on quite tight schedules. Drawing on their work in research articles directed toward an academic audience, they agreed to write about that work in a more accessible form.

A Framework for Response to Intervention in Literacy

Peter H. Johnston

W hat does it mean when a child has difficulty acquiring literacy? One historically common view has been that it indicates a lack of intelligence. Though this unhelpful and inaccurate view has not completely disappeared, it began to be displaced in the 1970s by a different view, the idea that, for some children, the problem lies not in a broad intellectual deficit but in a very specific cognitive impairment: a learning disability. In 1975, the Education for All Handicapped Children Act (EAHCA) institutionalized this view, providing an authorized diagnosis and a source of funds to support special instruction for such children. A specific learning disability became defined as

> a disorder in 1 or more of the basic psychological processes involved in understanding or in using language, spoken or written, which disorder may manifest itself in the imperfect ability to listen, think, speak, read, write, spell, or do mathematical calculations.... [The] term includes such conditions as perceptual disabilities, brain injury, minimal brain dysfunction, dyslexia, and developmental aphasia...[but] does not include a learning problem that is primarily the result of visual, hearing, or motor disabilities, of mental retardation, of emotional disturbance, or of environmental, cultural, or economic disadvantage. (U.S. Department of Education, n.d.b)

Since then, schools have been organized to recognize this category of disability, and a separate system with its own funding stream has been set up in schools to manage students who have been recognized as falling into this category.

EAHCA was reauthorized in 1990 as the Individuals with Disabilities Education Act (IDEA). The legislation still presented learning disability as a stable characteristic of the child, but a specific one rather than a more general one. At least in theory, children no longer needed to feel stupid when they had difficulty acquiring literacy. Their difficulty was a specific handicap that was beyond their control. Parents, too, were relieved of that burden and assured

RTI in Literacy—Responsive and Comprehensive, edited by Peter H. Johnston.
© 2010 by the International Reading Association.

that their child would get extra resources such as a reduced teacher–pupil ratio. Because the disability was still seen as a fixed trait beyond anyone's control, teachers, too, no longer needed to feel incompetent when a child was having difficulty acquiring literacy.

Unfortunately, the only way to tell whether a student had a learning disability was to rule out alternative explanations such as intelligence, poverty, culture, and instruction. In practice, this came down to ruling out low intelligence as the explanation. If an IQ test showed that the child was "normal" but reading well below what might be expected for such a student, then the child was considered to have a learning disability. On the other hand, if a test showed the child's IQ to be below normal, then limited reading development was "normal" and nothing needed to be done.

A second problem was that the disability was still considered to be a permanent trait. Consequently, even though the children were to get special education, there was no real expectation that it would eliminate the disability. Indeed, relatively few children exit special education (Carlson & Parshall, 1996). Viewing learning disability as permanent also made it possible to argue that schools should not be responsible for these children's normal growth in literacy, so many low-achieving children (disproportionately minorities) could be removed from accountability testing rolls by classifying them as learning disabled (LD). The numbers of students, particularly minorities, in special education ballooned. In some schools one in five children are classified as LD (e.g., www.education.com/schoolfinder/us/new-york/district/kingston-city-school-district/).

In the years leading up to the 2004 reauthorization of IDEA, other problems became apparent, particularly with the use of the IQ-achievement discrepancy approach to deciding whether a student had a learning disability (Aaron, 1997; Fletcher, 1992; Stanovich, 1991; Vellutino, Fletcher, Snowling, & Scanlon, 2004). Researchers realized that IQ tests were not as independent of culture or socioeconomic status as they were thought to be (Beiser & Gotowiec, 2000). Also, the assessment process provided no instructionally useful information (Vaughn, Levy, Coleman, & Bos, 2002). Another concern was that for some students who were experiencing difficulty it could take two years before the discrepancy was large enough for the child to be classified as LD and thus to have access to special education funding. Often referred to as the "wait to fail" problem, it meant, unfortunately, that once children were classified, the classification became permanent. In part, this was because intervention was begun too late. In part, it was also because special education instruction was not effective at accelerating children's literacy growth after classification.

At the same time, considerable evidence was accumulating showing that early intervention, before children were classified, substantially reduced the number of children entering special education (Scanlon, Vellutino, Small, Fanuele, & Sweeney, 2005; Schmitt, Askew, Fountas, Lyons, & Pinnell, 2005; Vellutino, Scanlon, & Sipay, 1997). Consequently, in 2004 when the U.S. Congress reauthorized IDEA, it made some important changes. In particular, the law allowed schools to use 15% of the money allocated for special education to initiate interventions designed to reduce the number of children classified as LD. This provision became referred to as Response to Intervention (RTI), though the term never actually appears in the legislation.

The logic of RTI was first clearly articulated by Marie Clay (1987) in a classic paper titled "Learning to Be Learning Disabled," in which she argues that learning disability is more often acquired through inadequate instruction than through genetics. Consequently, she argues, before claiming that someone has a learning disability we should rule out the possibility of inadequate instruction—as the law puts it, we must be sure "that underachievement…is not due to lack of appropriate instruction" (U.S. Department of Education, n.d.a).

How the Law Frames RTI in Schools

In the law, the concept of RTI is framed in two ways. The first is as an alternative assessment to the IQ-achievement discrepancy strategy for identifying students who have a learning disability. To accomplish this, the law requires that we document students' response to instruction—"data-based documentation of repeated assessments of achievement at reasonable intervals, reflecting formal assessment of student progress during instruction" (U.S. Department of Education, n.d.a). If a student is not acquiring literacy quickly enough, this frame proposes that the child likely has a learning disability. In other words, it turns our attention toward the qualities of the *student*.

The second framing is an expansion of the law's insistence on "appropriate instruction." The law requires that we use "data that demonstrate that prior to, or as a part of, the referral process, the child was provided appropriate instruction in regular education settings, delivered by qualified personnel" (U.S. Department of Education, n.d.a). However, the law does not specify the nature of instruction or how to determine its quality. If a student is not acquiring literacy quickly enough, this frame turns our attention toward the qualities of *instruction*.

How we frame RTI, then, has major consequences for how we organize our RTI strategy in schools.

RTI as Identification

When RTI is framed as primarily about identifying who is and is not LD, it becomes a measurement problem. The concern is for accurate identification of the disability. The focus is commonly on testing and standardization. The central problem is deciding whether the child is responding sufficiently to instruction. This often leads to frequent standardized testing to get a measure of rate of learning. Rate of learning is important in this frame because a slow rate of learning in response to what is considered scientifically correct instruction indicates a potential disability. Consequently, in this frame, standardization is equally important in instruction. Just as in drug studies, instruction is viewed in terms of standardized, pure, effective ingredients. It is thus common to argue for using standard instructional intervention packets (preferably scripted) for a standard (preferably short) amount of time. The instruction is essentially a standardized test item.

Instructional quality is established in this measurement frame by choosing an intervention shown to be successful, on average, in a research study. If the intervention has been verifiably taught exactly as it was in the research study (referred to as "treatment fidelity") then a child's failure to learn is seen as due to the child's disability. The language used reflects this view of fixed traits and includes terms like "dyslexic," "treatment resister" (Torgesen, 2000), or "chronic non-responder" (Fuchs, Stecker, & Fuchs, 2008).

In this identification-measurement frame, there are often levels, or tiers, of instructional intervention. For example, if a child showed inadequate growth in the classroom (Tier 1), there would be an intervention (Tier 2) that would quantifiably increase the "intensity" or "dosage" (Deshler, 2008) of the instruction. This might be a small-group intervention with more instructional time. If the child still showed inadequate growth, there might be another intervention (Tier 3), perhaps one-to-one instruction for twice the amount of time. If the child still did not improve adequately, a committee could use this failure as an indicator of the child's disability.

How do we know that the instruction is optimal? In this frame, the idea is to choose interventions that have been shown in a scientific study to be effective and to teach exactly as the teaching was done in that study. If the standardized, scientific intervention is not effective initially with a particular student then the dosage should be increased.

This view rests on erroneous assumptions about science and learning. Most important, it assumes that instruction that was effective *on average* with one group of students will be effective with *each* of a new group of students in a new setting and that increasing the amount of the instruction will increase the effectiveness. Wanzek and Vaughn (2008) offer an excellent example of why we cannot count on either of these assumptions. They developed a first-grade intervention and gave one group a "double dose" of instruction. They found the intervention to be effective, but they found no advantage for the additional instruction. Furthermore, although the intervention was effective on average, many students did not benefit from the intervention. In fact, quite a few actually got worse. The percentages of students getting worse by at least half a standard deviation were, in the single intervention, 14% in word identification and 24% in word attack—the primary targets of the intervention. The percentages for the double-dose intervention were 7% on word identification and 35% on word attack; in addition, 14% did worse on comprehension. Therefore, we cannot assume that instruction that was effective on average for one group in one situation will be effective for each student, particularly in a new situation. We cannot assume that when instruction is not effective for a student that providing more of it will make it effective.

The process of standardizing instruction, particularly by scripting it, to know how much instruction was received and whether it was exactly as prescribed has at least two problems. First, it underestimates the importance of human interactions and expertise. Insisting on treatment fidelity in this way is likely to reduce the teacher's ability to adapt instruction to individual students. For example, when a child reads a word incorrectly, a scripted program would prescribe a particular response. However, the response of a teacher with expertise would take into account the context, the nature of the error, the child's processing strategies, and the teaching opportunity offered by the error. Second, this focus on standardized interventions is entirely on children's identification of words rather than on literacy more broadly defined. In part, this is because the more complex the view of literacy the more standardization of instruction becomes transparently problematic.

RTI as Dependent on Effective Instruction

The second framing of RTI in the law presents RTI as centrally about ensuring "appropriate instruction" by "qualified personnel," optimizing instruction to *prevent* the need to classify children as LD. Again, the law requires "data that demonstrate that prior to, or as a part of, the referral process, the child was provided appropriate instruction in regular education settings, delivered by qualified personnel" (U.S. Department of Education, n.d.a). Framing RTI as an instructional problem means interpreting evidence that a child is not profiting from instruction as a reflection of the qualities of instruction more than the qualities of the child. It means assessment practices should provide instructionally relevant information about what the child knows and can do and about the qualities of instruction. This instructional frame emphasizes teacher expertise more than the measurement frame. This part of the law recognizes the evidence that teacher expertise is the most important factor in improving children's learning (Darling-Hammond & McLaughlin, 1999) and reflects the insistence in both the No Child Left Behind Act and IDEA on "highly qualified teachers."

Obviously, "highly qualified" does not mean that we should assign a person with a PhD to work with a child experiencing difficulty acquiring literacy, particularly if that PhD is in, say, urban planning or chemical engineering. Children experiencing the most difficulty acquiring literacy must have the most expert literacy teachers (Clay, 1972, 1985). In principle, this seems uncontroversial. In practice, however, this is often not the case. Often children have a scripted intervention "delivered" by a teacher aide, after which a school psychologist tests them and sends them to a special education teacher. Special education teachers' and school psychologists' training has often been directed toward a broad range of atypical aspects of children's development at a wide range of ages. In general, both have *less* specialized knowledge of literacy instruction than do classroom teachers and certainly literacy specialists. The law that gives us RTI pushes us to reevaluate our ways of thinking about the distribution of expertise and training and professional development of all parties.

How RTI Is Framed in This Book

Most books on RTI to date—and there are many—approach RTI through the measurement-identification frame. This frame preserves the status quo—the idea that we should expect a substantial group of students who have permanent disabilities in the area of literacy and who will likely always have such difficulties

(Fuchs & Fuchs, 2006; Shaywitz, 2003). But McDermott and Varenne (1995) pose the question, "What if the very act of saying there is something wrong, if improperly contextualized, makes [children's] situation worse?" (p. 339) and offer evidence that it is often the case. Because "identification" cannot be accomplished directly through assessment but only as a default interpretation after ensuring appropriate instruction, the first order of business should be providing appropriate instruction rather than identifying who is handicapped. Even if a child becomes classified as LD, the goal must remain the same: optimizing instruction for that child.

This is the approach taken in this book. To capitalize on the promise of RTI in literacy, we turn our attention away from the measurement-identification frame and focus on the instructional frame, emphasizing prevention models, the development of teacher expertise, and institutional learning. These threads run through all sections of the book; however, separate sections emphasize different dimensions of practice.

Section I, "The Logic of RTI in Literacy," consists of one chapter that provides a clear framework for thinking about RTI, and Section II, "High-Quality Classroom Literacy Instruction (Tier 1)," contains three chapters addressing how to optimize regular classroom instruction—what has come to be called Tier 1. Section III, "Literacy Assessment," provides a range of examples of productive assessment practices. Section IV, "High-Quality Interventions in Literacy," the longest section, offers examples of effective instructional interventions intended to avoid some of the problems with many current implementations. The four chapters in Section V, "Professional Development and Teacher Expertise," reveal the significance and nature of teacher expertise in the context of RTI. The final section, "Systemic Intervention," provides examples of systemic intervention, emphasizing the fact that RTI should not be a matter of simply applying quick fixes. At all levels of schooling, children encounter difficulties, and children, teachers, and administrators come and go. Schools must be able to provide a stable environment for learning both for children and for teachers.

Part of the stable environment should be a strong learning community. We assume that part of reading this book is to develop a learning community to figure out how best to engage RTI in particular school settings. To that end, there is a Discussion Guide provided as an appendix to the book. If you are reading the book in a group, this Discussion Guide should be read early on.

We have evidence that it is possible to prevent most children from developing serious difficulties in becoming literate, and RTI offers us an important opportunity to accomplish this. The chapters in this book offer ways to capitalize on this opportunity with a real sense of the complexity and the practical details of doing so. Based on the available research, we adopt the position that the bottom line in RTI is optimizing instruction for particular students in particular contexts. This requires increasingly expert teachers collecting instructionally useful data on each child and on their own teaching, and circumstances in which they can make productive use of it. None of this can be purchased in canned packages.

REFERENCES

Aaron, P.G. (1997). The impending demise of the discrepancy formula. *Review of Educational Research, 67*(4), 461–502.

Beiser, M., & Gotowiec, A. (2000). Accounting for native/non-native differences in IQ scores. *Psychology in the Schools, 37*(3), 237–252. doi: 10.1002/(SICI)1520-6807(200005)37:3 <237::AID-PITS4>3.0.CO;2-N

Carlson, E., & Parshall, L. (1996). Academic, social, and behavioral adjustment for students declassified from special education. *Exceptional Children, 63*(1), 89–100.

Clay, M.M. (1972). *Reading: The patterning of complex behaviour.* Auckland, New Zealand: Heinemann.

Clay, M.M. (1985). *The early detection of reading difficulties: A diagnostic survey with recovery procedures* (3rd ed.). Auckland, New Zealand: Heinemann.

Clay, M.M. (1987). Learning to be learning disabled. *New Zealand Journal of Educational Studies, 22*(1), 155–173.

Darling-Hammond, L., & McLaughlin, M.W. (1999). Investing in teaching as a learning profession: Policy problems and prospects. In L. Darling-Hammond & G. Sykes (Eds.), *Teaching as the learning profession: Handbook of policy and practice* (pp. 376–411). San Francisco: Jossey-Bass.

Deshler, D.A. (2008, July 1). Fidelity! Fidelity! Fidelity!—What about dosage? [Web log message]. Retrieved October 7, 2008, from www.rtinetwork.org/Connect/Blog/Fidelity-Fidelity-Fidelity-What-About-Dosage

Fletcher, J.M. (1992). The validity of distinguishing children with language and learning disabilities according to discrepancies with IQ: Introduction to the special series. *Journal of Learning Disabilities, 25*(9), 546–548.

Fuchs, D., & Fuchs, L.S. (2006). Introduction to Response to Intervention: What, why, and how valid is it? *Reading Research Quarterly, 41*(1), 93–99. doi:10.1598/RRQ.41.1.4

Fuchs, D., Stecker, P.M., & Fuchs, L.S. (2008). Tier 3: Why special education must be the most intensive tier in a standards-driven, No Child Left Behind world. In D. Fuchs, L.S. Fuchs, & S. Vaughn (Eds.), *Response to Intervention: A framework for reading educators* (pp. 71–104). Newark, DE: International Reading Association.

McDermott, R., & Varenne, H. (1995). Culture as disability. *Anthropology & Education Quarterly, 26*(3), 324–348. doi:10.1525/aeq.1995.26.3.05 x0936z

Scanlon, D.M., Vellutino, F.R., Small, S.G., Fanuele, D.P., & Sweeney, J.M. (2005). Severe reading difficulties, can they be prevented? A comparison of prevention and intervention approaches. *Exceptionality, 13*(4), 209–227. doi:10.1207/s15327035ex1304_3

Schmitt, M.C., Askew, B.J., Fountas, I.C., Lyons, C.A., & Pinnell, G.S. (2005). *Changing futures: The influence of reading recovery in the United States.* Worthington, OH: Reading Recovery Council of North America.

Shaywitz, S.E. (2003). *Overcoming dyslexia: A new and complete science-based program for reading problems at any level.* New York: Knopf.

Stanovich, K.E. (1991). Discrepancy definitions of reading disability: Has intelligence led us astray? *Reading Research Quarterly, 26*(1), 7–29. doi:10.2307/747729

Torgesen, J.K. (2000). Individual differences in response to early interventions in reading: The lingering problem of treatment resisters. *Learning Disabilities Research & Practice, 15*(1), 55–64. doi:10.1207/SLDRP1501_6

U.S. Department of Education. (n.d.a). Identification of specific learning disabilities [Topical brief]. In *Building the legacy: IDEA 2004.* Retrieved February 9, 2010, from idea.ed.gov/explore/view/p/%2Croot%2Cdynamic%2CTopicalBrief%2C23%2C

U.S. Department of Education. (n.d.b). Specific learning disability. In *Building the legacy: IDEA 2004.* Retrieved February 9, 2010, from idea.ed.gov/explore/view/p/%2Croot%2Cstatute%2CI%2CA%2C602%2C30%2C

Vaughn, S., Levy, S., Coleman, M., & Bos, C.S. (2002). Reading instruction for students with LD and EBD: A synthesis of observation studies. *The Journal of Special Education, 36*(1), 2–13. doi:10.1177/00224669020360010101

Vellutino, F.R., Fletcher, J.M., Snowling, M.J., & Scanlon, D.M. (2004). Specific reading disability (dyslexia): What have we learned in the past four decades? *Journal of Child Psychology and Psychiatry, and Allied Disciplines, 45*(1), 2–40. doi:10.1046/j.0021-9630.2003.00305.x

Vellutino, F.R., Scanlon, D.M., & Sipay, E.R. (1997). Toward distinguishing between cognitive and experiential deficits as primary sources of difficulty in learning to read: The importance of early intervention in diagnosing specific reading disability. In B.A. Blachman (Ed.), *Foundations of reading acquisition and dyslexia: Implications for early intervention* (pp. 347–380). Mahwah, NJ: Erlbaum.

Wanzek, J., & Vaughn, S. (2008). Response to varying amounts of time in reading intervention for students with low response to intervention. *Journal of Learning Disabilities, 41*(2), 126–142. doi:10.1177/0022219407313426

SECTION I

The Logic of RTI in Literacy

This first section of the book is composed of a single chapter, "Response to Intervention: An Overview: New Hope for Struggling Learners" by Donna M. Scanlon and Joan M. Sweeney. It provides a brief overview of the development and logic of RTI and a clear, perhaps prototypical example of a successful, thoroughly researched approach to RTI. The format of the approach—the three-tier model—is common to many RTI programs and is often viewed as standard operating procedure. What is unfortunately less common is Scanlon and her colleagues' (Scanlon, Vellutino, Small, Fanuele, & Sweeney, 2005; Vellutino & Scanlon, 2002) highly successful approach to instructional intervention, which is the key to the success of their efforts. Referred to as the Interactive Strategies Approach (ISA), its practicalities and logic are later described in some detail by these authors in Chapter 10, "Kindergarten Intervention: Teaching to Prevent Reading Difficulties." Interested readers can find a more theoretical elaboration in an article by Vellutino and Scanlon (2002). This instructional approach is also the foundation of the successful professional development intervention described in Chapter 14, "Reducing the Incidence of Early Reading Difficulties: Professional Development for Classroom Teachers Versus Direct Interventions for Children."

In this first chapter, Scanlon and Sweeney remind us of some concepts introduced by Marie Clay. First, to be successful, an intervention must enable the slowest literacy learners to learn faster than their average and above-average peers. Although this seems counterintuitive to many, unless it happens, the gap between the more and less successful will continue to grow. Second, they remind us of the importance of *early* intervention so the less successful students have less distance to cover to catch up to their more successful peers, and so that confusion and motivational issues are less likely to complicate their progress.

Prior to engaging in their successful intervention research, Scanlon and her colleague Frank Vellutino systematically researched and debunked many of the myths surrounding the concept of dyslexia (e.g., Vellutino, 1987; Vellutino, Fletcher, Snowling, & Scanlon, 2004). They have shown that there are specific cognitive and linguistic differences among students that make it harder for some children to acquire literacy (Vellutino, Scanlon, & Sipay, 1997; Vellutino et al., 1996). However, in that same research, through their intervention, they have shown how those cognitive and linguistic differences can be overcome so that not only can children who appear to have real handicaps be taught to read and write but, as a consequence, the cognitive and linguistic differences diminish. In other words, as these children learn to read, the cognitive and linguistic skill differences that appeared to predispose them to be unsuccessful in literacy learning begin to disappear.

REFERENCES

Scanlon, D.M., Vellutino, F.R., Small, S.G., Fanuele, D.P., & Sweeney, J.M. (2005). Severe reading difficulties, can they be prevented? A comparison of prevention and intervention approaches. *Exceptionality, 13*(4), 209–227. doi:10.1207/s15327035ex1304_3

Vellutino, F.R. (1987). Dyslexia. *Scientific American, 256*(3), 34–41.

Vellutino, F.R., Fletcher, J.M., Snowling, M.J., & Scanlon, D.M. (2004). Specific reading disability (dyslexia): What have we learned in the past four decades? *Journal of Child Psychology and Psychiatry, 45*(1), 2–40. doi:10.1046/j.0021-9630.2003.00305.x

Vellutino, F.R., & Scanlon, D.M. (2002). The Interactive Strategies approach to reading intervention. *Contemporary Educational Psychology, 27*(4), 573–635. doi:10.1016/S0361-476X(02)00002-4

Vellutino, F.R., Scanlon, D.M., & Sipay, E.R. (1997). Toward distinguishing between cognitive and experiential deficits as primary sources of difficulty in learning to read: The importance of early intervention in diagnosing specific reading disability. In B.A. Blachman (Ed.), *Foundations of reading acquisition and dyslexia: Implications for early intervention* (pp. 347–380). Mahwah, NJ: Erlbaum.

Vellutino, F.R., Scanlon, D.M., Sipay, E.R., Small, S.G., Pratt, A., Chen, R.S., et al. (1996). Cognitive profiles of difficult-to-remediate and readily remediated poor readers: Early intervention as a vehicle for distinguishing between cognitive and experiential deficits as basic causes of specific reading disability. *Journal of Educational Psychology, 88*(4), 601–638. doi:10.1037/0022-0663.88.4.601

Response to Intervention:
An Overview:
New Hope for Struggling Learners

Donna M. Scanlon and Joan M. Sweeney

Most children who are classified as learning-disabled are identified because of difficulties with reading. Since the 1970s, the process for identifying a child as learning-disabled, or reading-disabled more specifically, has had, as a central criterion, the requirement that there be a substantial discrepancy or difference between the student's measured intellectual ability and his or her measured reading achievement. This approach to LD classification was implicitly based on the belief that IQ and achievement should be strongly related. That is, it was believed that children whose IQ was unusually high should, in general, be relatively high achievers academically and that children whose measured IQ was relatively low should be relatively low achievers. When this close relationship was not evident, particularly when IQ was substantially higher than academic achievement, it was believed that there must be something inherently wrong with the student's ability to learn. In other words, it was believed that the student was unable to learn (i.e., he or she was learning-disabled). This foundational belief about the meaning of a discrepancy between intellectual ability and academic performance was institutionalized in the United States with the passage of Public Law 94-142 in 1975.

However, there were a variety of criticisms of this IQ-Achievement Discrepancy approach to the identification of learning-disabled students, and these criticisms led to a good deal of research, particularly in the area of early reading development, that demonstrated that the hypothesized close relationship between intellectual ability and reading ability does not exist in the early primary grades. In fact, there is only a weak relationship between intelligence

RTI in Literacy—Responsive and Comprehensive, edited by Peter H. Johnston, published by the International Reading Association. This chapter reprinted from Scanlon, D.M., & Sweeney, J.M. (2008). Response to Intervention: An Overview: New Hope for Struggling Learners. *Educator's Voice, 1*, 16–29.

and reading achievement in the early primary grades (Adams, 1990). Moreover, Vellutino, Scanlon, and Lyon (2000) demonstrated that, among children who experience difficulty in learning to read, there is little if any relationship between the children's measured IQ and their response to intervention designed to reduce reading difficulties. Findings such as these argue strongly against the use of an IQ-Achievement Discrepancy approach to learning disabilities classifications, particularly for children in the primary grades (see Vellutino et al., 2000 for a more comprehensive review).

Response to Intervention (RTI) is the most commonly cited alternative to the discrepancy approach. It involves identifying children who are not meeting grade-level expectations and who are presumably at risk for continuing to lag behind their peers early on and providing instructional modifications (interventions) for these children that are instituted early in their educational careers. The students' progress is closely monitored to determine whether and when additional modifications need to be made or whether the interventions can be discontinued because the student is performing at or close to grade level. The goal of the instructional modifications is to accelerate the children's rate of growth so that they will be able to meet grade-level expectations. In an RTI model, when appropriately intensified and targeted interventions fail to lead to accelerated progress in learning, the child would be considered for possible LD designation.

The call for using RTI as a major component of LD classification grew out of a substantial body of research that indicates that many children who demonstrate early reading difficulties can overcome those difficulties if provided with intensified assistance in developing literacy skills and strategies. The roots of that research may be traced to an article published by Marie Clay in 1987 titled "Learning to be Learning Disabled" in which she asserts that many children who are identified as learning-disabled (at least in reading) qualify for that classification not because there is some-thing inherently wrong with the child but because the child's early instruction was not sufficiently responsive to their instructional needs. Clay argued that consideration for LD classification should be delayed until substantial efforts had been made to help the child to overcome his or her early difficulties. Clay's Reading Recovery program, which is an intensive (one-to-one) intervention for struggling first-grade readers was, in fact, developed for the purpose of accelerating the progress of children who demonstrated difficulties at the early stages of learning to read. Clay argued that children who continued to demonstrate reading difficulties despite such intensive support may be appropriately identified as learning-disabled.

Since Clay's 1987 article, a substantial amount of research demonstrated that instructional interventions are effective in reducing the incidence of early reading difficulties. In fact, it is now widely acknowledged that, for the majority of children who demonstrate difficulties at the early stages of learning to read, long-term reading difficulties can be prevented through early and appropriately targeted reading intervention (Denton et al., 2005; Scanlon, Vellutino, Small, Fanuele, & Sweeney, 2005, Torgesen, Alexander, Wagner, Rashotte, Voeller, & Conway, 2001; Vellutino, Scanlon, Small, & Fanuele, 2006; Vellutino, et al. 1996; Vaughn, Linan-Thompson, & Hickman, 2003). Some of this research has also demonstrated that, for many children, classroom and small-group interventions can serve to accelerate the development of early reading skills, thereby reducing the number of children who need more intensive one-to-one interventions (O'Connor, Fulmer, Harty, & Bell, 2005; Scanlon, Gelzheiser, Vellutino, Schatschneider, & Sweeney (in press); Scanlon et al., 2005). Indeed, some have estimated that the provision of high-quality classroom instruction, by itself, could substantially reduce the incidence of early reading difficulties (Lyon, Fletcher, Fuchs, & Chhabra, 2006). However, without such instructional interventions, many children who struggle at the early stages of learning to read continue to struggle throughout their academic careers (Juel, 1988) and many are ultimately identified as reading-disabled (Vellutino et al., 1996; O'Connor et al., 2005).

These various strands of research stimulated federal legislation that sought to apply the scientific knowledge on a broad scale. The No Child Left Behind Act (2002) and the Individuals with Disabilities Education Improvement Act (IDEIA, 2004) were both driven by this research. Indeed, the IDEIA was the first federal legislation permitting and encouraging the use of alternative approaches, such as RTI, to the identification of learning-disabled children.

Most RTI models involve using a "tiered" approach to the implementation of instructional modifications. In a tiered approach, instruction is gradually intensified for low-performing students who do not show accelerated growth with less intensive instruction. Intensification may be accomplished by providing more time in instruction, smaller instructional groupings, or both. In most models, the first tier of intervention occurs at the classroom level and is provided by the classroom teacher. Children receiving such intervention are monitored for a period of time and, if they do not show accelerated progress, they are provided with an additional tier of instruction. Tier 2 instruction is generally provided in addition to (rather than instead of) classroom instruction and is provided by a specialist teacher in a small group context. Once again, the students' progress is monitored. In some RTI models, children who do not show accelerated progress when provided with Tier 2 intervention are considered for possible LD classification. In other models, an additional tier of intervention (Tier 3) is provided before consideration for LD classification. In either case, it is the documentation of limited progress over a protracted period of time, in spite of multiple attempts to adjust the amount or type of instruction the child receives, that serves as a major criterion in deliberations regarding classification.

Thus, there is fairly universal agreement that the characteristics of a child's instructional experiences must be weighed heavily in attempts to determine whether lack of progress is due primarily to underlying learning difficulties or to insufficient instructional intervention. Despite this area of agreement, there are many aspects of an RTI approach about which there is considerable diversity of opinion with regard to how aspects of an RTI approach might be operationalized in schools. To date, there is only limited scientific evidence to guide schools in their implementation planning. Thus, the goal of this article is not to attempt to answer the multiple questions that still exist, but rather to provide a brief description of what an RTI approach might look like in a school and to provide a structure that schools might use in thinking through the options that need to be considered in developing their RTI approaches. The model we present is consistent with the research that we and our colleagues have been engaged in over the last 15 years and with the general conceptualization of RTI.

A Suggested RTI Model

Drawing on the extensive research that we and our colleagues have done that has focused on preventing reading difficulties, in what follows, we describe a model for RTI implementation in the early primary grades that, in our view, would be reasonable. The model calls for beginning to address differences in literacy-related knowledge and skills as soon as they are noticed so as to maximize the likelihood that achievement gaps can be closed rather than allowed to grow.

Tier 1 Instruction

In this model, all entering kindergartners would be assessed on a measure of early literacy skills such as The Primary Reading Inventory (TPRI, Texas Education Agency, 2005) or the Phonological Awareness Literacy Screening (PALS; University of Virginia). These and other measures provide benchmarks that allow for the identification of children who are at increased risk of experiencing difficulties in learning to read. For children scoring below the benchmark, the classroom teacher would monitor their progress more closely and would provide more intensive and targeted instruction in early literacy skills. This does not mean the teacher would provide these children with an entirely different instructional program. Rather, the teacher would devote a portion of the time allocated for language arts instruction to providing children identified for close monitoring with small group instruction that specifically meets them where they are relative to the classroom curriculum. The children identified for close monitoring need to progress at a faster rate than their peers who are already meeting grade level expectations. Therefore, they need to learn more in a given period of time than do their higher-performing peers. Additional instructional support will be needed to accomplish this goal. Ideally, the classroom teacher would form small instructional groups of children who are similar in their early literacy status. This would allow the teacher to offer instruction that is specifically targeted to meet the differing needs of the children in the various groups (i.e., the instruction would be differentiated). Ideally, the children in the close monitoring group would receive instruction in smaller groups, more frequently, and/or for longer periods of time. In other words, they would receive more intensive instruction than would the children who began the school year with skills that were closer to or above grade-level expectations. Small group instruction would, of course, constitute only a portion of the language arts instruction provided during the course of the school day. Read alouds, shared reading, writing, and a variety of other aspects of language arts instruction would be offered in a whole class context.

As noted, the progress of the children in Tier 1 should be monitored more closely than that of the children in the rest of the class. Virtually all RTI models call for some formal documentation of progress. However, there is, at this point, no widely accepted standard for how often such assessments should be used. Indeed, recommendations regarding frequency vary substantially with some suggesting that assessments be conducted as often as twice per week (Christ, 2006; Safer & Fleischman, 2005) while others (such as ourselves) have utilized formal assessments only three or four times a year (Scanlon et al., 2005). However, it is generally agreed that a record of progress needs to be maintained as it is this record that is used to determine whether a change needs to be made in the intensity of support being offered to each child.

There are also substantial differences of opinion with regard to the type of instrument that should be used for progress monitoring. An extensive discussion of the issue of progress monitoring is beyond the scope of this article. However, it is important to note that, in the intervention research that we and our colleagues have done, we have used a combination of standardized assessments administered three or four times per year and informal, ongoing assessments guided by checklists completed by teachers to monitor progress. This approach to progress monitoring is distinctly different from approaches that involve frequent assessment of isolated skills such as the speed with which children can name letters or words, or segment words into phonemes. There is growing concern that the use of speeded measures of isolated skills as the sole index of progress will lead to the unintended consequences of children being fast and accurate in such things as word reading but inattentive to the meaning of what they are reading (Johns, 2007; Paris, 2005; Pearson, 2006; Samuels, 2007). We share this concern and would add that such assessments provide teachers with far less information upon which to base instructional decisions than do informal observations that take note of the children's knowledge, skills, strategies, and attitudes and not just how quickly they can apply isolated skills. In fact, we would argue that informal assessment should be an ongoing process that occurs during the course of instruction and thus, essentially, occurs in every instructional interaction as the teacher makes note of how the children respond to the lesson and reflects on how instruction might need to be modified in order to facilitate student learning.

It is important to note that the main purpose of frequent progress monitoring is to ensure that children who are not making sufficient progress toward meeting grade level expectations do not go unnoticed. Teachers who are knowledgeable about early literacy development and who are working closely with young children in small groups are likely to be acutely aware of which children are making limited progress. Indeed, classroom teachers are particularly likely to be able to identify children who are making limited progress because these teachers, unlike teachers who work exclusively with students who are receiving intervention, are working with children who demonstrate a broader range of literacy skills.

Tier 2 Intervention

Children who do not show the accelerated progress in Tier 1 that would allow them to attain benchmark performance levels by the end of the school year would be provided with additional instructional support or Tier 2 intervention.

Tier 2 instruction is provided in addition to ongoing Tier 1 classroom-based instruction and should be provided by a teacher who has specialized knowledge of how to promote development in the targeted area. Generally, Tier 2 instruction would be provided in a small group context (maybe three or four students) several times a week.

As with many aspects of RTI approaches, there is no general agreement regarding the relationship between Tier 2 intervention and the classroom curriculum. In implementing an RTI approach, schools sometimes assume that Tier 2 instruction should involve the implementation of a program that is different from the classroom program and specifically and exclusively targets foundational skills such as phonics or phonemic awareness. In our intervention research, on the other hand, we utilized an instructional approach that was tailored to the children involved and took into account both what the children knew and were able to do, and what they needed to learn in order to benefit from their classroom language arts instruction (Scanlon, et al., 2005; Vellutino et al., 1996; Vellutino, Scanlon, & Lyon, 2000). No packaged or scripted programs were employed. In contrast, Fuchs and Fuchs (2006) suggest that scripted and prescribed programs are reasonable alternatives for intervention purposes as they eliminate the need to have expert teachers engaged in the intervention. Clearly, there is a great need for additional research to address this issue. In the interim, there is reason to be cautious about broad scale implementation of tightly scripted programs that may limit the teachers' ability to respond to their students. Indeed, the U.S. Department of Education's What Works Clearinghouse, which has provided evaluations of several educational interventions, finds remarkably little evidence that widely marketed interventions have a positive effect on student learning (www.whatworksclearinghouse .org). And, at least as of the date that this article was finalized, the only program that this site identifies as having potentially positive impact on overall reading performance is Reading Recovery, an intervention approach which relies heavily on teacher decision-making.

It should also be noted that there is abundant research indicating that student outcomes in the general population are more closely tied to the quality of teaching than to characteristics of the instructional program adopted (Darling-Hammond, 2000; Haycock, 2003; Taylor & Pearson, 2002; Tivnan & Hemphill, 2005). We would argue strongly that the children who struggle the most with literacy acquisition need the most expert teaching if we are to help them achieve the kind of accelerated learning that is needed to close their initial achievement gaps. Thus, we would argue against the adoption of a tightly scripted intervention program at either Tier 2 or Tier 3 and would argue instead for an intervention approach that supports the children in learning the content of their classroom language arts curriculum.

Tier 3 Intervention

To return to the general model of a tiered approach, children who are receiving Tier 2 interventions are monitored closely as in Tier 1. In many cases, with the intensified instruction provided through the combination of Tier 1 and Tier 2 instruction, children experience accelerated gains and therefore interventions can be discontinued. However, some children continue to make limited progress. One option for these children is to intensify instruction even further by providing them with very small group or one-to-one instruction (Tier 3). While the notion of providing one-to-one instruction may sound formidably expensive, it is important to note that if Tiers 1 and 2 have been effective, there should be only a small number of children who qualify for Tier 3 intervention. However, children who qualify for Tier 3 intervention are likely to be in greatest need of expert teaching in order to accelerate their learning because for these children the teachers need to very carefully tailor the instruction offered such that it accounts for the child's current knowledge and skills and prepares the child to benefit from ongoing class-room instruction as much as possible.

Following a period of Tier 3 intervention (in this model), the children who demonstrate only limited or no growth following several months of intensive, expert instruction might be considered for classification as learning-disabled. However, it is important to note that such a designation should not be taken as a signal to discontinue efforts to build the student's literacy skills. It is just an acknowledgement of the fact that, given current funding realities in schools, it is generally not possible to continue intensive Tier 3 instruction indefinitely. Less-intensive instructional interventions, while they are likely to be less powerful, should nevertheless be maintained for the children who are ultimately identified as learning-disabled.

At far right is a graphic representation of the generalized three-tiered RTI model discussed above. To summarize the workings of the model, students who perform substantially below grade-level expectations at the beginning of the school year are identified for close monitoring and are provided with one or more tiers of intervention depending upon their degree of growth at each tier. Children who demonstrate accelerated growth at Tier 1 and perform at or above the desired level (however it is assessed) would exit the tiers and be served by the regular classroom program. Children who show limited or no acceleration in growth in Tier 1 would be provided with Tier 2 intervention which is provided by a specialist teacher in a very small group. Tier 2 intervention would be provided in addition to ongoing Tier 1 intervention. The progress of Tier 2 children would be monitored for a sufficient period of time to determine whether they show the growth needed to meet grade level expectations.[1] Those

METHODOLOGY

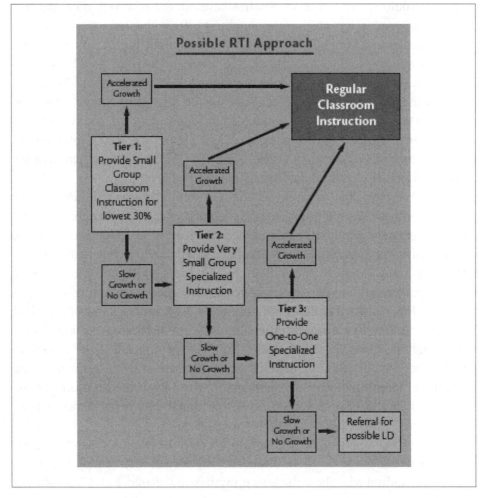

who demonstrate limited or no growth would receive Tier 3 intervention. This very intensive intervention would be provided in addition to Tier 1 supports. That is, the student would receive literacy instruction from both the classroom teacher (Tier 1) and the specialist teacher (Tier 3) to allow accelerated progress. Children who continue to show limited growth despite gradually intensifying interventions provided by expert teachers over a protracted period of time might ultimately be considered for LD classification.

In discussing the model provided above, we spoke in broad generalities and did not provide guidance on such important questions as when a child might enter the tiers and how long a student might spend at given tiers. There is little research to guide decision-making about these questions. Thus, a perusal of the literature would reveal that some studies have offered relatively short periods of intervention at each of the tiers while others offer longer term interventions.

The studies that have been done differ in terms of the types of interventions offered as well as the duration of each tier. Therefore it is not possible to confidently prescribe a timeline for interventions and decision-making. However, based on our research, we would advocate for the implementation of Tier 1 for the first two or three months of kindergarten followed by the addition of Tier 2 for children who are not showing accelerated progress. Tier 2 intervention would be maintained throughout the remainder of the kindergarten year for those children who continue to demonstrate limited growth.

At the beginning of first grade, all children would be assessed. Intervention planning for those scoring below the specified benchmark would depend on the children's performance levels and instructional history in kindergarten. Thus, children who demonstrated the most limited growth during kindergarten might begin Tier 3 at the start of the school year. Children who had been in Tier 2 in kindergarten and had demonstrated reasonably good growth might be continued in Tier 2 at the beginning of first grade. Children who never qualified for intervention in kindergarten or who made accelerated progress with Tier 1 alone, might be offered a period of Tier 1 only in first grade as their low initial performance may be due to limited literacy experience and engagement during the summer months. In general, intervention planning at the beginning of the school year should take the children's instructional and performance history into account.

As the school year progresses, performance on the progress monitoring assessments would guide decisions about the intensity of intervention that is offered with children who show the least growth being offered Tier 3 intervention for the longest period of time that is manageable given the resources available. In our opinion, a minimum of 15 to 20 weeks of daily Tier 3 intervention should be offered before a referral is made for special education or consideration of a learning-disabled classification. However, we should note that some children do not begin to show acceleration until they have had many weeks of intensive intervention. For these children, ideally, intensive intervention would be maintained once that acceleration begins and continued until the student consolidates his or her skills.

Summary

This paper provides an overview of response to intervention, which we argue is an important step forward in addressing the instructional needs of children who begin school with limited early literacy skills. Rather than providing children with "the gift of time," which was once thought to be the appropriate response to children who lagged behind their peers at the early stages of learning to read, an RTI approach involves attending to the instructional needs of young children as soon as those needs can be identified in the hopes of closing achievement gaps before they have the opportunity to grow and become debilitating. A substantial amount of research now indicates that early reading difficulties can be prevented through appropriate instructional interventions. Thus, a major value of an RTI approach is that it has the potential to reduce the number of children who are inappropriately identified as learning-disabled.

There are, at this point, more questions about RTI implementations than there are answers. While the research community will continue to explore these critical questions, federal and state legislation is encouraging schools to begin to utilize RTI as a preferred method for determining whether children should be considered for learning-disability designation. This is good news for children who experience early difficulties with school. It is now widely recognized that the "wait to fail" model in which struggling learners languished in schools while waiting for the discrepancy between their intellectual and academic abilities to grow large enough to qualify them for "services" is not acceptable. With the reauthorization of the IDEA, schools are encouraged to allocate instructional resources in a preventive fashion. As a result, schools have the potential to substantially reduce the number of children who are inappropriately identified as learning-disabled and to enhance the learning experiences of all children who struggle during the early school years.

In conclusion, it is important to note that the extant research that supports the use of an RTI approach to learning-disability classification focuses primarily on literacy learning in the early primary grades. There is little to no research on the applicability of an RTI model in the upper grades and in other academic domains. The lack of research in these areas does not, of course, argue against attempts to institute substantial remedial efforts before learning-disability classification is considered. On the contrary, efforts at remediation would seem to be the first response to any learning difficulties. However, the model that might be adopted in these situations might be substantially different than what was outlined above. For example, it may not make sense to institute a period in which an older child receives Tier 1 intervention only. Rather, older learners who are performing substantially below grade level expectations are likely to be in greater need of a swift and more intensive response to their difficulties. The absence of research to guide our thinking should not limit our response to children who are in need of intervention.

NOTE

[1] As with many aspects of RTI, there is no clear research evidence that provides guidance on how long children should be served at each tier before decisions are made regarding whether intervention should be intensified or discontinued. In our own research, interventions for kindergartners were provided for a total of approximately 50 half-hour sessions with sessions occurring twice per week for most of the school year. Children who continued to demonstrate substantial difficulty at the beginning of first grade received daily one-to-one (Tier 3) instruction for 75 to 125 sessions.

REFERENCES

Adams, M.J. (1990). *Beginning to Read: Thinking and Learning About Print*. Cambridge, MA: MIT Press.

Christ, T.J. (2006). Short-term estimates of growth using curriculum-based measurement of oral reading fluency: Estimating standard error of the slope to construct confidence intervals. *School Psychology Review, 35*, 128–133.

Clay, M. (1987). Learning to be learning disabled. *New Zealand Journal of Educational Studies, 22*, 155–173.

Darling-Hammond, L. (2000). Teacher quality and student achievement: A review of state policy evidence. *Education Policy Analysis Archives, 8*(1), 1–42.

Fuchs, D., & Fuchs, L.S. (2006). Introduction to response to intervention: What, why and how valid is it? *Reading Research Quarterly, 41*(1), 93–99.

Haycock, K. (2001). *Closing the achievement gap. Educational Leadership*. Alexandria, VA: Association for Supervision and Curriculum Development.

Johns, J. (2007). Monitoring progress in fluency: Possible unintended consequences. *Reading Today, 24*(6), 18.

Juel, C. (1988). Learning to read and write: A longitudinal study of 54 children from first through fourth grades. *Journal of Educational Psychology, 80*, 437–447.

Lyon, G.R., Fletcher, J.M., Fuchs, L., & Chhabra, V. (2006). Learning disabilities. In E. Mash & R. Barkley (Eds.), *Treatment of childhood disorders* (3rd ed., pp. 512–591). New York: Guilford.

Mathes, P.G., Denton, C.A., Fletcher, J.M., Anthony, J.L., Francis, D.J., & Schatschneider, C. (2005). The effects of theoretically different instruction and student characteristics on the skills of struggling readers. *Reading Research Quarterly, 40*(2), 148–182.

O'Connor, R.E., Fulmer, D., Harty, K.R., & Bell, K.M. (2005). Layers of reading intervention in kindergarten through third grade: Changes in teaching and student outcomes. *Journal of Learning Disabilities, 38*(5), 440–455.

Paris, S.G. (2005). Reinterpreting the development of reading skills. *Reading Research Quarterly, 40*(2), 184–202.

Pearson, P.D. (2006). Foreword. In Goodman, K.S. (Ed.), *The truth about DIBELS: What it is, what it does* (pp. v–viii). Portsmouth, NH: Heinemann.

Safer, N., & Fleischman, S. (2005). How student progress monitoring improves instruction. *Educational Leadership, 62*, 81–83.

Samuels, S.J. (2007). The DIBELS tests: Is speed of barking at print what we mean by reading fluency? *Reading Research Quarterly, 42*(4), 563–566.

Scanlon, D.M., Gelzheiser, L.M., Vellutino, F.R., Schatschneider, C., & Sweeney, J.M. (in press). Reducing the incidence of early reading difficulties: Professional development for classroom teachers vs. direct interventions for children. *Learning and Individual Differences.*

Scanlon, D.M., Vellutino, F.R., Small, S.G., Fanuele, D.P., & Sweeney, J.M. (2005). Severe reading difficulties—Can they be prevented? A comparison of prevention and intervention approaches. *Exceptionality, 13*(4), 209–227.

Taylor, B.M., & Pearson, P.D. (Eds.). (2002). *Teaching reading: Effective schools, accomplished teachers.* Mahwah, NJ: Erlbaum.

Tivnan, T., & Hemphill, L. (2005). Comparing four literacy reform models in high-poverty schools: Patterns of first-grade achievement. *The Elementary School Journal, 105*(5), 419–441.

Torgesen, J.K., Alexander, A.W., Wagner, R.K., Rashotte, C.A., Voeller, K.K.S., & Conway, T. (2001). Intensive remedial instruction for children with severe reading disabilities. *Journal of Learning Disabilities, 34*(1), 33–58.

Vaughn, S., Linan-Thompson, S., & Hickman, P. (2003). Response to treatment as a means of identifying students with reading/learning disabilities. *Exceptional Children, 69*(4), 391–409.

Vellutino, F.R., Scanlon, D.M., & Lyon, G.R. (2000). Differentiating between difficult-to-remediate and readily remediated poor readers: More evidence against the IQ—Achievement discrepancy definition of reading disability. *Journal of Learning Disabilities, 33*(3), 223–238.

Vellutino, F.R., Scanlon, D.M., Small, S.G., & Fanuele, D.P. (2006). Response to Intervention as a vehicle for distinguishing between reading disabled and non-reading disabled children: Evidence for the role of kindergarten and first grade intervention. *Journal of Learning Disabilities, 39*(2), 157–169.

Vellutino, F.R., Scanlon, D.M., Sipay, E.R., Small, S.G., Pratt, A., Chen, R., et al. (1996). Cognitive profiles of difficult-to-remediate and readily remediated poor readers: Early intervention as a vehicle for distinguishing between cognitive and experiential deficits as basic causes of specific reading disability. *Journal of Educational Psychology, 88*, 601–638.

SECTION II

High-Quality Classroom Literacy Instruction (Tier 1)

Educators' professional commitment demands that children receive high-quality instruction. IDEA requires it. This section of the book is about improving the quality of instruction in classrooms—the place where most children learn to read and write. Nonetheless, there are large differences across schools and classrooms in terms of the proportion of children for whom this is true. Although this is not the longest section of the book, it is probably the most important. If regular classroom instruction were optimal for each child, few if any children would find themselves handicapped by learning disabilities. If that happened, we would avoid the complications of interventions and additional layers of personnel and record keeping.

This section of the book, then, turns our attention to answering the question, What are the characteristics of high-quality instruction? The first chapter in the section, Chapter 2, "What I've Learned About Effective Reading Instruction From a Decade of Studying Exemplary Elementary Classroom Teachers" by Richard L. Allington, reviews the basic characteristics of effective literacy instruction. This work is based on his and others' research on the characteristics of exemplary teachers, particularly that supported by the federally funded Center on English Learning and Achievement project. His "six T's" of time, texts, teaching, talk, tasks, and testing provide a valuable heuristic for reflection on, and productive conversations toward, improving practice.

The second chapter in this section, Chapter 3, "Reading Growth in High-Poverty Classrooms: The Influence of Teacher Practices That Encourage Cognitive Engagement in Literacy Learning" by Barbara M. Taylor, P. David Pearson, Debra S. Peterson, and Michael C. Rodriguez, is based on their work in high-poverty urban classrooms in the federally funded Center for the Improvement of Early Reading Achievement project. They document classroom practices that encourage cognitive engagement in literacy learning. Their findings are particularly important in the context of current emphases in RTI instruction. For example, they found that in grades 2 through 5, the greater the emphasis on phonics instruction, the lower the growth in reading. They found that comprehension improves when teachers use higher level questions—which turn out to be more engaging. Placing routine skills instruction ahead of engaging conversation about books would be a poor instructional decision. The heart of successful classroom teaching, they remind us, lies in the decisions the teacher makes.

Taylor and her colleagues found that teachers who group students for instruction are more effective, and for literacy learning, the guided reading group is central. The final chapter in the section, Chapter 4, "Decisions, Decisions: Responding to Primary Students During Guided Reading" by Robert M. Schwartz, takes us inside the guided reading group to understand effective teachers' decisions more clearly. In contrast to the previous two chapters, this chapter offers a microanalysis of classroom interaction, in which Schwartz turns our attention to the nature and significance of the moment-to-moment decisions teachers make and how to make them more effective.

Each of these chapters makes clear the nature and significance of teachers' expertise, which, along with the importance of systemic commitment to the development of that expertise, forms the focus of Section V.

CHAPTER 2

What I've Learned About Effective Reading Instruction From a Decade of Studying Exemplary Elementary Classroom Teachers

Richard L. Allington

It seems that, finally, those who make education policy—at the local, state, and federal levels—have begun to recognize just how much good teachers matter. A series of studies have confirmed what was probably obvious from the beginning. Good teachers, effective teachers, matter much more than particular curriculum materials, pedagogical approaches, or "proven programs."[1] It has become clearer that investing in good teaching—whether through making sound hiring decisions or planning effective professional development—is the most "research-based" strategy available. If we truly hope to attain the goal of "no child left behind," we must focus on creating a substantially larger number of effective, expert teachers.

Effective teachers manage to produce better achievement regardless of which curriculum materials, pedagogical approach, or reading program they use. I am not going to try to understand why it has taken education so long to recognize what other industries recognized almost from the start—expertise matters. Instead, I am going to describe what the teaching of exemplary elementary teachers looks like and challenge school administrators to examine whether their daily practice and longer-term planning are designed to foster such teaching. In other words, I believe that school administrators should be crafting policies that ensure that more effective teachers are created each year in their schools.

For much of the past decade my colleagues and I at the National Research Center on English Learning and Achievement have been studying some of the

RTI in Literacy—Responsive and Comprehensive, edited by Peter H. Johnston, published by the International Reading Association. This chapter reprinted from Allington, R.L. (2002). What I've Learned About Effective Reading Instruction From a Decade of Studying Exemplary Elementary Classroom Teachers. *Phi Delta Kappan, 83*(10), 740–747.

best elementary school teachers in the U.S.[2] These teachers were selected primarily from schools that enrolled substantial numbers of poor children and schools that reflected the racial, ethnic, and linguistic diversity of the nation. We observed first- and fourth-grade teachers from six states (New York, Texas, New Hampshire, California, Wisconsin, and New Jersey). We spent at least 10 full instructional days, and often more, observing, interviewing, and videotaping in each teacher's classroom. Two books, a number of articles, and related technical reports provide documentary details (the books and articles are cited throughout, and the technical reports, along with research summaries, can be found at http://cela.albany.edu).

We studied teachers who had been found to be particularly effective in developing reading and writing proficiency. Over the course of the study, however, it became clear that the teachers we were studying developed students' academic proficiencies well beyond the ability to score higher on reading and writing achievement tests (though the evidence we gathered also demonstrated that these teachers produced significantly better performance on standardized tests as a matter of course).

The hundreds of days of classroom observation and the hundreds of interviews with teachers and students provided a clear picture of what good elementary teaching looks like. Below I sketch six common features—the six T's of effective elementary literacy instruction—that we observed in exemplary elementary classrooms.

Time

These teachers maintained a "reading and writing versus stuff" ratio that was far better balanced than is typically found in elementary classrooms.[3] In other words, these teachers routinely had children actually reading and writing for as much as half of the school day—around a 50/50 ratio of reading and writing to stuff (stuff is all the other things teachers have children do instead of reading and writing). In typical classrooms it is not unusual to find that children read and write for as little as 10% of the day (30 minutes of reading and writing activity in a 300-minute—five-hour—school day). In many classrooms, a 90 minute "reading block" produces only 10 to 15 minutes of actual reading—that is, less than 20% of the allocated reading time is spent reading. Worse, many classrooms devote only 20 minutes of the entire school day—less than 10%—to actual reading (including reading in science, social studies, math, and other subjects).[4]

When stuff dominates instructional time, warning flags should go up. This is true even when the activity, in some form, has been shown to be useful. For example, research supports activating students' background knowledge before reading[5] and holding discussions after reading.[6] But spending most of a 90-minute reading block on building background knowledge seems an unlikely strategy for improving reading proficiencies. Three to five minutes of this activity would be sufficient.

There is also a lot of stuff going on in less effective class rooms that is not supported by reliable evidence for *any* amount of use (e.g., going through test-preparation work books, copying vocabulary definitions from a dictionary, completing after-reading comprehension worksheets).

Extensive reading is critical to the development of reading proficiency.[7] Extensive practice provides the opportunity for students to consolidate the skills and strategies teachers often work so hard to develop. The exemplary elementary teachers we studied recognized this critical aspect of instructional planning. Their students did more guided reading, more independent reading, more social studies and science reading than students in less effective classrooms. But the teachers' instructional planning involved much more than simply allocating lots of time for reading and writing.

Texts

If children are to read a lot throughout the school day, they will need a rich supply of books they can actually read. This seems a simple statement of fact. But there also exists a large and potent research base that supports supplying children with books of appropriate complexity.[8] This research began in the 1940s and has continued into this new millennium.

Simply put, students need enormous quantities of successful reading to become independent, proficient readers. By successful reading, I mean reading experiences in which students perform with a high level of accuracy, fluency, and comprehension. When a 9-year-old misses as few as two or three words in each hundred running words of a text, the text may be too hard for effective practice. That text may be appropriate for instructional purposes, but developing readers need much more high-success reading than difficult reading. It is the high-accuracy, fluent, and easily comprehended reading that provides the opportunities to integrate complex skills and strategies into an automatic, independent reading process.

The exemplary teachers we studied too often had to teach against the organizational grain. They rejected district plans that required all children to be placed in the same textbook or trade book (and do the same worksheets on the same day). They recognized such schemes for what they are: truly anti-scientific, non-research-based fads designed more, it seems, to exert administrative power than to produce high levels of student achievement.

Unfortunately, these exemplary teachers too often had to spend both their personal time and their personal funds to locate and purchase the texts needed to effectively teach the children they were assigned. Some were lucky to work in "smart" organizations: organizations that supported them and provided a rich and expansive supply of texts to promote children's learning across the school day (multilevel texts for social studies and science as well as for reading classes); organizations that knew that "one-size-fits-all" contradicts virtually everything we have learned about effective teaching.

Students of all achievement levels benefited from exemplary teaching, but it was the lowest achievers who benefited most.[9] In the classrooms of exemplary teachers, lower-achieving students spent their days with books they could successfully read. This has not typically been the case in less effective classrooms.[10] In too many schools, lower achieving readers receive appropriate reading materials only when they participate in special-support instruction (e.g., special education resource rooms, Title I in-class support, bilingual education blocks). In other words, in too many cases the lower-achieving students receive, perhaps, an hour of appropriate instruction each day and four hours of instruction based on grade-level texts they cannot read. No child who spends 80% of his or her instructional time in texts that are inappropriately difficult will make much progress academically.

The exemplary teachers we studied noticed that the highest-achieving students 1) received a steady diet of "easy" texts—texts they could read accurately, fluently, and with good comprehension—and 2) consistently outgained both the average-achieving students and the lower-achieving students, year after year. They also noticed that motivation for reading was dramatically influenced by reading success. They acted on these observations by creating multi level, multisourced curricula that met the needs of the diverse range of students in their classrooms.

Teaching

Obviously, part of good teaching is planning instructional time and selecting appropriate books. But here I want to focus more on the notion of *active instruction*—the modeling and demonstration of the useful strategies that good readers employ. Much of what many administrators might consider teaching behaviors involves little or no active instruction.[11] Much of what many teachers consider teaching is little more than assignment and assessment. Somewhere along the way, active teaching—explicit explanation, direct teaching—has been lost in the shuffle of thinking about classroom instruction.

The exemplary teachers in our study routinely gave direct, explicit demonstrations of the cognitive strategies that good readers use when they read. In other words, they modeled the thinking that skilled readers engage in as they attempt to decode a word, self-monitor for understanding, summarize while reading, or edit when composing. The "watch me" or "let me demonstrate" stance they took seems quite different from the "assign and assess" stance that dominates in less effective classrooms.[12]

The dominance of the assign-and-assess model has been too little written about, but the truth is that "instruction" of this nature is of little benefit to all but the few students who have already acquired a basic understanding of the strategy that is the focus of the lesson. As Marilyn Jager Adams pointed out in her analysis of traditional phonics programs, when teachers assign a worksheet that requires children to fill in the missing vowel, only children who already know the correct response can successfully do the task.[13] And *they* don't need the practice. Children who do not know which vowel to put in the blank space cannot acquire that knowledge from the worksheet. They need actual teaching. In other words, the missing-vowel worksheet is an *assessment* of who already knows the vowel patterns, not an instructional activity that will teach the vowel pattern.

Likewise, when assigned a story to read and questions to answer at the end, children who have developed the appropriate strategy to use while reading can respond correctly, but those who have not developed it cannot.[14] And these latter children cannot acquire the strategy from the end-of-story questions. They need someone to actually teach it to them—someone who can model and demonstrate its use.[15]

The exemplary teachers seemed to realize that most commercial instructional packages provide no useful information on the direct and explicit teaching of skills or strategies. The scripts one typically finds in teachers' manuals accompanying commercial packages may offer a "definitional" model (for example, explaining that the main idea is the author's most important idea about a topic), but they offer little in the way of helping children develop useful reading strategies (for example, showing how to determine the relative importance of the various ideas an author might present on a topic).

Thus these teachers took on the responsibility of crafting explicit demonstrations of skills and strategies. For example, to demonstrate the use of the deletion strategy when teaching summarization, they would first list the various ideas an author presented in a persuasive paragraph through a line-by-line analysis—a watch-me-do-this lesson. Then they would demonstrate through a think-aloud process the strategy of deleting redundant, trivial, and subordinate information until they had arrived at the summary statement.

These teachers offered models of useful strategies—decoding strategies, composing strategies, self-regulating strategies—as separate lessons to the whole class, to targeted small groups, and to individual students in side-by-side instruction. In fact, it is this plethora of instructional activity that truly sets these teachers apart and explains much of their effectiveness with lower-achieving students.[16]

We have a wealth of studies demonstrating the power of active teaching, especially for children who struggle to learn to read and write. But expert teaching requires knowing not only how to teach strategies explicitly but also how to foster transfer of the strategies from the structured practice activities to students' independent use of them while engaged in reading. A real concern is that, when instruction becomes too explicit, children never learn when and how to use the strategies profitably and successfully in their independent reading.

Talk

Like the teaching component, classroom talk is under-researched. We saw fundamental differences between the nature of the classroom talk in the exemplary teachers' classrooms and the talk typically reported in classroom observational studies. First, we observed the exemplary teachers fostering much more student talk—teacher/student and student/student—than has previously been reported. In other words, these exemplary teachers encouraged, modeled, and supported lots of talk across the school day. This talk was purposeful talk, though, not simply chatter. It was problem-posing, problem-solving talk related to curricular topics.[17]

It wasn't just more talk but a different sort of talk than is commonly heard in classrooms. The interrogational nature of most classroom talk has been well documented. Teachers pose questions, children respond, teachers verify or correct. That is the dominant pattern observed in study after study, grade after grade.[18] The classroom talk we observed was more often conversational than interrogational. Teachers and students discussed ideas, concepts, hypotheses, strategies, and responses with one another. Teachers posed more "open" questions, to which multiple responses would be appropriate. For instance, consider the different types of after-reading questions below:

Question 1: So, where were the children going after all?

Question 2: So, what other story have we read that had an ending like this one?

Question 3: Has anyone had a problem with a pet, like the boy in the story?

Responses to question 1 are strictly limited to a single "correct" answer as dictated by the story content. But questions 2 and 3 offer the opportunity for multiple "correct" responses. In addition, while a response to the first question leads only to a teacher reply of "Right" or "Wrong," the others lead to follow-up teacher queries along the lines of "Explain how the endings are similar" and "Tell us more about how your pet problem was like the problem in the story." While question 1 allows the teacher to assess whether the student has used a strategy appropriately, questions 2 and 3 offer the opportunity to examine the thinking—the strategy as it is being used—and to continue instruction. Question 1 assesses recall; questions 2 and 3 assess a broader understanding and help make children's thinking visible.

The nature of classroom talk is complicated and too little understood. While there is evidence that more "thoughtful" classroom talk leads to improved reading comprehension,[19] especially in high-poverty schools,[20] we still have few interventions available that focus on helping teachers develop the instructional skill to create such classrooms, and few of the packaged programs offer teachers any support along this line. The classroom talk we observed was highly personalized, providing targeted replies to student responses. Teacher expertise was the key, not a scripted, teacher-proof instructional product.

Tasks

Another characteristic of these exemplary teachers' classrooms was greater use of longer assignments and less emphasis on filling the day with multiple, shorter tasks. In these classrooms students often worked on a writing task for 10 days or more. They read whole books, completed individual and small-group research projects, and worked on tasks that integrated several content areas (reading, writing, and social studies).

The work the children in these classrooms completed was more substantive and challenging and required more self-regulation than the work that has commonly been observed in elementary classrooms. We observed far less of the low-level worksheet-type tasks and found a greater reliance on more complex tasks across the school day and across subjects. Perhaps because of the nature of this work, students seemed more often engaged and less often off-task than researchers in other classrooms have reported.

Another factor related to student engagement was that the tasks assigned by exemplary teachers often involved student choice. We described the instructional environment as one of "managed choice." Students did not have an unlimited range of task or topic choices, but it was less common to find every student doing the same task and more common to observe students working on similar but different tasks. For instance, in a fourth-grade unit on insects, each child caught an insect and brought it to class. The students then sketched their insects using magnifying glasses to discover detail. These sketches were then labeled for body parts (thorax, abdomen, antennae, and so on). Students also observed the insects in their natural environments and jotted field notes about behaviors and habits. They wrote short descriptions based on these notes and constructed models of the insects from craft materials. Finally, they presented their insects to their classmates and then posted their sketches, models, and descriptions on the classroom wall, where classmates could review them.

Choice of this sort has been shown to lead to greater student ownership of and engagement with the work.[21] Another interesting outcome is that the diversity of student work makes it more difficult for students (and perhaps teachers) to rank that work from best to worst. A low-achieving student may have selected one of the more interesting insects to study and display. Peers see the new information on an interesting bug, instead of comparing the low-achieving student's work to their own on an identical insect worksheet.

Testing

Finally, these exemplary teachers evaluated student work and awarded grades based more on effort and improvement than simply on achievement. Thus all students had a chance to earn good grades. Achievement-based grading—whereby the best performances get the best grades—operates to foster classrooms in which no one works very hard. The higher-achieving students don't have to put forth much effort to rank well, and the lower-achieving students soon realize that even working hard doesn't produce performances that compare well to those of higher-achieving students. If you are a lucky low achiever, hard work gets you a C in an achievement-based grading scheme.

The complexity, though, of effort-and-improvement grading lies in the fact that teachers must truly know each of their students well in order to assign grades. They have to be able to recognize growth and to track or estimate the student effort involved. The exemplary teachers often used a rubric-based evaluation scheme to assign grades. Improvement was noted based on where students started and where they ended up, rather than on the latter alone.

Another impact of the effort-and-improvement evaluation model was that it shifted much of the responsibility for earning grades over to the students. Students could not assign bad grades to "unluckiness," since the evaluation scheme was rather transparent to them. The rubrics provided the information they needed to improve their grades.

The fourth-grade exemplary teachers we studied did acknowledge that the effort-and-improvement grading scheme required careful explanation to parents, who were more familiar with achievement-based grading. However, none of the teachers reported much parental resistance, perhaps because the teachers were typically able to describe in substantive detail just what a child needed to do to achieve a better grade.

I must also note that we observed almost no test-preparation activity in these classrooms. None of the teachers relied on the increasingly popular commercial test-preparation materials (e.g., workbooks, software). Instead, these teachers believed that good instruction would lead to enhanced test performance. The data bore out their beliefs. It was in the less effective teachers' classrooms (which we observed as part of a substudy) that we found test-preparation activity. It seems that less effective teachers truly don't know what to do and, as a result, drift toward the use of packaged test-preparation activities in the hope that they will make up for less effective teaching throughout the year.

Summary

In reducing a complex activity to a list of key features, there is always the risk of oversimplification. Such seems to be the case here. While the six T's offer a shorthand, of sorts, for describing exemplary teaching in the elementary grades, they also oversimplify the complex nature of good teaching. For instance, the six T's actually operate interactively. It seems highly unlikely that we could develop teaching that reflects any single T alone.

For instance, if we want to increase substantially the amount of reading that children do (and I would argue that this is one absolutely crucial step toward enhancing reading proficiency), it is important to give children books they *can* read and choices regarding which books they *will* read. Likewise, crafting a supportive conversational environment in which students talk to their teachers and to their peers about the books they are reading is an important component for sustaining increased reading. And active teaching of useful reading strategies expands the array of books that children are able to read. Finally, shifting evaluation to focus on effort and improvement enhances students' motivation for reading.

In other words, creating and supporting exemplary teaching of the sort we observed is complicated. It really seems unfortunate that so many of the exemplary teachers we studied were forced to teach against the organizational grain. These teachers had to reject school and district plans that put the same reader, trade book, textbook, or workbook on every child's desk. They had to reject scripted lessons, pacing schedules, and grading schemes that presented a one-size-fits-all model for instruction. Too often they had to search out appropriate instructional texts and materials on their own because the one text that the school or district provided was not of appropriate difficulty for most students and failed to offer the sort of accurate and engaging information that might entice students into sustained and effortful study. Worse, in too many cases, these teachers were forced to spend their own funds to purchase the materials they needed to teach the students they were assigned.

Exemplary teaching should not be so hard to accomplish. Schools and school districts must take more responsibility for providing instructional and curricular support so that exemplary teaching becomes more common and requires far less effort. Good teaching should not have to work against the organizational grain.

In closing, I will note that few of these exemplary teachers gave much credit to their school districts for the development of their expertise. Some pointed to administrators who allowed them to experiment, encouraged them to "break the mold," and told them not worry about test scores or about following the organizational plan. But most credited other exemplary teachers for supporting them and encouraging them to become better teachers and to assume greater professional responsibility for the success of their students. These teachers seemed to understand that professional responsibility meant choosing how to teach, what to teach, and with what sorts of curricular materials and tasks: they rejected the low-autonomy/high-account ability models that seem increasingly popular with advocates of "proven programs."[22]

Instead, these teachers elected a high-autonomy/high-accountability model. They seemed to feel no particular pressure from state testing schemes, perhaps because their students performed so well. At the same time, because they were the architects of the instruction offered in their classrooms, they reported a greater sense of responsibility for student outcomes. In other words, these teachers accepted the professional responsibility for developing high levels of reading proficiency but insisted on the autonomy to act on their expertise.[23]

Educational leaders might do well to consider the nature of the instruction these teachers offered. They might do well to ask whether current school policies seem likely to foster this sort of teaching. They might ponder how the organizational plan, including the professional development opportunities and the curricular schemes, currently work to foster or undermine the emergence of exemplary elementary classroom teaching.

In the end, enhanced reading proficiency rests largely on the capacity of classroom teachers to provide expert, exemplary reading instruction. Our study of these exemplary teachers suggests that such teaching cannot be packaged. Exemplary teaching is not regurgitation of a common script but is *responsive* to children's needs. In the end it will become clearer that there are no "proven programs," just schools in which we find more expert teachers—teachers who need no script to tell them what to do. The question for the education profession—teachers, principals, professors, and policy makers—is, Are we creating schools in which every year every teacher becomes more expert?

NOTES

[1] Richard L. Allington and Peter H. Johnston, "What Do We Know About Effective Fourth-Grade Teachers and Their Classrooms?," in Cathy Roller, ed., *Learning to Teach Reading: Setting the Research Agenda* (Newark, Del.: International Reading Association, 2001), pp. 150–65; Linda Darling-Hammond, *Teacher Quality and Student Achievement: A Review of State Policy Evidence* (Seattle: Center for Teaching Policy, University of Washington, 1999); Gerald G. Duffy, "Powerful Models or Powerful Teachers? An Argument for Teacher-as-Entrepreneur," in Steven Stahl and David Hayes, eds., *Instructional Models in Reading* (Mahwah, N.J.: Erlbaum, 1997), pp. 331–65; Michael

Pressley et al., "A Study of Effective First-Grade Literacy Instruction," *Scientific Studies in Reading*, vol. 5, 2001, pp. 35–58; William L. Sanders, "Value-Added Assessment," *School Administrator*, vol. 55, 1998, pp. 101–13; and Barbara M. Taylor et al., "Effective Schools and Accomplished Teachers: Lessons About Primary Grade Reading Instruction in Low-Income Schools," *Elementary School Journal*, vol. 101, 2000, pp. 121–65.

[2] Richard L. Allington and Peter H. Johnston, *Reading to Learn: Lessons from Exemplary Fourth-Grade Classrooms* (New York: Guilford, 2002); and Michael Pressley et al., *Learning to Read: Lessons from Exemplary First-Grade Classrooms* (New York: Guilford, 2001).

[3] Richard L. Allington, *What Really Matters for Struggling Readers: Designing Research-Based Interventions* (New York: Longman, 2001).

[4] Michael S. Knapp, *Teaching for Meaning in High-Poverty Classrooms* (New York: Teachers College Press, 1995).

[5] P. David Pearson and Linda Fielding, "Comprehension Instruction," in Rebecca Barr et al., eds., *Handbook of Reading Research, Vol. II* (New York: Longman, 1991), pp. 815–60.

[6] Randy Fall, Noreen M. Webb, and Naomi Chudowsky, "Group Discussion and Large-Scale Language Arts Assessment: Effects on Students' Comprehension," *American Educational Research Journal*, vol. 37, 2000, pp. 911–41.

[7] Stephen Krashen, "More Smoke and Mirrors: A Critique of the National Reading Panel Report on Fluency," *Phi Delta Kappan*, October 2001, pp. 119–23; and Keith E. Stanovich, *Progress in Understanding Reading: Scientific Foundations and New Frontiers* (New York: Guilford, 2000).

[8] Allington, op. cit.

[9] Allington and Johnston, *Reading to Learn*; and Pressley et al., "A Study of Effective First-Grade Literacy Instruction."

[10] Richard L. Allington, "The Reading Instruction Provided Readers of Differing Abilities," *Elementary School Journal*, vol. 83, 1983, pp. 548–59.

[11] NICHD Early Childcare Research Network, "The Relation of First-Grade Classroom Environments to Structural Classroom Features, Teacher and Student Behaviors," *Elementary School Journal*, in press.

[12] Marilyn Jager Adams, *Beginning to Read: Thinking and Learning About Print* (Cambridge, Mass.: MIT Press, 1990); and Dolores Durkin, "What Classroom Observations Reveal About Reading Comprehension Instruction," *Reading Research Quarterly*, vol. 14, 1978-79, pp. 481–533.

[13] Adams, op. cit.

[14] Durkin, op. cit.

[15] Duffy, op. cit.

[16] Taylor et al., op. cit.

[17] Allington and Johnston, *Reading to Learn*; and Peter Johnston, Haley Woodside-Jiron, and Jeni Day, "Teaching and Learning Literate Epistemologies," *Journal of Educational Psychology*, vol. 93, 2001, pp. 223–33.

[18] Courtney B. Cazden, *Classroom Discourse: The Language of Teaching and Learning* (Portsmouth, N.H.: Heinemann, 1988); and Martin Nystrand, *Opening Dialogue: Understanding the Dynamics of Language and Learning in the English Classroom* (New York: Teachers College Press, 1997).

[19] Fall et al., op. cit.; Johnston, Woodside-Jiron, and Day, op. cit.; and Nystrand, op. cit.

[20] Knapp, op. cit.

[21] Julianne C. Turner, "The Influence of Classroom Contexts on Young Children's Motivation for Literacy," *Reading Research Quarterly*, vol. 30, 1995, pp. 410–41.

[22] Jeni Pollack Day, "How I Became an Exemplary Teacher," in Pressley et al., *Learning to Read*, pp. 205–18.

[23] Anne McGill-Franzen, "Policy and Instruction: What Is the Relationship?," in Michael Kamil et al., eds., *Handbook of Reading Research, Vol. III* (Mahwah, N.J.: Erlbaum, 2000), pp. 891–908.

Richard L. Allington would like to thank the following people for their assistance in the project reported in this article: Peter Johnston and Michael Pressley, co-principal investigators for the fourth- and first-grade teacher studies respectively; the classroom teachers who allowed us to study their teaching practices; and the other researchers on the project, including Elizabeth Asbury, Kim Baker, Kim Boothroyd, Greg Brooks, Melissa Cedeno, Cathy Collins Block, John Cronin, Jeni Pollack Day, Gay Ivey, Haley Woodside-Jiron, Susan Layden, Anne McGill-Franzen, Lesley Morrow, Steven Powers, Jean Veltema, and Ruth Wharton-McDonald. This article is based on research supported in part under the Research and Development Centers Program (award number R305A6005) as administered by the Office of Educational Research and Improvement, U.S. Department of Education. However, the conclusions are the author's own. ©2002, Richard L. Allington.

CHAPTER 3

Reading Growth in High-Poverty Classrooms: The Influence of Teacher Practices That Encourage Cognitive Engagement in Literacy Learning

Barbara M. Taylor, P. David Pearson, Debra S. Peterson, and Michael C. Rodriguez

There is an unprecedented emphasis in the United States on improving the teaching of reading in elementary classrooms, and the press for improvement has been increased by the Reading First provisions of Title I, the No Child Left Behind Act of 2001 (2002). Fortunately, there is a great deal of research-based knowledge about effective reading instruction to guide teachers' efforts to become more accomplished reading teachers.

The National Reading Panel Report (NRP, 2000), central to the conceptualization of research and effective reading instruction in the No Child Left Behind legislation, is attracting most of the attention nationally and within states in terms of defining effective reading instruction. The National Reading Panel, charged with reviewing reading research to determine the effectiveness of various approaches to teaching children to read, focused on curricular components of an effective reading program. The NRP found five areas that merited immediate implementation: (a) phonemic awareness instruction, (b) explicit, systematic phonics instruction, (c) repeated oral reading practice with feedback and guidance, (d) direct and indirect vocabulary instruction, and (e) comprehension strategies instruction. It is important to note that the authors of the NRP report recognized that their report did not speak to many aspects of reading instruction because the research in

RTI in Literacy—Responsive and Comprehensive, edited by Peter H. Johnston, published by the International Reading Association. This chapter reprinted from Taylor, B.M., Pearson, P.D., Peterson, D.S., & Rodriguez, M.C. (2003). Reading Growth in High-Poverty Classrooms: The Influence of Teacher Practices That Encourage Cognitive Engagement in Literacy Learning. *The Elementary School Journal*, 104(1), 3–28.

those areas was neither definitive nor extensive. Moreover, even for those issues for which there was broad consensus (e.g., phonics and comprehension), the panel noted that many caveats were required to add the necessary nuance, qualification, and context that would be required to support valid policy recommendations. Other broad reviews, such as the Report of the National Academy of Education on Preventing Reading Difficulties in Young Children (Snow, Burns, & Griffin, 1998) and particular chapters of the third volume of the *Handbook of Reading Research* (Kamil, Mosenthal, Pearson, & Barr, 2000), have corroborated many of the NRP findings (albeit with substantial elaboration and nuance).

Knowledge about effective reading instruction has also come from the close examination of effective teachers of reading (e.g., Duffy et al., 1987; Knapp et al., 1995; Pressley et al., 2001; Taylor, Pearson, Clark, & Walpole, 2000). In an extensive study of teachers and students in 140 high-poverty classrooms, Knapp et al. (1995) found that effective teachers of reading stressed higher-level thinking skills in addition to lower-level skills. Knapp et al. posited that this extra emphasis on higher-level thinking increased students' understanding of what they were doing and encouraged them to be meaning makers. Even so, relatively few stimulating discussions took place in the classrooms Knapp et al. (1995) studied. Based on extensive examination of classrooms populated by low-income children, Knapp et al. urged teachers to promote students' understanding and to build the quest for meaning into their learning experiences.

Duffy, Roehler, and colleagues (Duffy et al., 1987; Roehler & Duffy, 1984) identified the cognitive processes supported by excellent teachers. More effective teachers engaged in modeling and explanation to teach students strategies they could use to decode words and understand texts. Implicit in their empirically based model of teaching effectiveness was the concept of scaffolding (what others have called coaching)—supportive actions by the teacher to move either an individual or a group of students to the next level of independence in completing a task, strategy, or activity. Pressley et al. (2001) found that effective primary-grade reading teachers provided a balanced literacy program. They taught skills, actively engaged students in a great deal of reading and writing, and fostered self-regulation through a combination of modeling, scaffolding, and providing informative feedback to students as they tried to apply strategies.

Based in part on work suggesting that "engaged" readers have better text comprehension and reading achievement than disengaged readers (Campbell, Voelkl, & Donahue, 1997; Cunningham & Stanovich, 1997), Guthrie and his colleagues (Baker, Dreher, & Guthrie, 2000; Guthrie, 1996; Guthrie et al., 2000) have stressed that teachers need to know how to promote reading engagement in order to teach reading well. Engaged readers are motivated, read to learn, use cognitive strategies, and interact in a classroom community (Guthrie, 1996). In a study of effective primary-grade reading teachers, Pressley et al. (2002) found that these teachers were skilled at providing motivating instruction, instruction that was as concerned about student involvement as it was about achievement. Chin, Anderson, and Waggoner (2001) looked at fourth-grade classrooms and found that in comparison to recitation, literacy discussions that stressed collaborative reasoning fostered greater engagement and higher-level thinking. These researchers explained this increase by suggesting that students had more control over and participation in the discussions, which in turn led to deeper and more productive cognitive processing. These findings point to instructional practices in which teachers "engage" students' cognitive functioning rather than simply cover key curricular components. In other words, they suggest that the "how" of instruction may be as important as the "what."

Our own work has supported the findings on effective teachers reported above. In an earlier study (Taylor et al., 2000) examining effective schools and teachers, we learned that primary-grade teachers in effective schools differed from their counterparts in less effective schools in a number of ways, including (a) providing more high-level questioning, (b) coaching students in strategies for applying their word-recognition skills to everyday reading, and (c) allowing students more active reading practice (more time for independent reading). When we examined the most effective teachers irrespective of the schools in which they taught, we also found that they, like the teachers in the effective schools, provided more higher-level questioning and emphasized applying word-recognition strategies. Additionally, they provided much more coaching and promoted a higher level of on-task behavior among their students than did the less effective teachers (Taylor et al., 2000).

Toward a Framework for Effective Reading Instruction Maximizing Cognitive Engagement in Literacy Learning

The overall purpose of the CIERA (Center for the Improvement of Early Reading Achievement) School Change study, which is the broader line of work in which this current study of classroom instruction is embedded, was to investigate the efficacy of a school-based reading improvement model. Within the wider scope of that study, we were struck by the consistency, even in the early stages of our work on effective schools and teachers (Taylor et al., 2000), with which particular instructional practices were associated with relatively high student growth. This finding prompted us to wonder whether this set of practices could be conceptualized as a more explicit framework of effective instruction. By moving back and forth between our data and the literature on effective reading instruction, we developed the current framework of teaching for cognitive engagement to partially account for what is known about effective reading instruction. A fundamental tenet of this framework is that what teachers do to maximize students' cognitive engagement in literacy activities will matter as much as what they cover in their instructional interactions with students.

The framework of instruction maximizing cognitive engagement in literacy learning that we are putting forth combines key ideas from the work of Knapp et al. (1995), which stresses teaching for meaning, with the engagement construct of Guthrie et al. (2000). Although the framework we are investigating does not account for all that is known about effective reading instruction (due to the constraints of our observation system, described below), it contains four teaching dimensions: (1) supporting higher-level thinking (in both talk and writing about text), (2) encouraging independent use of word-recognition and comprehension strategies during reading activities (both instruction and text reading), (3) using a student support stance (in contrast to a teacher-directed stance) during literacy lessons, and (4) promoting active, as opposed to passive, involvement in literacy activities.

In the present study, using an observation system designed to investigate multiple aspects of literacy lessons (Taylor & Pearson, 2000), we evaluated the relative contributions of an array of curricular and teaching variables to children's reading and writing growth. Because our system accounts for a wide range of curricular and teaching variables, not all were relevant to evaluation of the cognitive engagement framework. By the same token, our investigation into elements of effective reading instruction was limited by the aspects of reading instruction included in our observation coding scheme. Fortunately, however, two types of variables were relevant to our investigation—those included in the cognitive engagement framework and those that ran counter to it. Variables in the observation scheme that we were able to consider included explicit phonics skill instruction, instruction in applying word-recognition strategies to text, comprehension skill instruction, comprehension strategies instruction, lower- and higher-level thinking related to text, teachers' use of various interaction strategies (e.g., coaching, modeling, telling, and recitation), student time on-task, and active (as opposed to passive) pupil response to a reading lesson. (The observation system is described in the Method section.)

A key step in instantiating this framework for effective reading instruction was to identify its features in our coding scheme. In most instances, this process proved transparent. For example, the research on higher-level talk about text (Knapp, 1995; Taylor, Peterson, Pearson, & Rodriguez, 2002; Taylor et al., 2000) and use of reading strategies (Guthrie et al., 2000; Pressley et al., 2001) had been a part of our coding scheme from the outset. In the scheme (and in the research literature), when students are engaged in higher-level thinking about text, they are making connections to their prior knowledge, considering thematic elements of the text, interpreting characters' motives and actions, and so on. Similarly, during comprehension and word-recognition strategy instruction, students are engaged in metacognitive thinking and monitoring as they try to solve reading problems.

In contrast, one would expect the practices in the following list to stimulate more mechanistic or routine than active and strategic thinking by students and, hence, lead to relatively less reading growth when they occurred frequently: lower-level questioning, mechanical practice of comprehension skills, and explicit phonics skill instruction past grade 1. When engaged in lower-level thinking about text, students are typically responding to questions about detail or questions that require relatively little thought and can be answered with a word or two. With mechanical practice of comprehension skills, students may be completing a worksheet on a skill such as main idea or fact/opinion, or they may be responding to a teacher prompt to predict or retell in a turn-taking manner. In either case, these comprehension skill activities are likely to require less cognitive effort than when students are trying to apply comprehension strategies to actual reading. In kindergarten and grade 1, when the content is novel and students are attempting to grasp the alphabetic principle, students are likely to be cognitively engaged in phonics lessons. However, past grade 1, phonics lessons typically cover content that either most readers know or some have not yet mastered. In either case, phonics lessons past grade 1 are likely to involve most students in mechanical practice rather than in active cognitive engagement.

A close reading of the research leads one to expect more reading and writing growth in classrooms in which students are more actively engaged in their literacy learning than in other classrooms (Pressley et al., 2001; Taylor et al., 2002). The more students are performing literacy activities themselves, as opposed to listening to or watching others performing literacy activities, the greater their active involvement in learning and hence the greater their opportunity for growth. Within our observation scheme, we included many indicators of active responding (reading, writing, manipulating, chorally responding, and sharing ideas with a partner) as well as passive responding (reading turn-taking, oral turn-taking, and listening to the teacher).

Teacher stance, which we defined as the mode of interaction between a teacher and his or her students, is also implicated as an important instructional variable in the research on effective teaching (e.g., Duffy et al., 1987; Pressley et al., 2001; Taylor et al., 2000). A teacher's stance toward instruction is related to the nature of the literacy activity (e.g., level of questioning, strategy vs. skill instruction) and to the type of pupil responding being encouraged (e.g., active vs. passive responding). One would expect more reading and writing growth in classrooms in which teachers frequently coach, model, and provide feedback, all of which are important when students face challenging literacy activities (Duffy et al., 1987; Taylor et al., 2000). For example, in these challenging settings a teacher may need to coach students to answer a higher-level question, model for and coach students in the use of specific comprehension or word-recognition strategies, and offer feedback as students attempt to use those strategies during a guided reading activity. In contrast, the practice of telling students information about a comprehension skill or leading them in recitation with low-level questions about a story is likely to lead to less cognitive engagement by students than are more supportive actions.

In analyzing the data for the current study, we were able to fulfill two purposes: (a) to determine which elements of classroom instructional practice accounted for the greatest growth in student achievement across a school year to better understand effective reading instruction and (b) to evaluate the efficacy of a framework of teaching for cognitive engagement. If such a framework were supported, we reasoned, it would provide teachers with a coherent body of information, beyond that provided by the NRP report, about what they must do to improve teaching, learning, and reading achievement.

Method

Participants

Nine schools were part of the CIERA School Change Project in 2000–2001. All schools were high poverty, with 70%–95% of the students qualifying for subsidized lunch. Across schools, 2%–68% of the students were non-native speakers of English, and 67%–91% were members of minority groups. The nine project schools were from eight districts in a rural area in the Southeast, an eastern city, two small towns in the Midwest, a large city in the Midwest, and a large city in the Southwest. In order to become a project school, at least 75% of the teachers in a building had to agree to participate in the project. In all schools, two teachers per grade were randomly selected and invited to participate in the classroom observations and interviews. This article focuses on students' reading and writing growth in grades 1–5. A total of 88 teachers and 792 students across these grades participated in the data collection.

Teachers from each school varied in teaching experience, ranging from 0 to 35 years of service on average. Almost all teachers held a bachelor's degree in education or a related field, and about 40% at each school had a master's degree.

Because schools had different assessment procedures in place, teachers were asked to use their judgment to divide their classes into thirds (high, average, and low) in terms of reading ability so we could obtain a stratified, random sample. It was from these thirds that we randomly selected nine children in the fall as target students, three each from the high, middle, and low thirds of the classroom continua of reading ability.

Student Assessments

The children were assessed in the fall and spring on a number of literacy measures that varied depending on grade level. Although the study focused on reading instruction and, for the most part, reading achievement, we included a measure of writing ability to assess any serendipitous effect that the reading instructional practices we observed may have had on the highly related process of composition. Assessments included a standardized reading comprehension test (grades 1–5), a comprehension test from a basal reader program (grades 2–5), fluency (words correct per minute; Deno, 1985) (grades 1–5), and writing (responding to a common prompt) (grades 1–5), as well as tests considering letter-name knowledge (grade 1), phonemic awareness (grade 1), and word dictation (grade 1) (see Table A1).

In the fall in grade 1, children were individually assessed on letter-name knowledge and phonemic segmentation and blending (Taylor, 1991). Children were also assessed in small groups on word dictation. In the spring all students were individually assessed on reading fluency (in which students read aloud for

1 minute to obtain a score for the number of words read correctly; Deno, 1985) based on a grade-level passage from the Basic Reading Inventory (BRI; Johns, 1997). In a group setting, students took the reading comprehension subtest of the Gates-MacGinitie Reading Test (MacGinitie, MacGinitie, Maria, & Dreyer, 2000) and responded to a writing prompt (the same one as used in grades 2–5).

In the fall, students in grades 2–5 were assessed individually on fluency (words correct per minute, wcpm) based on their reading of a BRI passage one grade level below their grade placement. In a group they took the comprehension subtest of the Gates-MacGinitie Reading Test (MacGinitie et al., 2000), a comprehension test from a basal reader program (Houghton Mifflin, 1999) in which they read a two-page passage and answered five multiple-choice and five short-answer questions and responded to a writing prompt (Michigan Literacy Progress Profile, 1998). In the spring, all students were assessed on fluency on a passage at grade level (Johns, 1997), reading comprehension (Gates), basal reader comprehension, and writing to a prompt (using the same prompt as in the fall).

For the writing prompt, each paper was scored by one person according to a four-point rubric. Twenty-five percent of the writing samples at each grade level were scored by a second scorer with 83% agreement between the two scorers.

Use of the School Change Framework

Teachers in the project agreed to meet for a minimum of 1 hour a week, on average, in focused study groups. Study group activities included within-grade and/or across-grade groups that concentrated on particular aspects of classroom reading instruction and student work (e.g., comprehension instruction and phonemic awareness instruction). Groups were encouraged to review research and video clips on the CIERA School Change web site and to read and discuss articles on research-based practices related to their group's focus area. Members of study groups also raised issues, solved problems, and developed action plans related to their focus area in order to make changes in their classroom reading instruction.

Use of data emanating from the project was an important aspect of the process. At the beginning of the 2000–2001 school year, principals received a summary of the Beating the Odds research (Taylor et al., 2000) on characteristics of effective schools and teachers to share with teachers in their schools. The schools also received a report on the 1999–2000 project that presented means across schools on the school and classroom variables under investigation. Also, the report included correlations identifying school and classroom factors related to growth in students' reading and writing ability. Two purposes of this report were to help schools consider possible strengths and weaknesses in their classroom reading instruction and to help them determine topics to focus on in study groups.

Documenting Program Characteristics and Classroom Practices

Teachers participating in the data collection were interviewed in the fall, winter, and spring. Each interview lasted about 30 minutes. The interview data were used primarily to document school reading program features as well as participants' beliefs about school reform, leadership, collaboration, professional development, and parent partnerships. In this article, however, we used interview data in a very limited manner to shed light on the beliefs about reading instruction in the classrooms of 25 teachers who tended to ask higher- or lower-order questions. No quotes from the interviews are provided, and the interview questions are not given.

On three occasions (fall, winter, spring) each teacher was also observed for an hour during reading instruction to document her classroom practices in the teaching of reading. All observations were scheduled during the portion of a teacher's literacy block devoted primarily to reading instruction. The observers consisted of graduate students in literacy education and retired elementary teachers. They were trained to use the CIERA Classroom Observation Scheme (Taylor & Pearson, 2000) through an on-site visit by one member of the research team and through use of an observation training kit that contained a manual, a practice video, and a CD with video clips of teachers illustrating the various codes in their teaching. The observers then watched an inter-rater "test" video, and they had to demonstrate at least 80% agreement at each of the seven levels of the coding scheme with a "standard" coding (Taylor & Pearson, 2000) prior to conducting classroom observations.

The observation system (influenced by the work of Greenwood, Carta, Kamps, & Delquadri, 1995; Scanlon & Gelzheiser, 1992; and Ysseldyke & Christenson, 1993) combined note-taking with a quantitative coding process. The observer took field notes for a 5-minute period, recording a narrative account of what was happening in the classroom, including, where possible and appropriate, what the teacher and children were saying. At the end of this 5-minute period, the observer first recorded the proportion of all students in the classroom who appeared to be on-task (i.e., doing what they were supposed to be doing). Then the observer coded who was providing the instruction (level 1), the grouping pattern in use for that event (level 2), and the major literacy activity (level 3). Next, the observer coded the two or three most salient literacy events (level 4 codes) occurring during that 5-minute episode. For every level 4 event, the observer also coded the materials being used (level 5), the teacher interaction styles observed (level 6), and the expected responses of the students (level 7). An example of a 5-minute observational segment is provided in Appendix B. (See Table A2 for a list of the codes for the seven levels.)

The level 4 codes dealt primarily with curricular and teaching aspects of reading instruction. Through a curricular lens, we classified the content of instruction. For example, was it phonemic awareness, phonics, vocabulary, or comprehension instruction? We also attempted to capture the nature of the instruction. For example, when the teacher was teaching comprehension skills or strategies, was she treating them as elements to be rehearsed and practiced or as processes to be understood metacognitively and incorporated into students' independent reading? During talk or writing about text, was the teacher asking lower- or higher-level questions after reading? In the case of phonics, we distinguished between an explicit phonics lesson and a teacher's attempts to coach students to apply a range of word-recognition strategies as they read text. Level 6 codes dealt with teaching components of reading instruction (e.g., Was telling or coaching observed?) as did level 7 codes (e.g., Was the teacher having students engage in reading or reading turn-taking?).

The observations were used as a source of feedback to individual teachers. Teachers received a copy of each observation, a description of the codes, a brief summary of research related to the major categories of codes being analyzed for the project (e.g., incidence of whole-class instruction, incidence of higher-level questioning), and a table summarizing the data from the observation codes for a national sample of teachers at their grade level. External facilitators received training in how to interpret observations so they, in turn, could help teachers understand the information contained in their observations without interpreting it for them. Teachers were encouraged to go to the facilitators with questions.

Establishing Trustworthiness of the Observation Data

Because the core analyses in this project hinged on the trustworthiness of the data from the observations, we took several steps to ensure the reliability and validity of the codes recorded at each site. First, as mentioned earlier, each observer was required to meet a standard (i.e., achieving at least 80% agreement with a standard set of codes for an observation) prior to conducting the observations used in the data analysis. Second, while visiting each site one research team member conducted a fidelity check with each site observer to obtain data on the interrater reliability of the coding scheme. The two coded the same classroom for 30 minutes. The observer's codes for each 5-minute observation segment were compared with those of the research team member to determine consistency for each of the seven levels of the coding system. Across 12 observations, mean agreement with the research team member ranged from 82% to 95% across the levels of the coding system: 95% agreement at level 2 (grouping), 95% agreement at level 3 (major literacy focus), 82% agreement at level 4 (specific literacy activity), 87% agreement at level 5 (material), 85% agreement at level 6 (teacher response), and 82% agreement at level 7 (student response). The classroom teacher was always coded at level 1 because this was the person we were observing.

Although these indices of congruence meet conventional standards for interrater reliability, we remained concerned about the consistency and the validity of the codes, particularly for levels 4 and 7. Thus we undertook a post hoc review to enhance their validity. An expert observer, who had used the observation scheme for 2 years and had helped to revise and refine it, read the notes taken during each observation by each observer to assess the degree to which observers were using the codes consistently across sites. She did not code the observations "blind." Instead she recorded a different code if her reading of the notes prompted her to disagree with an observer's original code. For a random sample of 10% of the observations, the agreements between the observers and the expert observer at each of the levels of coding for the codes used in the data analysis (described below) were as follows: 97% agreement at level 2 (grouping), 96% at level 3 (major literacy focus), 84% at level 4 (literacy activity), 100% at level 5 (material), 81% at level 6 (teacher response), and 89% agreement at level 7 (student response). In all instances in which a discrepancy was noted, not only for the 10% sample but for the entire corpus, the code assigned by the expert was used in subsequent statistical analyses.

The variability between the observers and the expert, especially at levels 4 and 6, prompted us to undertake yet another reliability check. To ensure that we had not introduced any bias in this first review process, a second reviewer read the notes from the same 10% random sample of observations and assigned her own codes. She agreed with the first reviewer over 90% of the time, specifically:

99% agreement at levels 2 and 3, 91% at level 4, 99% at level 5, 93% at level 6, and 92% agreement at level 7. We were thus confident in the reliability and validity of the coding scheme; further, any slippage that may have occurred was detected and corrected during the post-hoc review process.

Observational Categories Used in the Analyses

Certain categories from classroom observations (i.e., those found to be important in previous research) were most relevant to the current study, that is, to determine which elements of classroom instructional practice accounted for the greatest growth in student achievement across a school year and to investigate the efficacy of our framework of teaching for cognitive engagement. The classroom practices (see App. C for descriptions of these categories) that we entered into our statistical analyses were as follows:

1. Whole class/large group
2. Small group
3. Phonemic awareness skill instruction
4. Phonics skill instruction
5. Coaching in word-recognition strategies
6. Active reading practice
7. Vocabulary instruction
8. Comprehension skill instruction
9. Comprehension strategy instruction
10. Lower-level questioning or writing about text
11. Higher-level questioning or writing about text
12. Telling
13. Recitation
14. Modeling
15. Coaching
16. Watching/listening/giving feedback
17. Students actively responding
18. Students passively responding
19. Time on-task

Statistical Analysis

We used hierarchical linear modeling (HLM; Bryk & Raudenbush, 1992) to investigate the effect of classroom-level characteristics on students' reading growth. Descriptive analyses were also conducted to elaborate on the quantitative findings.

HLM is a method of computing regression at multiple levels. The analyses in this study employed a two-level HLM model in which students were nested within classrooms. HLM estimates a regression within each classroom and combines them to see if there is a common regression across classrooms. When regressions (either the intercepts or slopes) vary across classrooms, researchers can examine classroom-level characteristics that may explain such variation. This is a common method for evaluating classroom factors and their effects on student outcomes. It would be inappropriate to use simple regression in these situations because one would be violating the independence assumption of regression.

In addition, HLM partitions variance components across levels, providing an estimate of variance in student performance that exists within classrooms or schools and between classrooms or schools. An unconditional HLM is one without an explanatory variable that allowed us to answer the question, How much variance in student outcome can be attributed to factors on which classrooms differ systematically from one another? This analysis is equivalent to a random-effects analysis of variance. Estimation using HLM rests on assumptions similar to multivariate multiple regression.

The formula for a correlation is $r = \text{cov}_{XY}/s_X s_Y$. The formula for a regression coefficient is $b = \text{cov}_{XY}/s^2_X$. To evaluate the relative importance of regression coefficients based on variables in different scales, one computes a standardized regression coefficient as $\beta = b s_X/s_Y = \text{cov}_{XY}/s^2_X s_X/s_Y = \text{cov}_{XY}/s_X s_Y$, which results in something like a partial correlation controlling for other variables in the equation (when there are more than one).

If the resulting effect, standardized beta, is 0.35, for example, we would interpret this as meaning that a change of one standard deviation in the predictor (observation scheme) variable is associated with a 0.35 standard deviation change in the outcome (achievement) variable.

Because of the improved estimation employed by HLM, including the use of maximum likelihood and empirical Bayes estimates, interpretation of statistical results can be broadened to include a larger p value associated with statistical tests. Also, statistical results with associated p values at or near 0.10 should be included in interpretation and explored in future studies with smaller numbers of cases (fewer teachers, in our case) because such results indicate that there are relations worth exploring further. For a more complete description of estimation in HLM, see Bryk and Raudenbush (1992, pp. 32–56). HLM (Raudenbush, Bryk, & Congdon, 2000) is recognized as a standard program for estimating multilevel models (Bryk & Raudenbush, 1992; Kreft & DeLeeuw, 1998).

Results

Reading Growth and Teacher Practices Across Schools

Through the HLM analyses we investigated the relation between teacher practices during literacy instruction and students' reading growth. Because six of nine schools were in their first year of the reform in year 2 of the project, we were unable to look at changes in instruction during the school year with only three observations per teacher. The analyses were conducted on the relationships between teacher practices and each of the major outcome variables: reading fluency, comprehension as measured by a standardized reading test, comprehension as measured by a basal reader test, and writing. Typical results of multi-level models yield 10%–33% of the variance between schools. In studies employing classrooms, some have found as much as 25%–50% of the variance between classrooms (Frank, 1998). Grade 1 data (see Table 1) were analyzed separately from grades 2–5 because different fall scores (e.g., word dictation in grade 1 vs. words correct per minute, comprehension from a standardized reading test in grades 2–5) were used as explanatory variables in the analyses.

Fluency. The HLM analysis (see Table 2) for grade 1 revealed that 35% of the variance in spring fluency scores was between teachers, after accounting for fall scores. Thirty-five percent of the between-teacher variance was accounted for by the variable of higher-level questioning. The average classroom mean spring fluency score was 53.0 (SD = 17.4). For every standard deviation increase in the coding of higher-level questioning (mean percentage of segments observed = 6%, SD = 13%), students' fluency score in a class increased by an average of 11.4 words correct per minute (β = 66).

For grades 2–5, fall scores and grade were used to adjust for differences in growth in fluency across grades. The HLM analysis (see Table 3) revealed that 46% of the variance in spring fluency scores was between teachers after accounting for fall scores. Of this between-teacher variance, coaching, active reading (as

Table 1. Means and Standard Deviations for Student Scores, Grades 1–5

Assessment Tool/Grade	N	Fall M	Fall SD	Spring M	Spring SD
Letter names (grade 1)	124	49.44	5.03		
Phonemic awareness (grade 1)	124	6.96	4.30		
Word-level dictation (grade 1)	125	14.70	9.39		
Gates comprehension (NCE):					
Grade 1	107			48.99	18.38
Grade 2	147	43.23	19.05	45.61	18.96
Grade 3	166	36.27	14.34	37.65	16.40
Grade 4	152	35.90	17.68	35.69	17.40
Grade 5	135	35.05	18.46	38.98	17.93
Basal comprehension:					
Grade 2	155	12.22	4.54	15.03	2.93
Grade 3	151	12.62	4.87	14.27	5.39
Grade 4	146	11.71	4.86	13.66	4.82
Grade 5	134	13.54	4.92	15.09	4.46
Fluency:					
Grade 1	135			52.41	31.63
Grade 2	146	54.52	29.85	80.78	31.07
Grade 3	128	79.16	31.94	86.87	30.42
Grade 4	154	105.12	37.12	122.03	38.76
Grade 5	135	121.33	40.31	139.96	42.06
Writing:					
Grade 1	123			2.04	.79
Grade 2	147	1.67	.60	1.99	.75
Grade 3	141	1.89	1.81	1.97	.79
Grade 4	123	1.71	.66	2.01	.76
Grade 5	135	2.02	.72	2.22	.79

opposed to turn-taking reading), and phonics instruction (negatively related) accounted for 13% of the variance. The average classroom mean spring fluency score was 107.9 wcpm (SD = 17.9). For every standard deviation increase in the coding of coaching (mean percentage of segments observed = 14%, SD = 14%), students' fluency score in a class increased by 4.2 wcpm on average (β = .23). For every standard deviation increase in the coding of active reading practice (M = 28%, SD = 12%), students' fluency score in a class increased by 3.0 wcpm on average (β = .17). For every standard deviation increase in the coding of phonics instruction (M = 6%, SD = 10%), students' fluency score in a class decreased by 5.2 wcpm on average (β = .29).

Table 2. HLM Analysis of the Relation of Grade 1 Reading Fluency to Higher-Level Questioning

	Variance Component	% Variance Between
Initial random effects:		
Classroom means	301.41	35
Student residual	544.51	
Total	845.92	

		% Variance Accounted for by Model
Final random effects:		
Classroom means	197.17	35
Student residual	543.89	

	Coefficient	t Ratio	df	p
Final fixed effects:				
Intercept (grand mean)	52.98	14.26	15	
High-level questioning	88.14	2.70	15	.017
Fall score	2.14	6.31	132	

Table 3. HLM Analysis of the Relation of Grade 2–5 Reading Fluency (After Accounting for Fall Scores and Grade) With Phonics, Active Reading, and Coaching

	Variance Component	% Variance Between
Initial random effects:		
Classroom means	319.84	46
Fall score slope	.03	
Student residual	368.69	
Total	668.56	

		% Variance Accounted for by Model
Final random effects:		
Classroom means	278.89	13
Fall score slope	.03	
Student residual	368.86	

	Coefficient	t Ratio	df	p
Final fixed effects:				
Intercept (grand mean)	107.85	47.44	58	.000
Grade	21.50	9.36	58	.000
Phonics	–51.98	–2.29	58	.025
Active reading	25.31	1.99	58	.051
Coaching	29.84	1.86	58	.068
Fall score	.83	22.88	62	.000

Reading Comprehension as Measured by a Standardized Test. The HLM analysis (see Table 4) for grade 1 revealed that 35% of the variance in spring comprehension scores was between teachers, after accounting for fall scores. Twenty-seven percent of the between-teacher variance was accounted for by the variable of higher-level questioning. The average classroom mean spring comprehension NCE score was 49.7 (SD = 9.8). For every standard deviation increase in the coding of higher-level questioning (*M* = 6%, SD = 13%), students' comprehension NCE score in a class increased by 5.7 on average (β = .59).

For grades 2–5, the HLM analysis (see Table 5) revealed that 48% of the variance in spring comprehension NCE scores was between teachers after accounting for fall scores. Of this between-teacher variance, higher-level questioning (positively related), classroom time on-task (positively related), comprehension skills (negatively related), and passive responding (negatively related) accounted for 20% of the variance. In grades 2–5 the average classroom mean spring comprehension NCE score was 40.3 (SD = 8.0). For every standard deviation increase in the coding of higher-level questioning (*M* = 19%, SD = 19%), students' NCE score in a class increased by an average of 2.5 (β = .33). For every standard deviation increase in the coding of time on-task (*M* = 91%, SD = 5.5%), students' NCE score in a class increased by 2.0 on average (β = .27). For every standard deviation increase in the coding of comprehension skill instruction (*M* = 13%,

Table 4. HLM Analysis of Grade 1 Reading Comprehension (Gates-MacGinitie, NCE) With Higher-Level Questioning

	Variance Component	% Variance Between		
Initial random effects:				
Classroom means	93.69	35		
Student residual	174.51			
Total	268.20			
		% Variance Accounted for by Model		
Final random effects:				
Classroom means	68.30	27		
Student residual	174.37			
	Coefficient	*t* Ratio	*df*	*p*
Final fixed effects:				
Intercept (grand mean)	49.65	20.72	14	.000
High-level questioning	44.06	2.30	14	.037
Fall score	1.30	7.23	122	.000

Table 5. HLM Analysis of Grade 2–5 Reading Comprehension (Gates-MacGinitie) With Higher-Level Questioning, Time On-Task, Comprehension Skills (Negatively Related), and Passive Responding (Negatively Related)

	Variance Component	% Variance Between		
Initial random effects:				
Classroom means	63.32	31		
Fall score slope	.03			
Student residual	142.68			
Total	206.03			
		% Variance Accounted for by Model		
Final random effects:				
Classroom means	53.70	16		
Fall score slope	.03			
Student residual	142.97			
	Coefficient	t Ratio	df	p
Final fixed effects:				
Intercept (grand mean)	40.27	38.70	61	.000
Higher-level questioning	13.99	2.57	61	.010
Time on-task	3.60	1.96	61	.049
Comprehension skills	−17.01	−2.37	61	.018
Passive responding	−14.25	−1.78	61	.075
Fall score	.67	14.42	65	.000

SD = 14%), students' comprehension NCE score in a class decreased by 2.4 on average (β = .30). For every standard deviation increase in the coding of passive responding (M = 72%, SD = 13%), students' NCE score in a class decreased by 1.8 on average (β = .23).

Reading Comprehension as Measured by a Basal Reader Test. For grades 2–5, the HLM analysis (see Table 6) revealed that 40% of the variance in spring comprehension scores was between teachers, after accounting for fall scores. Asking higher-level questions after reading accounted for 4% of the variance between teachers. The average classroom mean spring score was 14.5 (SD = 2.5). For every standard deviation increase in the coding of higher-level questioning, students' comprehension score in a class increased on average by .65 points (β = .26).

Writing. For grade 1, 39% of the variance in spring writing scores was between teachers, after accounting for fall dictation scores (see Table 7). Teaching

Table 6. HLM Analysis of Grade 2–5 Reading Comprehension (Basal Reader) With Higher-Level Questioning

	Variance Component	% Variance Between		
Initial random effects:				
Classroom means	6.31	46		
Fall score slope	.07			
Student residual	9.23			
Total	15.61			
		% Variance Accounted for by Model		
Final random effects:				
Classroom means	6.06	4		
Fall score slope	.07			
Student residual	9.24			
	Coefficient	t Ratio	df	p
Final fixed effects:				
Intercept (grand mean)	14.48	43.53	63	.000
High-level questioning	3.49	2.00	63	.045
Fall score	.46	9.97	64	.000

Table 7. HLM Analysis of Grade 1 Writing With Comprehension Strategies and Telling (Negatively Related)

	Variance Component	% Variance Between		
Initial random effects:				
Classroom means	.249	39		
Student residual	.387			
Total	.636			
		% Variance Accounted for by Model		
Final random effects:				
Classroom means	.067	73		
Student residual	.388			
	Coefficient	t Ratio	df	p
Final fixed effects:				
Intercept (grand mean)	2.03	23.46	13	.000
Comprehension strategies	3.07	3.86	13	.002
Telling	−1.02	−2.08	13	.058
Fall score	.023	2.75	119	.006

comprehension strategies and telling (negatively related) accounted for 73% of the variance between teachers. The average classroom mean writing score was 2.0 (SD = 0.5). For every standard deviation increase in the teaching of comprehension strategies (M = 6%, SD = 13%), students' writing score in a class increased by 0.4 points on average (β = .80). For every standard deviation increase in the coding of telling (M = 51%, SD = 19%), students' writing score in a class decreased on average by 0.13 points (β = .39).

For grades 2–5, 43% of the variance in spring writing scores was between teachers, after accounting for fall scores (see Table 8). The average classroom mean writing score was 2.0 (SD = 0.5). Asking higher-level questions after reading, and modeling accounted for 22% of the variance between teachers. For every standard deviation increase in the asking of higher-level questions (M = 19%, SD = 19%), students' writing score in a class increased by 0.2 (β = .38). For every standard deviation increase in the coding of modeling, students' writing score in a class increased on average by 0.13 points (β = .24).

Summary Across Measures. In three of four HLM analyses for grades 2–5, higher-level questioning contributed to students' growth in reading and writing. In grade 1, higher-level questioning contributed to students' improvement

Table 8. HLM Analysis of Grade 2–5 Writing With Higher-Level Questioning and Modeling

	Variance Component	% Variance Between		
Initial random effects:				
Classroom means	.255	43		
Student residual	.342			
Total	.597			
		% Variance Accounted for by Model		
Final random effects:				
Classroom means	.199	22		
Student residual	.342			
	Coefficient	t Ratio	df	p
Final fixed effects:				
Intercept (grand mean)	2.02	32.26	59	.000
Higher-level questioning	1.00	2.95	59	.005
Modeling	1.80	1.93	59	.058
Fall score	.36	4.82	49	.000

in reading comprehension and fluency. Relatively frequent phonics instruction, based on classroom observations, was negatively related to students' fluency growth in grades 2–5. Comprehension skill instruction was negatively related to students' growth on the standardized comprehension measure in grades 2–5, whereas comprehension strategy instruction was associated with students' writing growth in grade 1.

In terms of teacher stance and student engagement or mode of responding, time on-task was positively related to students' gains in standardized reading comprehension in grades 2–5, whereas passive responding was negatively related. Coaching and involving students in active reading (as opposed to the more passive practice of turn-taking during reading) were positively related to gains in fluency in grades 2–5. Modeling was related to improvement in writing in grades 2–5. Telling was negatively related to students' writing growth in grade 1.

Descriptive Data From the Classroom Observations

It is important to qualify the significant findings in these statistical analyses with a descriptive snapshot of the frequency of occurrence of these various instructional behaviors. These data (see Table 9) are important because they show that even those instructional practices that explained substantial growth in student achievement occurred, in real terms, so infrequently (or in the case of negative predictors, so frequently) as to suggest that much remains to be done in efforts to change instruction and improve professional development.

Grouping Practices. Across all grades, whole- and small-class/group instruction were coded with equal frequency except that there was more whole-group than small-group instruction coded in grade 5. In contrast, a greater occurrence of small- than whole-group instruction characterized the most effective schools in our earlier study of primary-grade reading instruction in schools that were beating the odds (Taylor et al., 2000). That being said, a framework of cognitive engagement would suggest that what is important is that students be actively involved in their learning, and this could occur in well-run small- or large-group instruction. Poor instruction, irrespective of the size or nature of the group experiencing it, may lead to a high number of students being off-task or may involve passive responding.

Reading Instruction. Not surprisingly, word-level activities during reading were observed more in grade 1 than in grades 2–3 or 4–5. Phonics instruction was coded for 22% of the reading segments in grade 1 but coded much less often

Table 9. Incidence (Percentages) of Classroom Factors, by Grade

Factor	Grade 1 (N = 17)		Grade 2 (N = 18)		Grade 3 (N = 17)		Grade 4 (N = 18)		Grade 5 (N = 17)	
	M	SD	M	SD	M	SD	M	SD	M	SD
Percentage of time (5-minute segments) coded:										
Whole group	.47	.29	.48	.37	.46	.28	.46	.38	.63	.30
Small group	.49	.32	.45	.34	.49	.20	.57	.35	.37	.30
Narrative text	.53	.24	.72	.22	.55	.22	.61	.28	.44	.30
Informational text	.06	.10	.06	.10	.18	.17	.21	.21	.21	.20
Telling	.51	.19	.54	.18	.52	.16	.61	.18	.55	.20
Recitation	.59	.23	.62	.19	.73	.20	.76	.16	.66	.17
Modeling	.05	.05	.04	.06	.03	.04	.05	.09	.05	.08
Coaching	.20	.16	.16	.11	.14	.11	.15	.19	.11	.15
Percentage of reading segments coded:										
Phonemic awareness	.09	.07								
Phonics instruction	.22	.17	.10	.13	.06	.09	.02	.03	.04	.11
Word-recognition strategies	.16	.14	.18	.19	.08	.07	.08	.10	.06	.07
Vocabulary	.22	.21	.23	.16	.32	.27	.29	.15	.23	.15
Comprehension skills	.12	.17	.08	.11	.18	.17	.15	.13	.13	.16
Comprehension strategies	.06	.13	.02	.05	.09	.10	.07	.14	.16	.15
Meaning of text:										
Lower level	.28	.20	.41	.24	.52	.21	.50	.22	.46	.26
Higher level	.06	.13	.11	.11	.20	.20	.21	.21	.26	.19
Active reading practice	.37	.26	.47	.20	.31	.21	.31	.15	.26	.19
Percentage of all codes for student responding:										
Active responding	.36	.14	.38	.09	.25	.13	.20	.07	.26	.12
Passive responding	.64	.14	.62	.09	.75	.13	.80	.07	.74	.12
Time on-task	.92	.05	.92	.03	.91	.38	.89	.05	.90	.08

in grades 2–5. Phonemic awareness instruction was seldom coded beyond grade 1. Coaching in word-recognition strategies during reading was coded with some regularity in grades 1 and 2 but with less frequency in grades 3–5. These findings are similar to those in our study of primary-grade reading instruction in schools beating the odds (Taylor et al., 2000), in which we found that word-level activities were infrequently observed in grade 3. The findings related to word skill activities also suggested that teachers are focused on phonics instruction in first grade. This finding is compatible with the National Reading Panel Report (2000) recommendation that "Phonics instruction taught early proved much more effective than phonics instruction introduced after first grade" (p. 2-85).

Little comprehension instruction was observed. Comprehension skill instruction was coded for 8%–18% of the reading segments across grades 1–5; comprehension strategy instruction was coded for 2%–9% of the segments in grades 1–4 and 16% of the segments in grade 5.

Across all grades, little higher-level questioning or writing related to texts was observed. This was coded for 6% of the reading segments in grade 1, 11% of the segments in grade 2, and 20%–26% of the segments in grades 3–5. In contrast, lower-level questioning was coded for 28% of the reading segments in grade 1, 41% of the segments in grade 2, and 46%–52% of the segments in grades 3–5. Similarly, a low incidence of higher-level questioning was found in our earlier study (Taylor & Pearson, 2000). However, in this earlier study, we did find that more accomplished teachers (based on experts' ratings) more frequently asked higher-level questions than did less accomplished teachers, just as in the current study more effective teachers (based on students' reading growth) asked higher-level questions more frequently than less effective teachers.

Materials. Across all grades, informational text was seldom a part of the lessons we observed; it was coded for only 6% of the segments in grades 1 and 2 and 18%– 21% of the segments in grades 3–5. In contrast, narrative text was coded for one-half to three-quarters of the segments in grades 1–4 and 44% of the segments in grade 5.

Teacher and Student Actions. Telling and recitation were common interaction styles of teachers in all grades, with telling coded for 51%–61% of the segments in grades 1–5. Recitation was coded for 59%–76% of the segments in grades 1–5. In contrast, modeling was coded for 3%–5% of the segments in grades 1–5. Coaching was only observed for 20% of the segments in grade 1, and from 11%–16% of the segments in grades 2–5. In our earlier study (Taylor et al., 2000), we also found that telling was a common interaction style, with the least accomplished teachers having a preferred style of telling children information, whereas the most accomplished teachers had a preferred interaction style of coaching.

Across all grades, students in the present study were coded as more often engaged in passive responding than in active responding. Passive responding, which included reading turn-taking (e.g., round robin reading), oral turn-taking, or listening to the teacher, was coded for 62%–64% of the student responses in grades 1 and 2 and 74%–80% of the student responses in grades 3–5. In contrast, active responding (reading, writing, and manipulating) was coded for 36%–38% of the student responses in grades 1–2 and 20%–26% of the student responses in grades 3–5.

Perhaps what is most important to remember about these descriptive data, in comparison to the HLM analyses, is that even modest levels of occurrence of these key variables, such as coaching and modeling or higher-level questioning, were associated with substantial growth in student achievement. One can only wonder, if a little goes such a long way, what would happen with wholesale changes in these practices.

Examples of Effective Reading Practices

One limitation of quantitative analyses is that it is difficult to get a picture of what the results look like in everyday practice. To offer a clearer sense of what was going on inside these classrooms, we describe teachers who aptly illustrate the practices identified as positive by the quantitative analyses. We also provide some counterexamples—classrooms in which low-level questioning was apparent and a heavily teacher-directed stance was prominent. Illustrations from the field notes are provided along with some of the conversation from teachers and students. To shed further light on one of the most consistent findings in the study, we conclude this section with a description of the teachers who frequently asked higher-level questions and contrast them with teachers who relied primarily on lower-level questions.

Grade 1. The HLM analyses showed that students improved more in comprehension and fluency when their teachers were coded as asking more higher-level questions than other teachers. Students grew more in writing when their teachers taught comprehension strategies and did not often tell students information. We searched the grade 1 teacher file and located one teacher who was higher than the mean in terms of asking higher-level questions and providing comprehension strategies instruction but lower in terms of telling students information. We also located one teacher who did a fair amount of lower-level questioning but little higher-level questioning, provided little comprehension strategies instruction, and exceeded the mean in terms of telling students information.

Ms. Hernandez (all names are pseudonyms), a first-grade teacher, engaged her students in a great deal of higher-level thinking during reading. She used small-group instruction extensively. While she worked with one group, the other students worked in centers, which included writing words/word families, math, computer, library, and reading signs and charts in the room.

On one day, as the students were reading a story, the teacher introduced a "GO" chart with columns that were labeled as follows: prediction, vocabulary, understanding, interpretation, connections, retelling. She prompted students to complete information on the chart by pointing to the "Prediction—I think the story is about..." column. Students gave their predictions based on the title and pictures. She asked them to check in the book to look for challenging vocabulary they thought they should add. Ms. Hernandez suggested a word that had the same meaning as house. They added cottage to the chart. The teacher asked, "Other interesting words? Another word for woods?" Students suggested forest. Ms. Hernandez referred to the "Understanding—I noticed" column of the chart. A student suggested, "The giant does interesting things." The teacher referred to the "Interpretation—I wonder" column. She encouraged students to think about what would happen next, to go beyond the story, to imagine what the characters could do together. "Think if you are one of the characters in the story how would you solve the problem. What connections can you make? What is the main thing you learned in the story?" A student explained it was about friends. Ms. Hernandez asked, "What maps can you use to help you retell the story?" Students suggested various graphic organizers such as story webs, circle maps, tree maps. The teacher asked how and why they could use each one. A student suggested they could use a bubble map to describe the character.

Another day Ms. Hernandez was working with a small group on informational texts. She referred to the "GO" chart. She told the students they would quickly review the steps without looking at the chart. Students responded, "I think this story is about (prediction)," "I noticed important words in the story (vocabulary)," "I noticed (understanding)," "I wonder (interpreting)," "This reminds me (connections)," and described maps/ story/illustration (retelling).

Ms. Metcalf, another first-grade teacher, primarily taught through small-group instruction, as did Ms. Hernandez. Unlike Ms. Hernandez, however, she typically did much of the work for the students, using a highly teacher-directed stance toward instruction. She minimized opportunities for students to engage in higher-level thinking by doing considerable talking about text herself. One day Ms. Metcalf was reading a story to the children. As they discussed the story, she interjected her own ideas and summarized for the group. She asked, "Why do you think they wrapped the [dinosaur] bones?" This could have served as a higher-level question, but the teacher simply acknowledged a brief answer from one student ("So they wouldn't break") and then provided a lengthy answer herself. She missed the opportunity to have the children express their ideas and elaborate on their thinking.

Grades 2–5. In grades 2–5 the HLM analyses revealed that students had greater growth in reading comprehension when teachers asked higher-level questions, maintained high levels of on-task behavior, and infrequently used comprehension skill instruction (comprehension taught as a routine as compared to a strategic approach to development of comprehension processes) or passive responding (e.g., turn-taking). Students showed more improvement in fluency when their teachers were more often observed coaching, engaging their students in active reading practice, and less often observed teaching phonics lessons. Greater writing growth was positively related to the incidence of higher-level questions and modeling. We searched the grade 2–5 teacher file and located two teachers: one who personified these findings (i.e., illustrated relatively high levels of the factors positively related to gains and low levels of the negatively related factors) and one contrasting teacher (i.e., who illustrated relatively low levels of factors positively related to gains and high levels of negatively related factors).

Mr. May, a fifth-grade teacher, provided many good examples of the "best practices" identified in the HLM analyses for grades 2–5. He stressed higher-level questions and active pupil involvement. As students were about to read the next chapter in the Best Christmas Pageant Ever (Robinson, 1972), Mr. May challenged them to think about what was happening in the story. "Do you think the children should be in the play?" He took a vote, which fostered active pupil involvement, and he had students defend their opinions. In their response journals, students were to answer the following higher-level questions: Do you think the Herdmans will do a good job? Why or why not? How do you think the audience will react? Give evidence from the story.

Mr. May provided small-group instruction to struggling readers while the rest of the class was reading independently. He coached the small group in the use of word-recognition strategies as they read the chapter, and he helped prepare them for the questions he would be asking in the whole-class setting.

Mr. May reconvened the whole class and they discussed their journal entries, after which students participated in small work groups. He asked the groups to write the meanings for two vocabulary words and answer a question they had been given. They recorded their answers on an overhead transparency in anticipation of showing their work to the rest of the class.

In contrast, Mr. Burns, a fourth-grade teacher, asked mostly lower-level questions, and students were engaged in considerable passive responding. During one lesson, students were divided into three groups. One worked with an aide, a second worked at their seats on worksheets, and a third met with Mr. Burns. The introduction to the story lasted 30 minutes. During that introduction, the teacher asked students about the meaning of words they would come across when they read: building, marketplace, celebration, foolishness, snickered, vow. When students could not answer, he told them what the word meant. Once the introduction had been completed, Mr. Burns began a round robin reading session. When a student got stuck on a word, the teacher told her/him the word. Questioning was a rapid fire of low-level questions: "Why did Mom miss Merritt? Did she use her cane when she had her guide dog with her? What did her daughter want her to do when she went on errands? What is the name of the school she is going to?" During this lesson, the teacher did almost all of the talking. Not surprisingly, pupil engagement was low.

Characteristics of Teachers Who Asked Higher-Level Questions. The most consistent finding in this study was that higher-level questioning was related to student literacy growth. We decided to see if we could "unpack" this finding in our attempt to better understand effective reading instruction. To that end, we engaged in a comparative analysis of the observations and interviews of teachers who asked more higher-level questions and those who asked relatively few.

First, we selected the observations and interviews of teachers who were relatively high, which we operationalized as one standard deviation above the mean, on the higher-level question index. Three teachers in grade 1, four in grade 3, two in grade 4, and four in grade 5 met this criterion, for a total of 13. We also selected a comparison group of teachers who were at or above the mean in terms of asking lower-level questions but below the mean in terms of asking higher-level questions. One grade 1 teacher, four grade 2, two grade 3, four grade 4, and 22 one grade 5 teacher met this dual criterion, for a total of 12.

We reread all of the classroom observations and coded activities related to talk or writing about text to add greater depth to the analysis than had been possible in the initial coding. Several promising subcategories of teacher-student interactions emerged from this analysis, that is, they occurred with enough frequency in the corpus of 25 teachers to provide some insights about the correlates of higher- versus lower-order questions. The list included questions that emphasized (a) theme, (b) character interpretation, (c) relating the text to one's life, (d) story events, (e) retelling or summarizing the text, and (f) making predictions before or during reading. We also found two activities that fell outside the questioning, (g) engaging students in a picture walk prior to reading a story or picture book and (h) asking students to work in pairs or small groups to discuss/answer questions about a text.

Table 10 reports the descriptive data for these analyses. The basic data reported were the percentage of teachers in the two groups—those who asked more higher-level questions (HLQ) and those who asked more lower-level questions (LLQ)—who engaged in the eight practices identified in the second, deeper reading of the observational and interview data. Chi-square tests were conducted to determine whether the relative percentages of teachers from the two groups differed for each of the eight practices. These analyses revealed that more HLQ teachers than LLQ teachers asked about theme and asked students to discuss text in a small group or with a partner. More LLQ than HLQ teachers asked about events from a story and engaged students in a picture walk.

We also read through the three teacher interviews, coding responses to questions that were related to teachers' reading comprehension instruction. When asked to relate the three critical components of their classroom reading program, 92% of the HLQ teachers mentioned reading comprehension, whereas 33% of the LLQ teachers mentioned comprehension. In contrast, 50% of the LLQ teachers but only 15% of the HLQ teachers mentioned small-group guided reading as a critical component of their classroom reading program.

Table 10. Percentage of High-Level Questioning and Low-Level Questioning Teachers Engaging in Story-Questioning Practices

Practice	High-Level Questioning Teachers (N = 13)	Low-Level Questioning Teachers (N = 12)
Theme[a]	46	8
Character	92	67
Relate to life	69	33
Events[a]	46	92
Retell	77	75
Predict	54	75
Picture walk[a]	8	42
Student discussion[a]	46	0

[a]Significant differences based on chi-square test.

When asked how they knew if their students were learning in reading, 62% of the HLQ teachers but only 20% of the LLQ teachers reported that they looked at students' responses to the questions they asked.

Discussion

One purpose of this study was to investigate the extent to which reading instruction maximizing students' cognitive engagement enhanced elementary students' growth in reading and writing. In general, results suggest that such an approach to reading instruction is effective. Below we discuss the relation of specific findings to this framework.

A second, related purpose of this study was to determine which aspects of reading instruction had the largest effect on students' reading growth. One consistent finding is that higher-level questioning matters. The more a teacher asked higher-level questions, the more growth the nine target students in her class experienced on a variety of measures. The teachers who asked more higher-level questions appeared to understand the importance of challenging their students to think about what they had read. In the process of asking more higher-level questions, at least two-thirds of the HLQ teachers emphasized character interpretation and connections to experience, and they focused more on thematic elements and student leadership in discussions than did LLQ teachers. In doing so, they implicitly implemented elements of the framework of cognitive engagement, especially in encouraging students to focus on higher-level thinking about what they had read.

Another set of findings suggests that routine practice on skills is not beneficial. The more that explicit phonics skill instruction was observed in grades 2–5, the lower the growth in reading achievement. Given that two-thirds of the students tested at these grades (e.g., average and above-average readers) were decoding well and thus probably had little to gain from phonics practice activities, the finding is not surprising. Furthermore, this finding is compatible with the recommendation in the NRP Report that phonics instruction should be concentrated in the earliest stages of schooling, mainly grades K–1, when it would provide novel information that might be cognitively engaging to students attempting to grasp the alphabetic principle.

The more that routine, practice-oriented approaches to teaching important comprehension processes were observed, the lower the growth in reading comprehension. A framework of cognitive engagement in literacy learning would predict that this more mechanical approach to comprehension processes (e.g., rehearsal related to comprehension skills) would not foster active thinking on the part of students and would not enhance their reading growth. In contrast, a strategic approach to the development of comprehension processes was found to be related to writing growth in grade 1. Interestingly, strategic comprehension instruction was explicitly acknowledged in the report of the National Reading Panel (2000). This finding suggests that how one teaches comprehension, mechanistically or strategically, is a key factor in determining the efficacy of comprehension instruction.

Other teaching variables such as passive responding (negatively related) and high engagement (positively related) were found to be associated with students' growth in reading comprehension. High levels of coaching and involving students in active reading enhanced students' growth in fluency. High levels of telling (negatively related) and modeling (positively related) predicted students' writing growth. Taken together, these findings suggest that two additional components of our framework of cognitive engagement—student support and active involvement—are important strategies to consider to improve reading instruction.

In the years following the current project, as we provide teachers and schools with data on teaching practices related to students' performance and as teachers continue to learn about effective reading instruction in study groups, we plan to investigate the degree to which classroom teaching practices shift over time toward reading instruction that maximizes students' cognitive engagement in literacy lessons. Additionally, we will evaluate the effects of those shifts on student achievement.

Limitations

This study involved schools that were engaged in a reform project that emphasized implementing researched-based reading practices of effective schools and teachers, thus limiting the generalizability of the findings. Teachers received data on their school's reading practices and their own reading practices that they compared to research on effective teaching of reading, and this may have affected the results. Another limitation is that we were only able to investigate classroom practices in nine schools. Finally, classroom information was gathered from three 1-hour observations per classroom per year. At best, we have only a snapshot of the reading instruction in these classrooms. These limitations are important to appropriately qualify our findings; what is perhaps more remarkable is that with a limited sample of teacher behavior, we were able to explain a great deal of the between-classroom variation in student growth.

Conclusions

The improvement of U.S. students' reading achievement is a national goal (Bush, 2001). Schools know that a wealth of information exists to help them move toward this goal, but knowing where to focus is often difficult for teachers, especially when they are bombarded with so many options. Our findings suggest that elements of a framework of reading instruction that maximizes students' cognitive engagement are important to consider when attempting to improve reading instruction. In addition to the reading curriculum, or what teachers teach, how teachers teach reading is of paramount importance.

The description of effective reading instruction emerging from our work encompasses teachers who challenge students with higher-level thinking and the application of reading strategies to their reading and writing. Effective teachers' questioning for texts is purposeful, and they assess students' learning through their answers to challenging questions. They actively involve students in literacy activities, often giving them responsibility for holding their own discussions about text, and they maintain high pupil involvement. Effective teachers use coaching and modeling to help students learn as well as to help them assume responsibility for their own learning. A challenge that remains is to help teachers translate research on effective reading instruction into practice through ongoing, quality professional development within their schools. We hope that the schools in our continuing project on school reform in reading will improve both the "what" (the curricular elements) and "how" (the teaching processes) of their classroom reading instruction with the end result of enhanced reading growth for all students.

NOTE

This research was conducted as part of CIERA, the Center for the Improvement of Early Reading Achievement, and supported under the Educational Research and Development Centers Program, PR/Award No. R305R70004, as administered by the Office of Educational Research and Improvement, U.S. Department of Education. However, the contents of the article do not necessarily represent the positions or policies of the National Institute on Student Achievement,

Curriculum, and Assessment, the National Institute on Early Childhood development, or the U.S. Department of Education, and readers should not assume endorsement by the federal government.

REFERENCES

Baker, L., Dreher, M.J., & Guthrie, J.T. (2000). Why teachers should promote reading engagement. In L. Baker, M.J. Dreher, & J.T. Guthrie (Eds.), *Engaging young readers: Promoting achievement and motivation* (pp. 1–16). New York: Guilford.

Bryk, A.S., & Raudenbush, S.W. (1992). *Hierarchical linear models*. Newbury Park, CA: Sage.

Bush, G.W. (2001). *No child left behind*. Washington, DC: Office of the President of the United States.

Campbell, J.R., Voelkl, K.E., & Donahue, P.L. (1997). *NAEP 1996 trends in academic progress*. Washington, DC: National Center for Education Statistics.

Chin, C.A., Anderson, R.C., & Waggoner, M.A. (2001). Patterns of discourse in two kinds of literature discussion. *Reading Research Quarterly, 30,* 378–411.

Cunningham, A.E., & Stanovich, K.E. (1997). Early reading acquisition and its relation to reading experience and ability 10 years later. *Developmental Psychology, 33,* 934–945.

Deno, S. (1985). Curriculum-based measurement: The emerging alternative. *Exceptional Children, 52,* 219–232.

Duffy, G.G., Roehler, L.R., Sivan, E., Rackliffe, G., Book, C., Meloth, M.S., et al. (1987). Effects of explaining the reasoning associated with using reading strategies. *Reading Research Quarterly, 20,* 347–368.

Frank, K.A. (1998). Quantitative methods for studying social context in multilevels and through interpersonal relations. *Review of Research in Education, 23,* 171–216.

Greenwood, C.R., Carta, J.J., Kamps, D., & Delquadri, J. (1995). *Ecobehavioral assessment systems software (EBHASS) practitioner's manual* (Version 3.0). Kansas City: University of Kansas, Juniper Garden Children's Project.

Guthrie, J.T. (1996). Educational contexts for engagement in literacy. *The Reading Teacher, 49*(6), 432–445.

Guthrie, J.T., Cox, K.E., Knowles, K.T., Buehl, M., Mazzoni, S.A., & Fasulo, L. (2000). Building toward coherent instruction. In L. Baker, M.J. Dreher, & J.T. Guthrie (Eds.), *Engaging young readers: Promoting achievement and motivation* (pp. 1–16). New York: Guilford.

Houghton Mifflin Invitations to Literacy. (1996). Boston: Houghton Mifflin.

Johns, J. (1997). *Basic reading inventory* (7th ed.). Dubuque, IA: Kendall Hunt.

Kamil, M., Mosenthal, P., Pearson, P.D., & Barr R. (Eds.). (2000). *Handbook of reading research* (Vol. 3). Mahwah, NJ: Erlbaum.

Knapp, M.S., Adelman, N.E., Marder, C., McCollum, H., Needels, M.C., Padilla, C., et al. (1995). *Teaching for meaning in high-poverty classrooms*. New York: Teachers College Press.

Kreft, I., & DeLeeuw, J. (1998). *Introducing multilevel modeling*. London: Sage.

MacGinitie, W.H., MacGinitie, R.K., Maria, K., & Dreyer, L.G. (2000). *Gates-MacGinitie Reading Tests* (4th ed.). Itasca, IL: Riverside.

Michigan Literacy Progress Profile 2000. (1998). Lansing: Michigan Department of Education.

National Reading Panel. (2000). *Report of the National Reading Panel*. Washington, DC: National Institute for Child Health and Human Development.

No Child Left Behind Act of 2001. Pub. L. No. 107-110, §115 Stat, 1425 (2002).

Pressley, M., Wharton-McDonald, R., Allington, R., Block, C.C., Morrow, L., Tracey, D., et al. (2001). A study of effective first-grade literacy instruction. *Scientific Studies of Reading, 5,* 35–58.

Pressley, M., Wharton-McDonald, R., Raphael, L.M., Bogner, K., & Roehrig, A. (2002). Exemplary first-grade teaching. In B.M. Taylor &

P.D. Pearson (Eds.), *Teaching reading: Effective schools, accomplished teachers* (pp. 73–88). Mahwah, NJ: Erlbaum.

Raudenbush, S.W., Bryk, A.S., & Congdon, R. (2000). *HLM: Hierarchical linear and nonlinear modeling (Version 5)* [Computer software]. Chicago: Scientific Software International.

Robinson, B. (1972). *The best Christmas pageant ever.* New York: Harper.

Roehler, L.R., & Duffy, G.G. (1984). Direct explanation of comprehension processes. In G.G. Duffy, L.R. Roehler, & J. Mason (Eds.), *Comprehension instruction: Perspectives and suggestions* (pp. 265–280). New York: Longman.

Scanlon, D.M., & Gelzheiser, L.M. (1992). Classroom observation manual. Unpublished manuscript, University of Albany, State University of New York, Child Research and Study Center.

Snow, C., Burns, S., & Griffin P. (Eds.). (1998). *Preventing reading difficulties in young children.* Washington, DC: National Academy.

Taylor, B.M. (1991). *A test of phonemic awareness for classroom use.* Minneapolis: University of Minnesota.

Taylor, B.M., & Pearson, P.D. (2000). *The CIERA School Change Classroom Observation Scheme.* Minneapolis: University of Minnesota.

Taylor, B.M., Pearson, P.D., Clark, K., & Walpole, S. (2000). Effective schools and accomplished teachers: Lessons about primary-grade reading instruction in low-income schools. *The Elementary School Journal, 101,* 121–166.

Taylor, B.M., Peterson, D.P., Pearson, P.D., & Rodriguez, M.C. (2002). Looking inside classrooms: Reflecting on the "how" as well as the "what" in effective reading instruction. *The Reading Teacher, 56,* 270–279.

Ysseldyke, J., & Christenson, S. (1993–1996). TIES: The instructional environment system— II. Longmont, CO: Sopris West.

Appendix A

Table Al. Assessments, Year 2

Ability Assessed	Assessment Tool/Description	Grades Tested Fall	Spring
Letter names	Letter Name subtest from Pikulski Emergent Literacy Survey, Houghton Mifflin. Students identified lowercase and uppercase letters.	1	
Phonemic awareness	Rhyming subtest from Pikulski Emergent Literacy Survey. Students were given a word and asked to say a word that rhymed with this word. Nonsense words were acceptable. Total of 8 points.	1	
	Classroom Segmentation and Blending Test (Taylor, 1991). Children were given six words to blend, "What is /c/ /a/ /t/?" Then they were given six words and asked to identify the first, middle, and last sound they heard in each word. "What sound do you hear first in 'sad'? What sound do you hear in the middle of 'sad'? What sound do you hear at the end of 'sad'?"		
Writing from word-level dictation	Graded lists from Right Start Project (Longmont, CO). Students were asked to write 15 dictated words. If they could write at least seven words correctly from the first list, they went on to a second list of 15 words. (Administered in a group.)	1	
Writing to a prompt	Michigan Writing Assessment. Students were asked to write to a prompt (e.g., Tell about a favorite place). The same prompt was used in the fall and spring. A scoring rubric was used to score papers from high (4) to low (1). (Administered in a group.)	2–5	1–5
Fluency	Words correct per minute on passage from Johns's Basic Reading Inventory (BRI; 1997). In fall, students read for 1 minute from a passage that was one level below grade level. In spring they read from a passage that was at grade level.	2–5	1–5
Comprehension:			
Basal	Retelling of Johns's BRI passage read in fall.	2–5	1–5
	Houghton Mifflin Baseline Test. After reading a three-page story, students answered five short-answer questions and five multiple-choice questions. Possible score is 20 (0, 1, or 2 points for each short-answer question and 2 points for each multiple- choice question correct). A score of 0–10 is considered low, 11–15 average, and 16–20 high. Narrative only, administered in a group.)		
Standardized test	Gates-MacGinitie Reading Test. Only the passage comprehension subtest was administered. Students read short passages and answered multiple-choice questions. (Administered in a group.)	2–5	1–5

Table A2. Codes for Classroom Observations

Level	Code	Level	Code
Level 1—Who:		Phonics:	
Classroom teacher	c	p1 = letter sound	p1
Reading specialist	r	p2 = letter by letter	p2
Special education	se	p3 = onset/rime	p3
Other specialist	sp	p4 = multisyllabic	p4
Student teacher	st	Word-recognition strategies	wr
Aide	a	Phonemic awareness	pa
Volunteer	v	Letter ID	li
No one	n	Spelling	s
Other	o	Other	o
Not applicable	9	Not applicable	9
Level 2—Grouping:		**Level 5—Material:**	
Whole class/large group	w	Textbook, narrative	tn
Small group	s	Textbook, informational	ti
Pairs	p	Narrative trade book	n
Individual	i	Informational tradebook	i
Other	o	Student writing	w
Not applicable	9	Board/chart	b
Level 3—General focus:		Worksheet	s
Reading	r	Oral presentation	op
Composition/writing	w	Pictures	p
Spelling	s	Video/film	v
Handwriting	h	Computer	c
Language	l	Other/not applicable	o/9
Other/not applicable	o/9	**Level 6—Teacher interaction:**	
Level 4—Specific focus:		Tell/give info.	T
Reading connected text	r	Modeling	m
Listening to text	l	Recitation	r
Vocabulary	v	Discussion	d
Meaning of text, lower:		Coaching/scaffolding	c
m1 for talk	m1	Listening/watching	l
m2 for writing	m2	Reading aloud	ra
Meaning of text, higher:		Check work	cw
m3 for talk	m3	Assessment	a
m4 for writing	m4	**Level 7—Expected pupil response:**	
Comprehension skill	c	Reading	r
Comprehension strategy	cs	Reading turn-taking	r-tt
Writing	w	Orally responding	or
Exchanging ideas/oral production	e/o	Oral turn-taking	or-tt
		Listening	l
Word ID	wi	Writing	w
Sight words	sw	Manipulating	m
		Other/not applicable	o/9

Appendix B

Sample of Observational Notes

9:40. A small group is discussing *The Best Christmas Pageant Ever* (Robinson, 1972). The teacher asks, "What happened in the barn? Who else takes part in this? What time of year is it? Let's predict how the family will be part of the pageant." Students offer predictions. Students then read and answer the questions on a sheet: What is a pageant? What is a bad reputation? Teacher circulates. 9:45 6/7 OT (On-task)

c/s/r	ml/n/r/or-tt	c/n/r/or-tt	r/n/l/r	v/s/l/w
levels 1/2/3	4/5/6/7	4/5/6/7	4/5/6/7	4/5/6/7

Appendix C

Description of Classroom Observation Categories Used in Data Analysis (Taylor & Pearson, 2000)

Percentage of time (5-minute segments) coded:

Whole class or large group: All of the children in the class (except for one or two or individuals working with someone else), or a group of more than 10 children. If there are 10 or fewer in the room, code this as a small group.

Small group: Children are working in two or more groups. If there are more than 10 children in a group, call this whole group.

Narrative text: The number of segments in which a narrative textbook (tn) or narrative trade book (n) was coded out of the total number of segments coded.

Informational text: The number of segments that an informational textbook (ti) or information trade book (i) was coded as being used out of the total number of segments coded.

Telling: Telling or giving children information, explaining how to do something.

Recitation: The teacher is engaging the students in answering questions, or responding, usually low-level q-a-q-a. The purpose primarily appears to be getting the children to answer the questions asked rather than engaging them in a formal discussion or fostering independence in terms of answering questions with more complete thinking.

Modeling: The teacher is showing/demonstrating how to do something or how to do a process as opposed to simply explaining it.

Coaching: The teacher is prompting/providing support that will transfer to other situations as students are attempting to answer a question or to perform a strategy or activity. The teacher's apparent purpose is to foster independence, to get a more complete thought or action rather than to simply get a student to answer a question.

Percentage of all reading segments coded:

Phonemic awareness instruction: Students are identifying the sounds in words or blending sounds together (an oral activity). The purpose is to develop phonemic awareness, not letter-sound knowledge (e.g., Sound Box technique would be coded as "pa" because the focus is on learning the sounds in words).

Phonics instruction: Students are focusing on symbol/sound correspondences (pl) or letter-by-letter decoding (p2) or decoding by onset and rime or analogy (p3), but this is not tied to decoding of words while reading. If students are decoding multisyllabic words, code as p4. We calculated the total number of phonics activities divided by the total number of times reading, coded at level 3.

Word-recognition strategies: Students are focusing on use of one or more strategies to figure out words while reading, typically prompted by the teacher.

Lower-level text comprehension (talk or writing about text): Students are talking (ml) or writing (m2) about the meaning of text that is at a lower level of thinking. The writing may be a journal entry about the text or a fill-in-the-blank worksheet on the text meaning (rather than on a comprehension skill or vocabulary words). The total number of "low-level text comprehension" activities at level 4 out of the total number of times reading, coded at level 3, was calculated.

Higher-level text comprehension (talk or writing about text): Students are talking (m3) or writing (m4) about the meaning of text that is engaging them in higher-level thinking. This is talk or writing about text that is challenging to the children and is at either a high level of text interpretation or goes beyond the text: generalization, application, evaluation, aesthetic response. Needless to say, a child must go beyond a yes or no answer (e.g., in the case of an opinion or aesthetic response). The total number of "high-level text comprehension" activities at level 4 out of the total number of times reading (as the major focus) at level 3 was coded.

Comprehension skill instruction: Students are engaged in a comprehension activity (other than a comprehension strategy) that is at a lower level of thinking (e.g., traditional skill work such as identifying main idea, cause-effect, fact-opinion).

Comprehension strategy instruction: Students are using a comprehension strategy that will transfer to other reading and in which this notion of transfer is mentioned (e.g., reciprocal teaching, predicting. If predicting was done but transfer was not mentioned, this would be coded as *c*).

Vocabulary instruction: Students are discussing/working on word meaning(s).

Active reading practice: Students are reading (not reading turn-taking) at level 7.

Percentage of all codes for student responding:

Active responding: Children are engaged in one or more of the following level 7 responses: reading, writing, oral responding, manipulating. The total number of "active responding" codes coded out of the total number of level 7 responding codes coded was calculated.

Passive responding: Children are engaged in one or more of the following level 7 responses: reading turn-taking, oral responding turn-taking, listening. The total number of "passive responding" codes coded out of the total number of level 7 responding codes coded was calculated.

Time on-task: At the end of the 5-minute note-taking segment, the observer counted the number of children in the room who appeared to be engaged in the assigned task out of all the children in the room. If a child was quiet but staring out the window or rolling a pencil on his desk, this was not counted as on-task.

CHAPTER 4

Decisions, Decisions: Responding to Primary Students During Guided Reading

Robert M. Schwartz

M s. Gallant glanced around the table at the six students in the guided reading group. The book introduction had gone well. The new book was a version of *The Three Little Pigs* (1976) story and everyone in the group was familiar with the basic story structure. Looking at a few of the pictures generated lots of discussion among the students and helped establish the basic story line for this version. As the students began to read the story quietly to themselves, Ms. Gallant turned toward Michael, who was seated on her left for today's lesson (all scenarios are based on actual observations, but the names are all fictitious). She listened to him read the text and prepared to teach if an opportunity presented itself.

On page 7, Michael substituted *home* for *house* in the sentence "The big bad wolf went to the house of the first little pig." Before he turned the page Ms. Gallant needed to make a decision, and quickly.

In her book, *Change Over Time in Children's Literacy Development*, Clay (2001) argued that as teachers we need a complex theory of literacy learning and instruction to support the early progress of struggling students. She stated, "I am certain that a view of complexity is the kind of understanding required to deliver results in an early intervention programme aiming to prevent subsequent literacy difficulties in as many children as possible" (p. 138). Classroom teachers have fewer opportunities to work individually with struggling readers. Still, as guided reading plays a larger part in primary-classroom programs (Dorn, French, & Jones, 1998; Fountas & Pinnell, 1996), we need to make teaching de-

RTI in Literacy—Responsive and Comprehensive, edited by Peter H. Johnston, published by the International Reading Association. This chapter reprinted from Schwartz, R.M. (2005). Decisions, Decisions: Responding to Primary Students During Guided Reading. *The Reading Teacher, 58*(5), 436–443.

cisions as we listen and respond to a beginning reader's attempts to read leveled texts (Pinnell & Fountas, 1999).

This is a complex professional task. My experience working with primary teachers suggests they are often very comfortable providing guided reading lessons with rich book introductions (Clay, 1991a) that prepare students to understand the meaning and structure of leveled books. They also follow the reading of these texts with discussions that help to build comprehension and word-recognition knowledge. The task becomes more complex as teachers try to provide immediate feedback as they listen to one student or a group of students reading the story aloud. This is the type of guidance that many struggling readers need to construct problem-solving strategies on the run as they read. Guided reading lessons give us the opportunity to provide this type of support.

What Makes Teaching Decisions Complex?

Consider the factors involved in deciding how to respond to the substitution of *home* for *house*. A simple decision theory based on accuracy would say this error is always a problem to be corrected. A simple theory based on meaning might always ignore this type of miscue. A complex theory would base such a decision on previous observations of the student and an assessment of his or her literacy development.

Early in literacy learning, a student might read a patterned book (Cowley, 1987a, p. 10) containing the sentence "I'm going to build a house." Given a meaningful introduction to the story, the student might read this text and attend to only a few print cues. One possible reading is "I'm going to make a home." Teaching to a miscue of *home* for *house* in this context could eventually result in an accurate reading, but it is unlikely to facilitate processing strategies that carry over to other texts. Deciding to focus on the make/build substitution might be far more productive for this student. Most students learn to recognize gross visual differences among words before they attend to more subtle difference in the middle or end of words (Clay, 2001; Juel & Minden-Cupp, 2000).

The teaching decision would be very different for a student whose response history indicates that he or she always notices substitutions that change the initial letter–sound relationship and when stuck on a word will reread and generate a prediction based on meaning, sentence structure, and the initial visual cue. Attention to the substitution of *home* for *house* in *The Three Little Pigs* (1976) example may be an excellent opportunity to extend his or her strategies to include sound-to-letter expectations beyond the initial letter (Schwartz, 1997).

For a more advanced reader, who has demonstrated the ability to use a wide range of print cues, the substitution of *home* for *house* may again be worth ignoring. This miscue can represent the operation of a fluent reader whose eyes are working ahead of his or her voice as he or she focuses attention on constructing the meaning of the next section of text.

What are the factors that influence teaching decisions during a student's oral reading of a new text? A.L. Brown (1982) used a tetrahedron as a conceptual framework to organize factors affecting reading and other complex cognitive tasks. This framework is one useful way to think about the combination of factors that influence our teaching decisions (see Figure 1).

Responding to students' oral reading is a topic that has received much attention in instructional materials and research (see K.J. Brown, 2003, for a recent review of this literature). If you are familiar with this literature, the current framework provides a way to organize your knowledge about theory, observation, and

Figure 1. Factors That Affect Teaching Decisions During Oral Reading

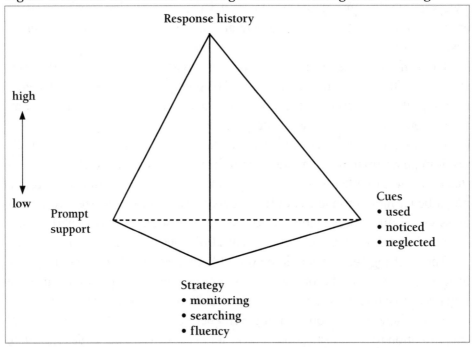

instruction. The combination of factors included in this framework should challenge even the most experienced primary teachers to refine their decision process to support struggling readers. For less experienced teachers the framework provides an introduction to factors that affect these decisions. In the following sections, I explore how each of the four factors in Figure 1 (i.e., response history, cues, strategies, and prompt support level) contributes to a complex theory of literacy learning and instruction. In the final section I return to the question of how to use this type of complex theory to guide teaching decisions.

Response History

Guided reading procedures and natural language texts that are leveled to provide a gradient of difficulty allow students to successfully read meaningful books as they build knowledge of letters, words, and how they are combined to form simple messages and texts. Careful observation and analysis of errors that students make as they read these texts can provide information to guide our teaching decisions.

Why are errors so important? Reading educators and theorists (Clay, 1982; Goodman, 1969) have long recognized the value of error analysis as an assessment of a student's developing strategies. Young students don't attend to all the information in texts, even when they read accurately. Beginning readers are extending the scope of information they can use. Analysis of the errors that a student makes and how the pattern of errors changes over time reflect developing processing strengths and strategies (Clay, 2001). Each error contains a partially correct response to the text. Focusing on the strengths reflected in the student's errors lets us build on what the student can do and focus our teaching decisions to extend that processing system.

To respond quickly and effectively to teaching opportunities during oral reading, we need a tentative but elaborate theory of a particular student's literacy development. Our analysis of the student's response history provides this theory. As beginning readers develop effective processing systems for literacy we need to keep adjusting our decisions to their shifting pattern of responses. High-progress students challenge our ability to adjust theory and instruction quickly enough to provide instruction that is contingent on observed patterns of responses. The good news is that these students need far less of this type of instruction. High-progress readers benefit from whole-class and small-group instruction and a wide variety of literacy opportunities to build effective processing systems (Clay, 1991b, 2001). A small amount of contingent or scaffolded instruction can support their continued rapid learning.

Struggling readers are less likely to shift their processing strategies without direct support in the context where strategic action is required. This is one reason that isolated phonics instruction has often failed to result in improved performance. Students may build the knowledge base needed to support word recognition, but they fail to use this knowledge in the context of reading texts. Contingent instruction during oral reading can support struggling readers to apply their letter–sound knowledge in context (Clay, 2001).

Cues

Teaching decisions and our analysis of the student's response history are further complicated by the number of different types of cues beginning readers may use, notice, or neglect in their reading of a text. Figure 2 displays some of the cues and knowledge sources that readers can use as they process a text (Schwartz, 1997).

Figure 2. Cues and Knowledge Sources to Support Monitoring and Searching Strategies

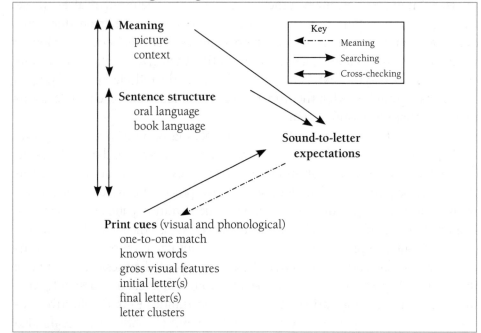

Note. Reprinted from Schwartz (1997).

Goodman (1969) has labeled his approach to error interpretation as "miscue analysis." This is a particularly apt term because every error, or miscue, uses some set of cues and ignores others. The pattern of cues used, noticed, or neglected in prior attempts at text reading is a central part of the student's response history and helps us decide the type of errors that might be most productive for future teaching.

The easiest leveled texts for guided reading lessons combine a repeated, single sentence pattern with high levels of meaning support from the pictures for any variation in the pattern. One such text begins, "The cat sat on the mat" (Wildsmith, 1982, unpaged). This is followed by five more sentences that repeat the same pattern except for a change in the animal name. The illustrations provide cues to the animal mentioned in the sentence and ingeniously manage to convey a story of tension, conflict, and resolution to complement the simple language of the text.

An adult reader would quickly and automatically process the high-frequency words with little attention to other cue sources to aid word recognition. The adult would be able to easily think about the developing story and the clever illustrations and perhaps add dramatic intonation and phrasing if reading this story aloud to a group of students.

A guided reading lesson for this text might begin with the teacher explaining that the book is about a cat that likes to spend his time sitting on his mat, but he doesn't like to share. On this page it says, "The cat sat on the mat." Turning to the next illustration the teacher asks, "What do you think it says on this page?" Given a correct prediction, the student could be asked to read the rest of the text aloud. A student with good oral language, a sense of how this type of book works, and a strategy of examining the illustrations for new information could accurately read the remainder of the text (with the exception of the page where letters are used to convey the sound the cat makes to scare away the other animals).

This type of emergent reading doesn't require a full analysis of the print, but it does provide opportunities for a student to notice, or a teacher to draw attention to, new or partially developed sources of information. A student might be learning how to match words in oral language with the directional conventions of print and an emergent concept of words in print (Morris, Bloodgood, Lomax, & Perney, 2003). Another student might notice high-frequency known words like *the* or *on*; the rhyming patterns in *cat*, *sat*, and *mat*; the sound-to-letter expectations for the initial letter in words like *dog* or *goat*; or the similarity of a known word, *how*, and a new word in this text, *cow*. All of these insights are possible, but most are probably inappropriate teaching points. An elaborate theory of the student, based on his or her previous response history, can guide a teacher's instructional decisions to focus on extending the set of cues the student attends to.

Leveled texts try to take advantage of the strengths that students bring to the reading task. Many students' greatest strengths are general knowledge from their immediate social environment and oral language ability. Other forms of beginning reading material focus attention on print, the least familiar aspect of the task for most beginning readers. These materials try to simplify the learning task by controlling the rate at which new reading vocabulary or letter–sound relationships are introduced into the materials. Picture cues are sometimes avoided in these materials to force attention to print, and many of the early materials can sound very artificial because of the limits imposed by control of vocabulary or sound relationships. These simple models of literacy learning and instruction give priority to one type of cue source. Simple models reduce the need for complex professional decisions, but they also provide only one route to literacy learning, and this route may not be effective for many students that struggle to construct an effective processing system for beginning reading (Clay, 1991b, 2001).

Strategies

An effective processing system for reading is made up of knowledge and mental strategies that are much more complex than the usual advice we give students. They take our advice, instruction, and their experience as readers to construct working systems that allow them to operate efficiently and effectively on increasingly complex texts (Clay, 2001). For beginning readers, two types of strategies that develop rapidly over the first few years are monitoring and searching strategies (Clay, 1991b; Schwartz, 1997).

Readers use searching strategies to generate an initial attempt to read a word and monitoring strategies to evaluate the attempt and initiate further searching if needed. Phonics, the use of context cues, and decoding by analogy are all forms of searching. They help students to make initial attempts to read words that are not recognized quickly as sight words. Searching strategies have played a major role in classroom reading programs and in the professional debate on early literacy instruction.

Monitoring strategies have received less attention. The opportunity to teach for monitoring strategies is often difficult to recognize. We need to let students make an error and allow enough time for them to notice their error independently. Usually this means at least letting students finish reading the sentence in which the error occurs. In a small-group read-aloud this might be impossible because the other students often interrupt the reading as soon as the error is made.

Whether to teach for monitoring or searching needs to become a more conscious part of the decision process when we listen to a student's oral reading. If readers don't notice errors that they make in oral reading (via monitoring strategies), they have no reason to search for additional cues or refine their searching strategies. Monitoring by a variety of cues to determine whether an attempt looks right and makes sense is a learning mechanism that drives students to refine their processing system.

Struggling readers often lack the feedback about their attempts that effective monitoring strategies can provide. Self-correction during oral reading is one observable indication of effective processing. Self-correction requires a combination of monitoring and searching strategies. Clay (1982) reported a marked difference in the self-correction rates for high- versus low-progress beginning readers.

Phonemic awareness has recently received considerable attention in the professional literature as a predictor of reading achievement. The mechanism by which phonemic awareness affects reading achievement is less clear (Morris et al., 2003). The hypothesized relationship seems to be that phonemic awareness supports the learning of searching strategies based on phonics. An additional or alternative mechanism is that phonemic awareness enables monitoring by sound-to-letter expectations that in turn lead to self-correction and increased independence in both monitoring and searching.

As shown in Figure 2, beginning readers may use searching strategies based on one cue source to generate a prediction and then cross-check that attempt with a prediction from another cue source. This is an early form of monitoring (Clay, 1993). A slightly more advanced reader might use multiple cue sources to generate a word-recognition attempt. The attempt provides expectations about sound-to-letter relationships that can be used to check whether the attempt matches additional print cues—a more complex form of monitoring.

For example, a beginning reader who is just learning how to gather information from print may use a searching strategy based on meaning and the initial visual cue to make the *home* for *house* substitution in *The Three Little Pigs* (1976). We could point to *house* and ask the student to sound it out, possibly resulting in an accurate response. This teaching sequence is unlikely to lead to increased self-corrections and independence because the student never noticed that her initial attempt conflicted with some of the available cues. Alternatively, we might allow the student to complete the sentence and then prompt, "That made sense, but check to see if it looks right." If the student's response history indicates that if she were asked to write a word like *home* she would include the major consonant sounds, then this prompt might be sufficient to help the student notice the discrepancy as she rereads the sentence, paying closer attention to the print (Clay, 1991b, 1993; Schwartz, 1997).

A large body of research evidence (Schwartz, 1980; Schwartz & Stanovich, 1981; Stanovich, 2000) indicates that adult readers, and even proficient younger readers, do not normally use meaning and structure cues to support word recognition while reading. This evidence suggests that effective readers recognize words based on rapid visual analysis while focusing attention on constructing meaning from the text. They continue to use meaning and structure cues to monitor this rapid visual processing but extend their strategies to include new forms of monitoring that operate at the message level and not just as a check on word recognition. This transition is a gradual process that continues well beyond a first-grade reading level.

Programs that encourage beginning readers to use cues from pictures and oral language structures to support word recognition in the easiest levels of text must ensure that students develop the knowledge and strategies of more proficient readers. We expect a change in a student's searching strategies over time. Running record assessments let us track these changes over time in the student's response history and plan our teaching decisions to support these changes (Clay, 2001, 2002; Schwartz, 1997).

Prompt Support Level

Even with a complex theory of literacy learning and instruction and a clear understanding of the student's current processing, contingent teaching decisions during oral reading are a challenge. In the original work on scaffolding, Wood, Bruner, and Ross (1976) found that independent performance on a puzzle-building task was enhanced when parents followed a prompting rule based on the student's response to previous prompts. The prompts varied in the level of adult support provided, increasing support when the student struggled and decreasing support when the student succeeded. Thus the scaffold, or support provided, was raised or lowered depending on immediate observation of performance to build independence on the task. Training graduate students to use these contingent rules with students was effective, but Wood (1988) noted that responding appropriately was difficult even in this simplified problem domain.

Reading is a much more complex domain. As shown in Figure 1, after an analysis of the student's response history, teachers need to decide what type of strategic processing to foster, what cues the student should use or notice, and how much support to provide for new learning. Teaching for independence requires a balance of all these factors in teaching decisions during reading. For example, if the student has made an error in oral reading, and, considering his or her response history, you feel there are cues that have been ignored that he or she should be able to notice, you might decide to prompt for self-monitoring. You still need to decide how much support to provide in that prompt. When the student completes the sentence or the page, showing no indication of noticing the error, you could ask, "Were you right?" (Clay, 1993, p. 41). This prompt, if not used exclusively when the student has made an error, encourages the student to monitor his or her reading consistently and independently. If you are trying to help the student extend the cues used for monitoring during reading, this prompt may not provide sufficient support for the student to notice the error. A higher level of support would be provided by a prompt that indicates what cues the student used in his or her response and what cues he or she ignored (i.e., "That makes sense; check to see if it looks right."). If this more supportive prompt is not sufficient to help the student identify the difficulty, then you could provide a demonstration or direct explanation. Future prompts in similar situations would shift toward providing less support. The goal of this sequence of teaching decisions is to extend the set of cues the student uses for independent self-monitoring.

Teaching From a Complex Theory

Listening to a student read a new or partially familiar text provides a variety of teaching opportunities. Decisions about when, what, and how to teach can be guided by the conceptual framework previously discussed and shown in Figure 1.

Table 1 lists a number of possible prompts (Clay, 1993) that respond to different readings of the text *What Would You Like?* (Cowley, 1987b). In this story a boy is making a sandwich. On each page an animal suggests something to put on the sandwich. A cat says, "Would you like a mouse?" (p. 6). A lizard says,

Table 1. Possible Substitutions, Support Types, and Strategy Prompts

Text: "Would you like a fat worm?" "No I wouldn't." (Cowley, 1987b, p. 10)			
Substitution for *fat*	Support type	Monitoring prompt[a]	Searching prompt[b]
purple	Independence	Were you right?	What can you try?
flat	Meaning support	Does that make sense?	Try that again and think what would make sense.
four	Structure support	Does that sound right?	Try that again and think what would sound right.
purple	Print support	Does that look right?	Try that again and get your mouth ready for the first sound.

[a]Child makes the substitution and finishes the sentence, showing no sign of noticing the error. Give the prompt without indicating where in the sentence the error might be. Use these prompts occasionally, following accurate reading so the prompt itself doesn't signal an error.
[b]Child notices that his or her initial attempt doesn't work or stops at the unknown word and makes no further attempt.

"Would you like a grasshopper?" (p. 8). In the example the pattern changes slightly with the addition of an adjective, *fat*. The table includes four possible substitutions for the word *fat*, along with various prompts for monitoring or searching and the type of support the prompt provides.

We can prepare to respond to a student by looking for patterns in the errors we observe in previous running records (Clay, 2002; Schwartz, 1997). First, think about the cues the student uses for initial attempts. From these errors we can infer the student's initial searching strategies. A student that substitutes *lady* for *woman* or *purple* for *fat* may be using meaning cues from the story or pictures to support initial attempts.

Second, look for a pattern in errors that the student notices versus those that are ignored. From these behaviors we can infer the types of cues the student uses to monitor his or her reading.

Many struggling readers may make substitutions like those mentioned above and keep right on reading with no sign of hesitation or doubt. They've used their searching strategy, and as far as they're concerned it worked. A prompt at the end of the sentence may be sufficient to get them to recheck using an additional cue source. This is teaching. What they can do with assistance they will eventually be able to do independently (Clay, 2001; Clay & Cazden, 1990).

Finally, when the student does notice an error, look for a pattern in the student's responses at that point. From these responses we can infer the types of searching strategies used at difficulty. For too many struggling readers, their first and only searching attempt at difficulty is to look at the teacher for help. Prompt them to search in the text. Ask the student, "What could you try?" (Clay, 1993, p. 49). Early strategies may involve rereading all or part of the sentence to combine meaning and sentence structure with some print cues. More advanced readers can retain the meaning while searching within the problem word for parts that are familiar from other known words.

The following is an example of what this analysis might involve. Sara's reading of *Baby Bear's Present* (Randell, 1994) shows 11 initial errors in the 206 words of text. Six of these errors are noticed and self-corrected, usually as she rereads the sentence from the beginning. Nine of her initial attempts combine meaning, the sentence structure up to the point of error, and the initial letter cue. For example, she used *store* for *shop* (twice), *look* for *like*, *train* for *toy*, *move* for *make*, and *let's* for *let*. Of these initial errors only the store/shop substitution is left uncorrected. It could be that Sara uses meaning, structure, and initial visual cues for initial attempts and then monitors her attempts by additional visual cues, but it could also be that she accepts these initial attempts unless they conflict with the subsequent sentence structure. The store/shop substitution of course causes no conflict, but the other substitutions do conflict. For example, *Please let's* sounds fine, but *Please let's me* doesn't sound right. In a similar manner, *I can move it* sounds fine, but before Sara reads the last word, *go*, she rereads the sentence and changes *move* to *make*.

Sara shows many strengths in her reading process, but she has more to learn. Her knowledge of visual cues will be enhanced and her processing more effective if she learns to monitor within words. She needs to learn how to check her attempts against visual cues in the target word based on sound-to-letter expectations from the attempt. Closer visual attention to monitor many successful and unsuccessful attempts should lead to faster visual searching strategies for her initial attempts, with less reliance on meaning and structure cues. This record analysis prepares me to look for opportunities to teach as I work with Sara in the future or to recognize her progress over time.

Effective Support for All Students

The guided reading lesson format provides a rich opportunity for teachers to observe and investigate early literacy. Listening to a student read a text that is only partially familiar allows us to apply and refine our theories of literacy learning and instruction. As classroom teachers arrange more opportunities to listen to and respond to developing readers, it would be useful to discuss your insights with teachers that work one-on-one with struggling readers. The contexts differ, so effective instruction in each setting will also differ, but discussion of teaching decisions that support students' learning can help us better understand the complexity of literacy learning and instruction.

Close observation of students during oral reading also has the potential to help move our profession beyond the endless debate over the most effective searching strategy for initial reading instruction (Chall, 1967). Teaching for self-monitoring is at least as important as any particular searching strategy for many students (Schwartz, 1997). There are many different paths to proficient reading, but students who struggle with initial literacy learning need a guide to help keep them on their path (Clay, 1998).

In the opening scenario, Ms. Gallant has only a moment to decide how to respond to Michael's reading. This decision process can be as complex as that engaged in by trial lawyers or emergency-room doctors. She needs to use her professional knowledge base and previous observation of the student to make moment-by-moment decisions that support one of the most culturally important and complex learning tasks. The challenge for all of us as teachers is to continue to refine our personal theories to a point where our teaching decisions can effectively support the literacy learning of all students.

REFERENCES

Brown, A.L. (1982). Learning how to learn from reading. In J.A. Langer & M.T. Smith-Burke (Eds.), *Reader meets author/bridging the gap* (pp. 26–54). Newark, DE: International Reading Association.

Brown, K.J. (2003). What do I say when they get stuck on a word? Aligning teachers' prompts with student development. *The Reading Teacher, 56*, 720–733.

Chall, J.S. (1967). *Learning to read: The great debate.* New York: McGraw-Hill.

Clay, M.M. (1982). *Observing young readers: Selected papers.* Portsmouth, NH: Heinemann.

Clay, M.M. (1991a). Introducing a new story-book to young readers. *The Reading Teacher, 45*, 264–273.

Clay, M.M. (1991b). *Becoming literate: The construction of inner control.* Portsmouth, NH: Heinemann.

Clay, M.M. (1993). *Reading Recovery: A guidebook for teachers in training.* Portsmouth, NH: Heinemann.

Clay, M.M. (1998). *By different paths to common outcomes.* York, ME: Stenhouse.

Clay, M.M. (2001). *Change over time in children's literacy development.* Portsmouth, NH: Heinemann.

Clay, M.M. (2002). *An observation survey of early literacy achievement.* (2nd ed.). Portsmouth, NH: Heinemann.

Clay, M.M., & Cazden, C.B. (1990). A Vygotskian interpretation of Reading Recovery. In L. Moll (Ed.), *Vygotsky and education: Instructional implications and applications of sociohistorical psychology* (pp. 206–222). Cambridge, UK: Cambridge University Press.

Cowley, J. (1987a). *Where are you going Aja Rose?* Bothell, WA: The Wright Group.

Cowley, J. (1987b). *What would you like?* Bothell, WA: The Wright Group.

Dorn, L.J., French, C., & Jones, T. (1998). *Apprenticeship in literacy: Transitions across reading and writing*. York, ME: Stenhouse.

Fountas, I.C., & Pinnell, G.S. (1996). *Guided reading: Good first teaching for all children*. Portsmouth, NH: Heinemann.

Goodman, K.S. (1969). Analysis of oral reading miscues: Applied psycholinguistics. *Reading Research Quarterly, 5*, 9–30.

Juel, C., & Minden-Cupp, C. (2000). Learning to read words: Linguistic units and instructional strategies. *Reading Research Quarterly, 35*, 458–492. doi:10.1598/RRQ. 35.4.2

Morris, D., Bloodgood, J.W., Lomax, R.G., & Perney, J. (2003). Developmental steps in learning to read: A longitudinal study in kindergarten and first grade. *Reading Research Quarterly, 38*, 302–328. doi:10.1598/RRQ.38.3.1

Pinnell, G.S., & Fountas, I.C. (1999). *Matching books to readers: Using leveled books in guided reading, K–3*. Portsmouth, NH: Heinemann.

Randell, B. (1994). *Baby Bear's present*. Petone, New Zealand: Nelson Price Milburn.

Schwartz, R.M. (1980). Levels of processing: The strategic demands of reading comprehension. *Reading Research Quarterly, 15*, 433–450.

Schwartz, R.M. (1997). Self-monitoring in beginning reading. *The Reading Teacher, 51*, 40–48.

Schwartz, R.M., & Stanovich, K.E. (1981). Flexibility in the use of graphic and contextual information in good and poor readers. *Journal of Reading Behavior, 13*, 264–269.

Stanovich, K.E. (2000). *Progress in understanding reading: Scientific foundations and new frontiers*. New York: Guilford.

The three little pigs: A British folk tale. (1976). In *Reading unlimited, level 3* (pp. 2–26). Glenview, IL: Scott Foresman.

Wildsmith, B. (1982). *Cat on the mat*. Oxford, UK: Oxford University Press.

Wood, D. (1988). *How children think and learn*. Cambridge, UK: Basil Blackwell.

Wood, D., Bruner, J.S., & Ross, G. (1976). The role of tutoring in problem solving. *Journal of Child Psychology & Psychiatry, 17*, 89–100.

SECTION III

Literacy Assessment

The introduction to this section is necessarily longer than the others. Assessment is consistently one of the most problematic aspects of RTI, primarily because of misconceptions, particularly about what the law requires. IDEA actually has very few requirements. It requires regular progress monitoring, data to inform instruction, and data on which to make decisions regarding the successfulness of an intervention. It requires data that allow responsible parties to determine "that underachievement...is not due to lack of appropriate instruction" (U.S. Department of Education, n.d.). According to the law, this means examining (a) "data that demonstrate that prior to, or as a part of, the referral process, the child was provided appropriate instruction in regular education settings, delivered by qualified personnel" and (b) "data-based documentation of repeated assessments of achievement at reasonable intervals, reflecting formal assessment of student progress during instruction" (U.S. Department of Education, n.d.).

Assessing the manner in which our instruction influences students' learning is a central requirement of IDEA. However, the law does not specify the nature and frequency of that assessment. As the researchers in this section of the book show, there are many sensible strategies. However, there are some that are not as useful as they might seem. For example, in recent years an assessment strategy called curriculum-based measurement (CBM) has become popular for monitoring students' literacy development. Stanley Deno developed this strategy in the 1970s in an attempt to find a simple progress-monitoring tool for reading (Alt & Samuels, in press). Because students were reading basal readers, Deno felt that counting the number of words they read accurately from the basal in a minute would be a useful proxy measure for reading ability, and it would not take time away from instruction. He felt that reading quickly and accurately required integrating all components of reading and thus would be a good indicator of progress. He also thought that it would not encourage special education teachers to distort the curriculum by focusing their attention on myriad subskills (which they were inclined to do).

The logic of such measures of speed and accuracy is seductively simple and received a boost from the report of the National Reading Panel (National Institute of Child Health and Human Development, 2000) when it popularized the apparently related concept of fluency. However, these measures are sustained by the following misconceptions:

- It is assumed that recognizing words quickly and accurately is a good indicator of reading fluency, or reading competence. It is not (Alt & Samuels, in press; Goodman, 2006).

- It is assumed that recognizing words quickly and accurately ensures comprehension. It does not (Samuels, 2007). Reading speed is not necessarily related to comprehension or even fluency (Cramer & Rosenfield, 2008; Pressley, Hilden, & Shankland, 2005).

- It is assumed that rapid identification of words integrates all the components of reading. It does not (Samuels, 2007).

Measures of speed and accuracy answer the question, How quickly and accurately can this student read material deemed appropriate for this grade level? Because this material is often too difficult for the students involved with RTI, the process they use to read such texts is not a good indicator of their competence. They are likely to use a different process on material of an appropriate difficulty, for example, monitoring their comprehension. Assessments of speed and accuracy do not provide instructionally useful information, particularly because they do not draw attention to the processes the students use. They make no record of self-correction or strategic processing of any kind and thus draw the teacher's attention away from strategic reading processes and their instruction. Indicators of writing development are no more promising, for example, simply counting changes in the number of words written (Gansle, Noell, VanDerHeyden, Naquin, & Slider, 2002). These are serious problems of construct and consequential validity.

Over the years, CBM has also changed. Now, just as with any test, the texts used are standardized passages, no longer from the curriculum the students are using (Fuchs, 2003). The measure is, in fact, no longer curriculum based. By contrast, the assessment strategies Anne McGill-Franzen and colleagues describe in Chapter 6 and those Linda J. Dorn and Shannon Coman Henderson describe in Chapter 7 show a different approach to assessment, one that is more accurately curriculum based, because it really does draw on the reading and writing the students are doing daily in the classroom. We might call this real curriculum-based assessment (RCBA). This form of assessment answers different questions, such as, Are materials of appropriate difficulty being used for instruction? Is the student in control of problem solving and monitoring for meaning making in reading and writing? How is the student using strategies and resources in the process of making meaning? The difference between the CBM and RCBA approaches to assessment lies in the goals they serve.

Assessment Goals

As the Introduction to this book points out, IDEA contains language that directs us toward two goals: designing instruction that reduces the number of children classified as learning disabled (LD) and identifying the children who have a learning disability. Although identifying a learning disability and preventing one can be seen as two sides of the same coin, they are in fact different activities. They require different tools and strategies (Fuchs, Stecker, & Fuchs, 2008) and they invoke different ways of representing children and literacy, and different relationships. Focusing on the goal of tidy and uncontestable decisions regarding which children have disabilities and which do not—a matter of identification—draws us into a measurement frame and an emphasis on standardizing the decision process as much as possible. For example, because the identification decision is based on students' response to an instructional intervention, we tend to standardize the instruction as much as possible, to script it, ensure that it takes place for a specific number of weeks, and check to make sure instruction is accomplished exactly as prescribed.

The chapters in this section approach RTI through an instructional frame in which the goal is first and foremost to prevent children from *becoming* LD. In this context, it is not enough to monitor how much a student is learning. Teachers need to have *instructionally relevant* information about the student's learning, acquired and examined in a way that makes it likely to be used. As we see in Chapters 6, 7, 16, and 17, collecting and attending to such information in a shared learning environment not only accomplishes change in student performance but also accomplishes teacher development (Gilmore, 2002).

Screening

There is no requirement in the law for screening. I mention this because there is a misconception that screening is required and that it must be universal.

Certainly, optimizing instruction, which is required, could lead to initial screening upon entry to school, when there is no other available information. But screening at that point can be relatively unsophisticated. For example, Frank Vellutino and his colleagues (Vellutino, Scanlon, Small, & Fanuele, 2006) used children's knowledge of the alphabet to screen them upon entry to kindergarten to decide which students would benefit from some focused small-group instruction. The measure was not really used as a measure of alphabet knowledge but rather as an indirect indicator (a proxy measure) of general literacy experience. When children enter kindergarten, this works because children with limited alphabet knowledge also generally have limited experience with other aspects of literacy. This simple test requires relatively little effort and provides some instructionally useful information. Although it is not particularly precise, it is sufficiently accurate to allow the relatively low resource prevention effort to begin immediately. Some children respond rapidly to such modest interventions and can be discontinued on the basis of ongoing classroom assessments, leaving more resources for those still in need. Alphabet knowledge could not be used as an ongoing measure of literacy development, both because once children enter school it is no longer a good proxy for literate experience and because teachers would focus on teaching each letter of the alphabet for its own sake rather than as part of the larger goal of literate development.

Screening is simply a strategy for deciding where to put instructional resources to maximize prevention and minimize costs. Where the costs are low, it does not matter if our assessment erroneously includes some children who may not need much help. Where the stakes are high, however, perhaps for deciding who gets one-to-one instruction, we need a more sensitive assessment. So, for example, in first grade we might choose one like the Observation Survey of Early Literacy Achievement (Clay, 2004). Although it takes more time, it documents the concepts and specific knowledge the child has about print and how it works and the strategies he or she uses to make sense with print. It not only screens well but also provides detailed, instructionally useful information (Denton, Ciancio, & Fletcher, 2006). An assessment like this need not be used for everyone. Neither the law nor common sense requires it. Teachers are actually quite good at distinguishing which students are at risk on the basis of ongoing classroom assessments (Taylor, Anselmo, Foreman, Schatschneider, & Angelopoulos, 2000) and do not need to assess the students who are obviously developing successfully. Thus they could assess in more detail the lower half of the students, allowing a buffer for error (Clay, 2004). In fact, if a teacher cannot determine which students are having more and less difficulty acquiring literacy after a couple months of school, it is unlikely that high-quality instruction is taking place. In other words, assessment and instruction are closely aligned dimensions of teacher expertise (Sato, Wei, & Darling-Hammond, 2008).

This Section of the Book

This section of the book opens with Chapter 5, "Thinking Straight About Measures of Early Reading Development," in which Scott G. Paris describes how to think about the qualities of assessment practices, such as reliability (or consistency) and construct and consequential validity, and how they relate to RTI. The chapter helps us to decide on useful assessment strategies for RTI and to evaluate the qualities of RTI research that has used particular kinds of assessment.

Chapter 6, "Responsive Intervention: What Is the Role of Appropriate Assessment?" by Anne McGill-Franzen, Rebecca L. Payne, and Danielle V. Dennis, offers practical, evidence-based examples of assessment practices that are effective for reducing the incidence of specialized language development. These assessments document and draw instructional attention to children's literate understandings and processes. McGill-Franzen and colleagues' approach also includes teachers collaboratively examining their data to improve their instruction, a theme picked up in Chapter 7, "A Comprehensive Assessment System as a Response to Intervention Process" by Linda J. Dorn and Shannon Coman Henderson. Both chapters point out the need for teachers to gather ongoing, up-close data to inform their instruction but then to engage in regular stocktaking with colleagues to take a more distanced view of students' progress. Because we all have areas of blindness with respect to particular students and our own teaching, we need to involve others in reflections on data. Indeed, as Wiliam (2008) points out, research suggests that such teacher learning communities focused on data analysis are "the most powerful single approach to improving student achievement" (p. 36). This theme is echoed in the work of Stuart McNaughton and Mei Kuin Lai in Chapter 16 and in Linda J. Dorn and Barbara Schubert's work in Chapter 17.

The final chapter in this section, Chapter 8, "Helping a Learning-Disabled Child Enter the Literate World" by Carol A. Lyons, takes a different approach. This chapter shows not only the importance of documenting student learning but also the importance of assessing the interactions between teacher and student, particularly for those students whom we find most challenging to teach. In this chapter, a successful Reading Recovery teacher fails to accelerate one student who happens to be classified as LD. The case study shows how her interactions with this student, which are different from those with other students, are responsible for his failure to accelerate. When the instructional interactions are changed, the student accelerates. To make this sort of adjustment, we need specific information about the nature of the interactions between teacher and student—data on the timing, wording, examples, focus, and control in teaching, as we shall see in Gwenneth Phillips and Pauline Smith's Chapter 12, "Closing the Gaps: Literacy for the Hardest-to-Teach."

Again, the law requires "data that demonstrate that prior to, or as a part of, the referral process, the child was provided appropriate instruction in regular education settings, delivered by qualified personnel" (U.S. Department of Education, n.d.). This section argues that the *process* of assessment must constantly make personnel more qualified. We revisit effective examples of this concept in later chapters.

REFERENCES

Alt, S.J., & Samuels, S.J. (in press). Reading fluency: What is it and how should it be measured? In A. McGill-Franzen & R.L. Allington (Eds.), *Handbook of reading disability research*. London: Routledge.

Clay, M.M. (2004). *An observation survey of early literacy achievement* (2nd ed.). Portsmouth, NH: Heinemann.

Cramer, K., & Rosenfield, S. (2008). Effect of degree of challenge on reading performance. *Reading & Writing Quarterly*, 24(1), 119–137. doi:10.1080/10573560701501586

Denton, C.A., Ciancio, D.J., & Fletcher, J.M. (2006). Validity, reliability, and utility of the Observation Survey of Early Literacy Achievement. *Reading Research Quarterly*, 41(1), 8–34. doi:10.1598/RRQ.41.1.1

Fuchs, D., Stecker, P.M., & Fuchs, L.S. (2008). Tier 3: Why special education must be the most intensive tier in a standards-driven, No Child Left Behind world. In D. Fuchs, L.S. Fuchs, & S. Vaughn (Eds.), *Response to Intervention: A framework for reading educators* (pp. 71–104). Newark, DE: International Reading Association.

Fuchs, L.S. (2003). Assessing intervention responsiveness: Conceptual and technical issues. *Learning Disabilities Research & Practice*, 18(3), 172–186. doi:10.1111/1540-5826.00073

Gansle, K.A., Noell, G.H., VanDerHeyden, A.M., Naquin, G.M., & Slider, N.J. (2002). Moving beyond total words written: The reliability, criterion validity, and time cost of alternative measures for curriculum-based measurement in writing. *School Psychology Review*, 31(4), 477–497.

Gilmore, A. (2002). Large-scale assessment and teachers' assessment capacity: Learning opportunities for teachers in the National Education Monitoring Project in New Zealand. *Assessment in Education: Principles, Policy & Practice*, 9(3), 343–361.

Goodman, K.S. (2006). *The truth about DIBELS: What it is, what it does*. Portsmouth, NH: Heinemann.

National Institute of Child Health and Human Development. (2000). *Report of the National*

Reading Panel. *Teaching children to read: An evidence-based assessment of the scientific research literature on reading and its implications for reading instruction* (NIH Publication No. 00-4769). Washington, DC: U.S. Government Printing Office.

Pressley, M., Hilden, K., & Shankland, R. (2005). *An evaluation of end-grade-3 Dynamic Indicators of Basic Early Literacy Skills (DIBELS): Speed reading without comprehension, predicting little.* East Lansing: Literacy Achievement Research Center, Michigan State University.

Samuels, S.J. (2007). The DIBELS tests: Is speed of barking at print what we mean by reading fluency? *Reading Research Quarterly, 42*(4), 563–566. doi:10.1598/RRQ.42.4.5

Sato, M., Wei, R.C., & Darling-Hammond, L. (2008). Improving teachers' assessment practices through professional development: The case of National Board Certification. *American Educational Research Journal, 45*(3), 669–700. doi:10.3102/0002831208316955

Taylor, H.G., Anselmo, M., Foreman, A.L., Schatschneider, C., & Angelopoulos, J. (2000). Utility of kindergarten teacher judgments in identifying early learning problems. *Journal of Learning Disabilities, 33*(2), 200–210. doi:10.1177/002221940003300208

U.S. Department of Education. (n.d.). Identification of specific learning disabilities [Topical brief]. In *Building the legacy: IDEA 2004.* Retrieved February 9, 2010, from idea .ed.gov/explore/view/p/%2Croot%2Cdynam ic%2CTopicalBrief%2C23%2C

Vellutino, F.R., Scanlon, D.M., Small, S., & Fanuele, D.P. (2006). Response to Intervention as a vehicle for distinguishing between children with and without reading disabilities: Evidence for the role of kindergarten and first-grade interventions. *Journal of Learning Disabilities, 39*(2), 157–169. doi:10 .1177/00222194060390020401

Wiliam, D. (2008). Changing classroom practice. *Educational Leadership, 65*(4), 36–42.

CHAPTER 5

Thinking Straight About Measures of Early Reading Development

Scott G. Paris

Measuring reading achievement is no longer limited to the educational practices of teachers, nor is it a research domain explored only by academics; it is a compelling political and commercial enterprise tied to educational standards, funding, and accountability. Since the passage of federal legislation in the No Child Left Behind (NCLB) Act in 2002, scientifically based reading research has become the foundation of reading assessment and education in the United States. Despite the virtues of using sound evidence and research for large-scale policies concerning reading education, there are fundamental problems in assessing early reading skills for a simple reason—they change rapidly. In this chapter, I describe the differences in developmental trajectories of various reading skills and show how fast-developing skills related to decoding yield unstable measures and misleading interpretations of assessment data.

Overwhelmed by Assessment Options

Teachers are exhorted to use assessments for both summative and formative purposes, yet they often fail to receive the training and resources needed to conduct classroom assessments well (Paris & Hoffman, 2004). That is why teachers often use the assessments provided by the school or commercial textbooks, and they often prefer quick and easy measures. The appeal of both options is clear for a busy teacher. Let's consider the kinds of early reading assessments available for teachers. One group of popular assessments is informal reading inventories (IRIs), which include measures of word knowledge, oral reading rate, oral reading accuracy and mistakes, retelling, and comprehension questions that can be given to students just learning to read as well as to proficient readers. These performance-based measures provide a wealth of information for the experienced teacher who listens to students read and respond to text because they reveal good and bad strategies used by students. However, IRIs require time-intensive one-on-one testing and considerable teacher expertise in observing students and evaluating the data. IRIs are appropriate measures of individual reading strengths and weaknesses, but they usually do not provide a common scale to track progress over time or compare students in a classroom.

A second group of measures are based on knowledge about reading and language, for example, knowing the alphabet and letter sounds, concepts about print, word boundaries, differences among genres, and functions of text. Students need to understand such concepts about their native language, but the knowledge enables rather than causes reading to develop. The basic concepts about print (e.g., word boundaries, direction of reading) are usually acquired in the first two years that students learn to read.

A third group of measures includes traditional reading comprehension tests that usually involve silently reading many short passages and either answering questions, filling in missing words (cloze passages), or writing short answers. These kinds of tests are difficult for beginning readers who may struggle to decode and understand the words, but as decoding becomes more skilled, comprehension tests reveal more about understanding and responding to ideas in text.

A fourth group of measures aims to assess automatic decoding skills, for example, how quickly students can recognize and say letters, words, and nonsense syllables and how quickly they can read connected text. The advantage of these kinds of reading fluency measures is that they are quick and quantitative. One-minute tests of how many letters on a page can be named or how many words in a text can be read are simple data to collect and easy data to use for screening, tracking progress, and monitoring growth in fluent decoding. Assessments of decoding fluency are the core measures in the Dynamic Indicators of Basic Early Literacy Skills (DIBELS; Good & Kaminski, 2002), a widely used battery of early reading assessments. Indeed, it has been modified for use with languages other than English in the Early Grade Reading Assessment toolkit (RTI International, 2009) and is now used globally to measure early reading development in many languages.

Early reading assessments found in commercial materials, state-designed assessment batteries, and teachers' daily use include tasks from all four groups, but measures of fluency and decoding predominate in K–2, because (a) the skills provide a necessary foundation for reading development, (b) they develop rapidly during this time frame, and (c) they are quick and quantitative. The data are seductively simple but may lead to two problems: One is the overemphasis on skills that are easy to measure in both assessment and instruction of early reading. A second problem is the misinterpretation of the data and exaggerated claims about the measures. Reading skills that change rapidly yield unstable data compared with other skills that may reflect more enduring abilities of students. In the rest of the chapter, I describe how differences in the growth trajectories of reading skills influence assessment data and can lead to exaggerated claims about rapidly developing skills.

Developmental Differences Among Reading Skills

Some skills that are required to learn to read are constrained in their scope or period of acquisition, and some skills are less constrained (Paris, 2005, 2009). (For more information about constrained skill theory, see Paris and Paris [2006] and Paris, Carpenter, Paris, and Hamilton [2005].) Learning the names of letters in the English alphabet is a good example of a constrained skill, whereas learning new vocabulary words is unconstrained over time and words. Most students master constrained skills quickly, such as learning the names and sounds of the 26 letters in the English alphabet. Within a year or two, students go from knowing a few letters to knowing all of them. Skills not related to decoding, such as vocabulary and comprehension, develop slowly and over a lifetime. The different developmental courses of acquisition, coupled with mastery levels of performance for constrained skills, mean that fast-developing constrained skills are unstable measures. Consider how the following skills develop rapidly.

Knowledge about print and text is acquired early and mastered almost completely in early childhood. Print knowledge entails a finite amount of information, and the fundamental concepts comprise small domains. For example, the 26 letters of the English alphabet are a small set, the sounds associated with the letters are only a slightly larger set, and the concepts about print that are usually assessed include fewer than 25 concepts (e.g., Clay, 1979). Understanding concepts about print (e.g., letters, words) and concepts about reading (e.g., matching of sounds to print, directionality of reading) begins as early as 2 to 3 years of age for some children and is mastered usually after a year or two of formal instruction, certainly by first grade for U.S. students. All students learn the same concepts to a very high level, even though the rates of mastery may vary widely depending on a student's specific literacy experiences.

Phonological awareness begins to develop with oral language in early childhood, and it continues to develop during childhood, but fundamental features are mastered in the primary grades. For example, by age 5 or 6, most students can identify onset-rime patterns, such as *cat–hat*, and they can rhyme words based on simple patterns. Segmenting phonemes in words and blending phonemes to create words are more difficult skills but are usually acquired as students are asked to decode words in early instruction. Phonological awareness develops most rapidly during primary grades and formal reading instruction.

Decoding skills (matching letters to sounds) are also constrained in scope (i.e., the domain is finite and small) and rate of learning (i.e., most students acquire decoding skills in a few years). It might be argued that the most central features of decoding skills, such as identifying initial consonant sounds and long and short vowels, are learned quickly. More subtle aspects of grapheme–phoneme correspondence may be acquired over several years, but mastery of decoding skills occurs in a relatively brief period for most students. Practice promotes automatic word identification and faster decoding, which are evident in fluent oral reading. Fluency includes reading text quickly, accurately, and with intonation (Kuhn & Stahl, 2003). First graders read about 50–70 words per minute and increase their rate by about 20 words per minute each year. Research suggests that accuracy and rate begin to reach ceiling levels by 10 to 12 years of age for most students, about 150 words read correctly per minute. Thus, oral reading fluency (ORF) measures provide the most discriminating information as students progress from deliberate, slow decoders to automatic, fast decoders, but less information after fluency becomes automatic.

Therefore, it appears that print knowledge, phonological awareness, and decoding skills are different from vocabulary and comprehension in at least two fundamental ways: First, the scope of the knowledge and skills is finite and small, and second, the knowledge and skills are mastered to a high level by most students in a short developmental period. Consequently, constrained skills show little growth or statistical variance after mastery. Both claims can be debated, but the issue is only about degree; that is, some might argue that the domains of print knowledge, phonological awareness, and decoding skills are larger than I portray them, so their acquisition curves are longer over time and never mastered completely. That may be true for some concepts and skills, but the essential, central, and prototypical knowledge and skills, which are exactly the kinds of knowledge and skills assessed in reading tests, develop from non-existent or modest at ages 4 to 5 to ceiling levels by ages 8 or 9. Before and after the period of rapid growth, assessments of constrained skills provide little variance and discriminating information.

Stable Versus Unstable Correlations Among Reading Skills

Knowledge and skills that are mastered during childhood reflect learning, so the status of learning any specific skill is always between 0% and 100%. Because the period of acquisition is relatively brief, researchers typically assess these skills during periods of volatile growth. For example, alphabet knowledge is near zero before age 4 and at 100% by age 7 for most students, so it is usually assessed during kindergarten and first grade. Alphabet knowledge has been shown by many researchers to be a strong predictor of reading development (e.g., McBride-Chang, 1999). For example, Lonigan, Burgess, and Anthony (2000) state, "knowledge of the alphabet (i.e., knowing the names of letters and the sounds they represent) at entry into school is one of the strongest single predictors of short- and long-term success in learning to read" (p. 597). However, there is decreasing strength of correlations between letter knowledge and later reading proficiency with increasing age (e.g., Johnston, Anderson, & Holligan, 1996; Muter, 1994). Knowledge of the alphabet is correlated strongly with subsequent reading achievement only during a period of acquisition when the alphabet is partially learned, a phase that coincides with kindergarten in the United States.

Similar patterns of correlations, initially strong and then decreasing in strength with age, have been observed for other reading skills, such as phonemic awareness. Researchers have been aware of the transitory strength of correlations between basic skills and reading achievement. In their five-year longitudinal study of early reading predictors, Wagner et al. (1997) note, "Our results suggest that the influence of individual differences in phonological processing abilities on subsequent reading skills is developmentally limited for (letter) naming and is less so for phonological awareness" (p. 477). Walsh, Price, and Gillingham (1988) suggest explicitly that letter knowledge is related to reading achievement in a transitory fashion. Adams (1990) suggests that the contribution of a particular skill to reading achievement depends on its level of development at the time of testing. Stanovich (2000) says that patterns of correlations among reading skills range from strong to nil depending on the level of skill expertise. This pattern suggests that some reading skills change markedly with learning and practice.

Constrained skills theory (CST) explains the transitory correlations as a consequence of skewed data distributions and brief periods of skill mastery. It is a narrow developmental period and a special case when the skill is partially acquired by most students that the variance in the sample approximates a normal distribution and can yield strong correlations. CST claims that many skills relevant to early reading are mastered in childhood and thus yield floor or ceiling performance with minimal variance before and after their relatively brief periods of learning. The transitory correlations between mastered skills and other measures of reading illustrate fundamental differences between constrained and unconstrained skills. Constrained skills yield correlations that are unstable over time and samples, because they reflect the degree of learning in a particular sample at a specific time. The relative degree of learning of a mastered variable is not a measure of a stable individual difference, so the correlations with other variables are always idiosyncratic and unstable. In contrast, variables that measure individual differences that are more enduring, such as speed of processing, memory, and comprehension abilities, yield more stable correlations over samples and time.

It is important to recognize that the correlations between constrained skills and knowledge that occur in beginning reading can vary over a wide range. The apparent consistency in correlations across research studies is due to a procedural artifact of assessing students of similar ages who are partway to mastering the alphabet. When those same students are assessed longitudinally, the pattern of correlations between alphabet knowledge and other skills or later achievement tracks a course over time from no relation to a strong relation to no relation. The variable and transitory correlations therefore should be expected if the assessment is measuring learning accurately. Alphabet knowledge, like any constrained skill, yields unstable correlations that are developmentally valid only for a short period of rapid learning.

Assessment–Instruction Connections

There is no doubt that students need to learn the alphabet, print concepts, and phonological awareness to learn to read. The knowledge and skills necessary to build automatic word decoding are fundamental for every student learning to read. In fact, one might argue that progress assessments of these skills are not needed, because the skills must be acquired, practiced, and automated. Certainly teachers and parents know this. However, early reading assessments have demonstrated consistently that the lack of fluency skills, at developmental levels comparable to their peers, places young students at risk for future reading difficulties. I think that this predictive correlation has been misinterpreted in a causal manner by many people and has led to prescriptive policies, such as mandatory training on constrained skills. The causal attribution ignores the transitory correlational patterns and interprets the simple correlations in isolation.

The causal link is explicit in RTI models, because fluency skills such as ORF are used to assess the status or progress of students, and if the fluency is inadequate, teachers provide explicit practice to build fluency. The success of the RTI model rests on the assessments used to allocate students to different tiers of instructional intensity and the validity with which the assessments measure successful reading. Teaching students to read faster is not the instructional antidote for struggling readers. Yes, if they exhibit poor fluency, then practice with repeated reading and other strategies can be helpful, but the danger is in what is omitted. Struggling readers may also need help with vocabulary and comprehension skills, oral language, written expression, and so forth. Just because those are more difficult to assess does not mean they are less important for students to learn.

Consider the schoolwide prevention model advocated by the DIBELS researchers (e.g., Kame'enui & Simmons, 1998). Using models of identification and intervention from special education, these researchers propose three layers of assessment and instruction to prevent reading difficulties. The primary level of prevention is "universal" and is designed to identify students at risk, so it involves administering DIBELS assessments three times during the school year to all students in grades K through 3. The instructional needs are defined as the DIBELS benchmarks at each grade. Secondary prevention is designed to provide intensive help to students who are not making adequate yearly progress in the regular classroom with the regular curriculum. Additional instruction delivered in the regular classroom on the DIBELS benchmarks (i.e., stage 1 skills) is intended to allow students with low literacy skills to catch up to their peers. Tertiary prevention is designed for students who exhibit sustained low literacy skills and associated complications, such as academic and behavioral problems. The remedial instruction is provided by a special educator, psychologist, speech pathologist, or other professional in small groups or one-on-one arrangements for at least 100 minutes per day. Progress monitoring on the DIBELS assessments occurs once each week.

There are many virtues of the DIBELS assessments and systematic model for grades K through 3 assessment and instruction. DIBELS is a schoolwide program that involves personnel beyond the classroom teacher. It provides clear procedures for administrators and educators to follow. The data are collected relatively quickly in one-minute tests. The data allow quantification for monitoring progress and charting accountability. There are successive levels of more intense intervention according to the progress of the student. Also, DIBELS is consistent with principles of early identification and intervention in public health and special education. Unfortunately, the liabilities of DIBELS have received less attention.

DIBELS claims to provide valid evidence about predictors of later reading achievement, but the data are suspect in light of CST, because the correlations are interpreted without regard for mastery constraints and sample dependency. On a practical level, DIBELS testing requires a great deal of time from teachers or others to administer individualized assessments. The one-minute tests focus on narrow skills, including letter naming fluency, initial sound fluency, phonemic segmentation fluency, and nonsense word fluency—all fluency skills that reflect phonics skills and automatic word recognition. The tests are given frequently and to all students. The focus of diagnosis is more detailed than necessary for mastered skills, and the differences in relative rates of learning become the criteria for assigning risk status. Oral reading fluency assesses only the number of words read correctly in one minute without consideration for comprehension, so the test privileges rate over understanding. Reading rate becomes the benchmark of reading success for students, teachers, and parents. Comprehension is not assessed or valued in DIBELS, so it is not a focus of assessment or instruction in the classroom or school that adopts the DIBELS prevention model.

The prescriptions for assessment are evident in many state-designed and commercial assessments. Moreover, basal reading series include batteries of assessments for screening, diagnostic, and progress-monitoring functions. Teachers and students in primary grades are overwhelmed with reading assessments and the time they require for administration, management, and interpretation (Paris & Hoffman, 2004). I think the assessment of fluency skills has become excessive, the importance attached to their acquisition has been inflated, and the assessments have taken time away from instruction as well as assessment of more important aspects of reading, such as vocabulary, compre-hension, and reading across content areas and texts. Teachers and critics who express frustration are regarded as opponents of accountability.

It seems evident in light of CST that assessment of early reading skills should focus on mastery, and perhaps the rate of mastery, and not on quantita-tive measures of partial mastery. It does not matter much when students know 5, 10, or 20 letters of the alphabet, when they segment the phonemes of 30%, 50%, or 80% of the words on a test, or when their ORF scores increase from 75 words per minute to 85 words per minute. Those data are unstable measures of learning not enduring individual differences, and they lead to misinterpreta-tions of correlations that are transitory and sample dependent.

What Data Reflect Favorably on Schools?

I realize that this is not the usual question teachers ask, but everyone knows that some interventions are easier than others and some data show progress better than others. CST explains why. Fast-developing constrained skills are excellent targets for intervention, because their knowledge and skills are ex-plicit and relatively fewer than those of unconstrained skills. Thus, teaching letter names and sounds to kindergartners yields big changes in performance in a few months, compared with teaching vocabulary words, for example. Kindergartners may learn 20% to 50% of the alphabet in a few months of inten-sive training but only a small percentage of their total vocabulary. Constrained skills are also learned as part of the embedded context of literacy learning, so over time without direct intervention, students show increases in fluency skills as part of their maturation. There is a practice effect, too. As students learn to name letters or nonsense syllables on a page or read words quickly, they improve their rate from practice alone. Thus, fluency measures are the "low-hanging fruit" of early reading assessments, because they are likely to increase for many reasons, in addition to the intervention, and show positive progress of students and reflect favorably on schools. In contrast, increasing students' read-ing comprehension dramatically is unlikely in a brief intervention, even if it is an excellent program, because the developmental trajectory of comprehension skills is slower than that of fluency skills.

However, interventions that target mastered skills show only temporary ad-vantages until peers acquire the same knowledge and skills through other means. If interventions create temporary boosts in students' skills and knowledge, the correlations may also reveal temporary and enhanced relations with other measures of reading. Thus, interventions aimed at skills that are about to blossom show large growth effects over short time periods. The developmental timing of the intervention is critical. It makes little sense to intervene with a treatment that is way beyond children's abilities, such as teaching phonemic awareness to 2-year-olds. It is also unreasonable to provide interventions for students who have already acquired most of the skills. That is exactly why researchers arrange interventions on constrained skills and knowledge for students who exhibit partial mastery of the target skills. Although these practices are common, they are effective because they accelerate learning to mastery without providing enduring benefits.

Conclusions

The general problems with research-based evidence on constrained skills can be summarized in two ways: First, failure to consider the constraints on rapidly developing skills has led researchers to treat all reading skills in the same manner when examining their growth or RTI. This error confuses temporary differences in levels of knowledge and skill proficiency during periods of partial mastery with enduring and stable individual differences that persist over time. It has led to trivial demonstrations that students' print knowledge or fluency skills can be accelerated by a variety of brief and intense treatments. However, the effects are transitory; they fail to generalize to other reading skills and knowledge, and they fail to lead to long-term advantages in reading achievement. I hasten to add that 4- to 7-year-olds need to be instructed on those skills early and persistently by teachers and parents, but not assessed compulsively or exclusively on those skills.

The second summary point about instructional effects or RTI emphasizes the developmental timing of the interventions. RTI on fluency skills is more dramatic than on other skills, because they are fast-developing skills. Thus, they exhibit rapid growth in grades K to 2 because of practice effects, maturation, and increasing automaticity. This means that treatments vary in their appropriateness and effectiveness according to the age and expertise of the student and developmental validity of the measures. What does this mean on a practical level? Assessments of fluency at beginning mastery will reveal disfluent readers who have difficulty reading and comprehending, because they cannot decode words readily enough to allow cognitive resources to be applied to text processing. Assessments of fluent readers (e.g., students reading 140 or more words per minute) will yield modest information because of small differences and variability among students. Automatic decoding sets a threshold to enable comprehension and text processing, but fluent reading does not guarantee good comprehension. Fluency assessments therefore are informative only for students who have partial mastery of decoding skills. They do not need to be given repeatedly to students who read very slowly or quickly. The widespread use of assessments of constrained skills are not justified by the time required or information derived from them. More prudent measures of constrained skills mastery can allow teachers to focus more on instruction than assessments of necessary foundation skills.

REFERENCES

Adams, M.J. (1990). *Beginning to read: Thinking and learning about print*. Cambridge, MA: MIT Press.

Clay, M.M. (1979). *Reading: The patterning of complex behavior* (2nd ed.). Portsmouth, NH: Heinemann.

Good, R.H., III, & Kaminski, R.A. (Eds.). (2002). Dynamic indicators of basic early literacy skills (6th ed.). Eugene, OR: Institute for the Development of Educational Achievement.

Johnston, R.S., Anderson, M., & Holligan, C. (1996). Knowledge of the alphabet and explicit awareness of phonemes in pre-readers: The nature of the relationship. *Reading and Writing*, 8(3), 217–234. doi:10.1007/BF00420276

Kame'enui, E.J., & Simmons, D.C. (1998). Beyond effective practice to schools as host environments: Building and sustaining a school-wide intervention model in beginning reading. *Oregon School Study Council Bulletin*, 41(3), 3–24.

Kuhn, M.R., & Stahl, S.A. (2003). Fluency: A review of developmental and remedial practices. *Journal of Educational Psychology*, 95(1), 3–21.

Lonigan, C.J., Burgess, S.R., & Anthony, J.L. (2000). Development of emergent literacy and early reading skills in preschool children: Evidence from a latent-variable longitudinal study. *Developmental Psychology*, 36(5), 596–613. doi:10.1037/0012-1649.36.5.596

McBride-Chang, C. (1999). The ABCs of the ABCs: The development of letter-name and letter-sound knowledge. *Merrill-Palmer Quarterly*, 45(2), 285–308.

Muter, V. (1994). The influence of phonological awareness and letter knowledge on beginning reading and spelling development. In C. Hulme & M.J. Snowling (Eds.), *Reading development and dyslexia* (pp. 45–62). London: Whurr.

Paris, S.G. (2005). Reinterpreting the development of reading skills. *Reading Research Quarterly*, 40(2), 184–202. doi:10.1598/RRQ.40.2.3

Paris, S.G. (2009). Constrained skills—so what? In K.M. Leander, D.W. Rowe, D.K. Dickinson, M.K. Hundley, R.T. Jimenez, & V.J. Risko (Eds.), *59th yearbook of the National Reading Conference* (pp. 34–44). Oak Creek, WI: National Reading Conference.

Paris, S.G., Carpenter, R.D., Paris, A.H., & Hamilton, E.E. (2005). Spurious and genuine correlates of children's reading comprehension. In S.G. Paris & S.A. Stahl (Eds.), *Children's reading comprehension and assessment* (pp. 131–160). Mahwah, NJ: Erlbaum.

Paris, S.G., & Hoffman, J.V. (2004). Reading assessments in kindergarten through third grade: Findings from the Center for the Improvement of Early Reading Achievement.

The Elementary School Journal, 105(2), 199–217. doi:10.1086/428865

Paris, S.G., & Paris, A.H. (2006). Assessments of early reading. In W. Damon, R.M. Lerner (Series Eds.), K.A. Renninger, & I.E. Sigel (Vol. Eds.), *Handbook of child psychology: Vol. 4. Child psychology in practice* (6th ed., pp. 48–74). Hoboken, NJ: Wiley.

RTI International. (2009). Early Grade Reading Assessment toolkit. Washington, DC: The World Bank Office of Human Development.

Stanovich, K.E. (2000). *Progress in understanding reading: Scientific foundations and new frontiers.* New York: Guilford.

Wagner, R.K., Torgesen, J.K., Rashotte, C.A., Hecht, S.A., Barker, T.A., Burgess, S.R., et al. (1997). Changing relations between phonological processing abilities and word-level reading as children develop from beginning to skilled readers: A 5-year longitudinal study. *Developmental Psychology, 33*(3), 468–479. doi:10.1037/0012-1649.33.3.468

Walsh, D.J., Price, G.G., & Gillingham, M.G. (1988). The critical but transitory importance of letter naming. *Reading Research Quarterly, 23*(1), 108–122. doi:10.2307/747907

CHAPTER 6

Responsive Intervention: What Is the Role of Appropriate Assessment?

Anne McGill-Franzen, Rebecca L. Payne, and Danielle V. Dennis

We believe that the purpose of RTI is to provide struggling students with instruction that will mitigate failure, not to identify students as failures. To teach responsively and responsibly, move students' development forward, and disrupt early patterns of confusion and failure, we first need to know what they know about reading and writing. To proceed otherwise—based on a test score and category of risk—would lead us to blindly implement an intervention program that purported to remedy broadly defined deficits. If, however, we identify students' strengths—what they know—we will not be overwhelmed by what they cannot yet do, and we will have a starting point for instruction that is personal and individual. This approach requires reliable, valid, and, most of all, useful assessments of what students can do at a particular point in time that are easy to implement, flexible, and timely.

Rather than compare students' scores on norm-referenced tests of skills involving phonology or other important—but isolated—components of literacy, teachers are in a position to observe and systematically record students' full engagement with reading and writing in the classroom. Such systematic recording of individual literacy behaviors constitutes authentic curriculum-based assessment appropriate for planning more focused and intensive instruction (i.e., intervention) and monitoring of students' progress. When combined with professional learning and collegial support for teachers, assessment can build teachers' capacity to interpret students' literacy behavior within a developmental framework, reflect on the efficacy of particular practices, and revise instruction to move each student forward along the road to reading proficiency.

RTI in Literacy—Responsive and Comprehensive, edited by Peter H. Johnston.
© 2010 by the International Reading Association.

In this chapter, we first challenge the assumption that struggling readers of any age are a homogeneous group needing the same kinds of intervention. Spear-Swerling and Sternberg (1996) propose a model of reading (dis)ability that makes this argument explicitly. Next, we identify the research base for disabusing educators of the idea that one size fits all. We establish the heterogeneity of struggling readers at different ages, from kindergartners to adolescents, and describe the role that assessment can assume in formulating effective instruction, albeit instruction interpreted in different ways in the studies cited. Finally, we describe a specific project—Kindergarten Literacy—that sought to build teachers' capacity so that the knowledge developed in an intervention with struggling readers was available to all students, and this knowledge deepened across the years of the project.

Literacy Development—A Multifaceted Path to Proficiency

Students move through phases of literacy development as they acquire new skills and make connections with existing knowledge. These skills build on one another as readers move toward proficiency, but not necessarily in a linear way. In many respects students' developmental paths may be compared to puddles and streams—at particular points some students may gain insight that propels their development forward, as in a stream, whereas others may spend more time in a particular phase, seeking more experience to consolidate their knowledge before moving forward.

Students who struggle in the earlier phases of development often lag behind their peers, making it difficult for them to catch up without appropriate intervention. To illustrate this notion of a continuum of reading development, we draw on the metaphor developed by Spear-Swerling and Sternberg (Spear-Swerling, 2004; Spear-Swerling & Sternberg, 1996) in their research on struggling readers. Becoming proficient is conceptualized as a path, and the metaphor summons ideas of movement, destination, and signposts. As students move along the path to becoming literate, they may experience periods of accelerated growth, in which things begin to make sense. Other times, they may face significant confusion and feel frustrated. This metaphor highlights the signposts or developmental insights that lead to proficiency and may help teachers locate what students already know, or what they use but confuse in the practice of literacy. A clear understanding of the metaphor and concomitant signposts may bolster a teacher's ability to assess student progress and diagnose problems along the way.

Drawing heavily on word-recognition studies by Ehri (1991), Spear-Swerling (2004) posits six phases on the path to proficiency. These phases do not encompass all processes involved in literate development; for example, she does not address the reciprocal relation between reading and writing and instead focuses more specifically on the acquisition of word knowledge. The first four phases (Visual-Cue, Phonetic-Cue, Controlled, and Automatic Word Recognition) describe students' deepening knowledge about the way print works—letter-sound relationships, the role of spelling patterns, decoding, and fluent or "at sight" recognition of words in text guided by oral language comprehension. The last two phases (Strategic and Proficient Reading) involve students' integration of skills for particular purposes and typically occur from the elementary grades through adulthood. For the purpose of this section, we focus on the first four phases to provide insight into patterns that Ehri and Spear-Swerling identify in students' acquisition of word knowledge, an important process in literacy development.

The metaphor of a path to proficiency (Spear-Swerling, 2004) provides a useful way of thinking about development over time. The early phases, in conjunction with Ehri's (1991) work, provide a framework for noting patterns in the acquisition of word knowledge, an important part of literacy development. Of course, literacy development involves more than word recognition. Literacy development begins before children enter school or receive any formal instruction and culminates in purposeful and varied kinds of interactions around text by adolescents or adults.

Visual-Cue Word Recognition

The path to reading proficiency begins with a child's first awareness of print and language. During this phase, Visual-Cue Word Recognition, children are considered *prealphabetic readers* (Ehri, 1991) and use visual cues (e.g., word shape, color, familiar logo) rather than phonetic cues in word recognition. Students in this phase have considerable oral language comprehension and benefit from listening to stories and talking about books, even though they are unable to read independently. This phase typically occurs in preschool and early kindergarten and is heavily affected by the child's experiences with literacy in the home. As a result, students come to school with varying amounts of exposure to literacy concepts and early assessment is important to establish a starting point for instruction.

Phonetic-Cue Word Recognition

The next phase, Phonetic-Cue Word Recognition, involves understanding the alphabetic principle—that there is a relationship between phonemes and the letters used to represent them. Readers show they are in this phase when they begin to use phonetic cues, such as the first and last letters of a word, in their writing and reading and are considered *partial alphabetic readers* (Ehri, 1991). They enter this phase by having increased phonemic awareness, which allows them to begin matching letter patterns to sounds.

Controlled Word Recognition

Students then move to a phase of Controlled Word Recognition. Considered *full alphabetic readers* (Ehri, 1991), these students make use of phonetic cues in word recognition and are generally accurate, but not automatic, in reading common words. Students now have an understanding of many letter–sound relationships, particularly consonants and short vowels, which supports decoding unfamiliar words with similar spelling patterns. Assessments during this phase should provide the teacher with information about students' abilities to read, write, and spell common words.

Automatic Word Recognition

As students become fluent in recognizing these spelling patterns in word reading and writing, they demonstrate Automatic Word Recognition. In this phase, students are *consolidated alphabetic readers* (Ehri, 1991) and recognize common words automatically and accurately. During this phase, students continue to integrate their understanding of letter–sound relationships with larger chunks of text (e.g., prefixes, suffixes, common rimes) and increase reading fluency through independent reading.

In the next section, we examine the work of McGill-Franzen (2006a), who conceptualizes literacy a bit more broadly than has been described previously. This view of literacy encompasses strategic processes and holds that reading and writing bear a reciprocal relationship to each other. McGill-Franzen thus complicates the construct of early literacy by viewing writing (i.e., spelling and creating text) as integral to and supportive of word knowledge and strategic reading.

Regardless of Grade, Students' Development Looks Different—So, Too, Must Literacy Instruction

All readers—and of particular concern here are all struggling readers—are not at the same place in their development regardless of their grade placement or age, underscoring the importance of ongoing, classroom-based assessment to identify what readers know and to provide appropriate, intensive instruction to get them on the path to proficiency. In this section we look closely at one grade level—kindergarten—and demonstrate the range of literacy development that may be found in kindergarten classes. McGill-Franzen (2006a) identifies patterns in literacy development that she has observed in kindergarten classrooms over the course of her research. She provides a way of thinking about these patterns by describing what readers at particular points in their literacy development can do. Understanding early literacy development requires teachers to recognize patterns as they systematically observe and document students' work with letters, sounds, and words and their strategic behavior as they read and write text. Multiple observations over time enable teachers to monitor the progress of individuals and revise the intensity or the emphasis of their instruction.

Being able to recognize constellations of patterns in literacy development helps teachers to form small groups and more appropriately differentiate instruction. For example, McGill-Franzen (2006a) refers to students who understand concepts of print, know some letters, and can create letterlike forms as "letters and sounds kids" because they are just beginning to understand the relation between sound and print. Students who are "almost readers" represent another constellation of patterns: they typically are able to track print with their finger, know most letters and sounds, recognize a few words when reading, and often spell using one letter to represent a word or idea. Almost readers can read back their own writing because it is personal and memorable, and they are on the verge of reading a conventional text. Students who are "readers" know almost all letters and sounds; use sight words from reading in writing; read familiar, leveled books by making an exact match between words spoken and the printed words; and are able to use what they know about words to decode and spell new words in their reading and writing. Clearly, instruction for students who are "letters and sounds kids" requires a different emphasis of skills and strategies than for students who are "readers." To determine what to teach, teachers need to become "evaluation experts" (Johnston, 1987). As such, they understand how students learn to read and the assessments necessary to provide information about their progress.

Early Literacy Observation and Assessment Tools

In *Kindergarten Literacy: Matching Assessment and Instruction in Kindergarten*, McGill-Franzen (2006a) presents a series of research-based literacy assessment tools designed to provide teachers with information about specific aspects of students' literacy development, such as the assessment tools outlined in the form in Figure 6.1. Two questions underscore these assessments: What does this student know about literacy? and What can this student do? Assessment of early literacy development should be systematic and include both work samples (e.g., writing and spelling drafts, oral reading records) and observed behaviors (e.g., sorts, word reading and writing fluency, print and book-handling concepts, voice–print match). The assessments, discussed in depth in *Kindergarten Literacy*, are presented here to illustrate how teachers can establish a starting point for appropriate instruction based on individual student needs. These assessments include letter–sound association, phonological awareness, print concepts, text writing, word writing, text reading, and word reading.

Letter–Sound Association

In the letter–sound association task, students are asked to identify the name and sound of individual letters from a randomized list of upper- and lowercase letters. Students point to each letter and say the name and sound (or a word beginning with that sound) as the teacher records the information on a separate sheet. This assessment should be done with students individually and takes a few minutes for each. It is important to know *precisely* which letters students know because some enter school knowing almost all the letters and sounds and some enter knowing few, if any. For students who know few, the standard curriculum of a letter a week would not provide information about all the letters and sounds until the end of the school year, placing them at a distinct disadvantage. Besides knowing which letters students can identify, and most important, which to teach, this assessment also provides information to the teacher about possible visual or sound confusions. For example, students who confuse

Figure 6.1. Knox County Kindergarten Literacy Assessment

Pupil Profile Sheet

Student _____ School _____

Teacher _____ Year _____

		Observation Dates		
		Beginning of Year	Midyear	End of Year
Letter and Sound Association	Names	/54		
	Sounds	/26		
	D'Nealian	/54		
Phonological Awareness	Rhyme	/10		
	Beginning sounds	/12		
Print Concepts	Book			
	Directionality			
	One-to-one match			
	Word			
	Letter			
	First and last			
	Punctuation			
	Total concepts	/12	/14	
Phonemic Segmentation and Representation	Spelling list 1	/20		
	Spelling list 2	/18		
Word Reading	List 1	/16		
	List 2	/16		
	List 3	/16		
Word Writing "Write all the words you know"				
Reading				
	Reads from memory			
	Reads own writing			
Level	Reads leveled text — Book title			
	Guided reading level			
	Accuracy			
	Rate/words correct per minute			
Writing "Draw a picture and write all about yourself"				
	Drawing and letterlike forms			
	Copied and random letters			
Level	Name			
	Words			
	Sentence			
	Text			

lowercase *b*, *p*, *d*, and *q* may need opportunities to explore the orientation of the "ball and stick" configuration by printing them on dry-erase boards and manipulating magnetic letters and tiles; also, matching of upper- and lowercase letters may alleviate visual confusion of *i* and *l*. Similarly, confusion of the sound of /w/ and the name of letter *y* (and other letter–name and sound confusions) would become apparent as the teacher analyzed students' responses and would provide a starting point for instruction.

Phonological Awareness

Teachers can assess students' phonological awareness using picture sorts to identify rhyming words and beginning sounds. Sorts are both a teaching and an assessment tool. As students note the dimensions of phonemes to which they should attend, they are learning; as teachers observe students' performance on sorts, they evaluate their understandings of rhyme and beginning sounds. In addition, once students understand sorting procedures they can categorize words along varying dimensions of language and print.

In the rhyme sort students manipulate picture cards that represent common words (e.g., *hen*, *bag*, *tag*, *rug*, *fan*) and arrange them in rhyming pairs. The beginning sound sort is similar in that students manipulate picture cards of common words, but this time they are matching pictures with the same beginning sounds. These assessments should be done individually or in small groups and again take a few minutes each, factoring in time to model each sort and provide students with the opportunity to practice.

Similarly, the group spelling assessment may help the teacher determine whether the student can hear sounds/phonemes in consonant-vowel-consonant words, segment these words into phonemes, and represent each of the phonemes with an appropriate letter. The teacher calls out five words, emphasizing the individual sounds that make up each word. Teachers analyze the results, looking for patterns within students' spelling and letter formation and ask themselves questions such as, Does the student write only letterlike forms or random letters? Can the student segment the word into phonemes and represent these with an appropriate letter? Does he or she attend to sounds at the beginning of the word? The middle of the word? The end of the word? Does the student include a vowel? Rather than simply asking students to segment and blend nonsense words, as required in many fluency assessments, the spelling task is an authentic and more sophisticated application of phonemic segmentation and one that is actually used by students to write.

Print Concepts

The print-concepts assessment is adapted from Clay's (1993) model and provides insight on students' understanding of basic print concepts including directionality, voice-to-print match (finger-point reading), and word, letter, and punctuation concepts. The teacher selects a predictable book that contains periods, question marks, and pictures that clearly support the text to engage the student in an informal conversation about specific aspects of the book (e.g., "Point to the title," "Show me with your finger which way you would go when you read," "Show me one word only," "Show me one letter"). The teacher records the student's responses, making this information available for on-the-spot teaching, shared reading, or small-group instruction.

Text Writing

The text-writing task taps into the familiar and encourages students to use what they know about writing. All students, regardless of their developmental level or experience, can participate equally in this assignment. The purpose of the text-writing task is to discover what young learners know about using writing to communicate. This task can be administered individually, to a small group, or to a whole class. Students are asked to "draw a picture and write all about yourself" and encouraged to use the resources in the classroom available to them (e.g., word wall, alphabet chart, vowel chart, personal dictionary). McGill-Franzen (2006a) provides a useful rubric with examples to describe what students know about the way print works. Noticing how students represent their message when they write (e.g., drawing and letterlike forms, copied and random letters, single letters or some spelling patterns, or memorized words; and the conventions they use, such as spacing, linearity, and directionality) helps teachers know what to emphasize in their instruction about print. Besides these aspects of print, teachers can learn how students organize their ideas in text—do they simply label or list, or do they write statements about events or attributes that demonstrate the beginnings of informational or story writing? These writing samples, when collected over time, can vividly represent a learner's development in writing and provide teachers with a road map for where to go next when conferring with or teaching each one.

The writing sample reproduced in Figure 6.2 ("I like to play with my friends") demonstrates not only that the young author understands that writing conveys a message, but also the concepts of linearity, directionality, and return

Figure 6.2. Student's Text-Writing Sample

sweep in reading and writing a sentence, plus print concepts of upper- and low-ercase letters (although not always when to use them), and the alphabetic principle that sounds are represented by letters, arranged in patterns to spell words (*mi* for *my*). The writer uses but confuses long-vowel patterns, as in *lik* for *like* and *pla* for *play*, and can segment and spell at least the beginnings of unfamiliar words (*fri* for *friends*). Clearly, an analysis such as this provides the teacher with information for teaching that builds on what the student knows and needs to learn, in this case, spacing, fluent spelling of high-frequency words (*my, like, I*), and attention to spelling patterns such as the *ay* in *play* that will be useful in decoding and writing new words.

Word Writing

While the text-writing task assesses a student's understanding of how writing conveys a message and can be used to communicate, the word-writing task enables the teacher to closely observe the student's word-writing fluency. Adapted from Clay's (1993) "Write All the Words You Know" assessment in the Observation Survey of Early Literacy Achievement, the word-writing task can be administered to a whole class. The teacher begins by modeling how to think of words she knows and begins with her name. After demonstrating several ways to come up with words (e.g., names of family members, friends, pets, colors), the teacher asks students to write their own list. Like the writing samples produced in the text-writing task, analysis of these word lists illustrates what each student knows about print—does the student have a store of memorized words; can he or she use familiar parts of words, such as word families, to spell new words; and how does the student's writing vocabulary show growth over time?

Text Reading

The text-reading assessment is designed to determine the level of text the learner is able to read. McGill-Franzen (2006a) describes a continuum of reading development often found in kindergarten classrooms that articulate what students can do—read from memory, read back writing, or read text. Based on classroom observation, the teacher should be able to gauge a starting point for this assessment. For students who "pretend read," that is, they make up a story based on the illustrations in a familiar book, McGill-Franzen states that they read from memory. Students who can read back their own writing composed during the text-writing task ("Write all about yourself") are "almost readers" in the conventional sense, and they demonstrate knowledge that words are invariant, that is, spelled and read the same way regardless of the context. For students who can read text, that is, guided reading levels A through D, teachers need to conduct running records to determine a more precise match between the reader and the appropriate level of text, noting reading behaviors that the student exhibits and his or her reading fluency. After reading, the student is asked to retell the story as if to a friend who has not heard it. Depending on performance, the teacher can develop instruction that takes into account how the student perceives reading and what strategies he or she employs.

Word Reading

The word-reading task is a corollary to the text reading described previously and provides the teacher with important information about the high-frequency words students can recognize automatically. The 20 or so words included in the word list are words that students are most likely to see in reading and to need to use in writing. Any unknown words become a corpus that the teacher must teach each student to automatically read and spell.

Ruth, a teacher portrayed in *Kindergarten Literacy* (McGill-Franzen, 2006a), used information from these assessments to personalize her whole-group literacy routines, such as shared reading, and create small groups to provide each student with appropriate and meaningful instruction—which is a characteristic of more successful teachers (Taylor, Pearson, Clark, & Walpole, 2000)—and to identify those students who needed more intensive small-group or side-by-side teaching. For example, while her "letters and sounds kids" were using personal alphabet books to learn letter names and sounds, Ruth's "readers" were learning strategies for reading less predictable text. Likewise, Ruth's "almost readers" were reading back their own writing. Ruth engaged all of her students in authentic, meaningful literacy activities based on their individual profiles that were put together from the early literacy assessments she administered to inform her instruction. Student heterogeneity within classrooms, however, does not end once students develop early literacy skills.

Evaluation of Literacy Beyond the Early Grades

Assessment must continue to support teachers' instructional decisions throughout a learner's schooling. Buly and Valencia (2002) tested the assumption that students who failed the state reading assessment were all missing decoding skills. They administered a variety of reading assessments to 108 fourth-grade students from 13 elementary schools who failed the Washington Assessment of Student Learning. Although some of the fourth-grade students demonstrated slow word identification, most experienced difficulty reading fluently and reading for meaning. Thus, the majority of these struggling readers demonstrated adequate decoding and word-recognition skills but limited development of the skills and strategies necessary for reading with understanding. Therefore, providing these students with intensive intervention in decoding was, at best, superfluous and a waste of teachers' and students' instructional time, and at worst, instructional malfeasance, because the instruction was unrelated to what the students needed to learn. Additionally, Buly and Valencia demonstrated that the students in the study represented a heterogeneous group, all of whom could not be taught through implementation of one commercial reading program or a single instructional emphasis.

Influenced by the work of Buly and Valencia (2002), Rupp and Lesaux (2006) conducted a study investigating the diagnostic profiles of students across proficiency levels on a mandated standardized assessment of reading.

The researchers used multiple assessments to determine 1,111 fourth-grade students' reading abilities. The assessments used in the study tested the assertion that "all children with reading problems have deficits in phonological processing, working memory and short-term memory, and syntactic awareness" (Siegel, 2003, p. 160). Rupp and Lesaux reported strong heterogeneity among the students in the study at all levels of proficiency, indicating that the capacity to use skills and strategies varies regardless of achievement level. Thus, teachers must first learn which skills and strategies students use proficiently and then build on those with increasingly more challenging text.

Similarly, Hargis (2006) reports that many young adolescent readers are capable of reading text, but the variation among reading levels is great. For example, Hargis noted that seventh-grade students with average achievement, those who scored in the second and third quartiles on the Peabody Individual Achievement Test, demonstrated reading levels between grades 5 and 10. These "average achievement" students, then, were all readers but not all were capable of reading text based on grade-level expectations. Buly and Valencia (2002) addressed this same condition in their assertion that "for many struggling students, grade-level standards are goals rather than immediate needs" (p. 234). In other words, even though the students were able to read text, the reading abilities demonstrated by these adolescents varied greatly, representing a range of instructional strengths and needs to which a middle-grades teacher must respond.

Much like Buly and Valencia (2002), Dennis (2009) administered multiple literacy assessments to 94 middle school students. The assessments measured students' knowledge of phonics, decoding, fluency, vocabulary, and comprehension. The findings supported the idea that students who struggle with reading represent heterogeneous abilities that cannot be captured by a proficiency category on a single measure, nor by a failing designation on a state assessment. Assessments such as the Qualitative Reading Inventory (Leslie & Caldwell, 2006) and the Spelling Inventories from *Words Their Way* (Bear, Invernizzi, Templeton, & Johnston, 2004), provide sensitive data that teachers can easily analyze to determine the most appropriate instruction for each student, or for small groups of students with similar abilities. By the same token, a one-size-fits-all instructional approach will not support the development of students whose profiles suggest varying patterns of strengths and needs.

In a single case study of a middle school student who scored below proficient on a state-mandated assessment, Dennis (2008) discusses the mismatch between the student's literacy abilities and the curriculum required by the school district. Jennifer, the sixth-grade student described in the study, participated in a variety of literacy assessments, including an Individual Reading Inventory that indicated her independent reading level was a grade equivalent of 5 and her spelling ability a grade equivalent of 4. Jennifer reported that she read books for pleasure both at home and school. Despite her literacy abilities, Jennifer received instruction in a curriculum mandated for all students who failed the state test. The curriculum focused on decoding skills and offered no opportunities for students to read independent-level text. Instead, students were placed within the program based on a test of nonsense word reading, on which Jennifer scored at a first-grade equivalency. Rather than using multiple assessments of authentic tasks to make instructional decisions, the school district assumed that all middle school students who failed the state assessment were missing the phonological and decoding skills required of early readers. Had the district instead looked for patterns of students' literacy abilities and recognized that Jennifer's ability to decode and comprehend real words—those actually encountered in text—was consistent with her grade level, they would be more likely to respond to the needs of the heterogeneous population of students who face difficulty on high-stakes tests.

Responsive Interventions Can Build Teacher Capacity

If struggling readers demonstrate different profiles of strengths and needs, as research cited in the previous section suggests, then instruction that builds on what students know should be more effective than instruction that is broadly focused on presumed phonological deficits that may or may not be missing from the students' repertoires of practice. A series of studies conducted by Carol Connor and her colleagues at Florida Center for Reading Research (FCRR) have demonstrated just that. Connor and colleagues (2009) contrasted the effectiveness of two core reading programs, with and without differentiated instruction, and found that students made more progress in comprehension when instruction was differentiated, regardless of the program. In a similar study of first graders with entering abilities that varied considerably along the dimensions of vocabulary and phonics, Connor, Morrison, and Katch (2004) found that students benefited from different kinds of instruction—those with weaker phonics benefited from explicit teacher-managed instruction, whereas those with stronger vocabulary and decoding were more successful with student-managed interactions, which involved independent reading.

Ultimately, Connor and colleagues (2009) developed algorithm-guided individualized reading instruction that teachers were able to access via a computerized assessment system, and to which these researchers attribute significant achievement gains by struggling readers. In summing up the work of FCRR in this area, Connor et al. assert the following:

> We have found that instruction that a) is intentionally planned to accommodate the individual differences among children within the classroom, b) relies on careful assessment of students skills, and c) is responsive to each student's changing status (cognitive, behavioral, social-emotional) is generally more effective than instruction that treats the classroom environment more globally, less diagnostically, more intuitively, and less dynamically. (p. 95)

Unfortunately, to accomplish the kind of individualization or responsive instruction described in the FCRR studies, teachers would need to use a proprietary system rather than rely on their own expertise to assess individual students and attend responsively to patterns of reading development in their instruction. Professional development was provided in these studies, but it focused on using the proprietary system, not on enabling teachers on their own to assess and teach a range of learners, regardless of particular curricular or assessment systems in place.

A two-year kindergarten professional development project, Kindergarten Literacy, developed by McGill-Franzen in collaboration with others, reported in a number of presentations at the National Reading Conference (McGill-Franzen, Payne, Dennis, & Jordan, 2008; McGill-Franzen, Solic, Mathson, & Payne, 2006) and the International Reading Association (McGill-Franzen, 2006b), also enabled teachers to differentiate instruction and improve the achievement of struggling students, but accomplished these goals by a different route. A joint project of Knox County, Tennessee, schools and the University of Tennessee, the kindergarten project sought to build teacher capacity. A major component of the project was teachers' participation in practice-based professional development similar to a reading specialist practicum. Teachers identified the students who struggled most in their classes, that is, those who entered kindergarten knowing 10 or fewer letters of the alphabet—typically 4–6 students—and taught them after school for about an hour Monday–Thursday. Once a month on a Friday, teachers met in a collaborative group to view unedited video clips of particular students, discuss professional reading that supported their work, and at the end of the year, to present a case study of one student. A small number of teachers participated in this project over two years, and the gain scores for all their students, in addition to the gain scores for their intervention students, were analyzed for growth. Assumptions of the project were the following:

- Teachers would develop deep expertise about literacy development through responsive interactions with struggling students, professional reading, and knowledge-building talk with colleagues.

- This expertise would be available to all students in these classes, not just the struggling readers in the after-school intervention.

Analyses of the gain scores in assessments of letter recognition, letter sounds, phonological awareness, spelling, word reading and writing, and text reading and writing demonstrated significant differences ($p < 0.01$) between struggling kindergartners who participated in the after-school intervention and matched comparison students who received different instructional support (packaged curriculum program, computer instruction, Success for All tutoring, and so on). Most important, more than one third of intervention students read at Guided Reading Level C or above at the end of the year, compared with 16% of comparison students; further, only 12% of intervention students could not read Guided Reading Level A text, whereas almost one third of comparison students were unable to read this level of easy text. Retention rates were significantly higher for comparison students as well (11% retained or placed in transition versus 3.6% for intervention students), indicating that teachers did not believe that these students would be as successful in first grade as those who participated in the intervention.

Besides improving the achievement of struggling students beyond that of comparison students who entered kindergarten at the same level, a series of repeated-measures analyses between all students in participating teachers' classrooms in year 1 and year 2 of the project revealed significant ($p < 0.01$) gains in spelling, word-reading, and text-reading and -writing levels in the second year. In other words, teachers were able to accelerate the development of all students in their classes, lending support to our thesis that practice-based professional development builds teacher capacity and makes expertise and responsive teaching available to every student.

A corollary to our analyses of gains scores was our qualitative analyses of teachers' talk about the struggling readers they were teaching. Of course, teachers started our project from different places in their knowledge about literacy development and experiences teaching reading. Nonetheless, we saw patterns in the ways they described their case study students between year 1 and year 2 of the project—moving from descriptions of students' families ("look at where he came from...") and behaviors ("he's not a risk taker...") to more detailed observations of the students' development ("he has that concept of directionality...") and more elaborated reflections on their teaching ("I needed to provide more support to help him read back his writing...").

Appropriate assessments as used in this project, that is, systematic observation and documentation of students' reading and writing behaviors, enabled teachers to do the following:

- Notice the trajectories of students' development over time
- Ground their collaborative talk about students' performance and progress in actual observed behaviors
- Provide the impetus for reflection and revisions in their teaching practices, and ultimately, in the view they hold of their struggling students and their ability to teach them

In summary, these are the characteristics of responsive intervention—attention to individual students' patterns of development, rethinking instruction so that it supports students' learning, and building on the strengths of students, not marking their failures. Appropriate assessment can help build teachers' capacity to develop, evaluate, and revise intervention so that it is truly responsive.

REFERENCES

Bear, D.R., Invernizzi, M., Templeton, S., & Johnston, F. (2004). *Words their way: Word study for phonics, vocabulary, and spelling instruction* (3rd ed.). Upper Saddle River, NJ: Prentice-Hall.

Buly, M.R., & Valencia, S.W. (2002). Below the bar: Profiles of students who fail state reading assessments. *Educational Evaluation and Policy Analysis, 24*(3), 219–239. doi:10.3102/01623737024003219

Clay, M.M. (1993). *An observation survey of early literacy achievement.* Portsmouth, NH: Heinemann.

Connor, C.M., Morrison, F.J., Fishman, B.J., Ponitz, C.C., Glasney, S., Underwood, P.S., et al. (2009). The ISI classroom observation system: Examining the literacy instruction provided to individual students. *Educational Researcher, 38*(2), 85–99. doi:10.3102/0013189X09332373

Connor, C.M., Morrison, F.J., & Katch, L.E. (2004). Algorithm-guided individualized reading instruction. *Scientific Studies of Reading, 8*(4), 305–336. doi:10.1207/s1532799xssr0804_1

Dennis, D.V. (2008). Are assessment data really driving middle school reading instruction? What we can learn from one student's experience. *Journal of Adolescent & Adult Literacy, 51*(7), 578–587. doi:10.1598/JAAL.51.7.5

Dennis, D.V. (2009). "I'm not stupid": How assessment drives (in)appropriate reading instruction. *Journal of Adolescent & Adult Literacy*, 53(4), 283–290. doi:10.1598/JAAL.53.4.2

Ehri, L.C. (1991). Learning to read and spell words. In L. Rieben & C.A. Perfetti (Eds.), *Learning to read: Basic research and its implications* (pp. 57–73). Hillsdale, NJ: Erlbaum.

Hargis, C.H. (2006). Setting standards: An exercise in futility? *Phi Delta Kappan*, 87(5), 393–395.

Johnston, P. (1987). Teachers as evaluation experts. *The Reading Teacher*, 40(8), 744–748.

Leslie, L., & Caldwell, J. (2006). *Qualitative reading inventory-4* (4th ed.). New York: Allyn & Bacon.

McGill-Franzen, A. (2006a). *Kindergarten literacy: Matching assessment and instruction in kindergarten*. New York: Scholastic.

McGill-Franzen, A. (2006b, May). *Kindergarten rules! Literacy teaching that can change lives.* Paper presented at the International Reading Association Annual Convention, Chicago, IL.

McGill-Franzen, A., Payne, R., Dennis, D.V., & Jordan, J. (2008, November). *Practice-based professional development: Building teacher expertise as intervention for struggling kindergartners.* Paper presented at the National Reading Conference, Orlando, FL.

McGill-Franzen, A., Solic, K., Mathson, D., & Payne, R. (2006, November). *Teacher expertise as intervention: A practice-based model of learning for teachers and extra support for at-risk kindergarteners.* Paper presented at the National Reading Conference, Los Angeles, CA.

Rupp, A.A., & Lesaux, N.K. (2006). Meeting expectations? An empirical investigation of a standards-based assessment of reading comprehension. *Educational Evaluation and Policy Analysis*, 28(4), 315–333. doi:10.3102/01623737028004315

Siegel, L.S. (2003). Basic cognitive processes and reading disabilities. In H.L. Swanson, K.R. Harris, & S. Graham (Eds.), *Handbook of learning disabilities* (pp. 158–181). New York: Guilford.

Spear-Swerling, L. (2004). A road map for understanding reading disability and other reading problems: Origins, prevention, and intervention. In R.B. Ruddell & N.J. Unrau (Eds.), *Theoretical models & processes of reading* (5th ed., pp. 517–573). Newark, DE: International Reading Association.

Spear-Swerling, L., & Sternberg, R. (1996). *Off track: When poor readers become "learning disabled."* Bolder, CO: Westview.

Taylor, B.M., Pearson, P.D., Clark, K., & Walpole, S. (2000). Effective schools and accomplished teachers: Lessons about primary grade reading instruction in low-income schools. *The Elementary School Journal*, 101(2), 121–165. doi:10.1086/499662

CHAPTER 7

A Comprehensive Assessment System as a Response to Intervention Process

Linda J. Dorn and Shannon Coman Henderson

The frustration on Sarah's face was sincere as she expressed her concerns about Leonardo's reading difficulties: "He just isn't making progress. I have tried everything, but he is still reading at a level B." When the literacy coach prompted Sarah to describe the child's problem-solving behaviors, she responded, "He has been at a level B for three weeks now. His entry-level DIBELS scores were PSF 9, NWF 18, and ORF 6. When I progress monitored yesterday they were PSF 12, NWF 28, and ORF 10."

The coach probed further, "But what have you observed about how Leonardo problem solves during the reading of a book?"

"He can't," she explained, "he just stops when he doesn't know the word."

The coach inquired, "What do you do to help him learn the word in the story he didn't know?"

"I just tell him," she sighed.

The link between assessment and intervention is reciprocal. If a teacher is unable to explain how assessment is used to inform instruction, then the assessment is of little value. In the previous scenario, Sarah was unable to use assessment to help Leonardo with solving problems during reading; therefore, the assessment process was meaningless. The International Reading Association and National Council of Teachers of English (2009) *Standards for the Assessment of Reading and Writing* explain that the primary purpose of assessment is to improve teaching and learning. If students are not learning from instruction, then the assessment system might be inappropriate for informing the teaching.

One goal of RTI is to develop more valid procedures for assessing and identifying students who are at risk of reading failure. Assessments should be

RTI in Literacy—Responsive and Comprehensive, edited by Peter H. Johnston.
© 2010 by the International Reading Association.

direct measures of specific skills and strategies that are needed for success in the general education classroom. A reading program should provide opportunities for differentiated instruction to meet the needs of individual learners; consequently, assessment must reflect how students are responding to curriculum and instruction. Some questions for linking assessment to instruction are, How does the student respond to instruction in a small reading group? Is the book appropriate for the student's learning level? What strategies does the student use to solve problems? How much teacher assistance is needed? Does the student generalize knowledge learned in an instructional setting to independent work?

An important goal of learning is to transfer knowledge from an assisted situation (e.g., guided reading group) to an unassisted situation (e.g., independent reading). This implies that assessment is a measure for studying the link between teaching and learning, and if a student is not responding to instruction, the problem is with the instruction and not with the student.

Teachers and administrators in our schools are swimming (or drowning) in a sea of data. They have data in the form of screening data, progress-monitoring data, anecdotal notes, formal observations, state tests, and national tests. These data are compiled by teachers, computers, and proctors and are primarily used to evaluate student progress. The problems we typically encounter in schools are not caused by a lack of data but rather by not knowing how to use the data to differentiate and design instruction that improves student literacy outcomes.

In this chapter we share how educators can design a comprehensive literacy assessment system as an RTI method. First, we describe the process of dynamic assessment as a diagnostic, decision-making practice. Then we present details for implementing two comprehensive assessment measures: (1) comprehensive assessment system (CAS), including core assessments for measuring student progress at the individual and school level, and (2) comprehensive literacy diagnostic (CLD) for matching a student to the appropriate intervention service. Finally, we share how schools can implement an assessment wall for progress monitoring as a component of RTI.

Dynamic Assessment

Dynamic assessment (DA) is a process for understanding the differences within individual learners and their responsiveness to instruction (Lidz & Gindis, 2003). It is grounded in an interactive model that examines the relationship between teaching and learning. DA is based on the belief that teaching leads development; therefore, instruction (intervention) must be aimed toward creating environments that activate a student's potential to learn. The goal is to discover whether and how much the learner will change under the influence of scaffolding activities (Lidz & Gindis, 2003). This means that dynamic assessment is a diagnostic measure that occurs in the child's zone of proximal development (see Vygotsky, 1978), and the teacher (not a program) is the primary agent of assessment and instruction.

From an RTI perspective, DA is especially relevant because it embeds intervention within the assessment procedure. Teachers conduct assessment for purposes of designing instruction, and instruction is focused on awakening the student's learning potential. Vygotsky (1978) insisted that assessment of the child's ability to learn through instruction was a better predictor of future cognitive functioning than a measure of independent performance through traditional tests (Kozulin, 1998). Consequently, DA emphasizes what a student can do with assistance, which may provide better insights into the student's learning capabilities than what the student can accomplish without help.

Assessment is a reflection of instruction; therefore, it must provide evidence of the student's learning at two levels: the independent level and the instructional level. Teachers should understand the purpose of assessment as it relates to a student's learning level.

The student's independent level is defined as the zone of actual development. This is the level where a student is able to accomplish successfully a task without teacher assistance. Assessments that measure a student's independent level are considered summative in nature, and they generally include standardized procedures, cut scores, and benchmark levels. Some examples of summative measures are text-reading levels, spelling placements, benchmark examinations, and district or state assessments.

The student's instructional level is defined as the zone of proximal development. This is the level where a student is able to learn from instruction. Assessments that measure a student's instructional level are formative in nature, and they include curriculum-based measures that directly reflect the impact of teaching on students' learning. Formative assessments in the form of teacher observations, anecdotal notes, checklists, rubrics, running records, and writing samples are used to make instructional decisions on a day-by-day, student-by-student basis.

A Comprehensive Assessment System

In this section, we describe the components of a CAS. The goal of the CAS is to create a systemic, decision-making model for engaging educators in the assessment and instruction process. The CAS is based on an interactive design that views assessment as a recursive and generative process. At the center of the CAS is the teacher—one who understands how to use assessment to inform and guide instruction.

The CAS includes four essential components: (1) a battery of core assessments at each grade level that represent the student's ability to respond to the core curriculum and district-level expectations, (2) a battery of diagnostic assessments for identifying students who are not responding to the core instruction and need an appropriate intervention, (3) an assessment wall for displaying the progression of individual students and designated subgroups (e.g., transient, learning disabled, English-language learners) on the core assessments, and (4) an intervention team that meets frequently to collaborate on student learning, including selecting appropriate interventions and monitoring progress across classroom and intervention settings.

Core Assessments

Core assessments are defined as universal assessments for all students in a particular grade. It is important to note that teachers may have other assessments, but these are not defined as the core system. The first step in the CAS is for teachers to identify a battery of core assessments at each grade level that present a comprehensive analysis of student learning. Generally, schools select five to nine core assessments, which should include both summative and formative measures at the particular grade level. The summative measures reflect student performance on district- or state-level assessments, while the formative assessments reflect student performance in response to the classroom curriculum. In the CAS, an emphasis is placed on formative assessments that provide evidence of how well the teacher is differentiating the instruction to accommodate the student's learning.

In Figure 7.1, we present an example of a CAS from Washington School for Comprehensive Literacy in Sheboygan, Wisconsin. You will notice that the assessment grid is divided into five assessment intervals: beginning of year, end of first quarter, end of second quarter, end of third quarter, and end of year. At each interval, an assessment window for data collection is identified. The

Figure 7.1. Example of Schoolwide Comprehensive Assessment System (CAS)

Beginning of Year
- Assessment and 2-Week Observation: September 4–21
- Benchmark Books: September 24–28
- Data Sheet: October 1
- Intervention Wall: October 2

End of First Quarter
- Assessment Window: November 5–16
- First Quarter Ends: November 9
- Data Sheet: November 19
- Intervention Wall (on your own): November 19, 20, 21

End of Second Quarter
- Assessment Window: January 14–24
- Second Quarter Ends: January 24
- Data Sheet: January 28
- Intervention Wall (on your own): January 29

End of Third Quarter
- Assessment Window: March 31–April 11
- Third Quarter Ends: April 8
- Data Sheet: April 14
- Intervention Wall (on your own): April 15

End of Year
- Writing and Spelling Window: April 28–May 16
- TRL Window: April 28–May 22
- Data Sheet: May 22
- Intervention Wall: May 27

	Beginning of Year		End of First Quarter		End of Second Quarter		End of Third Quarter		End of Year	
	Summative (Formal)	Formative (Informal)	Summative (Formal)	Formative (Informal)	Summative (Formal)	Formative (Informal)	Summative (Formal)	Formative (Informal)	Summative (Formal)	Formative (Informal)
Kindergarten	Observation Survey (Letter ID; CAP; Writing Vocabulary; Sentence Dictation; TRL)	2-Week Reading Observation	Letter ID	Reading Conference Notes	Benchmark Book* • 90%–94% Accuracy • Fluency • Comprehension • SC Rate	Reading Conference Notes	Benchmark Book* • 90%–94% Accuracy • Fluency • Comprehension • SC Rate	Reading Conference Notes	Observation Survey (Letter ID; CAP; Writing Vocabulary; Sentence Dictation; TRL)	
	Clay Writing Assessment	2-Week Writing Observation	Concepts About Print (CAP)	Writing Conference Notes	Letter ID	Writing Conference Notes	Letter ID	Writing Conference Notes	TRL • 90%–95% Accuracy • Fluency • Comprehension • SC Rate	
	Oral Language Acquisition Inventory			Writing Portfolio Rubric	CAP	Running Records	CAP	Running Records	Clay Writing Assessment	
					Oral Language Acquisition Inventory	Writing Portfolio Rubric		Writing Portfolio Rubric	Oral Language Acquisition Inventory	

(continued)

A Comprehensive Assessment System as a Response to Intervention Process   137

Figure 7.1. Example of Schoolwide Comprehensive Assessment System (CAS) *(continued)*

	Beginning of Year • Assessment and 2-Week Observation: September 4–21 • Benchmark Books: September 24–28 • Data Sheet: October 1 • Intervention Wall: October 2		End of First Quarter • Assessment Window: November 5–16 • First Quarter Ends: November 9 • Data Sheet: November 19 • Intervention Wall (on your own): November 19, 20, 21		End of Second Quarter • Assessment Window: January 14–24 • Second Quarter Ends: January 24 • Data Sheet: January 28 • Intervention Wall (on your own): January 29		End of Third Quarter • Assessment Window: March 31–April 11 • Third Quarter Ends: April 8 • Data Sheet: April 14 • Intervention Wall (on your own): April 15		End of Year • Writing and Spelling Window: April 28–May 16 • TRL Window: April 28–May 22 • Data Sheet: May 22 • Intervention Wall: May 27	
	Summative (Formal)	Formative (Informal)	Summative (Formal)	Formative (Informal)	Summative (Formal)	Formative (Informal)	Summative (Formal)	Formative (Informal)	Summative (Formal)	Formative (Informal)
1st Grade	Spring TRL From Assessment Folder • 90%–94% • Accuracy • Fluency • Comprehension • SC Rate	2-Week Reading Observation	Benchmark Book • 90%–94% • Accuracy • Fluency • Comprehension • SC Rate	Reading Conference Notes	Benchmark Book • 90%–94% • Accuracy • Fluency • Comprehension • SC Rate	Reading Conference Notes	Benchmark Book • 90%–94% • Accuracy • Fluency • Comprehension • SC Rate	Reading Conference Notes	TRL • 90%–94% • Accuracy • Fluency • Comprehension • SC Rate	
	Clay Writing Assessment	2-Week Writing Observation		Writing Conference Notes	Spelling Inventory	Writing Conference Notes		Writing Conference Notes	Personal Narrative Writing Prompt	
	Spelling Assessment	2-Week Spelling Observation		Running Records	Oral Language Acquisition Inventory	Running Records		Running Records	Spelling Inventory	
	Benchmark Book • 90%–94% • Accuracy • Fluency • Comprehension • SC Rate			Independent Reading Rubric		Independent Reading Rubric		Independent Reading Rubric	Oral Language Acquisition Inventory	
	Oral Language Acquisition Inventory			Writing Portfolio Rubric		Writing Portfolio Rubric		Writing Portfolio Rubric		

(continued)

Figure 7.1. Example of Schoolwide Comprehensive Assessment System (CAS) *(continued)*

	Beginning of Year		End of First Quarter		End of Second Quarter		End of Third Quarter		End of Year	
	• Assessment and 2-Week Observation: September 4–21 • Benchmark Books: September 24–28 • Data Sheet: October 1 • Intervention Wall: October 2		• Assessment Window: November 5–16 • First Quarter Ends: November 9 • Data Sheet: November 19 • Intervention Wall (on your own): November 19, 20, 21		• Assessment Window: January 14–24 • Second Quarter Ends: January 24 • Data Sheet: January 28 • Intervention Wall (on your own): January 29		• Assessment Window: March 31–April 11 • Third Quarter Ends: April 8 • Data Sheet: April 14 • Intervention Wall (on your own): April 15		• Writing and Spelling Window: April 28–May 16 • TRL Window: April 28–May 22 • Data Sheet: May 22 • Intervention Wall: May 27	
	Summative (Formal)	Formative (Informal)	Summative (Formal)	Formative (Informal)	Summative (Formal)	Formative (Informal)	Summative (Formal)	Formative (Informal)	Summative (Formal)	Formative (Informal)
2nd Grade	Spring TRL From Assessment Folder • 90%–94% • Accuracy • Fluency • Comprehension • SC Rate	2-Week Reading Observation	Benchmark Book • 90%–94% • Accuracy • Fluency • Comprehension • SC Rate	Reading Conference Notes	Benchmark Book • 90%–94% • Accuracy • Fluency • Comprehension • SC Rate	Reading Conference Notes	Benchmark Book • 90%–94% • Accuracy • Fluency • Comprehension • SC Rate	Reading Conference Notes	TRL • 90%–94% • Accuracy • Fluency • Comprehension • SC Rate	
	Spring Writing Prompt From Assessment Folder	2-Week Writing Observation		Writing Conference Notes	Spelling Inventory	Writing Conference Notes		Writing Conference Notes	Personal Narrative Writing Prompt	
	Spring Spelling From Assessment Folder	2-Week Spelling Observation		Thoughtful Log Entry Rubric	Oral Language Acquisition Inventory	Literature Discussion Rubric		Literature Discussion Rubric	Spelling Inventory	
	Benchmark Book • 90%–94% • Accuracy • Fluency • Comprehension • SC Rate	Independent Reading Rubric				Thoughtful Log Entry Rubric		Thoughtful Log Entry Rubric	Oral Language Acquisition Inventory	
	Oral Language Acquisition Inventory	Writing Portfolio Rubric		Independent Reading Rubric		Independent Reading Rubric		Independent Reading Rubric		
				Writing Portfolio Rubric		Writing Portfolio Rubric		Writing Portfolio Rubric		

(continued)

Figure 7.1. Example of Schoolwide Comprehensive Assessment System (CAS) (continued)

Beginning of Year
- Assessment and 2-Week Observation: September 4–21
- Benchmark Books: September 24–28
- Data Sheet: October 1
- Intervention Wall: October 2

End of First Quarter
- Assessment Window: November 5–16
- First Quarter Ends: November 9
- Data Sheet: November 19
- Intervention Wall (on your own): November 19, 20, 21

End of Second Quarter
- Assessment Window: January 14–24
- Second Quarter Ends: January 24
- Data Sheet: January 28
- Intervention Wall (on your own): January 29

End of Third Quarter
- Assessment Window: March 31–April 11
- Third Quarter Ends: April 8
- Data Sheet: April 14
- Intervention Wall (on your own): April 15

End of Year
- Writing and Spelling Window: April 28–May 16
- TRL Window: April 28–May 22
- Data Sheet: May 22
- Intervention Wall: May 27

3rd Grade

Beginning of Year — Summative (Formal)	Beginning of Year — Formative (Informal)	End of First Quarter — Summative (Formal)	End of First Quarter — Formative (Informal)	End of Second Quarter — Summative (Formal)	End of Second Quarter — Formative (Informal)	End of Third Quarter — Summative (Formal)	End of Third Quarter — Formative (Informal)	End of Year — Summative (Formal)	End of Year — Formative (Informal)
Spring TRL From Assessment Folder • 90%–94% Accuracy • Fluency • Comprehension • SC Rate	2-Week Reading Observation	Benchmark Book • 90%–94% Accuracy • Fluency • Comprehension • SC Rate	Reading Conference Notes	Benchmark Book • 90%–94% Accuracy • Fluency • Comprehension • SC Rate	Reading Conference Notes	Benchmark Book • 90%–94% Accuracy • Fluency • Comprehension • SC Rate	Reading Conference Notes	TRL • 90%–94% Accuracy • Fluency • Comprehension • SC Rate	
Spring Writing Prompt From Assessment Folder	2-Week Writing Observation		Writing Conference Notes	Writing Portfolio Rubric	Writing Conference Notes	Writing Portfolio Rubric	Writing Conference Notes	Personal Narrative Writing Prompt	
			Literature Discussion Rubric		Literature Discussion Rubric		Literature Discussion Rubric		
Spelling Inventory			Thoughtful Log Entry Rubric	Spelling Inventory	Thoughtful Log Entry Rubric		Thoughtful Log Entry Rubric	Spelling Inventory	
Benchmark Book • 90%–94% Accuracy • Fluency • Comprehension • SC Rate	Independent Reading Rubric		Independent Reading Rubric	Oral Language Acquisition Inventory	Independent Reading Rubric		Independent Reading Rubric	Oral Language Acquisition Inventory	
Oral Language Acquisition Inventory	Writing Portfolio Rubric		Writing Portfolio Rubric		Writing Portfolio Rubric		Writing Portfolio Rubric		

(continued)

Figure 7.1. Example of Schoolwide Comprehensive Assessment System (CAS) (continued)

Beginning of Year
- Assessment and 2-Week Observation: September 4–21
- Benchmark Books: September 24–28
- Data Sheet: October 1
- Intervention Wall: October 2

End of First Quarter
- Assessment Window: November 5–16
- First Quarter Ends: November 9
- Data Sheet: November 19
- Intervention Wall (on your own): November 19, 20, 21

End of Second Quarter
- Assessment Window: January 14–24
- Second Quarter Ends: January 24
- Data Sheet: January 28
- Intervention Wall (on your own): January 29

End of Third Quarter
- Assessment Window: March 31–April 11
- Third Quarter Ends: April 8
- Data Sheet: April 14
- Intervention Wall (on your own): April 15

End of Year
- Writing and Spelling Window: April 28–May 16
- TRL Window: April 28–May 22
- Data Sheet: May 22
- Intervention Wall: May 27

	Beginning of Year — Summative (Formal)	Beginning of Year — Formative (Informal)	End of First Quarter — Summative (Formal)	End of First Quarter — Formative (Informal)	End of Second Quarter — Summative (Formal)	End of Second Quarter — Formative (Informal)	End of Third Quarter — Summative (Formal)	End of Third Quarter — Formative (Informal)	End of Year — Summative (Formal)	End of Year — Formative (Informal)
4th Grade	Spring TRL From Assessment Folder • 90%–94% • Accuracy • Fluency • Comprehension • SC Rate	2-Week Reading Observation	Benchmark Book • 90%–94% • Accuracy • Fluency • Comprehension • SC Rate	Reading Conference Notes	Benchmark Book • 90%–94% • Accuracy • Fluency • Comprehension • SC Rate	Reading Conference Notes	Benchmark Book • 90%–94% • Accuracy • Fluency • Comprehension • SC Rate	Reading Conference Notes	TRL • 90%–94% • Accuracy • Fluency • Comprehension • SC Rate	
	Spring Writing Prompt From Assessment Folder	2-Week Writing Observation		Writing Conference Notes	Spelling Inventory	Writing Conference Notes		Writing Conference Notes	Personal Narrative Writing Prompt	
	Spring Spelling Inventory	2-Week Spelling Observation		Literature Discussion Rubric	Oral Language Acquisition Inventory	Literature Discussion Rubric		Literature Discussion Rubric	Spelling Inventory	
	Benchmark Book • 90%–94% • Accuracy • Fluency • Comprehension • SC Rate			Thoughtful Log Entry Rubric		Thoughtful Log Entry Rubric		Thoughtful Log Entry Rubric	Oral Language Acquisition Inventory	
	Oral Language Acquisition Inventory			Independent Reading Rubric		Independent Reading Rubric		Independent Reading Rubric		
				Writing Portfolio Rubric		Writing Portfolio Rubric		Writing Portfolio Rubric		

(continued)

Figure 7.1. Example of Schoolwide Comprehensive Assessment System (CAS) (continued)

5th Grade	**Beginning of Year** • Assessment and 2-Week Observation: September 4–21 • Benchmark Books: September 24–28 • Data Sheet: October 1 • Intervention Wall: October 2		**End of First Quarter** • Assessment Window: November 5–16 • First Quarter Ends: November 9 • Data Sheet: November 19 • Intervention Wall (on your own): November 19, 20, 21		**End of Second Quarter** • Assessment Window: January 14–24 • Second Quarter Ends: January 24 • Data Sheet: January 28 • Intervention Wall (on your own): January 29		**End of Third Quarter** • Assessment Window: March 31–April 11 • Third Quarter Ends: April 8 • Data Sheet: April 14 • Intervention Wall (on your own): April 15		**End of Year** • Writing and Spelling Window: April 28–May 16 • TRL Window: April 28–May 22 • Data Sheet: May 22 • Intervention Wall: May 27	
	Summative (Formal)	Formative (Informal)	Summative (Formal)	Formative (Informal)	Summative (Formal)	Formative (Informal)	Summative (Formal)	Formative (Informal)	Summative (Formal)	Formative (Informal)
	Spring TRL From Assessment Folder • 90%–94% Accuracy • Fluency • Comprehension • SC Rate	2-Week Reading Observation	Benchmark Book • 90%–94% Accuracy • Fluency • Comprehension • SC Rate	Reading Conference Notes	Benchmark Book • 90%–94% Accuracy • Fluency • Comprehension • SC Rate	Reading Conference Notes	Benchmark Book • 90%–94% Accuracy • Fluency • Comprehension • SC Rate	Reading Conference Notes	TRL • 90%–94% Accuracy • Fluency • Comprehension • SC Rate	
	Spring Writing Prompt From Assessment Folder	2-Week Writing Observation		Writing Conference Notes	Spelling Inventory	Writing Conference Notes		Writing Conference Notes	Personal Narrative Writing Prompt	
	Spring Spelling Inventory	2-Week Spelling Observation		Literature Discussion Rubric	Oral Language Acquisition Inventory	Literature Discussion Rubric		Literature Discussion Rubric	Spelling Inventory	
	Oral Language Acquisition Inventory			Thoughtful Log Rubric		Thoughtful Log Rubric		Thoughtful Log Rubric	Oral Language Acquisition Inventory	
	Benchmark Book • 90%–94% Accuracy • Fluency • Comprehension • SC Rate			Independent Reading Rubric		Independent Reading Rubric		Independent Reading Rubric		
				Writing Portfolio Rubric		Writing Portfolio Rubric		Writing Portfolio Rubric		

Note. Special thanks to Katie Meyer and Brian Reindl, Literacy Coaches, Sheboyan School District, Wisconsin. TRL = text-reading level.

summative assessments at the beginning of the year are followed by a two-week observation period. The CAS places an emphasis on teacher observation as a tool for documenting how a student is responding to classroom instruction. In this example, the CAS includes the following formative assessments: anecdotal notes from reading and writing observations, running records, writing portfolio rubric, independent reading rubric, thoughtful log entry rubric, and literature discussion rubric. These formative assessments are a reflection of the classroom literacy program, which focuses on a reading and writing workshop approach with guided reading, literature discussion groups, independent reading, and reading/writing conferences.

From an RTI perspective, the CAS meets two assessment purposes: identification and progress monitoring. First, it serves as a universal screener to determine students who may be at risk of reading failure based on their lack of progress on the core assessments. Therefore, if a student is scoring below his or her classmates, the student may be referred for a CLD. Second, the CAS provides a measure for monitoring the progress of students on assessments that reflect the classroom curriculum and instruction, and if a student is not progressing, the problem might be with the curriculum rather than the student.

Comprehensive Literacy Diagnostic

A CLD is defined as a battery of literacy assessments for planning and monitoring student progress in a particular intervention (Dorn & Soffos, in press). The identification process begins with the classroom teacher, who recommends a student for diagnostic assessment based on the student's difficulty in the classroom literacy program. The reading specialist administers the appropriate assessment battery to diagnose the student's strengths and needs. For example, if a first-grade student exhibits at-risk behaviors in early reading, an appropriate assessment would be the Observation Survey of Early Literacy Achievement (Clay, 2004), which includes a six-part battery of literacy assessments (letter identification, word test, concepts about print, phonological measure, writing test, and text reading). A critical aspect of the Observation Survey of Early Literacy Achievement is the diagnostic summary—a measure for triangulating literacy behaviors across the subtasks and identifying learning patterns in related areas.

Assessments that make up the CLD include a range of summative and formative assessments, such as (a) diagnostic summary of all entry assessments,

(b) classroom observation checklists, (c) running records, (d) selected work samples from the classroom, (e) test results from district or state assessments, and (f) informal rubrics and checklists. The CLD greatly reduces the problem of misidentification—providing intervention to students who do not need it (false positives) or denying intervention to students who do need it (false negatives).

In the CLD, the most important assessments are formative assessments, which are used to monitor a student's progress and to inform instructional decisions. Data are collected at regular intervals to systematically monitor a student's progress in a particular intervention and include (a) systematic and periodic assessments of learning behaviors, (b) measuring and comparing growth over time, and (c) using assessment to plan next steps. These data are graphed to compare screening and baseline data to benchmark expectations for each assessment period and to grade-level end-of-year expectations.

Using Text-Reading Levels for Progress Monitoring. We are frequently asked whether schools should use text-reading levels and running records for monitoring students' progress in RTI. We believe that text-reading levels provide a valid measure for predicting future reading success, and running records are the tools for determining a student's ability to read a particular level with fluency and comprehension. Dunn (2007) provides a good rationale for why text-reading levels are important measures for progress monitoring. He describes how a beginning text level relates to RTI's dual-discrepancy component in two ways: (1) It helps determine the degree of the student's low performance with reading skills, and (2) it provides a baseline for measuring reading growth over time. Text-reading levels have established benchmark levels for reading proficiency at designated intervals; therefore, teachers can compare the reading growth of students who receive interventions with that of average-performing students at specific points in time. This criterion is important because it allows the teacher to examine the impact of the intervention on the student's learning, and if the student is not progressing at an expected rate, the problem might be the intervention. For example, the student might require a more intensive intervention or a different type of intervention.

Running Record. The running record is a diagnostic tool for measuring a student's ability to integrate multiple sources of information and apply problem-solving strategies while reading texts of graded difficulty. Running records can function as both a formative and summative assessment (it is the purpose that determines whether a measure is considered formative or summative) for providing teachers with a way to (a) assess individual students' reading (i.e., accuracy, self-correction, text level, fluency, strategic behaviors, and growth over time), (b) determine appropriate book choice (taking into consideration background knowledge and motivational factors as well as text level), and (c) inform teaching.

In Figure 7.2, we provide an example of how a teacher uses running records and text-reading levels for progress monitoring in a reading intervention. The first step focuses on recording the beginning- and end-of-year benchmark levels on a graph. Then the student's beginning text-reading level is plotted, and an "aim line" is drawn from the beginning-of-year benchmark to end-of-year grade-level expectation for text-reading level. This aim line marks the path a teacher needs to take to move a student from his or her current level of performance to grade-level norms. By drawing a line from a student's current benchmark to end-of-year expectations, the teacher can determine whether the student is progressing (accelerating) enough to reach grade-level norms by the end of the

Figure 7.2. Example of Using Text-Reading Levels and Running Records to Track a Student's Trajectory of Progress

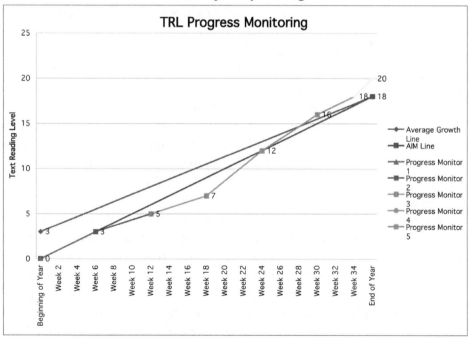

school year. As long as the student's performance is at or above the aim line, the teacher can be reasonably assured that the intervention is instructionally appropriate. However, if the student's performance falls below the aim line, the teacher must consider other instructional approaches or interventions to meet the individual student's needs.

Consolidating Core Assessments on the Assessment Wall

The assessment wall[1] is a critical component of the CAS. The wall provides the school with a way to make the data visible, and promotes problem-solving discussions focused on how students are responding to instruction. The wall serves three purposes as an assessment method: (1) identifying and monitoring the progress of individual students, (2) identifying and monitoring the progress of particular subgroups, and (3) monitoring the progress of the school's literacy program for increasing overall literacy achievement.

Identification and Progress Monitoring of Students. As described earlier, all students in a school are evaluated using common core assessments that align with the universal curriculum. These core assessments then serve as a universal screener for students who may be at risk for literacy failure. After the core assessment battery is administered, the data from these assessments are aggregated (not averaged) and instructional teams meet to classify students into predetermined categories such as (a) below basic, (b) basic, (c) proficient, or (d) advanced. This classification is noted and then transferred to individual student cards devoid of identifying information (e.g., the code "02-03-15" represents a student in grade 2, assigned to teacher number 3, with a corresponding student number of 15). The initial core assessments assist the teachers in determining where students' individual cards will be placed on the assessment wall (Figure 7.3). Those students falling into the "below basic" or "basic" range (approximately the lowest 20%) are then provided with a CLD to better pinpoint literacy strengths and weaknesses.

After completion of the core assessments, teachers come together in intervention team meetings to analyze the results and to reevaluate initial placement of student cards identified as "below basic" and "basic" during the screening process. Armed with curriculum-relevant assessment data, these teams collaboratively discuss and problem solve how to best meet individual learners' literacy needs based on students' strengths. If the team determines that an intervention is the most appropriate response, an intervention planner is completed

Figure 7.3. Photo of an Assessment Wall With Identification Categories

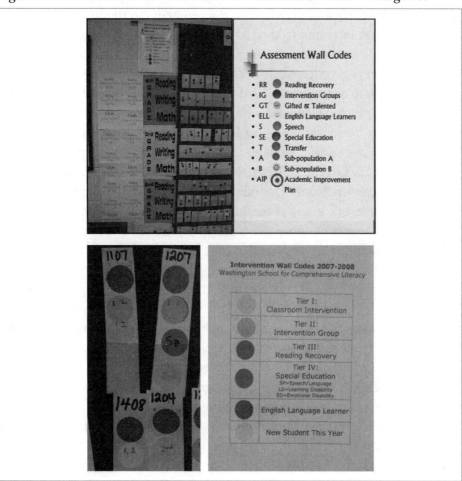

(see Dorn & Henderson, 2010, for a description of the intervention planner). This planner is then placed in a student's intervention portfolio where progress in the intervention is closely monitored and documented using both formative and summative assessments. At predetermined times during the year (usually grading periods) teachers reconvene in their grade-level teams to assess student progress on common core curriculum and to move individual cards. The expectation is that all students' cards will reflect forward progress (not just the intervention students) on the assessment wall, indicating that all have achieved a higher level of literacy skill.

Identification and Progress Monitoring of Subgroup Populations. After teachers apply corresponding identification numbers to the individual student cards, they meet in teams to discuss what they have observed and hypothesize what might be impeding literacy progress in their classrooms and school. Through a process of collective discussion, decisions are made as to which categories they wish to code onto the cards using colored file folder dots. Frequently occurring codes include students who speak English as a second (or third) language, receive a free or reduced-cost lunch, have been previously served in an intervention, or are transfer students.

Applying codes to the individual student cards enables schools to detect gaps in instruction not only for individual students but entire subgroups, as well. For example, one group of teachers we worked with decided to code their student cards for gender. Once the cards were placed on the assessment wall, it became apparent that kindergarten and first-grade boys were significantly behind the girls in reading prowess. In their literacy team meeting, teachers problem solved why this was occurring. An investigation of kindergarten and first-grade book collections evidenced that there were very few books in K–1 that boys chose to read. As a result, the school petitioned for and was granted permission to purchase informational books and stories that might motivate boys instead of adopting the district reading series. Within one year, the reading gap between K–1 boys and girls was significantly reduced.

In another example, a school we worked with noticed that while many of their students had moved from the below-basic category to basic as a result of implementing comprehensive interventions, it appeared that "green dot students" (students who had transferred in from outside their district) across the grade levels were not making adequate progress. As a result, the school assembled a triage team to assess any transfer student within 48 hours of enrolling in their building. When this step did not produce accelerated results, the team reconvened to problem solve yet again. This time, the interventionists proposed a plan whereby transfer students who scored below the basic level were prioritized and placed in an intervention group as soon as a slot was available. As a result, literacy outcomes for the "green dot students" improved.

The assessment wall provides stakeholders with a visual medium that facilitates detection of patterns in subgroups that might otherwise go undetected in a computerized or composite assessment system. It is a powerful tool for identification, monitoring, and problem solving of specific populations of students in a building. In Table 7.1, we present the procedures for constructing an assessment wall in the school.

Table 7.1. Procedures for Constructing an Assessment Wall

Step	Description
1. Locating the wall	Assessment walls are placed in areas where stakeholders can easily gather to examine, analyze, and share information about their students. Typically, assessment walls are not placed in an administrator's office or conference room.
2. Constructing the wall • 4 large pocket charts • address labels • markers • index or mini flash cards (one color per grade level) • colored file folder dots (used to represent categories/codes) • assessment notebooks • camera for recording purposes	Construction of the assessment wall involves hanging pocket charts side by side horizontally to represent four categories of students who are determined to be at (1) below basic, (2) basic, (3) proficient, or (4) advanced levels of literacy progress in reading and writing. On the left side of the first pocket chart, grade levels are marked with each row on the pocket chart designated for a specific grade level with a separate row for both reading and writing. Index or mini flash cards are used to represent students, but each card is devoid of student information and assigned a number. Each grade level is assigned a different color card to visually distinguish the grades on the assessment wall (e.g., yellow for kindergarten, blue for first grade, pink for second grade, green for third grade). Separate cards are constructed for both reading and writing. Colored dots are used to represent designated categories/codes.
3. Examining students' key assessment data	Teachers come together in grade-level teams to determine the categories of information that should be represented on the student cards (e.g., sex, socioeconomic status, home language) and to determine which students should be provided with a CLD.
4. Coding of cards • student number • student information • interventions • other information	Each student is represented by a number. Colored dots are then strategically placed on cards to represent different categories of student information. There is no uniform number of codes or code list. Codes are used only for categories of information that may affect student performance relative to a particular school.
5. Placing cards on the assessment wall	Teachers come together in grade-level teams to place their individual student cards on the assessment wall. Once teachers have completed the process, the wall is analyzed for possible trends and target areas for improving instruction.

Monitoring Schoolwide Literacy Achievement

At the beginning of each academic year, but after the initial placement of student cards, a picture is taken of the assessment wall as a visual artifact to gauge how a school progressed at a systems level. At the end of each academic year, stakeholders assemble to evaluate literacy progress not only in terms of how individual students or subpopulations improved but also to question how successful the school community was in moving entire cohorts of literacy learners. This visual artifact in conjunction with numerical data provides a detailed picture of how the school is addressing the needs of its learners across grade levels at all levels of instruction (Figure 7.4).

Figure 7.4. Samples From a School Assessment Wall at the Beginning and End of Year

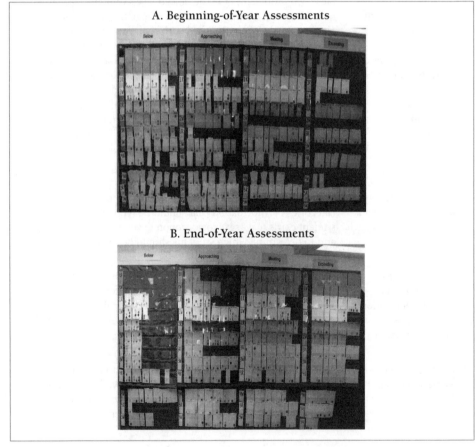

Assessment walls, as described in this chapter, are fundamentally different from other RTI assessment systems and are a critical part of the dynamic approach to RTI that we describe throughout this chapter. Unlike computerized data management systems (e.g., AIMSweb), the assessment wall facilitates an environment where teachers and administrators gather, analyze, explore, and converse over multiple data sources about their students, school, and communities to make better instructional decisions. Further, use of an assessment wall provides stakeholders with a *shared* visual representation of key assessment measures to monitor progress of individual students, specific subpopulations, and the overall literacy achievement of the school. In comparison with computerized assessment systems, the assessment wall provides a medium for interaction, conversation, and collaboration among literacy professionals in the building to improve literacy achievement for all students. The CAS is a problem-solving, decision-making cycle, and the teacher is the true agent of the assessment and intervention process (Figure 7.5).

Figure 7.5. Comprehensive Assessment System (CAS) as a Problem-Solving, Decision-Making Cycle

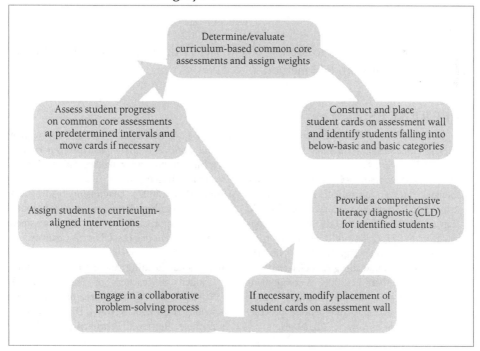

Final Thoughts

In Sarah's school, conversations such as the one that began this chapter were typical. Since the introduction of the comprehensive intervention model (Dorn & Henderson, 2010; Dorn & Schubert, 2008; Dorn & Soffos, in press) and the CAS, we have witnessed a remarkable change in the discourse surrounding students who experience literacy difficulties. The most noticeable shift is that teachers no longer spend precious time in grade-level meetings discussing why particular students are unable to perform at grade-level norms. Collaborative conversations in team meetings and hallways are grounded in an analysis of curriculum-aligned assessments with a focus on how students are responding to instruction both in the classroom and during small-group interventions.

Johnston (1987) states, "The most fundamental goal of all educational evaluation is optimal instruction for all children and evaluation practices are only legitimate to the extent that they serve this goal" (p. 744). Use of the CAS, as outlined in this chapter, assists schools in ensuring that optimal instruction is provided to all students and that both formative and summative evaluation practices adequately measure what we have identified that students need to learn about the reading and writing process.

NOTE

[1] We owe special thanks to literacy coach Vicki Atland for conceptualizing the assessment wall as an RTI method.

REFERENCES

Clay, M.M. (2004). *An observation survey of early literacy achievement* (2nd ed.). Portsmouth, NH: Heinemann.

Dorn, L.J., & Henderson, S.C. (2010). A comprehensive intervention model: A systems approach to Response to Intervention. In M.Y. Lipson & K.K. Wixson (Eds.), *Successful approaches to RTI: Collaborative practices for improving K–12 literacy* (pp. 88–120). Newark, DE: International Reading Association.

Dorn, L.J., & Schubert, B. (2008). A comprehensive intervention model for preventing reading failure: A Response to Intervention process. *Journal of Reading Recovery, 7*(2), 29–41.

Dorn, L.J., & Soffos, C. (in press). *Interventions that work: A K–3 comprehensive intervention model for preventing reading failure.* Boston: Allyn & Bacon.

Dunn, M.W. (2007). Diagnosing reading disability: Reading Recovery as a component of a Response-to-Intervention assessment method. *Learning Disabilities: A Contemporary Journal, 5*(2), 31–47.

International Reading Association & National Council of Teachers of English. (2009). *Standards for the assessment of reading and writing* (Rev. ed.). Newark, DE; Urbana, IL: Authors. Retrieved February 3, 2010, from

www.ncte.org/library/NCTEFiles/Resources
/Books/Sample/StandardsDoc.pdf

Johnston, P. (1987). The state of assessment in reading. *The Reading Teacher, 40*(8), 744–748.

Kozulin, A. (1998). *Psychological tools: A sociocultural approach to education.* Cambridge, MA: Harvard University Press.

Lidz, C., & Gindis, B. (2003). Dynamic assessment of the evolving cognitive functions in children. In A. Kozulin, B. Gindis, V.S. Ageyev, & S.M. Miller (Eds.), *Vygotsky's educational theory in cultural context* (pp. 99–116). New York: Cambridge University Press.

Vygotsky, L.S. (1978). *Mind in society: The development of higher psychological processes* (M. Cole, V. John-Steiner, S. Scribner, & E. Souberman, Eds. & Trans.). Cambridge, MA: Harvard University Press.

CHAPTER 8

Helping a Learning-Disabled Child Enter the Literate World

Carol A. Lyons

The learning disability field has been plagued by contradictions and controversy for the past twenty-five years. A major reason for the obvious confusion is that leading researchers in the field have never agreed on how to define learning disability or how to identify children as learning disabled (Ysseldyke, Algozzine, & Epps 1983). Berry and Kirk (1980) evaluated the best scientific studies in the field and concluded that the results were uninterpretable because the subjects in the studies could not be clearly defined. Yet in some school districts in the United States, children are tested by local professionals and classified as learning disabled at the beginning of first grade (Lyons 1989).

In addition to the problems associated with a term that defies definition, the learning-disability field has been marked by a lack of effective instructional programs with well researched successful results (Gittelman 1985). In a review of the research on various treatments for learning disabilities, Clay (1987) concludes that children who are below their classmates in reading achievement are learning to be learning disabled, because the teaching they receive in class is not appropriate for their idiosyncratic needs. Furthermore, when special small-group or individual instruction is available, it is focused on small segments of reading and writing, rather than directed toward reconstructing and restoring the whole, integrated response network involved when one reads (Clay 1987).

There is, however, an early intervention program, Reading Recovery, that has been rigorously researched (Lyons 1989a; 1989b) and found to be very successful with first-grade children who fall into the bottom 20 percent of their respective classes and who are further classified as learning disabled by professionals

RTI in Literacy—Responsive and Comprehensive, edited by Peter H. Johnston, published by the International Reading Association. This chapter reprinted from Lyons, C.A. (1991). Helping a Learning-Disabled Child Enter the Literate World. In D.E. DeFord, C.A. Lyons, & G.S. Pinnell (Eds.), *Bridges to Literacy: Learning From Reading Recovery* (pp. 205–216). Portsmouth, NH: Heinemann.

prior to placement in the program. A research study (Lyons 1989b) compares two groups of Ohio first-grade students having reading difficulties. The students in one group were diagnosed as learning disabled; the other group was composed of students who were *not* diagnosed as learning disabled but who were having reading difficulties. Both of these groups received daily, thirty-minute Reading Recovery instruction in the first grade. Examination of their reading strategies at the beginning of the Reading Recovery program showed that the group identified as learning disabled tended to overrely on visual/auditory cues and to ignore supporting language, while the group not identified as learning disabled tended to overrely on meaning and structure and to underemphasize visual/auditory cues. In an average of 63.13 lessons of Reading Recovery instruction, 73.3 percent of the students identified as learning disabled reached average reading levels in their respective classrooms and were discontinued (released) from the program. These results suggested that students identified as learning disabled often received exactly the wrong kind of special early instruction, which typically stresses limited reading strategies. Reading Recovery offered a promising way to help such students develop the full range of reading strategies they needed to become successful readers and thus prevented many of them from being mislabeled as learning disabled.

Reading Recovery is *not*, however, a learning-disability program. The program is designed to provide instruction to the least able 20 percent of first-grade readers in the education system—not excluding anyone—and to help them reach a level of achievement equal to the average of their class, thus placing them out of the remedial track. Research (Lyons 1989a) also suggest that the program can help educators define the term *learning disabled* more accurately and thus provide a way to eliminate some of the burgeoning population of students diagnosed as learning disabled (Singer & Butler 1987).

Reading Recovery *is* a second-chance first-grade program with daily, thirty-minute individual lessons supplementing regular classroom instruction for twelve to twenty weeks. It was developed and initiated in New Zealand by Marie Clay, a developmental child psychologist. The goal of the program is accelerated progress. Acceleration is achieved as the child takes over the learning process and works independently, continuously discovering new things and relating them to prior knowledge.

According to Clay, "acceleration depends upon the teacher's selection of the clearest, easiest, most memorable examples with which to establish a new response, skill, principle, or procedure" (1979, p. 53). It is essential that the teacher follow the child, designing a superbly sequenced program determined by the child's needs and then making highly skilled decisions throughout the lesson, moment by moment, to help the child make accelerated progress.

Reading Recovery teachers learn how to observe and asses the reading and writing strengths of children and design intervention strategies to meet individual learning needs in a yearlong inservice program. Some Reading Recovery teachers, however, become more skillful in implementing *effective* individual programs than others. For example, during the 1986–1987 school year, 25 of the 310 Reading Recovery teachers in Ohio successfully discontinued three or more children in forty lessons (eight weeks) or less (Lyons 1987). Further examination of their instructional programs revealed that these teachers recognized the teachable moments throughout the lesson: moments when the students could be taught how to use what they knew to develop new understanding. These effective teachers used a repertoire of actions and responses to facilitate accelerative progress. One of these very successful teachers, however, failed in her attempts to help Ryan, a child identified in kindergarten as learning disabled. Mary initially thought Ryan's inability to accelerate was the result of his learning disability. In this chapter you will learn how and why Mary changed her mind.

Instructionally Disabled, Not Learning Disabled

Mary was very concerned about the lack of progress of a first-grade boy she had been tutoring in the Reading Recovery program for six weeks. Ryan had been stuck on level 5, equivalent to a preprimer 1, for more than three weeks. This was the first time Mary had ever experienced difficulty in accelerating a child in the three years she had been teaching Reading Recovery.

Mary had asked several colleagues to observe her teaching Ryan. All concluded that the major reason Ryan was not accelerating was that he belonged to that group of children Marie Clay refers to as third-wave children, who need to be referred to professionals for further testing and placement (Clay 1987). Decisions for removing a student from the program are always carefully weighed and require a second opinion from an experienced teacher leader. (Teacher leaders prepare Reading Recovery teachers.) Therefore I was asked to confirm the teacher's suspicions and recommend that Ryan be removed from Reading Recovery and placed in a special program. Before making that decision, however, I asked to observe not only Ryan's lesson but the lessons of the other Reading Recovery students Mary taught. The following portions of each of the four childrens' lessons reveal how Mary enabled all but one of her students to develop strategies that facilitated accelerative learning. That one student was Ryan.

Mary and Melissa

Melissa is in her third week of lessons. She is attempting to integrate the meaning, structure, and visual cuing systems. To become an independent reader, the child must learn to search for and use all three types of cues in flexible ways. Mary's questions and Melissa's responses demonstrate early stages of developing the strategy to search for cues in sentence structure (syntax), cues from the message (semantics), and cues from the letters (graphics). The text reads: "I wave to my friend, the car driver."

> Melissa: (*Reading*) "I will to my friend, the car driver."
>
> Mary: You said, "I will to my friend, the car driver." Does that sound right?
>
> Melissa: No.

The teacher is developing the child's ability to search for cues in sentence structure. Melissa is a competent language user and Mary is teaching her to use her oral language and personal grammar to read the words.

> Mary: "I will to my friend, the car driver." Does that make sense?
>
> Melissa: No, that sounds silly!

The teacher is developing the child's ability to search for meaning cues. Mary is asking the question "Does that make sense?" to help Melissa understand that reading involves messages expressed in language that must make sense. The teacher, through appropriate questioning, is demonstrating that when Melissa reads, she should use her knowledge of oral and written language to gain meaning. Melissa is being taught a set of operations or strategies for problem solving in order to read more difficult bits of text. Mary is deliberately teaching Melissa how to solve new problems (figuring out the word *wave*) with familiar information.

> Mary: You said, "I will to my friend, the car driver." Does this word (*points to the word* wave) look like the word *will*?
>
> Melissa: No.
>
> Mary: What letters would you expect to see if the word was *will*?

Melissa:	*W, L*
Mary:	What letters do you see?
Melissa:	*W, A, V, E.*
Mary:	Look at the picture. What is the boy doing? What is the car driver doing?
Melissa:	They are waving to each other.
Mary:	What do you think the word could be?
Melissa:	*Wave.*
Mary:	Does *wave* make sense?
Melissa:	Yes. "I wave to my friend, the car driver."
Mary:	Does "wave to my friend, the car driver" sound right?
Melissa:	Yes.
Mary:	Does the word look right?
Melissa:	The letters make *wave*.
Mary:	I like the way you figured that all out.

The teacher's questioning shows the child how to cross-check the meaning and structure cue with graphic information. Melissa is able to predict the letter she expects to see if the word is *will*. She knows that the word can't be *will* because she doesn't see any *l*'s. The teacher redirects her attention to a meaning cue (the picture on the page) and then asks her to cross-check the meaning cue with a structure cue ("Does that sound right?"). The teacher is teaching for the cross-checking strategy. She is teaching Melissa how she can search for and use structure, meaning, and visual cues to predict an unknown word and then how to check one kind of cue against another. The preceding questioning techniques focus on meaning while Melissa is reading connected text. There are no isolated word or letter drills.

Mary and Mark

Mark is in his tenth week of lessons. He had read level 9 fluently, searching for and integrating the meaning, structure, and visual cues as Melissa is attempting to do. However, when reading his new text (level 10), Mark hesitates and shows signs of uncertainty when he comes to a difficult word. The text reads: "Lamb went to the bull."

Mark:	"Lamb went to the…"
Mary:	Why did you stop?
Mark:	I don't know that word.
Mary:	(*Attempts to direct Mark's attention to meaning*) Look at the picture.
Mark:	Lamb went to the cow.
Mary:	(*Fosters cross-checking on cue [meaning] with another cue [visual] by covering the word* bull *with her finger*) If that word was *cow*, what would you expect to see?
Mark:	C.
Mary:	(*Uncovers the word*) Could that be *cow*?
Mark:	No, it doesn't begin with a C.
Mary:	Can you think of another word that would make sense in the sentence and begins with a B?
Mark:	*Bull.*
Mary:	Check to see if what you read looks right [visual], sounds right [syntax/structure], and makes sense [meaning].
Mark:	"Lamb went to the bull." Yes, that is the word.
Mary:	How do you know?
Mark:	Because there is a picture of a bull [meaning cue] and the word begins with a letter *b* [visual clue].
Mary:	Great, I like the way you worked at that all by yourself.

Mary's first question, "Why did you stop?" tells Mark that she wants him to monitor his own reading. The fact that he is checking on his own behavior and recognizes that something is wrong is positive. Mary's next set of questions develops Mark's ability to search for and use meaning and visual cues to cross-check one kind of cue against another. She reinforces his self-monitoring and cross-checking attempts.

Mary and Janis

Today is Janis's fifty-sixth lesson. She has been in the program for eleven weeks and is reading at level 15. Mary notes that Janis is monitoring her reading, searching for and cross-checking at least two types of information, and self-correcting most of her own errors. This evidence suggests that Janis is ready to be discontinued from the program, but Mary is concerned that Janis relies on her too much. Today Mary is attempting to make Janis more independent by not asking questions when she stops at the word *splits*. The text reads: "The pupa splits. A butterfly comes out."

Janis: "The pupa (*long hesitation*) spits. A butterfly comes out."

Mary: You made a mistake on that page. Can you find it? (*Janis points to the word* splits.)

Mary: Yes, how did you know?

Janis: It doesn't make sense.

Mary: What are you going to do?

Janis: Start over and think of a word that sounds right and makes sense and has the right letters. "The pupa (*long hesitation*) splits. A butterfly comes out."

Mary: I like the way you solved that all by yourself. How did you do it?

Janis: I know another word that started with *spl* and that word is *splash*. I knew a little word in *splits*—*its*. Then I just put everything together.

Mary had previously taught Janis how to analyze words in text visually by helping her read in chunks. Janis independently applies this knowledge (attaching the *spl* sound to a group of letters rather than each letter) in order to figure out an unknown word (*splits*) from two known words (*splash* and *its*). Janis has demonstrated strategies for independent problem solving.

Mary and Ryan

Ryan is beginning his sixth week of lessons and has been reading level 5 books for the past three weeks. Ryan relies on visual information exclusively and does not attempt to make sense of what he is reading by using meaning or structural information as Melissa is learning to do in her third week of lessons. In this story, Fantail, a bird, is offered several things to eat. Ryan's substitutions are noted in brackets.

Ryan: "Fantail, Fantail, have some [said] cheese [church]." "No. No. No. I don't like [little] cheese [church]."

Mary:	Look at this word (*points to* some). Look at the third letter. What is that letter?
Ryan:	*M.*
Mary:	What sound does *m* make?
Ryan:	Mmmmm.
Mary:	Does the word *said* have the *m* sound?
Ryan:	No.
Mary:	That word is *some*. Look at this word (*points to* cheese). Look at the fifth letter, what is that letter?
Ryan:	*S.*
Mary:	What sound does *s* make?
Ryan:	Sssss.
Mary:	Does this word have the letter *s* in it?
Ryan:	No.
Mary:	Could that word be *church*?
Ryan:	No.
Mary:	The word is *cheese*. Look at this word (*points to* like). What is the third letter?
Ryan:	*T.*
Mary:	Say your alphabet. What comes after *J*?
Ryan:	*K.*
Mary:	What sound does *k* make?
Ryan:	Tuh, I mean kuh.
Mary:	The word is *like*.
Ryan:	"Fantail, Fantail have some [said] peas." "No. No. No. I don't like [little] peas." "Fantail, Fantail, have some [said] pie." "No. No. No. I don't like [little] pie." "Fantail, Fantail, have this [said] pie."
Mary:	(*Spells the word* said *with magnetic letters*) Ryan, here is the word *said*. Does this word (*points to the word* some *in the text*) look like this (*points to word* said)?
Ryan:	No.
Mary:	What do you hear at the end of the word *said*?
Ryan:	*D.*

Mary:	Does this word (*points to* some) have a *D* sound in it?
Ryan:	No.
Mary:	The word is *some*. Find the word *some* in the book. (*Ryan points to the word* some.)
Mary:	Find the letter *m*. (*Ryan points to the* m.)
Mary:	What is that word?
Ryan:	*Some*.
Mary:	How do you know?
Ryan:	Because it has the letter *m* in it.
Mary:	Good.

When the lesson is over I ask Ryan what reading is. He replies, "Saying the right letters."

After the observation, Mary and I discussed Ryan's progress. Mary recalled only one real strength Ryan had—little difficulty in generating a sentence for the writing portion of the lesson. She was quick to add, however, that Ryan experienced more difficulty generating the sentence as the weeks progressed. This concerned her because Ryan had adequate language and was one of the more articulate children she had worked with in the Reading Recovery program over the past three years. She attributed this to the fact that he was in a literature-based reading program and had many classroom opportunities to discuss and share ideas orally.

Mary was able to discuss and describe in detail Ryan's problems. Ryan's major weakness, demonstrated in all parts of the lesson, was his inability to use visual information. He did not integrate the meaning, structure, and visual cuing systems as the other three children did, because "he did not know his sounds." Lately, he was even experiencing difficulty remembering the letter names and sounds, which I observed in the lesson. This too was a surprise because he had scored 50 out of a possible 54 in letter identification on the Diagnostic Survey (Clay 1985).

Ryan seemed to have control of some of the early strategies (e.g., one-to-one matching, directional movement), but he couldn't locate an unknown word or letter even when prompted with a visual cue. Since Ryan did not have control of these very early strategies, Mary was not having any success teaching for strategies. He did not monitor his reading, search for other cues, cross-check one cue with another, or self-correct. Mary concluded that Ryan was "stuck because he could not use visual information."

As I listened to Mary discuss Ryan's lack of progress, several questions came to mind. First, why, when working with Ryan, did Mary abandon what she knew about teaching for strategies? Second, why did she have a less flexible view of Ryan's strengths? Third, why did Mary's attitude about Ryan's ability change? Finally, why did Mary change her instructional program so drastically when she taught Ryan?

I repeated some of the specific questions Mary asked Ryan, commenting on how they differed from ones she asked the other three children. Mary said that she had to shift her questioning techniques because Ryan was learning disabled and therefore needed a firm foundation in sound/symbol relationships before she could begin to teach for specific strategies. When Ryan began to regress in spite of an instructional program specifically designed to meet his needs, Mary concluded that Ryan should be placed in a learning-disabled class.

I supported Mary's concerns about Ryan's lack of progress and opened our conversation by repeating something she had said at the beginning of the conference: Ryan had adequate language and was one of the more articulate children she had ever taught in the Reading Recovery program. If he was a competent language user in the classroom and brought his knowledge of the world and experience to gain meaning in the beginning of the program, why had his behavior changed to exclude the supportive language he had good control of? We discussed the parts of the lesson that demonstrated Ryan's overattention to visual information. I asked Mary what Ryan had said at the close of the lesson when I asked him what reading is. Mary recalled that Ryan said "saying the right letters." She concluded that he was behaving in a way that really supported what he thought reading was—that is, he was saying the right letters.

Next I asked Mary what reading is. She quickly responded, "Gaining meaning from the printed page." We then looked at the type of questions Mary asked Ryan throughout the lesson. It didn't take her long to realize that she was confirming Ryan's assumption that reading is "saying the right letters"!

In examining parts of the other three children's lessons, it was obvious that Mary's questions supported the integration of all three cuing systems and were meaning-driven. For three of the four children, Mary's actions supported her definition of reading. For the fourth student, Ryan, Mary thought she needed to devise a different instructional plan. After examining her teaching decisions,

Mary understood that once she taught Ryan how to use and integrate strategies for independent problem solving, he too would accelerate.

The following week I observed Ryan's lesson. The text reads: "Up, up, up came little spider, to see what he could see."

Ryan: "Up, up, up can, I mean came, little spider, to see what he can, could, see."

Mary: I like how you changed *can* to *came*. Why couldn't that word be *can*?

Ryan: Because "up, up, up can little spider" doesn't sound right.

Mary: That's right! I like how you started over and tried to make the sentence sound right. Does it make sense too?

Ryan: Yes.

Mary: You also made another good self-correction when you said to see what he could see. How did you know to change that?

Ryan: Because if it were *can*, I would see an *n* and there is no *n*, so it has to be a word with a *d* and *could* is the word with a *d* that sounds right.

Mary: I am so proud of how you are making sense of what you read and checking to see if the words look right. That is just what good readers always do.

It was obvious that Mary had started to teach for strategies and that Ryan was now on his way to accelerative learning. Seven weeks later he was discontinued from the program.

Conclusion

Ryan's initial oral pattern of response, overattention to visual information, is consistent with studies examining oral reading behaviors of "learning disabled" students receiving Reading Recovery instruction (Lyons 1989b). Students diagnosed as learning disabled tend to rely on visual information and ignore or exclude the supportive language they control. Once the teacher brings in the language side, as Mary did, accelerative learning does occur.

The findings in this study also suggest that differences in reading patterns of behavior among "learning disabled" and other failing children are learned, and therefore can be unlearned. The earlier the instructional emphasis is changed, the sooner the child shifts to more appropriate responses. Clay (1987) argues that only a small percentage of low-achieving readers (1–2 percent) will not make accelerative progress in the Reading Recovery program. Although not the case in the data analyzed here, this small percentage of children may have neurological problems and require more extensive testing.

Finally, Ryan's definition of reading may have contributed to his reading problems. Unwittingly, Mary reinforced and confirmed his notion of reading by asking questions that focused on visual information to the exclusion of meaning and language structure. The instructional program thus helped Ryan learn to be learning disabled. If he were placed in a program for learning-disabled youngsters, would his concept of reading be confirmed and reinforced?

In every classroom in the elementary school, teachers are confronted with children who are having difficulty learning to read. In light of the findings reported in this chapter, classroom teachers should ask themselves several questions. First, what is their definition of reading? Second, does the instructional program they implement adequately reflect and support what their definition of reading implies? Third, do they believe the concept of reading is different and must change to meet the needs of specific populations of children such as learning-disabled readers? Fourth, does their instructional program change to fit a different concept of reading for special populations? Finally, are they excellent teachers who may have fallen into the same trap Mary did?

We need to reexamine our beliefs and instructional programs for all at-risk readers, especially those classified as learning disabled. Perhaps some of these children are not learning disabled but instructionally disabled, and, as Marie Clay (1987) argues, learning to be disabled.

REFERENCES

Berry, P., & D.A. Kirk. (1980). "Issues in Special Learning Disabilities: Towards a Data Base for Decision Making." *Exceptional Child* 27:115-25.

Clay, M.M. (1979). *The Early Detection of Reading Difficulties.* 2d ed. Portsmouth, N.H.: Heinemann.

Clay, M.M. (1987). "Learning to Be Learning Disabled." *New Zealand Journal of Educational Studies* 22: 155–73.

Gittelman, R. (1985). "Controlled Trials of Remedial Approaches to Reading Disability." *Journal of Child Psychiatry* 26: 843–46.

Lyons, C.A. (1987). "Helping Slow Readers Make Accelerated Progress: Teacher Responses and Knowledge." Paper presented at the annual meeting of the National Reading Conference, St. Petersburg, Florida.

Lyons, C.A. (1989a). "Reading Recovery: An Effective Early Intervention Program That

Can Prevent Mislabeling Children as Learning Disabled." *Spectrum* 7: 3–9.

Lyons, C.A. (1989b). "Reading Recovery: A Preventative for Mislabeling Young 'At-Risk' Learners." *Urban Education* 24: 125–39.

Singer, J.D., & J.A. Butler. (1987). "The Education for All Handicapped Children Act: Schools as Agents of Social Reform." *Harvard Educational Review* 57: 125–82.

Ysseldyke, J., B. Algozzine, & S. Epps. (1983). "A Logical and Empirical Analysis of Current Practice in Classifying Students as Handicapped." *Exceptional Children* 50: 160–66.

High-Quality Interventions in Literacy

In spite of our best efforts in classrooms, some students still do not acquire literacy as quickly as they might. This is particularly likely when there are large numbers of students in a classroom or when teachers are ill-prepared or not well supported in their own development. Even when these sources of difficulty are addressed, some students still encounter difficulties. When this happens, we need to intervene. Therefore, this section contains examples of productive, research-based interventions.

IDEA emphasizes the need for research-based interventions, and there is no doubt that research has been informative about useful dimensions to consider when teaching children to read. The National Reading Panel in its original meta-analysis offers some useful considerations and cautions (National Institute of Child Health and Human Development, 2000). However, current efforts at RTI have been informed largely by research that focuses on the word level or below and a view of what needs to be learned by children to read words rather than by a view of how children acquire literacy or what makes literacy learning possible. Intervention programs often have been based on a very narrow view of literacy, reducing it to reading (not writing) and reducing reading to speed and accuracy of word recognition.

Recently, even proponents of these programs have begun to recognize that any benefits are limited in important ways. Al Otaiba and Torgesen (2007), reviewing a range of such intervention programs viewed as successful, argue that

> given that [state tests] require a much broader range of knowledge and skill than the word-level tests used to estimate success rates in this review, it is likely that poor and minority students, in particular, will not achieve the same success rates on them as for the simpler tests that assess only word reading accuracy. (p. 220)

In other words, most of these interventions address little beyond word identification, and not only do they not generalize to more important aspects of literacy development, but also we should expect that benefits will be unequally distributed. Their solution is to add a subsequent intervention to build comprehension, assuming that word knowledge necessarily precedes comprehension.

We see in this section that comprehension and writing can be developed at the same time as word knowledge. Indeed, as we see in Stuart McNaughton and Mei Kuin Lai's Chapter 16 in Section V, instruction focusing on comprehension can improve word knowledge along the way rather than the other way around. Teaching for students who make meaning with reading and writing in a range of genres and subjects can be a primary goal rather than one to work for after improving word knowledge.

The first chapter in this section, Chapter 9, "Reading Recovery: A Major Component of Many RTI Models" by Salli Forbes, Beth Swenson, Tonya Person, and Jolene Reed, reviews evidence for Reading Recovery used as a component of many RTI models. Reading Recovery remains the only intervention on the U.S. Department of Education Institute of Education Sciences What Works Clearinghouse website (ies.ed.gov/ncee/wwc/) that shows effects at all levels including comprehension and fluency. Chapter 10, "Kindergarten Intervention: Teaching to Prevent Reading Difficulties" by Donna M. Scanlon and Joan M. Sweeney, is based on the highly effective Interactive Strategies Approach (Vellutino & Scanlon, 2002). The chapter shows the overall structure and logic of the intervention along with considerable practical instructional detail.

Although each of the interventions described in the first two chapters in this section includes a writing component, Chapter 11, "An Adapted Interactive Writing Intervention for the Kindergarten Classroom: Creating a Framework for Responsive Teaching" by Sharon A. Craig, provides an example of early intervention focused on interactive writing. This chapter, based on a more extensive research publication, provides not only the evidence for effectiveness but also the details and logic of the instructional practices. It is particularly important because writing has been systematically neglected in early interventions, particularly when it comes to models of RTI.

Virtually all current approaches to RTI assume that if intense one-to-one instruction is unsuccessful in accelerating a student's literacy development, then the problem must lie with the student. Indeed, that is seen as the defining feature in learning-disability identification and applies to between 1% and 2% of children (Al Otaiba & Torgesen, 2007; Clay, 1990; Vellutino et al., 1996). The final chapter in this section, Chapter 12, "Closing the Gaps: Literacy for the Hardest-to-Teach" by Gwenneth Phillips and Pauline Smith, takes a different approach. Phillips and Smith assumed instead that the problem might still be with their instruction. Their chapter reports their successful intervention in which, by focusing their assessment as much on their instructional practices as on the students' learning, they were able to bring three quarters of the students with whom they had not been successful into the average range of performance. These students would normally be classified as learning disabled and placed in special education, but would that have resulted in such finely tuned instruction?

REFERENCES

Al Otaiba, S., & Torgesen, J. (2007). Effects from intensive standardized kindergarten and first-grade interventions for the prevention of reading difficulties. In S.R. Jimerson, M.K. Burns, & A.M. VanDerHeyden (Eds.), *Handbook of Response to Intervention: The science and practice of assessment and intervention* (pp. 212–222). New York: Springer.

Clay, M.M. (1990). The Reading Recovery programme, 1984-88: Coverage, outcomes and education board district figures. *New Zealand Journal of Educational Studies*, 25(1), 61–70.

National Institute of Child Health and Human Development. (2000). *Report of the National Reading Panel. Teaching children to read: An evidence-based assessment of the scientific research literature on reading and its implications for reading instruction* (NIH Publication No. 00-4769). Washington, DC: U.S. Government Printing Office.

Vellutino, F.R., & Scanlon, D.M. (2002). The Interactive Strategies approach to reading intervention. *Contemporary Educational Psychology*, 27(4), 573–635. doi:10.1016/S0361-476X(02)00002-4

Vellutino, F.R., Scanlon, D.M., Sipay, E.R., Small, S.G., Pratt, A., Chen, R.S., et al. (1996). Cognitive profiles of difficult-to-remediate and readily remediated poor readers: Early intervention as a vehicle for distinguishing between cognitive and experiential deficits as basic causes of specific reading disability. *Journal of Educational Psychology*, 88(4), 601–638. doi:10.1037/0022-0663.88.4.601

Reading Recovery: A Major Component of Many RTI Models

Salli Forbes, Beth Swenson, Tonya Person, and Jolene Reed

Introduction

Salli Forbes

The response to intervention (RTI) initiative is contained in the 2004 reauthorization of the Individuals with Disabilities Education Act (IDEA). The purpose of RTI is to provide struggling readers with expert intervening instruction so that these students will not need special education placement and services. The 2004 IDEA reauthorization allows local school districts to allocate up to 15% of their funding targeted for students with disabilities to be used for general education interventions. The goal of this initiative is to significantly reduce the numbers of struggling readers who are identified as students with disabilities.

Marie Clay (1987) advanced the argument that many struggling readers are in fact "instructionally disabled" because they have not received appropriate instructional opportunities. Vellutino and Fletcher (2004) summarized research that supports this argument, stating that, "many poor readers are impaired because of inadequate instruction or other experiential factors" (p. 2). The RTI initiative is intended to provide high-quality instructional opportunities to struggling readers to minimize this problem.

Although IDEA funding is intended for students with disabilities, the RTI portion of that funding does not require that special education teachers deliver the intervention instruction. In fact, Richard Allington (2007) has called for schools to use the most-qualified and expert reading teachers to deliver the interventions.

Although there is no legal requirement to use any particular model of intervention, many districts and states are conceptualizing RTI as a three-tier model.

RTI in Literacy—Responsive and Comprehensive, edited by Peter H. Johnston, published by the International Reading Association. This chapter reprinted from Forbes, S., Swenson, B., Person, T., & Reed, J. (2008). Reading Recovery: A Major Component of Many RTI Models. *The Journal of Reading Recovery, 7*(2), 53–56.

Tier I is high-quality classroom instruction for all students. Tier II provides additional instruction for those students who need it, from either the classroom teacher or a reading specialist. Tier III is more intensive instruction delivered one-to-one or in small groups by teachers with special expertise in diagnosis and remediation of reading difficulties.

Two models of RTI are explained in this article. Reading Recovery is a major component of each model, although each model is uniquely designed for the needs of the students and teachers in each district. Both the Brainerd (Minnesota) District model and the Rio Rancho (New Mexico) Public School District model have been carefully developed with an emphasis on continuity of instructional goals, teacher professional development, and collaboration among all the teachers. The Brainerd model uses a three-tier approach in which Reading Recovery is the intervention at Tier II. The Rio Rancho model provides Reading Recovery training to special education teachers who then become 'literacy processing specialists' in their schools.

A third district which includes Reading Recovery in its RTI model is in Walled Lake, Michigan. Information about the Walled Lake model can be found in the International Reading Association (2007) document "Implications for Reading Teachers in Response to Intervention," and in the RRCNA briefing paper (Lose et al., 2007) "Reading Recovery and the IDEA Legislation: Early Intervening Services (EIS) and Response to Intervention (RTI)."

Brainerd, Minnesota

Beth Swenson and Tonya Person

The Brainerd School District has developed a dynamic districtwide multi-tiered response to intervention (RTI) model using a common literacy processing theory that links general education, Title I, special education, and administration. The model embraces an assessment tool that becomes the lens through which to view learners, allowing all educators in a team to see learners as a field of possibilities rather than a burden of discrepancy.

Brainerd uses a continuum of tools that follow the same learning theory to form a common growth model K–12. For this article, we will focus on the early intervention piece that happens in K–4. Brainerd schools are K–4 in the elementary; most districts run the model K–6. The assessment tools include Clay's (2002) Observation Survey, text leveling, High Frequency Word Test

(Swenson, 2007), and the Spelling Continuum (Bear, Invernizzi, Templeton, & Johnston, 2005), all graphed using the North Star Educational Tool (northstaret .com) graphing system. The North Star web-based data collection system creates a variety of graphs—diagnostic classroom, progress monitoring intervention, screening summary, and districtwide summary—providing a common lens through which to view students and creating highly effective problem-solving intervention teams. The assessment tool one looks through sets the foundation for instruction. Assessment can't follow instruction; it has to be used for screening, diagnostics, and progress monitoring.

The Brainerd RTI model is a capacity-building model that allows for the formation of a complex metacognitive processing system in every learner, beginning in kindergarten, and flowing through to adult learning. It allows each learner to have one instructional language to learn through; every person in the child's learning life has the same goals, language, vision of possibility, and growth goals K–6. The system for thinking is laid in kindergarten, develops thinking capacity strongly in first, and deepens the thinking in Grades 2–4. There is less time spent laying a new learning foundation each year and more time spent interconnecting grade levels, allowing for the building of more-complex thinking systems over time.

Tier 1: Literacy Collaborative Professional Development and Coaching Model

The key to RTI is a strong Tier 1 model that allows for differentiation within the classroom. The Literacy Collaborative is not a curriculum, but rather an intensive professional development and coaching model that has highly trained coaches (350 hours of training the first year and continuous training each subsequent year) that facilitate professional learning communities which construct the continuum of reading, writing, word study, and thinking K–6. The continuums allow teachers to view each learner in their classroom as an individual at different places on each different continuum. The teachers learn how to collect and utilize data that allow them to teach right within each learner's zone of proximal development. Teachers begin seeing what each learner knows, what each needs to know next, and which tools to use to construct the different pathways for the steepest learning trajectories possible. The inquiry coaching and professional development model allows for adults to build a more sophisticated way of using data for problem solving around student processing over time, allowing learning to be woven constructively across all grade levels.

Tier 2: Reading Recovery

Brainerd has Reading Recovery—a research-based one-to-one intervention—as its second tier. With the strong foundation of Tier 1 differentiation and in-classroom interventions in Literacy Collaborative kindergarten, most learners have developed the foundation of a complex metacognitive processing system in kindergarten. Reading Recovery allows the lowest 20% of learners to engage in a one-to-one intervention that uses the same language of learning as the classroom. Instructed one on one, beginning learners are able to construct a full foundation of internal language processing systems. A highly trained teacher (115 hours of training the first year and ongoing professional development each subsequent year) constructs an individualized intervention that builds on the learner's current understandings and fills the processing holes in each learner while integrating new learning to form a complete processing system that becomes the foundation for literacy learning. The capacity-building coaching and professional development model in Reading Recovery allows for teachers to develop the ability to take a more sophisticated look at data and use it to inform instruction.

Tier 3: Leveled Literacy Intervention (Small Group, Research Based)

Seventy-five percent of all Reading Recovery learners construct an effective processing system that allows for self-extension in the regular classroom without additional intervention. The most-naive learners need to continue their construction of the processing system through small-group supplemental intervention, using the same language of learning. Small-group instruction and whole-classroom instruction involve a more-sophisticated ability to have conversations around thinking, where each individual provides a piece of the thinking and stacks thinking. Guided reading, interactive read-aloud, community writing, and most whole-classroom learning depends on a child being able to be a part of the collective thinking around the text. Leveled Literacy Intervention continues the complex reading, writing, and word study continuums, while at the same time teaches attending skills that reach those very lowest-achieving learners and continues with the learning trajectory started in Reading Recovery.

Staying within the same theory of learning allows a child to construct a complete processing system rather than restarting in many different languages of instruction creating learning disabilities.

After these interventions designed to quickly close learning gaps, a very few learners (5%) will still show physiological needs for long-term interventions. The early intervention data from the first three tiers help to identify learners who should be tested for special education and receive long-term, comprehensive remediation and support.

Problem-Solving Teams

Common language and common assessment tools that capture small changes in student learning allow each classroom problem-solving team to spend 1-1/2 hours each trimester to discuss and design research-based interventions for an entire classroom of children. Using this model, specialists are not assigned to classrooms permanently, but reassigned because of student growth and student need. Assigning people based on student needs allows for careful interventions based on the North Star data. Using resources wisely, fewer adults can more powerfully meet the specific needs of children. Children also are allowed to grow to independence.

Results

The pilot school in Brainerd has dropped learning disability rates by 66% since launching this RTI model. Before starting this process, Title I and Reading Recovery were life preservers, keeping children from drowning while receiving services. But once that scaffolding was removed, others continued to see some of those children as "broken learners." Now, children are no longer seen as discrepant, but filled with possibilities. Classrooms are no longer islands of learning; the entire school is a village surrounding each child, allowing each child to grow to his fullest potential. The coaching and staff development follows each teacher, allowing them to grow to their fullest potential as well.

Rio Rancho, New Mexico

Jolene Reed

Since first implementing Reading Recovery 10 years ago, Rio Rancho Public Schools have been committed to the goal of making Reading Recovery available for all students in need of the intervention. Rio Rancho initially implemented Reading Recovery at each elementary school by training two teachers at each campus. Despite the district's continued dedication to quality implementation, rapid growth in student population and higher need at individual campuses prevented some students from receiving Reading Recovery. Discussion between the Reading Recovery teacher leader and the executive director of special services resulted in a solution that would ultimately benefit both Reading Recovery implementation in the district and the special education department. In addition to its core group of Reading Recovery teachers, Rio Rancho made the decision to provide Reading Recovery training to its special education personnel.

Reading Recovery training provides special education teachers with additional knowledge and expertise in the literacy acquisition process. Special education teachers who complete the Reading Recovery training are designated as "literacy processing specialists." During their training year, the literacy processing specialist's time is divided equally between two portions of the duty day. The Reading Recovery portion of the day entails one-to-one teaching of four general education first-grade students. The other half of the duty day is spent providing reading instruction to special education students individually or in small groups. The literacy processing specialist-in-training does not have a specific special education caseload during the training year.

Training of literacy processing specialists in Rio Rancho began in the 2006–07 school year. During that year, four specialists were trained at four of the eight elementary schools in the district. During the 2007–08 school year, these original four specialists returned to their full-time special education duties. An additional six special education teachers are currently receiving training as literacy processing specialists. Ongoing monthly continuing professional development for the four teachers who received training during the 2006–07 school year is being provided.

Training special education teachers as literacy processing specialists serves two important purposes. First, it gives special education teachers a 1-year professional development opportunity. During this time, teachers learn high-level reading instruction theory and practices that will enhance their classroom teaching when they return to the special education classroom. Second, it supports general education in a response to intervention model by providing Reading Recovery as an intervention to additional students experiencing difficulty in their literacy learning.

Rio Rancho Public Schools has experienced multiple benefits from the implementation of this model including

- professional development for special education teachers, resulting in an increased understanding of the literacy acquisition process by participating teachers;
- additional staff for providing Reading Recovery as an RTI model, resulting in more students receiving Reading Recovery services;
- alignment of school district interventions; and
- support of a common vision among all staff to meet the needs of all students.

Providing Reading Recovery training to special education teachers has proven to be a win-win solution that benefits all stakeholders—students, parents, teachers, and administrators.

REFERENCES

Allington, R., & Welmsley, S. (Eds.). (2007). *No quick fix, the RTI edition: Rethinking literacy programs in America's elementary schools*. New York: International Reading Association and Teachers College Press.

Bear, D., Invernizzi, M., Templeton, S., & Johnston, F. (2005). *Words their way* (3rd ed.). Columbus, OH: Pearson, Merrill Prentice Hall.

Clay, M.M. (1987). Learning to be learning disabled. *New Zealand Journal of Educational Studies, 22*, 155–173.

Clay, M.M. (2002). *An observation survey of early literacy achievement* (2nd ed.). Portsmouth, NH: Heinemann.

International Reading Association. (2007). *Implications for reading teachers in response to intervention*. Available online at www.ira.org/resources/issues/focus_rti.html

Lose, M.K., Schmitt, M.C., Gómez-Bellengé, F.X., Jones, N.K., Honchell, B.A., & Askew, B.A. (2007). *Reading Recovery and the IDEA legislation: Early intervening services (EIS) and response to intervention (RTI)* [Briefing paper]. Worthington, OH: Reading Recovery Council of North America. Available online at www.rrcna.org/reading_recovery/issues/index.asp

Swenson, E. (2007). North Star Educational Tools [web-based data collection software]. www.northstaret.com

Vellutino, F.R., Fletcher, J.M., Snowling, M.J., & Scanlon, D.M. (2004). Specific reading disability (dyslexia): What have we learned in the past four decades? *Journal of Child Psychology and Psychiatry, and Allied Disciplines, 45*(1), 2–40.

CHAPTER 10

Kindergarten Intervention: Teaching to Prevent Reading Difficulties

Donna M. Scanlon and Joan M. Sweeney

A great deal of attention has been focused on the RTI process, but most of that attention has focused on the progress monitoring and data-based decision-making aspects. Far too little attention has been devoted to the interventions themselves. However, the instruction is perhaps *the* critical factor in determining how students who demonstrate early difficulties will respond to intervention. There is considerable debate in the field regarding what interventions should look like for students who have difficulty at the early stages of learning to read, but there is little research that explicitly compares the highly scripted and controlled interventions that are sometimes recommended with intervention approaches that are more tailored to the needs of the students and support the students in their classroom language arts programs. In our intervention research, we have always adopted the latter type of approach (Scanlon, Gelzheiser, Vellutino, Schatschneider, & Sweeney, 2008; Scanlon, Vellutino, Small, Fanuele, & Sweeney, 2005; Vellutino et al., 1996).

The purpose of this chapter is to describe the kindergarten intervention approach used by Scanlon and her colleagues (2005; see also Vellutino, Scanlon, Small, & Fanuele, 2006). That study demonstrates that small-group intervention for students who are identified at kindergarten entry as being at increased risk of experiencing early reading difficulties could substantially reduce the number of students who need literacy intervention in first grade. The Scanlon et al. study also demonstrates that students who participate in the kindergarten intervention program and continue to need intervention in first grade fare better

---

RTI in Literacy—Responsive and Comprehensive, edited by Peter H. Johnston.
© 2010 by the International Reading Association.

in reading by the end of first grade than do similar students who do not receive intervention in kindergarten.

It should be noted that our study was initiated before the notion of RTI was formalized, and therefore it did not include an explicit classroom intervention (Tier 1) component. However, consistent with a tiered approach, all of the students who participated in the kindergarten intervention were also provided with the instruction normally available to them in their classrooms.

The Kindergarten Intervention Study in Action

The study was conducted in schools that served primarily working class and middle class families. Parents of all entering kindergartners in the 11 participating schools in the northeastern United States region received a consent form asking them to enroll their children in a study of reading development. More than 90% of the parents consented.

The students were assessed on measures of alphabet knowledge and phonological skills during the first few weeks of school. Students who scored below the 30th percentile on the letter-identification subtest of the Woodcock Reading Mastery Tests–Revised were identified as being at increased risk of experiencing difficulty in learning to read. This single measure was used rather than a more elaborate assessment of early literacy skills, because we had found in earlier research (Scanlon & Vellutino, 1996, 1997) that a measure of letter–name knowledge administered at kindergarten entry was as effective in identifying which students might ultimately demonstrate reading difficulties as was a more elaborate and time-consuming battery of assessments.

Assignment to Experimental Groups

As our intention was to test explicitly the efficacy of a small-group intervention approach to preventing early reading difficulties, we used an experimental design in which students were randomly assigned to either an intervention group, which received 30 minutes of instruction twice each week from a certified teacher employed by the research center, or to a comparison group, which received only the instruction provided by the school. Random assignment was done at the level of the teacher (i.e., half of the students who scored in the at-risk range for each participating classroom teacher were randomly assigned to the intervention group, and the other half were assigned to the comparison group).

By assigning students from each classroom to both the intervention and comparison conditions, we substantially reduced the likelihood that differences in classroom instruction would affect the outcomes of the study.

Assessments

Students in both the intervention and comparison groups were assessed formally in the early fall (September–October), December, March, and June of their kindergarten year, as well as at the beginning of first grade. For purposes of this chapter, we report on a limited number of the assessments used in the study. The letter-identification subtest of the Woodcock Reading Mastery Tests–Revised was used to identify the students who were considered to be at risk and as an outcome measure.

In addition, end-of-year outcomes are reported for the Yopp-Singer Test of Phoneme Segmentation (Yopp, 1995), which requires students to segment spoken words into their component sounds (phonemes). End-of-year results are also reported for several measures developed for the study by our research team, including a measure of letter–sound knowledge on which the students were asked to provide the sounds for letters presented in isolation, a measure of sight word knowledge on which the students were asked to read 25 high-frequency words, and a measure of decoding skill on which the students were asked to read one-syllable nonsense words.

Kindergarten Intervention

The instructional intervention was provided to students in groups of three. The groups met twice each week for 30 minutes. The intervention began in mid- to late October and continued until late May. On average, each group participated in approximately 50 half-hour sessions over the course of the school year.

One important goal of the kindergarten intervention was to support the students in their classroom language arts program. The intention was to increase the students' ability to profit from classroom instruction rather than to compete with classroom instruction by introducing skills and concepts in a different order, using different terminology, and so forth. To accomplish this goal, the intervention teacher began by meeting with each kindergarten classroom teacher to learn about the classroom language arts program. Important topics in these meetings included the following:

- The literacy skills that students were expected to demonstrate by the end of kindergarten

- The approach used to teach about the alphabet and decoding skills more generally

- Whether students were explicitly taught word-identification strategies and, if so, what strategies were taught

- The terminology used for important concepts such as upper- and lower-case letters and word families (e.g., chunks, phonograms, keys)

- The themes or instructional units that were to be covered and at what points in the school year

The intervention teachers were encouraged to use the information from these interviews to plan instruction for the student groups.

One of the primary ways in which the coordination with the classroom program was realized occurred in the context of teaching about the alphabet. Thus, for example, for students from classrooms that used a "letter of the week" approach, intervention teachers would place higher priority on helping students to learn the letters that had already been covered in class than on letters that had yet to be taught. Further, if the classroom teacher explicitly used a set of keywords to help students remember letter–sound correspondences, the intervention teacher would use the same keywords.

The kindergarten intervention program was guided by the basic premises of the Interactive Strategies Approach (ISA; Scanlon, Anderson, & Sweeney, 2010; Vellutino & Scanlon, 2002; note that the Scanlon et al. text describes a more fully developed and comprehensive version of the ISA than was used in the study reported by Scanlon et al., 2005), which argues that, to a great extent, students learn to read by reading and that one of the most important roles for the teacher is to help students develop the foundational skills and strategic approaches that are needed to make progress in reading. Thus, the kindergarten intervention approach placed heavy emphasis on the development of foundational skills, such as phonemic analysis and letter–sound knowledge, as phonological skills tend to be a major stumbling block for students who experience early reading difficulties. Intervention also placed heavy emphasis on teaching students to use code-based strategies with meaning-based strategies as a vehicle for identifying unfamiliar written words encountered in emergent-level texts.

Ultimately, the coordinated and confirmatory use of both code- and meaning-based strategies was intended to enable a student to learn words encountered in text so effectively that they become part of the student's sight vocabulary (i.e., words that can be identified effortlessly) with relatively few exposures. Having an extensive sight vocabulary ultimately allows students to devote most of their cognitive resources to interpreting the meaning of the texts that are read rather than having to devote extensive cognitive effort to the process of word identification. At the kindergarten level, our goal was to lay the foundation for establishing a strategic approach to word identification and help the students learn how to apply what they were learning about letters and their sounds when reading emergent-level texts and engaging in emergent writing.

The kindergarten intervention lessons were organized around a set of eight goals focused on foundational literacy skills and attitudes that were intended to support the students in the development of a strategic approach to word identification. Each goal is listed and discussed in the sections that follow.

Goal 1: Motivation to Read and Write

The student will develop the belief that reading and writing are enjoyable and informative activities that are not beyond his or her capabilities.

This goal appears first on the list because the intervention teachers were expected to keep this as a primary concern. Kindergarten is a formative time for students and has the potential to substantially affect their sense of themselves as learners. Repeatedly placing students in a situation in which they are asked to do things that are too challenging can lead them to become frustrated and avoidant.

In intervention of the sort we offered, teachers were able to carefully plan instruction that provided enough challenge to move the students forward but not so much as to frustrate them. Moreover, in this small-group context, teachers were able to do such things as incorporate books that were likely to be of particular interest to individual students, differentiate the level of support provided to individual students based on the teacher's observations of how each student was progressing in particular skill areas, and in general, keep the students more thoroughly and actively engaged.

In hopes of promoting intrinsic motivation for reading and writing, teachers were also cautioned against the use of extrinsic motivators such as stickers and encouraged to use activities that helped build literacy skills and interests as motivators (e.g., providing some choice about what book would be read, using a preferred medium such as chalkboards and whiteboards for practice activities). The opportunity to read emergent-level books, with guidance, appeared to be one of the biggest motivators for many of the students.

Goal 2: Phonemic Awareness

The student will have a conceptual grasp of the fact that words are made up of somewhat separable sound segments. Further, the student will be able to say the individual sounds that comprise single-syllable words spoken by the teacher and blend separate sounds to form whole words.

Numerous studies have documented that students who demonstrate difficulties in the early stages of learning to read also demonstrate difficulties with analyzing words into their component sounds (phonemes). Indeed, many in the research community believe that difficulties with phonemic analysis are a primary cause of early reading difficulties, and there is a substantial body of evidence indicating that instruction designed to attune young students to the phonemic nature of spoken language is effective in improving their word reading and spelling skills (e.g., Adams, 1990; Blachman, 2000). Therefore, instruction to promote phonemic awareness was an important component of our kindergarten intervention program.

In early lessons, teachers read books that included rhyme or alliteration (or both) to their intervention groups. The teacher and students would discuss sound commonalities (e.g., words that rhyme or have the same sound at the beginning). These read-alouds were also used to address other instructional goals, including motivation for reading and writing, letter–name and letter–sound identification, and print concepts. Many students become attuned to the phonemic nature of spoken language through experiences such as book reading and learning poetry and the lyrics of songs. However, a substantial proportion of young students do not develop phonemic awareness through such experiences (estimates vary around 30%), and these students benefit from more explicit instruction that helps them focus on the sounds in words. The majority of the students who qualified for the kindergarten intervention program needed such instruction.

To guide informal and ongoing assessment of students' phonological analysis skills and to inform instructional planning, teachers were provided with a checklist of skills to guide their thinking about what individual students were able to do and what they were ready to learn next. Three types of instructional activities were used to promote the development of phonemic analysis skills:

1. Picture sorting, in which students were taught to group picture cards by similarity in sounds in particular positions in the words

2. Phoneme blending, in which students were taught to blend sounds articulated by the teacher to form whole words

3. Phoneme segmentation, in which students learned to analyze spoken words into their constituent sound components

For each of these types of activities, teachers were provided with information about the relative difficulties of different types of items that might be used. For example, intervention teachers were encouraged to use words with stretchable consonant sounds when first teaching a particular phonemic analysis skill, as it is easier to draw students' attention to sounds that can be elongated without distortion (e.g., /mmm/, /sss/) than it is to draw their attention to stop consonants that cannot be pronounced in isolation without the addition of a vowel sound (e.g., /tuh/, /buh/). Teachers were also encouraged to use words with stretchable sounds in practice activities until the students could readily demonstrate the particular skill and then to incorporate words with stop consonants.

Thus, the teachers were not given a specific teaching program to promote phonemic awareness. Rather, they were given guidelines for decision making around how to adjust the level of challenge posed by a task for individual students. Such guidance was also provided for many other aspects of the instruction during the course of intervention. In general, teachers were expected to make informed decisions about what to teach and when to teach it, based on the knowledge and skills of the students, the expectations of the classroom program, and the guidance provided to the teachers during the course of professional development.

Goal 3: Letter Identification

The student will be able to name, rapidly and accurately, the upper- and lowercase versions of all 26 letters of the alphabet.

The ability to effortlessly identify the letters of the alphabet is critical for a variety of reasons. One major reason is that effortless letter identification frees up cognitive resources for higher level aspects of the reading process. Another is that, for many letters of the alphabet, the name of the letter includes the sound that the letter represents (e.g., the name of the letter *B* includes the phonemes /b/ + /ē/, the name of the letter *M* includes the phonemes /ĕ/ + /m/). Students who are beginning to learn to read often implicitly rely on this relationship between a letter's name and its sound, and this inclination is especially evident in their writing, in which teachers will often note that the students make logical substitutions by using a letter whose name includes the sound that the students wish to represent. For example, a student might spell the word *wait* with the letters *yat*, having chosen the letter *y* because the sound at the beginning of the name of the letter *Y* is the same as the sound heard at the beginning of the word *wait*.

Because knowing letter names is so helpful to learning letter sounds (for most letters), and because students who are identified in kindergarten as being at increased risk for reading difficulties generally know the names of few if any letters, in our kindergarten intervention approach, we focused initially on teaching letter names rather than teaching letter names and sounds simultaneously, as is often done in kindergarten. To establish the names of the letters as soon as possible, most early intervention lessons included whole-alphabet activities, such as singing the alphabet song and pointing to the letters, and reading and discussing alphabet books. In addition to whole-alphabet activities, we typically focused on one or more letters in a lesson. For each letter, we worked to make sure that the students knew its name before we made a specific effort to teach about its sound.

For all letter–name learning activities, the students were encouraged to use the letter name frequently, as it is the recollection of the name of the letter and remembering which name goes with which letter form that is particularly challenging for young students.

Goal 4: Letter–Sound Association

The student will be able to associate the sounds of the majority of consonants with their printed representations.

As noted previously, for many letters the name of the letter includes the most common sound for that letter. Thus, learning letter names goes a long way to supporting the development of letter–sound knowledge. However, we also found it useful to employ keywords for each letter as an additional aid to letter–sound learning, especially for the consonants *H, W,* and *Y,* whose names do not include their sounds. Keywords are also useful in helping students remember the short-vowel sounds, as these are generally not part of the name of the letter (i.e., the short sound of the letter *E* cannot be heard in its name). The students were explicitly taught how to use the keywords as a resource (e.g., a picture of an apple for the short *a*) during both reading and writing activities.

Goal 5: Alphabetic Principle

The student will understand that the letters in printed words represent the sounds in spoken words. Further, the student will be able to change single consonants at the beginnings or ends of one-syllable words in accord with requests made by the teacher (e.g., change mat *to* bat).

Three instructional activities were used to support the students' understanding of this principle:

1. Word building, which engaged the students in using movable letters to make words dictated by the teacher
2. Word reading, which involved the students in reading words that the teacher made or wrote
3. Written spelling, which required the students to write words dictated by the teacher

Early on, word families were used to limit the challenge imposed by these tasks. For example, the teacher might provide and name a word family (e.g., *at*) and then ask the students to change *at* to *mat*, *mat* to *sat*, *sat* to *fat*, and so on. Or, the teacher might show the students the word *sat,* name the word, and then ask them to change *sat* to *mat*, *mat* to *fat*, and so forth. As these tasks only required the students to attend to the beginning letters, this was a productive way to help them develop some automaticity in the application of letter–sound correspondences. Once the students demonstrated some facility with changes at the beginnings of words, the level of challenge was increased a bit, and changes were made at both the beginnings and ends of words. For example, the students might be asked to change *sat* to *fat*, *fat* to *fan*, *fan* to *tan*, and so on. Students who were proficient in analyzing and making changes at the beginnings and ends of words would begin to work with medial vowels as well.

As soon as students began to learn about letter–sound correspondences, they were taught how to apply that knowledge in attempting to identify words encountered in text. Consistent with the ISA, they were encouraged to use letter–sound knowledge with picture cues and the context of the sentence or emergent-level book in attempting to identify unfamiliar words. Students were also encouraged to apply emerging letter–sound knowledge in the context of writing. Thus, during shared writing activities the teacher might ask the students in the group to think of what letter would come at the beginning or end of a particular word. Once the students knew several letter–sound correspondences and some high-frequency words, they were often engaged in writing a sentence or two during the intervention lesson. They were encouraged to use sound spelling, which would serve to reinforce and extend their phonemic awareness and understanding of the alphabetic code.

Goal 6: Print Awareness

The student will understand that the purpose of print is to communicate.

Students who arrive in kindergarten with limited early literacy experiences sometimes have little or no understanding that print is a form of communication. Clearly, students who do not understand this will have limited interest in learning to read and write and will find the entire educational enterprise rather confusing, particularly if it is too tightly focused on the alphabetic code.

Instruction intended to promote an understanding of the purposes of print was integrated into other discussions about reading and writing. For example, the teacher might ask for a prediction concerning what would happen next in the story and then say, "Let's read the words [*while pointing to the print*] to find out...." Or, the teacher might engage the students in a shared writing activity that had the purpose of telling parents about a book that was read in the group by saying, "Let's write a note to your parents to tell them about this book."

Goal 7: Print Conventions

The student will understand some of the most basic print conventions, such as the left-to-right and top-to-bottom sequencing of print, where to begin reading a book, and the concepts of letter and word.

Students who are first learning to read generally need explicit guidance to understand the conventions that literate adults often take for granted. In the intervention lessons, this guidance was provided in several different ways in the context of reading and writing with the students. For example, while reading to the students, the teacher would often point to the words if the print was large enough for the students to see. In addition, after the students had engaged in reading an emergent-level book, the teacher might lead a discussion of how many words were on a particular page, how many letters were in particular words, how to tell where one word ended and the next one began, and so forth. Similar discussions would occur in the context of writing activities.

Goal 8: High-Frequency Word Identification
The student will learn to recognize, at sight, a set of high-frequency words.

High-frequency words are those that occur very often in both print and speech. Because these words occur so frequently, being able to identify them effortlessly will make it easier to read just about any text encountered. Knowing the high-frequency words also facilitates the students' ability to puzzle through unfamiliar words encountered in context, because the known high-frequency words (e.g., *the*, *in*, *it*) typically are included in the context needed to support the identification of the unknown words.

The high-frequency words taught in kindergarten intervention were selected from a list compiled by Eeds (1985), with the highest priority given to the high-frequency words that the students were learning in their classroom program. To teach a high-frequency word, the teacher would select an emergent-level text that includes the word multiple times. The teacher would present the word and name it, discuss its spelling, and have the students read the word and name the letters in it. Then, the students would typically read the book that contained the word. Afterward, they would look through the text to find and name the word each time it occurred. Subsequent practice activities with the word could include reading or writing it several times, often in the context of game-like activities, and reading additional books that include it. Teachers also kept a display of the high-frequency words that had been taught (akin to a word wall) and encouraged the students to refer to the display when they wanted to use the word in their writing. Encouraging conventional spelling of these high-frequency words was intended to facilitate the development of automaticity in the identification of these words.

Intervention Lesson Components

In addition to the specific instructional goals discussed earlier, intervention teachers were urged to be sure, throughout their interactions with the students, that the focus on the meaning of the texts that were read and written remained central. Teachers were encouraged to discuss and enjoy the texts with the students and develop in the students the attitude that what they read was supposed to make sense. In a later iteration of the ISA (Scanlon et al., 2008; Scanlon et al., 2010), two new goals were explicitly added for kindergarten: one focused on the development of vocabulary and oral language skills and one focused on the development of comprehension and the world knowledge that enables comprehension. These goals were not formally articulated in the earlier version of the ISA, but were certainly addressed during the course of instruction.

Instruction in the kindergarten intervention program was provided by certified teachers who participated in a professional development workshop prior to beginning their work with the students. The intervention teachers were observed individually and provided with feedback at least once every six weeks. In addition, all intervention teachers met as a group with the research team once every two or three weeks.

As previously mentioned, the intervention began in mid- to late October and continued through late May or early June. A few of the students made such limited progress in the small-group setting that it was difficult to meet their needs without hindering the progress of the other students in the group. For these students, we generally tried to provide one-to-one instruction if scheduling allowed. However, many students made strong progress in the intervention program. Because the students were involved in an experimental study, we did not discontinue their involvement in the intervention, although this would be a logical move in a nonresearch context. Each intervention lesson was typically composed of four or five of the following components.

Reading or Listening to a Book

In the earliest lessons, the teacher read a book to the group. During this component, the teacher worked to establish an interest in and enthusiasm for reading (motivation) as well as to develop knowledge of letters and their sounds, print concepts, and the like. In later lessons, this segment of the lesson involved the students in rereading emergent-level books that they had read in previous sessions.

Phoneme Analysis

Initially, explicit instruction in phonemic analysis was presented in isolation of talking about letters and their sounds. Ultimately, however, the two skill areas were brought together in a mutually supportive way.

Letter Work

As noted previously, in the earliest lessons, instruction was focused on the alphabet and the names of individual letters. Once the students knew the name of an individual letter, its sound would become a focus of instruction. As the students began to learn about the sounds of letters, the phonemic analysis and letter-work segments of the lessons were brought together, so students could more readily understand the purposes of both phonemic analysis and letter–sound instruction.

Reading

In most lessons, the students read one or more emergent-level books. This provided the teacher with the opportunity to coach the students in word-solving strategies. Texts were always discussed to maintain a focus on reading for meaning rather than simply for the purpose of accurate decoding. The students were typically explicitly prepared to read the book through the teaching of one or two high-frequency words or a decoding element that would be encountered several times in the new text.

Writing

In many lessons, the students did some writing either in the context of sound spelling individual words, writing sentences from dictation, or for more authentic purposes, such as writing a response to a book or note to communicate with parents. The writing component was intended to reinforce the students' phonemic analysis and alphabetic mapping skills, as well as their understanding of the purposes and conventions of print. It also served to build their confidence in their emerging skills.

High-Frequency Words

This component was added once the students knew the names of some of the letters of the alphabet and knew something about the purposes of print. Specific high-frequency words were introduced in preparation for the reading of a new book. However, as the number of words that students were expected to know increased, a few minutes of each intervention lesson were devoted to reviewing and practicing the words that the students were expected to know.

Results of the Study

Table 10.1 presents the results of the letter-identification assessment administered at the beginning of kindergarten for students who qualified as at risk and who were randomly assigned to either the treatment or comparison group. Examination of these data makes it clear that the students in the two groups were quite similar in their performance levels. Table 10.2 presents the assessment data collected at the end of kindergarten. Here, it is evident that the two groups were performing at substantially different levels, with the kindergarten intervention group consistently outperforming the comparison group.

Table 10.1. Performance Levels on Measures Administered at Kindergarten Entry to At-Risk Students Who Were Randomly Assigned to Intervention and Comparison Groups

Performance Measure		Intervention Group (n = 232)	Comparison Group (n = 230)
WRMT-R letter identification raw score	M	5.33	6.29
	SD	4.01	4.40
WRMT-R letter identification standard score	M	83.53	84.71
	SD	5.98	6.13

Note. M = mean; SD = standard deviation; WRMT-R = Woodcock Reading Mastery Tests–Revised.

Table 10.2. End-of-Kindergarten Performance Levels on Measures of Early Literacy Skills for the Intervention and Comparison Groups

Performance Measure (Maximum Possible Score)		Intervention Group (n = 214)	Comparison Group (n = 214)	Effect Size
WRMT-R letter identification	M	28.91	27.07	0.29
	SD	5.13	6.33	
Phoneme segmentation (22)	M	6.22	2.76	0.65
	SD	7.45	5.27	
Letter sounds (35)	M	24.49	20.80	0.41
	SD	7.80	9.05	
Sight words (25)	M	6.68	4.32	0.57
	SD	5.18	4.14	
Decoding skills (30)	M	6.51	4.15	0.52
	SD	6.50	4.56	

Note. M = mean; SD = standard deviation; WRMT-R = Woodcock Reading Mastery Tests–Revised.

All group differences at the end of kindergarten were statistically significant. The effect sizes reported in the last column of Table 10.2 provide an estimation of the magnitude of the group differences on the various measures. By convention, effect sizes of 0.3 or less are considered to be small, effect sizes of 0.3 to 0.7 are considered to be moderate, and effect sizes larger than 0.8 are considered to be large (Cohen, 1988). The results suggest that the ISA intervention had a moderate effect on most of the skills assessed.

Although the differences displayed in Table 10.2 suggest that the small-group intervention was effective, it should be noted that the results displayed may actually underestimate the effects of providing small-group intervention in kindergarten, because a number of the participating schools offered their own form of intervention for the students who had been assigned to the comparison group. Although these schools did not have a kindergarten intervention program in place when they were recruited for the study, we suspect that in the process of explaining what our study was intended to do, we were a bit too convincing about the potential utility of beginning to intervene in kindergarten.

As a result, some schools mustered their resources in such a way that they were able to provide more instructional support to the students in the comparison group than was offered to the students in the treatment group. For example, in some schools, the comparison group students participated in 30 to 60 minutes of additional literacy-focused instruction up to five times a week. Therefore, to conduct a stronger test of the effects of providing intervention for early literacy difficulties at the kindergarten level, we reanalyzed the data, eliminating schools that had provided their own form of kindergarten intervention for the students in the comparison group. The outcomes derived from this smaller sample of schools are provided in Table 10.3. It is clear that the differences between the intervention and comparison groups are much larger than when all of the schools are included in the analysis.

One of the rationales for providing intervention in kindergarten was that it would help to reduce the number of students who qualified for more intensive (and expensive) supports in first grade. Therefore, at the beginning of first grade, we reassessed all of the students who had been identified as at risk at kindergarten entry and were still attending the participating school. A variety of measures of early literacy skill were administered to each of these students, and these measures were used to derive a composite score for each individual.

We used the midpoint of the first-grade composite score distribution for the kindergarten intervention group as the cutoff for identifying students who were

Table 10.3. End-of-Kindergarten Performance Levels on Measures of Early Literacy Skills for the Intervention and Comparison Groups in Schools That Did Not Offer Intervention to Students in the Comparison Group

Performance Measure (Maximum Possible Score)		Intervention Group (n = 48)	Comparison Group (n = 65)	Effect Size
WRMT-R letter	M	28.52	24.37	0.51
identification	SD	3.86	8.14	
Phoneme segmentation (22)	M	6.25	1.05	1.66
	SD	7.50	3.13	
Letter sounds (35)	M	24.69	15.23	0.99
	SD	7.17	9.54	
Sight words (25)	M	4.38	2.06	1.07
	SD	3.30	2.16	
Decoding skills (30)	M	6.81	2.36	1.30
	SD	7.51	3.42	

Note. M = mean; SD = standard deviation; WRMT-R = Woodcock Reading Mastery Tests–Revised.

considered to be at continued risk for reading difficulties. Thus, the bottom half of the students who had participated in our kindergarten intervention program were identified as being at continued risk. This same cutoff score was applied to the comparison group. The logic was that if kindergarten intervention was effective in reducing the incidence of early reading difficulties, a larger proportion of students from the comparison group than from the intervention group should qualify as being at continued risk for reading difficulties.

Figure 10.1 presents the results of this analysis for the entire sample and for only those schools that did not institute their own kindergarten intervention programs. Inspection of the data for the entire sample reveals that although, by definition, 50% of the students who were in the intervention group as kindergartners qualified as being at continued risk, 60% of the students in the comparison group qualified as being at continued risk for reading difficulties at the beginning of first grade. This suggests a clear but modest advantage for the kindergarten intervention approach. However, when the analysis was limited to schools that did not provide their own version of kindergarten intervention, 83% of the students in the comparison group qualified as being at continued

Figure 10.1. Percentage of Students Who Were Identified as At Risk at Kindergarten Entry Who Continued to Score in the At-Risk Range at the Beginning of First Grade

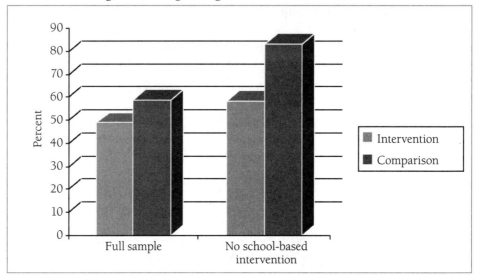

risk at the beginning of first grade. Interestingly, in these schools, a higher percentage of the students who participated in the ISA-based intervention program qualified as being at continued risk. This may suggest that the classroom language arts program that was offered in these schools was somewhat less effective in promoting early literacy skills.

Discussion

In this study, we identified students who were at increased risk of experiencing difficulties at the early stages of learning to read owing to their limited knowledge of the alphabet at kindergarten entry. The students were randomly assigned to either a treatment group, in which they were provided with ISA-based small-group literacy support services (a form of Tier 2 intervention in a RTI format), or to a comparison group, in which they received only the instruction offered by their school. The intervention approach used encouraged the intervention teachers to plan instruction that was both responsive to the needs of their students and took account of the expectations of the classroom language arts program. An important objective was that the instruction offered in the intervention setting be as congruent with the classroom program as possible so that the students would be better prepared to profit from classroom language arts instruction.

The outcomes reveal that students involved in the ISA-based kindergarten intervention substantially outperformed students in the comparison group at the end of kindergarten. This was especially true in schools that did not offer their own form of kindergarten intervention. The results also indicated that at the beginning of first grade, fewer students in the kindergarten intervention group qualified for reading support services. Thus, although the intervention offered in kindergarten was not very intensive (a hallmark of Tier 2 interventions), it was sufficient to accelerate the progress of many of the kindergartners who were initially identified as at risk. Students who did not show accelerated progress when provided with Tier 2 intervention were eligible for a more intensive (Tier 3) intervention in first grade. A more detailed description of the results of this intervention study can be found in Scanlon et al. (2005) and Vellutino et al. (2006). It should be noted, however, that many of the students who did not show accelerated growth during the course of Tier 2 intervention did show rapid gains when provided with daily one-on-one instruction in first grade.

Whereas it is not possible to clearly identify the most important ingredients in the intervention described in this chapter, as is true for many intervention approaches, we suspect that one important characteristic was the effort to support students in their classroom language arts program. Students who find it challenging to learn to read and write are apt to suffer additional confusion and challenge when they receive incongruent instruction in multiple settings. The implementation of vastly different instructional programs in classroom and intervention settings has the potential to interfere with, rather than promote, the development of literacy skills among young students.

NOTE

This study was supported by a grant from the National Institute of Child Health and Human Development (Grant #1RO1HO34598). We wish to express our sincere appreciation to the many students, teachers, school administrators, and clerical staff who participated in or facilitated this study. We wish to express our gratitude to our colleagues Sheila Small and Diane Fanuele, who made this work possible. Thanks are also due to the teachers who provided the intervention services in this study.

REFERENCES

Adams, M.J. (1990). *Beginning to read: Thinking and learning about print.* Cambridge, MA: MIT Press.

Blachman, B.A. (2000). Phonological awareness. In M.L. Kamil, P.B. Mosenthal, P.D. Pearson, & R. Barr (Eds.), *Handbook of reading research* (Vol. 3, pp. 483–502). Mahwah, NJ: Erlbaum.

Cohen, J. (1988). *Statistical power analysis for the behavioral sciences* (2nd ed.). Hillsdale, NJ: Erlbaum.

Eeds, M. (1985). Bookwords: Using a beginning word list of high frequency words from children's literature K–3. *The Reading Teacher, 38*(4), 418–423.

Scanlon, D.M., Anderson, K.L., & Sweeney, J.M. (2010). *Early intervention for reading difficulties: The Interactive Strategies Approach.* New York: Guilford.

Scanlon, D.M., Gelzheiser, L.M., Vellutino, F.R., Schatschneider, C., & Sweeney, J.M. (2008). Reducing the incidence of early reading difficulties: Professional development for classroom teachers versus direct interventions for children. *Learning and Individual Differences, 18*(3), 346–359.

Scanlon, D.M., & Vellutino, F.R. (1996). Prerequisite skills, early instruction, and success in first-grade reading: Selected results from a longitudinal study. *Mental Retardation and Developmental Disabilities Research Reviews, 2*(1), 54–63. doi:10.1002/(SICI)1098-2779(1996)2:1<54::AID-MRDD9>3.0.CO;2-X

Scanlon, D.M., & Vellutino, F.R. (1997). A comparison of the instructional backgrounds and cognitive profiles of poor, average, and good readers who were initially identified as at risk for reading failure. *Scientific Studies of Reading, 1*(3), 191–215. doi:10.1207/s1532799xssr0103_2

Scanlon, D.M., Vellutino, F.R., Small, S.G., Fanuele, D.P., & Sweeney, J.M. (2005). Severe reading difficulties—can they be prevented? A comparison of prevention and intervention approaches. *Exceptionality, 13*(4), 209–227. doi:10.1207/s15327035ex1304_3

Vellutino, F.R., & Scanlon, D.M. (2002). The Interactive Strategies approach to reading intervention. *Contemporary Educational Psychology, 27*(4), 573–635. doi:10.1016/S0361-476X(02)00002-4

Vellutino, F.R., Scanlon, D.M., Sipay, E.R., Small, S.G., Pratt, A., Chen, R.S., et al. (1996). Cognitive profiles of difficult-to-remediate and readily remediated poor readers: Early intervention as a vehicle for distinguishing between cognitive and experiential deficits as basic causes of specific reading disability. *Journal of Educational Psychology, 88*(4), 601–638. doi:10.1037/0022-0663.88.4.601

Vellutino, F.R., Scanlon, D.M., Small, S., & Fanuele, D.P. (2006). Response to Intervention as a vehicle for distinguishing between children with and without reading disabilities: Evidence for the role of kindergarten and first-grade interventions. *Journal of Learning Disabilities, 39*(2), 157–169. doi:10.1177/00222194060390020401

Yopp, H. (1995). Yopp-Singer Test of Phoneme Segmentation. *The Reading Teacher, 49*(1), 20–29.

CHAPTER 11

An Adapted Interactive Writing Intervention for the Kindergarten Classroom: Creating a Framework for Responsive Teaching

Sharon A. Craig

Investigations into effective literacy practices have shifted the pedagogical focus from program to teacher, linking teachers' instructional skills and students' literacy achievement (Block, Hurt, & Oakar, 2002; Hall & Harding, 2003; Wray, Medwell, Fox, & Poulson, 2000). Evidence across studies suggests that the most effective literacy teachers provide responsive, differentiated instruction that builds on students' existing knowledge and creates the optimal instructional match for their specific learning needs. They analyze data to make informed instructional decisions, implement high-quality classroom instruction, continually monitor progress, and engage in critical reflection to evaluate and improve their own practice (Snow, Griffin, & Burns, 2005).

High-quality classroom instruction delivered by knowledgeable, skilled teachers is a critical component of an RTI model of instruction (Howard, 2009). In primary classrooms, high-quality instruction not only provides adequate support for most students but also may even decrease the occurrence of literacy difficulties (Lyon, Fletcher, Fuchs, & Chhabra, 2006); however, some students fail to succeed despite the quality of this instruction and, consequently, need more intensive, targeted support. To accommodate all learners, teachers must continually monitor students' responsiveness to instruction and supply effective classroom interventions before they fail (Gersten et al., 2008). Recognizing the adaptive limitations of many prescriptive approaches, effective teachers seek more flexible interventions that can be tailored to accommodate students' changing strengths and needs.

One evidence-based intervention that offers this level of flexibility is an adapted interactive writing framework (Craig, 2006). A contextualized approach to instruction, this intervention integrates explicit instruction, modeling, and practice of phonological awareness and alphabetic skills into reading, writing, and word study. The instructional context balances experiences with words, sentences, and texts (Wray et al., 2000), linking students' skill work to meaningful, strategic reading and writing. Interactive writing shares the key elements of other evidence-based early literacy interventions. A synthesis of effective primary interventions published in peer-reviewed journals between 1995 and 2005 identified the following four characteristics across programs (Scammacca, Vaughn, Roberts, Wanzek, & Torgesen, 2007):

1. Explicit instruction in phonological awareness, decoding, and word study
2. Guided and independent reading with texts of increasing complexity
3. Comprehension strategy instruction and application
4. Opportunities for writing

This chapter documents the effectiveness of an adapted interactive writing intervention, providing a detailed description of the teaching strategies used in the intervention and the research behind them. The following sections establish a rationale for a writing-based intervention, summarize study findings, and describe the reading, interactive writing, and word-study components in the cyclical intervention framework.

Rationale for an Adapted Interactive Writing Intervention

Research provides a strong rationale for a writing-based intervention. This section discusses the facilitative effects of interactive writing on the interrelated processes of phonological awareness, reading, and spelling, describing an interactive literacy context that supports engagement.

Phonological Awareness, Reading, and Spelling: Interrelated Processes

Early literacy studies have consistently identified phonological awareness and alphabetic knowledge as powerful predictors of beginning reading and writing

(Juel, Griffith, & Gough, 1985; Share, Jorm, Maclean, & Matthews, 1984). Learners who develop awareness of phonemes in speech and successfully use knowledge of letter–sound correspondences to spell and read words demonstrate the greatest gains in reading and spelling in first grade and sustain these gains in subsequent years of schooling (Byrne & Fielding-Barnsley, 1995; Byrne, Fielding-Barnsley, & Ashley, 2000; National Institute of Child Health and Human Development, 2000).

The relationship between spelling and word reading suggests mutual facilitation, the interconnected processes accessing the same knowledge sources (Ehri, 1998) and exerting reciprocal influences during early literacy acquisition (McGuinness, McGuinness, & Donohue, 1995; Perfetti, Beck, Bell, & Hughes, 1987; Stahl & Murray, 1994). Investigating this interdependent relationship, some researchers suggest an order in the developmental progression, theorizing learners' earliest alphabetic insights emerge in writing prior to reading (Burns & Richgels, 1989; Chomsky, 1971, 1979; Frith, 1985; Read, 1975). Frith's (1985) integrative reading–writing model lends support to this theory, proposing alternating "pacemaker" roles for reading and writing across logographic, alphabetic, and orthographic stages of literacy development, with alphabetic writing leading and facilitating alphabetic reading. Ehri and Wilce (1987) provide evidence of this facilitative effect, finding kindergartners trained to invent spellings for phonetically regular words engaged in phonetic-cue or partial alphabetic reading when identifying words. Uhry and Shepherd (1993) observe that integrating invented spelling and explicit phonemic-segmentation instruction appears to enhance this effect, supporting students' early word reading and passage comprehension. This evidence suggests that teachers can support students' early literacy acquisition with developmentally appropriate writing instruction that provides explicit connections among phonemic segmentation, spelling, and reading (Ball & Blachman, 1991; Tangel & Blachman, 1992).

Writing as a Context for Early Literacy Instruction

Designing the optimal instructional context for early literacy learners, however, involves more than implementing evidence-based principles and practices. Quality literacy instruction builds on learners' existing knowledge and experience and extends their capacity to think and problem solve during actual reading and writing. Linking instruction in phonological awareness and alphabetic skills to connected texts supports students' meaningful connections among word, sentence, and text levels, scaffolding their strategic use of knowledge and skills during reading and writing (see Calfee, 1998; Dahl, Scharer, Lawson, & Grogan, 1999; Mathes et al., 2005; Pressley et al., 1998; Wray et al., 2000).

For young learners, writing provides a functional context for explicit instruction in phonological awareness and alphabetic skills. Converging evidence from spelling research indicates a causal relationship between invented spelling and early word reading (Clarke, 1988; Ehri & Wilce, 1987; Uhry & Shepherd, 1993), one that may be enhanced with developmentally appropriate feedback (Ouellette & Sénéchal, 2008; Rieben, Ntamakiliro, Gontier, & Fayol, 2005). When inventing spellings, learners use phonemic segmentation to complete internal analysis of known words (Griffith, 1991), mapping graphemes to phonemes as they encounter them, a process that imposes less stress on memory than decoding (Treiman, 1998). These "phonemic maps" provide visual depictions of pronunciations (Ehri, 2005), producing lexical representations that may eventually support students' reading (Ouellette & Sénéchal, 2008).

Writing as an Interactive Process Supporting Engagement

Responsive teaching within writing contexts requires interactive, supportive talk to facilitate students' engagement and understanding. Mariage (2001) documents how one teacher used conversational strategies to compose a morning message. Acting as scribe and facilitator, the teacher scaffolded students' problem solving, adapting interactions as needed to foster their involvement with the process and content. An analysis of the teacher's comments highlighted eight conversational moves (e.g., voicing a student's response, rereading the text, providing supporting comments) during message construction, showing that the teacher continually adapted prompts and explanations to engage students.

Whereas Mariage (2001) views interaction in terms of dialogue, Pinnell and McCarrier (1994) expand support to involve students directly in the writing process, sharing a pen to record a negotiated text. A collaborative partnership, interactive writing provides a context for modeling the writing process and developing students' phonemic awareness, print concepts, phonics principles, and language choices before, during, and after composing (Button, Johnson, & Furgerson, 1996; Pinnell & McCarrier, 1994). During an interactive writing lesson, the teacher uses students' strengths as the basis for instruction and collaborates with group members to record a message, stepping in as needed to provide strategy prompts, model unfamiliar print concepts, or demonstrate conventional spelling, capitalization, and punctuation. When teachers share the pen, they slow the writing pace to scaffold students' problem solving, making the abstract composing processes more concrete. During the writing process, responsibilities continually shift, with learners assuming control over the print concepts and spelling processes (e.g., segmentation, letter–sound correspondences) they already control and teachers stepping in to model the conventional elements that may be unfamiliar.

Although sharing the pen provides optimal support in the earliest stages, it may limit students' engagement as they develop competence with print concepts, phonemic segmentation, and letter–sound correspondences. Once they demonstrate understanding of the modeled processes, students may benefit more from an adapted form of interactive writing that promotes independent structured practice yet retains interactive discourse to support their problem solving (see Table 11.1 for a comparison of the two approaches). In the adapted individual response format (Craig 2003, 2006), a single chart is replaced with individual dry-erase boards for each student to record the group's negotiated message.

This adapted format differs from sharing the pen in another aspect: Learners problem solve their own spellings, producing both conventional spellings and

Table 11.1. Interactive Writing: Comparing Approaches

Element	Sharing the Pen (Pinnell & McCarrier, 1994)	Individual Response (Craig, 2003, 2006)
Purposes	• Introduce students to the writing process • Develop awareness of the structures and patterns of written language • Model print concepts, phonemic awareness, alphabetic principles, and orthographic features to support students' encoding and decoding • Collaborate to compose a readable text	• Extend students' understanding of the writing process • Support students' application of print concepts, phonemic awareness, alphabetic principles, and orthographic features to encode and decode a text • Independently compose a readable text
Context	• Individual, small group, or whole group • Single message • Shared text/group chart • Single pen/writing implement	• Individual, small group, or whole group • Single message • Individual dry-erase boards/paper • Individual writing implements

(continued)

Table 11.1. Interactive Writing: Comparing Approaches (*continued*)

Element	Sharing the Pen (Pinnell & McCarrier, 1994)	Individual Response (Craig, 2003, 2006)
Teacher's Role	• Negotiate a text with students • Share the pen with students to compose the text • Model concepts and conventions using think-alouds and demonstrations • Interact with individuals/group to facilitate participation in the composing process • Step in to provide skills students do not control for themselves	• Negotiate a text with students • Support students as they problem solve and independently compose the text, monitoring the pace to keep students together during the problem-solving phase • Interact with individuals/group as needed to draw students' attention to the teaching point, point out successful problem solving, question students' thinking, or provide strategy prompts • Following the composing process, model conventional spellings, capitalization, punctuation, letter formation, and spacing as students check/correct their own texts
Conventions	• Conventional spelling • Conventional capitalization, punctuation, and letter formation	• Invented and conventional spelling • Conventional capitalization and letter formation

predictable developmental variations as they individually record each word in the message. Interactions before and during composing typically take the form of strategy prompts, questioning, and individualized coaching. At the end of the composing phase, the teacher models conventional spelling, focusing the interactions more on strategy use, phonics principles, orthographic patterns, and writing conventions. The modeling continues to involve the students in problem solving, providing brief opportunities for them to achieve closer approximations. Each interaction is designed to foster independent applications of the skills beyond the interactive writing context.

The Study: Interactive Writing Intervention in the Classroom

Interactive writing in its original and adapted formats served as the basis for a writing-based intervention study of 98 kindergartners. The 16-week investigation examined the effects of two early literacy interventions, interactive writing–plus and metalinguistic games–plus, on students' phonological awareness, alphabetic knowledge, and spelling development (Craig, 2003, 2006). A form of contextualized instruction, the interactive writing–plus framework integrated reading, writing, and word study in a cyclical three-part intervention.

Each week, interactive writing–plus teachers introduced a shared text, responded to the reading using interactive writing, and concluded the instructional cycle with related word study. Teachers adopted a responsive approach and adapted instruction as needed, building on students' competencies and providing appropriate challenges to foster continual growth. Following a structured program of language games, metalinguistic games–plus teachers implemented the prescribed instructional sequence in the evidence-based program *Phonemic Awareness in Young Children: A Classroom Curriculum* (Adams, Foorman, Lundberg, & Beeler, 1998), supplementing this program with explicit code instruction. Language games and activities focused on explicit explanations and practice with words, syllables, onset-rime units, and phonemes.

Highly qualified teachers from both interventions met each week with small homogeneous groups outside the classroom for four 20-minute lessons. Teachers in both groups provided high-quality developmentally appropriate instruction that blended explicit explanations, modeling, and scaffolded practice. During debriefing sessions, they revisited lesson objectives and brainstormed applications for classroom-based reading and writing tasks.

These theoretically different models targeted the same phonological awareness and alphabetic skills but diverged on instructional stance. Throughout the investigation, teachers in the metalinguistic games–plus group adhered to the recommended sequence of the Adams et al. (1998) program and its supplemental code component, developing interactive sessions that were ordered according to task and linguistic complexity. In contrast, teachers in the interactive writing–plus group continually assessed students' performances and used their data to differentiate instruction, varying their content and techniques to accommodate students' responsiveness to their instruction.

Pretest and posttest measures provided between-group comparisons on students' phonological awareness, spelling, and reading development. On the basis of pretest letter knowledge, students in both groups were also designated as low, middle, or high initial literacy level learners. Posttest analyses measured the differential effects of these three levels and the two interventions on spelling and reading measures.

Reading assessments consisted of pseudoword reading, word identification, and passage comprehension. In addition, students' real-word and pseudoword reading responses were reanalyzed using a four-point scale derived from Ehri's (1995, 1998) four-phase model of word-reading development. These results provided evidence of learners' word-reading strategies, placing them along the developmental continuum from the prealphabetic and partial alphabetic phases to the more advanced full and consolidated alphabetic phases.

Results for phonological awareness, spelling, and pseudoword reading post-tests indicated substantial gains for the students in both interventions, with the groups demonstrating comparable performances on all three measures. Despite differences in instruction, the students in the interactive writing–plus and metalinguistic games–plus interventions demonstrated a strong grasp of phonemic segmentation and letter–sound mapping on encoding and word-attack tasks.

Similarly, posttest measures of real-word reading and comprehension indicated significant normative growth for both interventions; however, the interactive writing–plus group outperformed the metalinguistic games–plus group at all three literacy levels on word reading and comprehension. On the comprehension measure, effect sizes (Cohen, 1988) for between-group differences ranged from moderate to large: 0.49 for the low initial literacy level, 0.65 for the middle initial literacy level, and 1.03 for the high initial literacy level.

This training advantage extended to the students' word-reading development. By the end of the investigation, a greater percentage of interactive writing–plus students had reached the full and consolidated alphabetic phases of word reading (Ehri, 1995, 1998). Learners in the more advanced phases not only demonstrated phonemic segmentation and blending but also analogizing with intrasyllabic units (e.g., using *op* in the known word *top* to decode the unfamiliar word *hop*), providing evidence of a more sophisticated level of decoding (Ehri & Robbins, 1992).

These results verify the efficacy of a contextualized, responsive approach to teaching phonological awareness and alphabetic skills. Specifically, the writing and word-study experiences that support students' invented spellings with interactive talk and feedback appear to develop the phonological and orthographic skills required for early word reading (see Frith, 1985; Ouellette & Sénéchal, 2008). Moreover, the findings suggest that these benefits extend to students' passage comprehension. Although there is insufficient evidence to suggest a causal relationship for the comprehension outcome, it is important to note that the three integrated phases of the intervention framework shared a meaningful context, allowing for explicit connections among text, sentence, and word levels (see Wray et al., 2000). Within each phase, teachers focused on developing the analytical skills and strategies to construct meaning, concluding each session with a discussion of practical applications to reading and writing. This intentional integration of decoding instruction into text reading may provide an immediate return on decoding practice that transfers to comprehension (McCandliss, Beck, Sandak, & Perfetti, 2003).

Adapted Interactive Writing Framework: Classroom Applications

During the investigation, highly qualified teachers provided small-group instruction in a pull-out setting; however, the instructional components and processes of the interactive writing–plus condition also present implications for the classroom as an instructional framework for general education and supplemental interventions.

The adapted interactive writing intervention is a cyclical framework consisting of three integrated phases: text reading, interactive writing, and related word study (see Figure 11.1). Teachers begin the intervention cycle with the introduction of a new text using either shared (Holdaway, 1979) or guided reading (Fountas & Pinnell, 1996), selecting the instructional approach that matches the

Figure 11.1. Three Phases of the Adapted Interactive Writing Intervention

Integrated Components: Reading, Interactive Writing, and Word Study		
Day 1	Day 2	Day 3
Text Reading ⟶	Interactive Writing ⟶	Word Study
Instructional Options[a]		
Shared Reading Guided Reading	Sharing the Pen Individual Response	Word Spelling/Reading Unit: Letter–Sound Word Spelling/Reading Unit: Onset–Rime

[a]The instructional approach should build on students' problem-solving abilities and challenge them to perform at a more complex level.

students' abilities and optimizes engagement. On the second day of the cycle, the teacher and students negotiate a response to the text and use interactive writing to record the group message, with the teacher either sharing the pen (Pinnell & McCarrier, 1994) or implementing an adapted individual response format (Craig, 2003, 2006) that engages learners in each aspect of message construction. On the final day of the instructional cycle, the teacher incorporates multiple approaches to phonics instruction to teach a challenging word pattern from the reading or interactive writing lesson, developing students' phonological awareness as well as their encoding and decoding skills. Word study begins with individual letter–sound correspondences and progresses to larger orthographic units once students demonstrate understanding of the alphabetic principle in writing and reading (see Christensen & Bowey, 2005; Ehri & Robbins, 1992).

Following the word-study lesson, the three-phase cycle begins again, starting with the introduction of a new text, proceeding to interactive writing, and then continuing to word study. The descriptions that follow provide implementation guidelines for integrating the phases, selecting teaching techniques, and making instructional decisions.

Implementing the Text Phase

An engaging fiction or nonfiction text establishes a meaningful context for the adapted interactive writing intervention. To create the optimal context, select the reading level, genre, and instructional approaches that build on the students' existing knowledge and maximize their engagement in the reading experience. When previewing a new text, access and develop students' prior knowledge, guiding their analysis of illustrations, text features, and print, intentionally building their anticipation of text concepts and language. During the preview, encourage students to generate flexible predictions, make connections to the text, identify important ideas, and construct inferences. As learners encounter new information, challenge them to check their predictions and confirm or revise them to accommodate the evolving text. Select developmentally appropriate instructional techniques to match the students' reading abilities. During shared readings, model fluent, expressive reading and develop students' understanding of directionality, one-to-one correspondence, and concepts of letter, word, and sentence. Invite learners to interact with the text at appropriate points to interpret story ideas, to make text-to-self connections, and to identify language patterns. When implementing shared readings, support students' participation, encouraging them to join in on a familiar refrain or predictable text segment. Once students transition to guided reading (see detailed description in Fountas & Pinnell, 1996), foster their independent problem solving, providing strategic prompts as necessary to support their decoding, vocabulary development, and meaning construction (Iaquinta, 2006).

Following the reading, discuss the text, exploring relationships among story elements in goal-based narratives and summarizing textually important ideas in nonfiction texts. Encourage learners to examine and extend their meaning by sharing their questions, connections, and inferences. During the discussion, negotiate responses to the text, developing the language and ideas that may serve as the message for the interactive writing session. For example, a discussion of the story *No Dogs Allowed* (Hardin, 1997) might address the mischief caused by the dogs Max and Toby when they wander onto a beach and cannot read the sign that forbids dogs. As the discussion progresses, students may choose to generate a list of rules for owners who want to bring their dogs to the beach. The ideas generated for a new sign provide sentence options for the interactive writing session.

Implementing the Interactive Writing Phase

Sharing the Pen. Once students have read and discussed the text, they are ready to compose a written response to the reading. To support students' writing, provide a group chart with a large alphabet-sound card attached as a spelling resource. Revisit the text and discussion from the previous session and finalize the response to be recorded, repeating the sentence with students and counting the words in the message. Share the pen with students, encouraging them to demonstrate print concepts such as directionality, spacing, letter/word/sentence boundaries, capitalization, and punctuation. For single-syllable decodable words, have students orally segment the word into sounds and match individual sounds to letters or letter combinations using the alphabet-sound card as needed.

When appropriate, introduce visuals and manipulatives to make these concepts more concrete. For example, if spelling a three-sound decodable word, draw three connected sound boxes on the chart to represent the orally segmented sounds. If students are unable to supply conventional spellings, capitalization, or punctuation, the teacher should take responsibility for recording and model with a demonstration and think-aloud. As each new word is added to the chart, reread the entire message to ensure a focus on meaning. Following the composing phase, briefly return to the new message to develop or reinforce the print and alphabetic concepts discussed during the writing process (e.g., "Can you find a word that has three sounds?"; see McCarrier, Pinnell, & Fountas, 2000).

Adapted Interactive Writing: Individual Response. Select the individual-response approach if students are beginning to demonstrate knowledge of phonological awareness, alphabetic knowledge, and print concepts. Provide each student with a dry-erase board, marker, eraser, and alphabet-sound card, seating them in a formation that encourages interaction with other group members. Begin the writing session by revisiting the story, commenting on explicit and implied meanings. Rehearse the negotiated message, repeating the full sentence and noting the number of words. Encourage students to record the first word, prompting them to use the most appropriate strategy, which may involve locating a phonogram or irregular spelling on a resource wall or segmenting a word into phonemes and identifying logical letter–sound correspondences on the alphabet-sound card. Accept all invented spellings but intervene to correct letter reversals and uppercase/lowercase confusions as they occur.

As with sharing the pen, reread the message from the beginning each time a new word is added. Throughout the composing process, keep learners together but individualize interactions to support each student's problem solving. Once students have completed their writing, model the conventional spellings and print concepts, providing brief teaching points to illustrate effective problem solving. Conclude with a debriefing session, reviewing the learning objectives and discussing applications to other writing contexts. The individual response approach to adapted interactive writing is shown in the example that follows.

In this sample lesson, the teacher implemented a shared reading of the story *There Was a Mouse* by Patricia Blanchard and Joanne Suhr (2003). The predictable rhyming story follows a mouse as she chews through a boy's closet, his sneaker, and finally his backpack. On the last page, the mouse, now surrounded by baby mice, appears in the pocket of the boy's jacket. The boy ends the story with the question, "Now what do I do?"

Following the text reading, students discussed solutions to the boy's problem (all names are pseudonyms). The teacher and class members decided to list their solutions, beginning with the idea they considered most important. Suggestions for the list included the following:

- Make a bed for the baby mice.
- Get the mice some food.

- Tell or don't tell his mom about the mice.
- Take the mice to the pet store.

After some negotiation, the students agreed to begin the list with the sentence, "Make a bed for the baby mice."

The primary teaching point for the lesson was phonemic segmentation, with a focus on three-sound words. The teacher used sound boxes to support the students' understanding of this process.

Teacher: Yesterday we agreed that the little boy needed to help the mother mouse and her babies. We had so many good ideas, but we decided to start with one idea, the one that we thought most important. What did we say the boy needed to do first?

Anna: He had to make a bed.

Teacher: That's right. We wanted the boy to make a bed for the baby mice. We decided that our sentence should say, "Make a bed for the baby mice." Let's say that sentence together. [*As the teacher and students repeat the sentence, the teacher holds up a finger for each word in the sentence.*]

Teacher: How many words do we have in our sentence?

Students: Seven.

Teacher: We have seven words to write today. Who can remember the first word in our sentence?

Owen: *Make.*

Teacher: I want each of you to point to where you will begin writing the word *make*. [*All of the students point to the upper left corner on their dry-erase boards.*]

Teacher: The word *make* is a new word for us. Listen carefully while I say the sounds in the word *make*: /m/-/a/-/k/. How many sounds do you hear?

Students: Three.

Teacher: Say each sound with me. [*The students segment the word with the teacher and then individually.*]

Teacher: Say the first sound and find the letter that matches that sound. [*The class members vocalize the /m/ sound. Anna, Ryan, and Lauren immediately write the letter* M, *whereas Owen checks the alphabet-sound card before writing a lowercase* m.]

Teacher: Did you use an uppercase or lowercase letter?

Lauren: Uppercase.

Teacher: Why?

Lauren: Because it's the first word. [*Without further prompting, Owen erases his letter and uses the uppercase form.*]

Teacher: That's right; it's the first word in our sentence, so the first letter should be uppercase. What sound comes after /m/? Say the sounds to yourself. [*Each student says the next sound and writes the letter* a. *As he writes, Owen comments that the letter says its own name.*]

Teacher: Now say each sound again so you can hear the last sound in the word *make*. [*Each student says the final sound. Anna and Lauren immediately write the letter* k. *Ryan searches the alphabet-sound card before writing the letter* k. *Owen points to the cat on the alphabet-sound card and writes the letter* c. *No one writes the final* e.]

Teacher: Let's read the first word in our sentence. [*The teacher and students read the word* make.]

Teacher: What's the next word in our sentence?

Students: *a*

Teacher: This is a word that we all know. Write the word *a* on your board. [*The teacher pauses as the students write.*] Now let's read what we've written.

Teacher and
Students: "Make a"

Owen and
Lauren: "bed"

Teacher: Yes, *bed* is our next word. This is a new word, so I want you to listen as I say each sound in the word *bed*: /b/-/e/-/d/. How many sounds do you hear?

Students: Three.

Teacher: Say those sounds with me. [*The class members segment the word with the teacher and then individually.*]

Teacher:	I want you to draw three sound boxes for the word *bed*, one box for each sound. Watch as I draw them on my board. [*The teacher draws three sound boxes. Anna, Ryan, and Lauren draw three sound boxes on their boards, but Owen struggles with the task. The teacher uses her own marker to help Owen draw the sound boxes.*]
Teacher:	Now point to each box as we say the sounds in the word *bed*. [*The students point to the corresponding boxes as they segment the word.*]
Teacher:	Say the first sound and find the letter that makes that sound. [*All four learners isolate the initial sound. Anna, Ryan, and Owen write the letter* b. *Lauren writes the letter* d. *The teacher points to Lauren's alphabet-sound card and asks her to show the letter she is writing. Lauren points to the* b *on the alphabet-sound card. The teacher prompts Lauren to check her letter against the letter on the card. Lauren changes the* d *to a* b.]
Teacher:	Now I want you to use your vowel pinch strip. As you say the next sound in the word *bed*, pinch the picture that begins with that sound. [*Ryan and Lauren pinch the picture of the igloo and write the letter* i *in the second sound box. Anna pinches the picture of the elephant and writes the letter* e *in the second sound box. Owen chooses the picture of the apple and writes the letter* a *in his sound box.*]
Teacher:	Now say the last sound in the word *bed* and write the letter that matches that sound. [*All four students isolate the final sound and write the letter* d *in the last sound box.*]
Teacher:	Let's put our sounds together: /b/-/e/-/d/—bed.
Teacher and Students:	/b/-/e/-/d/—bed
Teacher:	Let's read the words we've written so far.

The students continued to record each word in the sentence. The teacher interacted with individual students as well as the group to support their problem solving. Following the composing session, the teacher displayed her board and demonstrated the conventional spellings for each word in the sentence. During this time, the teacher briefly commented on students' performances, drawing attention to their successes as well as to new spellings and phonics principles.

Teacher: I want you to watch as I write the words in our sentence. First, I can see that all of you heard the sounds in the word *make* and matched each sound with a letter. [*The teacher writes* Mak. *Students check off the letter–sound correspondences on their own boards.*]

Teacher: There's another letter that we need to add to end of this word. It's a tricky one because we don't hear a sound for this letter. Does anyone know what this letter is?

Ryan: Magic *e*.

Teacher: There is an *e* at the end of the word *make*. [*As the teacher writes the letter* e, *the students add the letter to their spellings. The teacher points to the completed spelling and reads the word.*]

Teacher: Everyone knew the word, *a*, so give yourselves a check as I write it on my board. Now, let's look at the next word, *bed*. You drew three sound boxes, one box for each sound. [*The teacher draws the sound boxes.*] Each of you matched the /b/ to the letter *b*. [*The teacher writes* b.] I can see that we have different ideas for our next sound, so let's solve this one together. [*The teacher and students isolate the sound and then use the vowel pinch strip to locate the match.*]

The teacher completed the spelling demonstration and concluded the session with a debriefing. During the debriefing, the teacher revisited the lesson objective and discussed segmentation. Students concluded the session by sharing how they intended to apply this skill in their classroom literacy tasks. Following the debriefing, the teacher made note of the students' invented spellings, ordering them according to phonogram frequency/utility (Fry, 1998). The teacher selected a high-utility phonogram to develop during the word-study lesson.

When using the individual-response approach, it is important to remember that it is the journey, not the destination, that matters. Slow the pace, keeping learners together so they have an opportunity to observe one another problem solve. Interact with the group as a whole or with individuals to question thinking, to prompt or point out strategy use, and to coach. When modeling conventions at the end of the writing session, focus on the process and build on students' approximations. Continue the conversational involvement, interacting with students to identify conventional print concepts, spelling, capitalization, and punctuation, encouraging them to check their own responses, to comment on their choices, and to make corrections as needed.

Implementing the Word-Study Phase

Selecting Words. Word study, the final phase in the integrated framework, is grounded in the interactions that occur in students' text experiences and interactive writing lessons. Observe learners during the reading and interactive writing sessions to collect and analyze data on their strategies for identifying and spelling words. Note and bring to their attention areas for growth in their word learning. Record the words that challenged students' spelling or reading, and select a word on the basis of segmentation abilities, alphabetic knowledge, and the utility of the word pattern itself (e.g., select a consonant-vowel-consonant word with a high-utility phonogram, a spelling pattern shared by other words). Also consider students' spelling and word-reading development when choosing the size of the orthographic unit, beginning with phonemes for learners in the early stages of code development and progressing to larger orthographic sequences, including onset-rime units and syllables.

Spelling Words. After selecting a word with a high-utility phonogram, rewrite the full sentence from the text or interactive writing session on sentence strips, inserting a blank box for the target word. Place the sentence strip(s) in a pocket chart and display sound boxes, letter tiles, and an alphabet-sound card to support word-building activities. Begin the lesson by reading the sentence with students, encouraging them to identify the missing word. Say the word slowly, enunciating each sound in the sequence. After modeling segmentation, support learners as they practice segmenting the word and clapping the sounds. Encourage them to count the segmented sounds and place the corresponding number of sound boxes in the blank word box. Invite students to construct the word, matching each segmented sound to a letter or letter combination. Have students repeat each letter's sound and then blend the letter sounds to say the word. Check the constructed word against the model and, if necessary, make corrections.

After spelling the target word in its original context, lift it from the sentence for further analysis. Encourage students to reconstruct the word using their own letter tiles, independently segmenting the word into sounds and mapping letter sounds. Dictate related words, coaching students as they construct each word using individual letter sounds. Once students are capable of segmenting and spelling consonant-vowel-consonant words, introduce an analogy strategy for spelling. For each new word, encourage students to retain the rime unit in the target word and substitute onsets to generate new words, beginning with single-consonant onsets and progressing to clusters. (An onset is the initial consonant or consonant cluster that precedes the vowel in a syllable, e.g., *stop*; a rime is a vowel and any consonants that follow, e.g., *stop*.)

Reading Words. Following spelling practice, shift the focus to reading the words students have spelled. Beginning with the target word, display each letter in sequence, model the corresponding sounds, and blend the letter sounds to pronounce the word. Disassemble the word and select a different onset. Again, display the individual letters in sequence and model the blending process, combining individual letter sounds to identify the word. Continue to present individual letters or letter combinations, gradually releasing responsibility for the blending task to students.

Learners who have progressed to an analogy strategy will blend onset-rime units. With each new word, remove the onset and have students identify the remaining rime unit (e.g., "What do you have left when you take the /t/ off *top*?"). Select a new onset and have students produce the sound(s). Place the onset in front of the rime unit and encourage students to blend the two parts to pronounce the word (e.g., /m/-/op/ to *mop*). Add new onsets (singletons and clusters) and blend the onset-rime units to identify words.

Increase the word-reading challenge with fully spelled words. Present a complete word spelled with letter tiles and prompt students to segment the word into individual letter sounds or onset-rime units, physically separating the tiles to demonstrate their analysis. Encourage them to repeat the sounds or sound units and then blend the parts to identify the word.

Developing Word Fluency. End with a Quick Write/Quick Read to develop spelling and reading fluency. Dictate words from the word family and encourage students to spell them quickly on dry-ease boards. Once students have spelled the dictated words, challenge them to read each word several times, varying the word order.

To conclude the lesson, return the target word to its original context and read the sentence together, once again demonstrating its use in a meaningful context. Most important, communicate an expectation for word use. The end of the word-study session signals the beginning of transfer opportunities, so foster enthusiasm for locating, applying, and sharing the words from the lesson, supporting students' intrinsic motivation for word learning.

Implications

An adapted interactive writing intervention provides a flexible framework for differentiated, responsive literacy instruction; however, the program's effectiveness rests on the professional expertise of the teacher implementing it. Knowledgeable, analytic teachers make data-based instructional decisions that build on learners' strengths and develop their areas for growth. They continually analyze students' performances, adapting instruction as needed to maximize their engagement and learning.

In reality, teachers may lack the literacy knowledge, pedagogical skills, or professional dispositions to assume responsibility for these complex decisions, suggesting a need to focus professional development and resources on building teacher capacity (Darling-Hammond, 1996). Facing heightened accountability, teachers must be prepared to collect and analyze data, design developmentally appropriate instruction, monitor progress, and, when necessary, intervene with supplemental instruction (Richards, Pavri, Golez, Canges, & Murphy, 2007). To achieve this level of expertise, school systems must commit to high-quality differentiated professional development and provide sustained support for continual growth, preparing proactive, responsive teachers for the early literacy classroom.

REFERENCES

Adams, M.J., Foorman, B.R., Lundberg, I., & Beeler, T. (1998). *Phonemic awareness in young children: A classroom curriculum*. Baltimore: Paul H. Brookes.

Ball, E.W., & Blachman, B.A. (1991). Does phoneme awareness training in kindergarten make a difference in early word recognition and developmental spelling? *Reading Research Quarterly*, 26(1), 49–68. doi:10.1598/RRQ.26.1.3

Block, C.C., Hurt, N., & Oakar, M. (2002). The expertise of literacy teachers: A continuum from preschool to grade five. *Reading Research Quarterly*, 37(2), 178–206. doi:10.1598/RRQ.37.2.4

Burns, J.M., & Richgels, D.J. (1989). An investigation of task requirements associated with the invented spellings of 4-year-olds with above average intelligence. *Journal of Reading Behavior*, 21(1), 1–14.

Button, K., Johnson, M.J., & Furgerson, P. (1996). Interactive writing in a primary classroom. *The Reading Teacher*, 49(6), 446–454.

Byrne, B., & Fielding-Barnsley, R. (1995). Evaluation of a program to teach phonemic awareness to young children: A 2- and 3-year follow-up and a new preschool trial. *Journal of Educational Psychology*, 87(3), 488–503. doi:10.1037/0022-0663.87.3.488

Byrne, B., Fielding-Barnsley, R., & Ashley, L. (2000). Effects of preschool phoneme identity training after six years: Outcome level distinguished from rate of response. *Journal of Educational Psychology*, 92(4), 659–667. doi:10.1037/0022-0663.92.4.659

Calfee, R. (1998). Phonics and phonemes: Learning to decode and spell in a literature-based program. In J.L. Metsala & L.C. Ehri (Eds.), *Word recognition in beginning literacy* (pp. 315–340). Mahwah, NJ: Erlbaum.

Chomsky, C. (1971). Write first, read later. *Childhood Education, 47*(6), 296–299.

Chomsky, C. (1979). Approaching reading through invented spelling. In L.B. Resnick & P.L. Weaver (Eds.), *The theory and practice of early reading* (Vol. 2., pp. 43–65). Hillsdale, NJ: Erlbaum.

Christensen, C.A., & Bowey, J.A. (2005). The efficacy of orthographic rime, grapheme-phoneme correspondence, and implicit phonics approaches to teaching decoding skills. *Scientific Studies of Reading, 9*(4), 327–349. doi:10.1207/s1532799xssr0904_1

Clarke, L.K. (1988). Invented versus traditional spelling in first graders' writings: Effects on learning to spell and read. *Research in the Teaching of English, 22*(3), 281–309.

Cohen, J. (1988). *Statistical power analysis for the behavioral sciences* (2nd ed.). Hillsdale, NJ: Erlbaum.

Craig, S.A. (2003). The effects of an adapted interactive writing intervention on kindergarten children's phonological awareness, spelling, and early reading development. *Reading Research Quarterly, 38*(4), 438–440. doi:10.1598/RRQ.38.4.1

Craig, S.A. (2006). The effects of an adapted interactive writing intervention on kindergarten children's phonological awareness, spelling, and early reading development: A contextualized approach to instruction. *Journal of Educational Psychology, 98*(4), 714–731. doi:10.1037/0022-0663.98.4.714

Dahl, K.L., Scharer, P.L., Lawson, L.L., & Grogan, P.R. (1999). Phonics instruction and student achievement in whole language first-grade classrooms. *Reading Research Quarterly, 34*(3), 312–341. doi:10.1598/RRQ.34.3.4

Darling-Hammond, L. (1996). What matters most: A competent teacher for every child. *Phi Delta Kappan, 78*(3), 193–200.

Ehri, L.C. (1995). Phases of development in learning to read words by sight. *Journal of Research in Reading, 18*(2), 116–125. doi:10.1111/j.1467-9817.1995.tb00077.x

Ehri, L.C. (1998). Grapheme-phoneme knowledge is essential for learning to read words in English. In J.L. Metsala & L.C. Ehri (Eds.), *Word recognition in beginning literacy* (pp. 3–40). Mahwah, NJ: Erlbaum.

Ehri, L.C. (2005). Learning to read words: Theory, findings, and issues. *Scientific Studies of Reading, 9*(2), 167–188. doi:10.1207/s1532799xssr0902_4

Ehri, L.C., & Robbins, C. (1992). Beginners need some decoding skill to read words by analogy. *Reading Research Quarterly, 27*(1), 13–26. doi:10.2307/747831

Ehri, L.C., & Wilce, L.S. (1987). Does learning to spell help beginners learn to read words? *Reading Research Quarterly, 22*(1), 47–65. doi:10.2307/747720

Fountas, I.C., & Pinnell, G.S. (1996). *Guided reading: Good first teaching for all children.* Portsmouth, NH: Heinemann.

Frith, U. (1985). Beneath the surface of developmental dyslexia. In K.E. Patterson, J.C. Marshall, & M. Coltheart (Eds.), *Surface dyslexia: Neuropsychological and cognitive studies of phonological reading* (pp. 301–330). London: Erlbaum.

Fry, E.B. (1998). Teaching reading: The most common phonograms. *The Reading Teacher, 51*(7), 620–622.

Gersten, R., Compton, D., Connor, C.M., Dimino, J., Santoro, L., Linan-Thompson, S., et al. (2008). *Assisting students struggling with reading: Response to Intervention and multi-tier intervention in the primary grades. A practice guide* (NCEE 2009-4045). Washington, DC: U.S. Department of Education. Retrieved February 4, 2010, from ies.ed.gov/ncee/wwc/pdf/practiceguides/rti_reading_pg_021809.pdf

Griffith, P.L. (1991). Phonemic awareness helps first graders invent spellings and third graders remember correct spellings. *Journal of Reading Behavior, 23*(2), 215–233.

Hall, K., & Harding, A. (2003). A systematic review of effective literacy teaching in the 4 to 14 age range of mainstream schooling. London: EPPI-Centre, Social Science Research Unit, Institute of Education, University of London. Retrieved February 4, 2010, from eppi.ioe.ac

.uk/EPPIWebContent/reel/review_groups/TTA/English/English_2003review.pdf

Holdaway, D. (1979). *The foundations of literacy.* Portsmouth, NH: Heinemann.

Howard, M. (2009). *RTI from all sides: What every teacher needs to know.* Portsmouth, NH: Heinemann.

Iaquinta, A. (2006). Guided reading: A research-based response to the challenges of early reading instruction. *Early Childhood Education Journal, 33*(6), 413–418. doi:10.1007/s10643-006-0074-2

Juel, C., Griffith, P.L., & Gough, P.B. (1985). Reading and spelling strategies of first-grade children. In J.A. Niles & R.V. Lalik (Eds.), *Issues in literacy: A research perspective* (34th yearbook of the National Reading Conference; pp. 306–309). Rochester, NY: National Reading Conference.

Lyon, G.R., Fletcher, J.M., Fuchs, L., & Chhabra, V. (2006). Learning disabilities. In E. Mash & R. Barkley (Eds.), *Treatment of childhood disorders* (3rd ed., pp. 512–591). New York: Guilford.

Mariage, T.V. (2001). Features of an interactive writing discourse: Conversational involvement, conventional knowledge, and internalization in morning message. *Journal of Learning Disabilities, 34*(2), 172–206. doi:10.1177/002221940103400206

Mathes, P.G., Denton, C.A., Fletcher, J.M., Anthony, J.L., Francis, D.J., & Schatschneider, C. (2005). The effects of theoretically different instruction and student characteristics on the skills of struggling readers. *Reading Research Quarterly, 40*(2), 148–182. doi:10.1598/RRQ.40.2.2

McCandliss, B., Beck, I.L., Sandak, R., & Perfetti, C. (2003). Focusing attention on decoding for children with poor reading skills: Design and preliminary tests of the word building intervention. *Scientific Studies of Reading, 7*(1), 75–104. doi:10.1207/S1532799XSSR0701_05

McCarrier, A., Pinnell, G.S., & Fountas, I. (2000). *Interactive writing: How language & literacy come together, K–2.* Portsmouth, NH: Heinemann.

McGuinness, D., McGuinness, C., & Donohue, J. (1995). Phonological training and the alphabetic principle: Evidence for reciprocal causality. *Reading Research Quarterly, 30*(4), 830–852. doi:10.2307/748200

National Institute of Child Health and Human Development. (2000). *Report of the National Reading Panel. Teaching children to read: An evidence-based assessment of the scientific research literature on reading and its implications for reading instruction* (NIH Publication No. 00-4769). Washington, DC: U.S. Government Printing Office.

Ouellette, G., & Sénéchal, M. (2008). Pathways to literacy: A study of invented spelling and its role in learning to read. *Child Development, 79*(4), 899–913. doi:10.1111/j.1467-8624.2008.01166.x

Perfetti, C.A., Beck, I.L., Bell, L.C., & Hughes, C. (1987). Phonemic knowledge and learning to read are reciprocal: A longitudinal study of first grade children. *Merrill-Palmer Quarterly, 33*(3), 283–319.

Pinnell, G.S., & McCarrier, A. (1994). Interactive writing: A transition tool for assisting children in learning to read and write. In E. Hiebert & B. Taylor (Eds.), *Getting reading right from the start: Effective early literacy interventions* (pp. 149–170). Needham, MA: Allyn & Bacon.

Pressley, M., Wharton-McDonald, R., Allington, R., Block, C., Morrow, L., Tracey, D., et al. (1998). *The nature of effective first-grade literacy instruction* (Report Series 11007). Albany: University of Albany, State University of New York, National Research Center on English Learning & Achievement.

Read, C. (1975). *Children's categorization of speech sound in English.* Urbana, IL: National Council of Teachers of English.

Richards, C., Pavri, S., Golez, F., Canges, R., & Murphy, J. (2007). Response to Intervention: Building the capacity of teachers to serve students with learning difficulties. *Issues in Teacher Education, 16*(2), 55–64.

Rieben, L., Ntamakiliro, L., Gontier, B., & Fayol, M. (2005). Effects of various early writing practices on reading and spelling. *Scientific Studies of Reading, 9*(2), 145–166. doi:10.1207/s1532799xssr0902_3

Scammacca, N., Vaughn, S., Roberts, G., Wanzek, J., & Torgesen, J.K. (2007). *Extensive reading interventions in grades K–3: From research to practice.* Portsmouth, NH: RMC Research.

Share, D.L., Jorm, A.F., Maclean, R., & Matthews, R. (1984). Sources of individual differences in reading achievement. *Journal of Educational Psychology, 76*(6), 1309–1324. doi:10.1037/0022-0663.76.6.1309

Snow, C.E., Griffin, P., & Burns, M.S. (2005). *Knowledge to support the teaching of reading: Preparing teachers for a changing world.* San Francisco: Jossey-Bass.

Stahl, S.A., & Murray, B.A. (1994). Defining phonological awareness and its relationship to early reading. *Journal of Educational*

Psychology, 86(2), 221–234. doi:10.1037/0022-0663.86.2.221

Tangel, D.M., & Blachman, B.A. (1992). Effect of phoneme awareness instruction on kindergarten children's invented spelling. *Journal of Reading Behavior, 24*(2), 233–261.

Treiman, R. (1998). Why spelling? The benefits of incorporating spelling into beginning reading instruction. In J.L. Metsala & L.C. Ehri (Eds.), *Word recognition in beginning literacy* (pp. 289–313). Mahwah, NJ: Erlbaum.

Uhry, J.K., & Shepherd, M.J. (1993). Segmentation/spelling instruction as part of a first-grade reading program: Effects on several measures of reading. *Reading Research Quarterly, 28*(3), 218–233. doi:10.2307/747995

Wray, D., Medwell, J., Fox, R., & Poulson, L. (2000). The teaching practices of effective teachers of literacy. *Educational Review, 52*(1), 75–84. doi:10.1080/00131910097432

LITERATURE CITED

Blanchard, P., & Suhr, J. (2003). *There was a mouse.* Katonah, NY: Richard C. Owen.

Hardin, S. (1997). *No dogs allowed.* Katonah, NY: Richard C. Owen.

CHAPTER 12

Closing the Gaps: Literacy for the Hardest-to-Teach

Gwenneth Phillips and Pauline Smith

This short report gives an overview of the national research project, "Achieving literacy for the hardest-to-teach". It outlines the aims and some important aspects and outcomes of the project. These, together with analysis and discussion, are elaborated in the major report, *A Third Chance to Learn*.

We now know that:

- the hardest-to-teach can achieve
- ways have been developed that can get them back to function with their same-aged peers
- getting what has been achieved into practice (including training for teachers) is a matter of urgency.

The project dealt with some complex processes which are not readily simplified without the possibility of misinterpretation. However, we believe that the findings of the project, which are summarised in this abridged version, are exciting and worthy of closer examination.

Our grateful thanks go to all those who resourced the project in various ways, and especially to the teachers who worked so valiantly to help bring about successful outcomes for hardest-to-teach children.

We now have an achievable challenge for the future.

RTI in Literacy—Responsive and Comprehensive, edited by Peter H. Johnston, published by the International Reading Association. This chapter reprinted from Phillips, G., & Smith, P. (1997). *Closing the Gaps: Literacy for the Hardest-to-Teach*. Wellington: New Zealand Council for Educational Research.

Introducing the Project

Background

Teaching children to read and write is a major task for teachers during the first years of formal schooling. New Zealand has quality classroom programmes to teach reading, and these can be supplemented by Reading Recovery, which provides an intensive one-to-one boost for children who fall below the average range during their first year at school. Studies in this country have demonstrated the efficiency and effectiveness of this two-pronged effort.[2] Fully implemented, the two-pronged approach could enable most—98–99%—of the approximately 53,000 children who start school each year to be well under way with reading and writing before the age of seven.

The success of the second change Reading Recovery programme has demonstrated that most of the lowest achieving children in reading and writing after one year at school can be helped to speed up their progress and catch up with their classmates.[3] However, there remains a small percentage of children—less than 2%, or approximately 1000 each year—who are identified as needing more help than the two prongs can offer. These children, the "hardest-to-teach", need a third chance to learn. They come from a wide range of areas and ethnic and social groups.

Research shows that very few of them receive specialist help in reading and writing.[4] Without effective, specialised help, they are doomed to school failure, illiteracy, and severely limited life chances. Some view which may prevent them from receiving extra tuition are that "these children":

- have already had their share of extra help, and are taking scarce resources away from other needy children who would benefit more;

- are developmentally delayed, and cannot be expected to achieve accelerated progress which would enable them to catch up with their peers;

- have such peculiar problems and needs that they are not able to learn, as others do, through daily reading and writing programmes;

- are unable to read and write at the level of their classmates because they have language and/or cognitive deficiencies, which no amount or type of extra help can remedy.

These commonly held views about hardest-to-teach children imply that the problem lies with the child, not with the quality of instruction.

The Aims of the Project

This project was based on a different assumption: that if these hardest-to-teach children had not yet learned how to read and write, it was because we, the educators, had not yet learned how to teach them. The main aim was to develop new ways of working which would enable these clearly identified children to catch up to their peers before the age of eight.

More precisely, the project set out to answer the following questions:

1. Through a process of colleague interaction and joint problem-solving, can more refined ways of observing children's reading behaviour, more adaptive teaching responses, and more detailed ways of recording teacher-child behaviour be developed, in order to guide more effective teaching practice?

2. In the context of developing these new ways of working:

   • Do the planned interventions result in more rapid progress for hardest-to-teach children?

   In particular, does colleague interaction, under the guidance of the researchers, make a difference to the progress of individual children? Is this effect enhanced as the new ways of working develop?

   • What proportion of recently referred, most needy hardest-to-teach children can make accelerated progress, and can be returned able to function within the average range for their age group?

The Teachers

Two teams of teachers, 8 in all, were recruited from different locations. As a group, they had a wide range of professional qualifications and experience. Five had degrees, including 2 who had MAs in reading difficulties, and 3 had completed university or Advanced Studies for Teachers papers within the preceding five years. Three had trained and worked as Reading Recovery teachers within the last 10 years. All had some experience as a Resource Teacher of Reading or reading specialist, and were teaching children with difficulties before the project began.

These teachers incorporated the project children into their full-time workload. The aim was to work with each child for a half an hour, once a day, five days a week. Travelling to each child's school (often in their lunch and tea breaks), the teachers worked in conditions varying from a congenial, quiet space which was always available, to a passageway, sickbay, staffroom, or cluttered resource room which might suddenly be required for another purpose.

The Children

In total, 35 children were involved. They entered the project at different times. They were all recently referred from Reading Recovery, and had been identified as needing long-term specialised tuition. On average they were aged 6 years 11 months when they entered, and were reading at the beginning of Yellow level on the Ready to Read series (Reading Recovery level 6). They were the lowest achieving hardest-to-teach children in each teacher's catchment area.

Fifteen were girls, and 20 were boys. They came from differing socioeconomic backgrounds, and a range of ethnic groups: 14 were Maori, 9 were Pacific Island children, 7 were Pakeha, 2 were from other ethnic groups, and 3 were of mixed ethnicity with no stated preference.

Of the 21 who had learned English as their first language, 20 used only English at home. Thirteen had first learned another language, and 6 used only this at home, while 8 were living in families where both English and another language were used. During the project, each teacher identified one child who was making the slowest progress. These children were called the *very* hardest-to-teach.

Each child was matched with a child of the same age (plus or minus 3 months) who was making average progress in their own school and reading at an appropriate level for their chronological age. Most 7-year-olds in the New Zealand system can read books at the end of the Blue level or beginning of the Purple level on the Ready to Read series (Reading Recovery levels 18 to 19).

Transfer

In order for a child to be transferred out of the project, their achievements had to be at least comparable with that of their matched peer. This was measured by comparing the two children's achievements in:

- processing passages of previously seen and unseen text
- reading and writing words and sentences
- taking part in regular group instruction.

Some Outcomes

Given the children's learning histories, the outcomes of the project were surprising.

Within the lifetime of the project, 24 children completed their programmes. Nineteen of these children (79.2%) were able to transfer out of the project and read and write in a group with their matched peer.

Sixteen children achieved this within an average time of 20.4 lesson weeks (see Table 1). On average, their book level at transfer (Reading Recovery level 20.8) corresponded to the beginning of the Dark Yellow level on the Ready to Read series. Two others took an average of 34 lesson weeks to reach their target transfer levels. One other child transferred, but his exact time in the programme was unclear.

A further 11 children did not complete 20 lesson weeks of instruction because they entered the project at a later stage, or they left, or their teacher left.

Eight of these children also met their acceleration rates. On average, these children had 13.3 lesson weeks of instruction. Had the project continued, these 8 children would also have been transferred successfully within 20 lesson weeks, and before they reached the age of 8.

Three of those who did not complete their programmes, and 5 of those who did—a total of 8 children—did not transfer. All made substantial gains, but they did not or would not have reached a level corresponding to that of their peers by the age of 8. Five of them were identified as the *very* hardest-to-teach. It was demonstrated during the project that particular factors adversely influenced their progress.

Children from different ethnic and language backgrounds were successful.[5] Of the 14 Maori children who entered the project, 12 (85.7%) either transferred

Table 1. Average Scores for Children Transferred in 20.4 Lesson Weeks and Matched Peers (*n* = 16)

Group	Age	Reading Recovery Text Levels*	Burt Word Test	Salford Sentence Reading Test	Peters Spelling
Transferred	7y 6m	20.8	28.1	7y 0m	14.4
Matched peers	7y 6m	20.2	27.9	7y 1m	16.1

*Reading Recovery book level 20 corresponds to the end of the Purple level on the Ready to Read series.

back to their classroom age group, or met their target acceleration rates. This was also the case for 10 (76.9%) of the 13 children from non-English speaking backgrounds.

Writing was not the main focus of the project. However, children also made progress in writing.[6] This included an increase in control over writing vocabulary. Many children achieved rates of near one new word learned per lesson.

The project outcomes also showed that teachers can help the majority of hardest-to-teach children to accelerate their progress immediately, without a long getting-to-know-you period.

The following sections outline how these outcomes were achieved, some of the factors affecting children's progress, the need for training, and how classroom teachers could help to support children engaged in "a third chance to learn".

How These Outcomes Were Achieved

Assumptions

The ways of working that emerged in this project were underpinned by the following assumptions about the process of learning to read:

- Children are *active participants* in their own learning.

- Reading and writing are message-gaining, *problem-solving* activities which involve *self-regulation.*

- Learning "what is relevant" and how to use it is the task to be learnt. This involves children learning the *relevance* of their own language systems, their own life experiences and their own understandings of print.

- What is relevant is embedded in the interactions which take place between the learner and someone who already knows what the task is about. This means that interactions between the teacher and the child *must focus* on the task to be learnt.

- Learning itself is an interactive process in which the *language of instruction* plays a crucial role.

Given these basic understandings, it is clear that the key to improving learning opportunities for hardest-to-teach children is to improve the interactions between them and their teachers as they share in literacy tasks.

The nature of these interactions changes over time. As the learner takes more control, the teacher withdraws her support. For the duration of this project, we focused our attention on the interactions that took place between teacher and child at points of critical behaviour.

Critical Behaviour

Critical behaviour was defined as behaviour that could be observed when a child:

- read or wrote text *correctly*
- made *undetected* errors
- knew they were *at a difficulty*.

Children who experienced the greatest obstacles to learning needed help to respond appropriately in each of these areas.

For example, children very frequently had to be alerted to the fact that *they had made an error*. Then they required help to find the error. If they were to learn how to regulate their own behaviour, they needed to learn how to do these two things before they could correct a mistake.

They also needed help to learn how to solve problems, when they knew they were *at a difficulty*. This involved learning how to search for relevant information, and how to integrate all sources of information in a flexible way.

Our job as teachers was to help them self-monitor, read accurately, and respond to the message. If the children were to be successful, we had to become expert at recognising critical behaviour whenever it occurred.

The Operational Guide

Basing our work on the assumptions and understandings outlined above, we, as researchers, gradually developed an Operational Guide.[1] We drew on our own experience, as well as the available knowledge in the field and in the literature.

This guide was designed to support and refine teaching practice. It consisted of four interrelated parts: observation, expectations for the child, a skeleton of powerful prompts, and a framework for the teacher. These four parts supported, and were held together by a process of teacher self-monitoring.

Updating these four components involved the teachers in very close observation, detailed daily on-the-run recording, clinical analysis of the child's

An Operational Guide for Teacher-Child Interaction

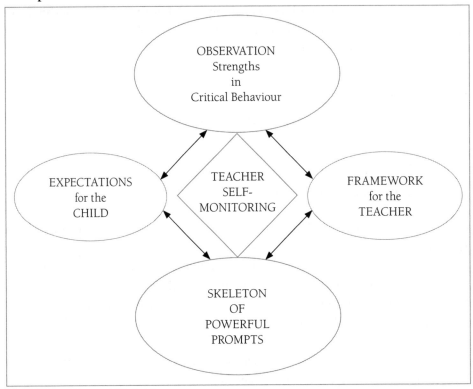

responding, and careful, articulated planning ahead of time as to how they would respond to each child when critical behaviour occurred.

Observation. Observation of reading and writing behaviour began when the child entered the project. Formal observation at entry was supplemented with a period of "extended observation". Observation then became an integral part of lessons on a daily and weekly basis.

This process was too complex, and the behaviour was too fleeting, to be held in the teacher's head. She therefore wrote down and updated a careful analysis of each child's strengths and problems in reading and writing. She captured her daily observations on Running Records and lesson plans.

Marie Clay stresses how important it is not to "overlook important behaviours when they occur, or to misinterpret them, or to deny their existence" (Clay 1991, p. 156). Faulty observation will result in faulty expectations.

Expectations for the Child. After formally observing the child, the teacher wrote expectations based on the child's strengths and problems. These stated what she expected each child to achieve, in both the short and the long term.

This task was new to all the teachers involved. They discussed and workshopped how to use their knowledge of the child's limited strengths as a basis for writing their expectations. They were encouraged to update these regularly as the child's programme evolved.

Skeleton of Powerful Prompts. The researchers sifted "prompts" from the literature. These prompts provided a range of responses for teachers to use selectively when critical behaviour occurred: when the child read correctly, made an undetected error, or was at a difficulty.

These prompts were listed and grouped according to how they functioned in terms of the reading task: to confirm correct reading, or to help the child find the error, fix the error, or solve the difficulty *for themselves*. The prompts within each functional group were ranked according to the amount of support they offered as the child worked at the reading task.

Using this skeleton of powerful prompts, the teacher then decided which ones to use with each child, according to:

- the function which the prompt had to perform
- the amount of support it had to provide, at that particular time in the child's progress.

Using her knowledge of the child's strengths, her expectations, and her understanding of the task, the teacher selected a prompt which would provide the *minimum* amount of support that the child needed, in order to be successful at the task. The prompt itself provided the bridge between what the child could do for him/herself, and what s/he could not do without that help.

To function effectively, the prompts had to be used consistently. They also had to offer *only* the minimum amount of support which the child required at each point. As the child gained skill and confidence, the teacher selected another prompt which performed the same function, but which offered less support.

Framework for the Teacher. Using a specially designed form, the teacher wrote down the specific prompts she had selected to use with the individual child. These were to be used at points of critical behaviour during the next

FRAMEWORK FOR TEACHING		
Date: _____ Child: _____ Text Level: _____ Teacher: _____	**CORRECT READING**	**WORD WORK**
	AFTER ERROR (how to find)	**WRITING** **Getting a Story** **Known Words** Practice: Extending:
	PROBLEM SOLVING (at difficulty—fixing)	**Solving Unknown Words** Multisyllabic words: Sound analysis: Spelling patterns: Analogy:

lesson. This framework encapsulated the expectations the teacher had for herself and was used to guide her interactions with the child.

Teacher Self-Monitoring

By using an updating the components of the Operational Guide, the teacher was constantly encouraged to redefine the task as the child constructed it. Then, in the light of the child's construction, as inferred from the teacher's observation, she had to change her expectations in order to build in the child's new understandings. She also had to change her own responses, in order to bring about further changes in behaviour.

This process was called "teacher self-monitoring". It involved the teacher in a constant process of monitoring her use of the components of the Guide, and her own behaviour.

In this way, the Operational Guide provided the basis for self-sustaining teaching practice.

Formal Teacher Self-Monitoring. The fragile strengths of these hardest-to-teach children called for teacher responses to be more finely tuned, more closely related to specifically defined reading behaviour, and more consistently delivered than ever before. In other words, precision teaching was required.

Using the components of the Operational Guide, we (the teachers) developed a plan for each child which involved precision teaching. But the key to its effective use and successful tuition was the teacher's self-monitoring. So it was necessary to develop procedures which enabled teachers to formally monitor their own interactions, particularly with the children not making accelerated progress. The aim of these procedures was to help the teachers check that their plans were put into practice.

Teachers tape-recorded specific lessons with their *very* hardest-to-teach children, and analysed their own responses to their child's critical behaviour. They checked what they had planned to do against the recordings showing what they actually did do in practice. Then they had to modify their own behaviour wherever this was necessary.

Teachers became aware of confusions. They commented on how uncomfortable it was for them to listen to their own tapes. They also realised how difficult it was to change their own behaviour. Here are some of the typical responses from the teachers:

> "The taped sessions…were an initial source of devastation which I found hard to listen to at first."

> "I was able to hear areas where I was causing confusion for the child, simply by my inexact questioning and comments."

> "I've been given amazing insight into how a child can be influenced by various questioning techniques and the teacher's attitudes."

> "It has been useful to consider the confusions the teacher's prompts could be creating or reinforcing—overcoming these is the challenge ahead."

These comments by teachers prompted the researchers to make a subsequent analysis of tapes and records. This analysis confirmed that difficulties and confusions did occur in some teacher-child interactions.

Guidelines for Self-Monitoring

The researchers wrote some guidelines for self-monitoring.[1] These were based on the understandings that underpinned the Operational Guide, and their own observation of teacher-child behaviour. These guidelines also began to flesh out the skeleton of powerful prompts. They stated that the teacher must:

1. Clearly understand and focus on the task to be learnt by the child.

2. Act consistently across interactions.

3. Assume that the child is making sense in terms of his/her own understandings.

4. Check that the chosen prompts function as intended.

5. Carefully select places to intervene.

The researchers then untangled some misunderstandings that occurred in tape-recorded lessons. They did this to make these guidelines and the teacher self-monitoring process itself more explicit. The process was complex, and confusions were often hard to untangle.

It is important to stress that the teachers in the project did not have the advantage of this analysis when using these new ways of working. This may have been an important factor in their struggle to interact effectively with their most difficult children. The following examples and the descriptions of interactions are included here with the intention of making the guidelines and the teacher self-monitoring process more explicit, and to guide future practice. The interactions occurred on the run as the teachers were working with their *very* hardest-to-teach children.

Guideline 1: The teacher must clearly understand and have a consistent focus on the task to be learnt by the child.

To help the child find an error, the teacher has a two-fold task. The teacher must alert the child to the fact that an error has been made, and provide sufficient information for *the child* to find the error.

In example 1.1 the teacher's prompt is successful. The child engages appropriately in a task-related search and finds an error. However, because the child's successful response is ignored, the teacher appears *not* to be focused on finding an error—the current task to be learnt.

Example 1.1
Text: The net was fishy. So he jumped in a dishy.

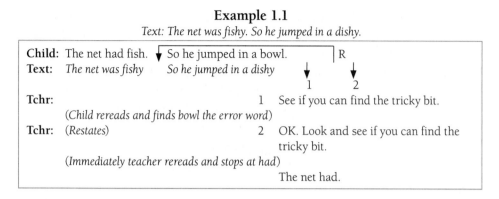

Child:	The net had fish.	So he jumped in a bowl.		R
Text:	*The net was fishy*	*So he jumped in a dishy*		
			1	2
Tchr:			1	See if you can find the tricky bit.
	(Child rereads and finds bowl the error word)			
Tchr:	*(Restates)*		2	OK. Look and see if you can find the tricky bit.
	(Immediately teacher rereads and stops at had)			
				The net had.

There is potential in this example for the child to become confused about the task itself. The child may well ask "What does the teacher want of me? Does she want me to search for and find my error, or to know her word *had*?"

Guideline 2: The teacher must act consistently across interactions.
When the child participates in recurring interactions involving the same words in the same context with the same meaning, learning is made easier and clearer. Inconsistencies have the potential to confuse the learner and make the task more difficult.

The following examples, 2.1, 2.2, and 2.3, come from one teacher's data. They occurred in different lessons. This teacher often used the same "Mmmm" prompt and frequently repeated the child's words. This "Mmmm" prompt and/or repetitions occurred in different contexts for different purposes: sometimes confirming correct reading, and sometimes altering the child to error. However, to the child, there is no difference between reading in which an *undetected* error is made, and correct reading. Thus, from the child's point of view, the context of the teacher's statements remains the same. As interpretations of statements and actions are dependent on the context in which they occur, it is difficult for the child to learn what the teacher means by what she says. The child becomes confused.

In example 2.1, the teacher repeats the child's words, the correct reading of the text, as if to confirm or respond to the story. The repetition of the child's words in this example signals *correct* reading.

Example 2.1
Text: I'm not too little.

Child:	I'm not too little.	
Text:	*I'm not too little.*	
Tchr:		Mmmm, I'm not too little said Baby Bear.

In example 2.2, the repetition of the child's words signals *incorrect* reading, and the child becomes confused. In this story about Julie, the teacher repeats the child's incorrect reading. The teacher is apparently requiring the child to search for the error, but the child interprets the repetition as a confirmation of correct reading, as in example 2.1 above. Now thinking "Jelly likes me" is correct, the child proceeds to use this phrase in the rest of the story wherever "*Just like me*" recurs in the text.

Example 2.2
Text: Just like me. (This is a recurring phrase in the story.)

Child:	Jelly*	likes me	
Text:	*Just*	*like me* ↓	
Tchr:			Jelly likes me?

* "Jelly" appears to be a name—the child's interpretation of Julie.

In example 2.3, the teacher uses "Mmmm" as in example 2.1, where it was used as if to confirm correct reading. But this time it is used to alert the child to an error. The teacher has used the same prompt, but its function has changed. To distinguish the different meanings for "Mmmm", the child has to become attuned to the different tonal qualities of the teacher's voice.

Example 2.3
Text: I frighten kids and I jump.

Child:	I frighten kids and the	I SC	
Text:	*I frighten kids and I*	↓	*jump.*
Tchr:		Mmmm	

In these 3 examples the same prompts, "Mmmm" and repetition, were used to convey different and, at times, opposing meanings. When language is used inconsistently, the child learns to respond appropriately to one meaning, but then is confronted with another. Learning is made more difficult. The changing patterns of interactions also make teacher self-monitoring more difficult.

Guideline 3: The teacher must assume the child is making sense in terms of his/her own understandings.

This involves the teacher in a constant search for the child's point of view, particularly when discrepancies occur between her intentions and the child's understanding. Discrepancies can occur between the child's responses to the teacher's talk or to the task itself, and those expected by the teacher.

In example 3.1, ambiguity in the teacher's requests leads to a discrepancy between the teacher's intention and the child's interpretation of her text-related talk. She is trying to imply "Does that (what you said) sound right?"—a directive to the child to query the syntax of his/her own language. The child's interpretation is clearly different from this. The child has interpreted the teacher's first question as a request to repeat the phrase.

Example 3.1
Text: Bill stood by the door.

Child:	Bill stand standed	by the door. ↓	
Text:	*Bill stood*	*by the door.*	
Tchr:			Sam, would you say Bill standed by the door?
Child:	(*obligingly*)		Bill standed by the door.
Tchr:	(*tries again*)		Is that the way you'd say it?
Child:	(*this time with much expression*)		Bill, standed by the door!

The teacher did not acknowledge the child's interpretation and re-phrased her request. This suggests that the teacher may not have recognised the ambiguity in her prompt, and consequently did not understand the child's interpretation. This time the child focuses on one aspect of processing, expressive reading, and the teacher on another, finding an error. Neither of the teacher's prompts function as the teacher intended, and an opportunity for the child to learn how to self-monitor is lost.

Next, in example 3.2, the teacher's focus appears to be on the text and not the child's processing. The teacher's first prompt is relevant if, and only if, she is concentrating single-mindedly on the error word in the context of the sentence. By intervening at the end of the text sentence with *her* meanings in mind, she interrupts the child's construction of meaning, and does not take into account the meaningfulness of the child's attempt. From the child's point of view, her prompt is irrelevant and confusing. If the teacher had suspended her own mind set and assumed the child was making sense, she would have avoided the disruption and allowed the child an opportunity to notice the error.

Example 3.2
Text: Ali put the monkey in the cage. He locked the cage.

Child:	Ali put the monkey in the cage. He locked the monkey....	
Text:	*Ali put the monkey in the cage. He locked the cage.* ↓	
Tchr:		Can you lock a monkey?
		What can you lock?

Guideline 4: The teacher must check that her prompts function as intended.
The intended function of prompts-to-find is to alert the child to the fact that an error has been made and to help *the child* learn "how to" search for and find the undetected error. To achieve these goals, prompts must be used in specific physical and linguistic settings. The following examples illustrate lost opportunities, because important aspects of the setting were overlooked. Prompts were not used as intended because teachers:

- found the error for the child through the use of their voice and actions, and/or denied the child the opportunity to search and find by intervening too quickly (see examples 4.1, 4.2, and 4.3)
- focused on fixing before finding the error (see example 4.3)
- used them in linguistic settings which robbed them of their power (see example 4.6).

On many occasions, the setting in which prompts occurred after undetected error involved several of these undermining characteristics (see example 4.5).

Teacher Finds Error and Child's Opportunity Is Denied. In example 4.1, by repeating the error word, the teacher finds the error for the child before she asks the question that would engage the child in an active search.

Example 4.1

Text: Bangers and Mash sit on the rug.

Child:	Bangers and Mash sit on the floor.
Text:	*Bangers and Mash sit on the rug.* ↓
Tchr:	Floor? Does that look right?

In example 4.2, the teacher intervenes immediately at the point of error and indicates exactly where the error is by rereading, stopping, and repeating the error (questioningly).

Example 4.2

Text: Mash puts the jam pot on his head.

Child:	Mash puts the jam jar
Text:	*Mash puts the jam pot* ↓
Tchr:	*(intervenes immediately and rereads)* Mash puts the jam jar. Jar?

In example 4.3, the teacher asks a self-monitoring question, but prevents the child searching by pointing up and emphasising the error with her voice and actions.

Example 4.3
Text: Which hole shall I have?

Child:	Which hole will	I have?
Text:	*Which hole shall*	*I have?* ▼
Tchr:		You said, which hole <u>will</u> I have.
		Are you sure?
		Look at this part.

Fixing Before Finding. In example 4.4, the teacher immediately tries to fix the error *before* helping the child to find it.

Example 4.4
Text: Father Bear and Baby Bear went down to the river.

Child:	Father Bear and Baby Bear went by
Text:	*Father Bear and Baby Bear went down* ▼
Tchr:	Where did they go? Did they go down to the river?

Example 4.5 illustrates all the above in combination. This teacher uses a partial self-monitoring prompt. By intervening at the point of error, rereading, stopping, and focusing on the initial letter of the error word (to fix), she effectively prevents the child self-monitoring.

Example 4.5
Text: Dad had a turn.

Child:	Dad had a ride	
Text:	*Dad had a turn.* ▼	
Tchr:		It could be ride
Tchr:	*(Rereads)*	Dad had a tttt…

Prompts Robbed of Power. In example 4.6, the teacher alerts the child to the fact that an error has been made, but does not take into account the meaningfulness of the child's substitution. Her chosen prompt "Does that make sense?" does *not* draw the child's attention to the source of information that would help the child find the error. In this linguistic context, her question is inappropriate. It has the potential to cause cognitive confusion and to hinder the child's processing. This example illustrates the importance of the linguistic context if prompts are to function as intended.

Example 4.6

Text: Bangers has a red hat.

Child:	Bangers hat is a red hat
Text:	*Bangers has—a red hat.* ↓
Tchr:	Does that make sense?

Guideline 5: The teacher must carefully select places to intervene.
The child will not gain equally from all errors. Working at too many is likely to disrupt the child's sense of phrasing and his/her meaning-making. The teacher must "select the clearest, easiest, most memorable examples with which to establish a new response, skill, principle or procedure" (Clay 1993, p. 8).

Some Factors Influencing Progress

Levels of Support for Teachers

As the project developed, interventions or changes were made. These provided the teachers with different levels of support in each phase.[1]

Level 1: Baseline. In this phase, teachers worked in their regular way with no support. This occurred twice: for 6 to 8 weeks at the beginning of the project, and again at the end of the project in the final phase. These periods provided a baseline for comparison.

Level 2: Interactive/Developmental Intervention. Teachers took part in fortnightly colleague interaction sessions. They each taught live lessons behind a one-way screen, while their colleagues observed, analysed and discussed the lesson.

During these sessions we shared our understandings of critical behaviour and focused attention on teaching responses at these points, gradually developing new understandings. Throughout this period we (the researchers) were introducing the components of the Operational Guide.

Level 3: Formal Teacher Self-Monitoring Intervention. As explained earlier, teachers tape-recorded specific lessons with their *very* hardest-to-teach children, in order to check on their own responses. This took place when all the components of the Operational Guide were being used and when our attention was focused on the children making the slowest progress. Teachers continued to participate in interaction sessions.

The research design allowed us to evaluate the effect which these different levels of teacher support had on the children's progress.

Graph 1 shows that compared with the first baseline period, there was an increase in the children's progress when teachers interacted with their colleagues in sessions focusing on critical behaviour. This increase was statistically significant. When teachers received no support, relatively little progress was made by most children.

Graph 1. Progress of Baseline Children (*n* = 8) During Phase 1 and 2

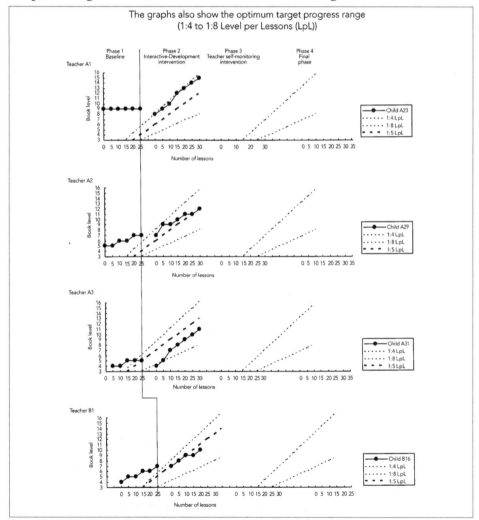

Note. The graphs also show the optimum target progress range (1:4 to 1:8 Level per Lessons (LpL)).

Graph 1. Progress of Baseline Children (*n* = 8) During Phase 1 and 2 (*continued*)

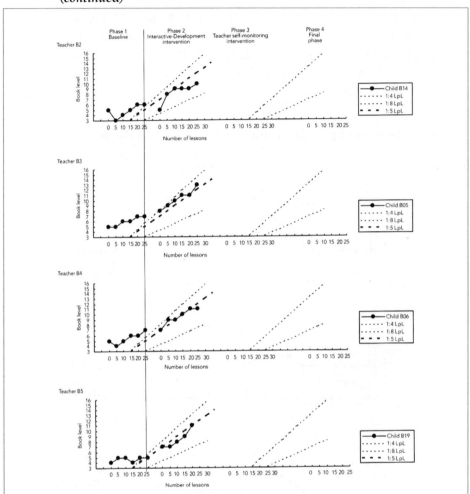

Note. The graphs also show the optimum target progress range (1:4 to 1:8 Level per Lessons (LpL)).

Graph 2 shows that children as a group made relatively slow progress when teachers had no support. The greatest acceleration was achieved when teachers were participating in interaction sessions *and* using all the components of the Operational Guide, *as well as* engaging in formal teacher self-monitoring.

We found that when teachers received this amount of support, all but one of the 9 hardest-to-teach children who entered the project during this phase speeded up their progress to meet their target transfer rate. This suggests that

Graph 2. Mean Book Level Gains Between Lessons 5 and 25 for Children Taught by Teachers Receiving Different Levels of Support

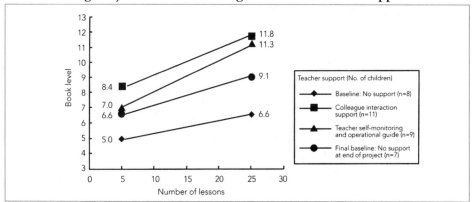

Note. A two-tailed T-test indicated there was a significant group difference ($p < 0.05$) for both colleague interaction support and teacher self-monitoring. There was no significant difference ($p > 0.05$) between the mean entry level of the latter and either baseline or final baseline.

had all children received the advantage of such support, an even greater proportion may have transferred.

Teacher-Dependent Patterns

The levels of acceleration which children achieved also varied between teachers. Graph 3 shows the progress of all children taught by two teachers over the same period of time. Distinct patterns of progress can be seen for *all* children taught by the *same* teacher. The upward acceleration for Teacher A contrasts with the big dip in progress shown in the graph for Teacher B.

Patterns of progress can reflect our expectations, our assumptions or biases in our own teaching. It is possible that one teacher expected children's progress to fall off after the summer vacation whereas the other did not. The teacher whose children showed a big dip in progress commented:

> "Progress slowed following long holiday due to my failure to bring children quickly back to previous levels."

Whatever the cause, such teacher-dependent patterns can:

- influence a child's acceleration
- alert us to re-examine our teaching decisions.

Graph 3. Progress in Book Levels for All Children Taught by Teachers A and B During the Same Period (From the End of 1993 and After Summer Vacation 1994)

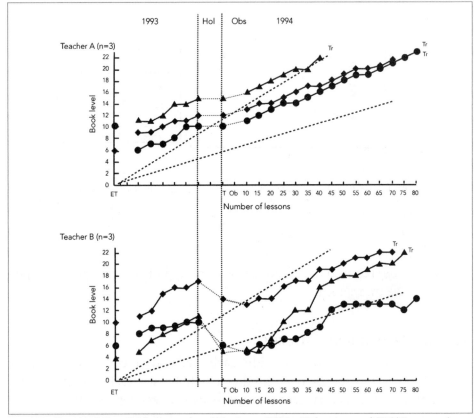

Note. ET = Entry level; Tr = Child was transferred; T = Re-test 1994—Highest text read (90(+)% accuracy);
------ = Target acceleration range (1 text level in 4 lessons to 1 text level in 8 lessons).

Missed Lessons

The children missed, on average, 7 lesson weeks of instruction each. This meant that for some children, their age increased more quickly than their opportunities to learn.

Missed lessons had a marked influence on children's progress. The effect was shown to be negative on both reading and writing. Not only did the child lose chances to practice using fragile strengths, but the teacher was in a constant state of uncertainty as to what was coming under control. This had the potential

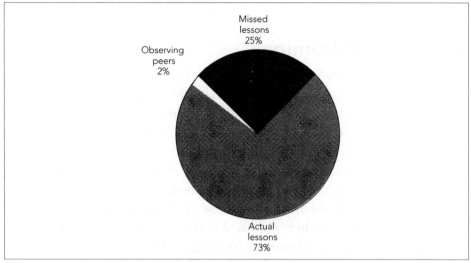

to affect the teacher's ability to choose the appropriate books or prompts to use with the child.

Why Were Lessons Missed?

There were two broad reasons: either the teacher was not available, or the child was not available. These two reasons each accounted for a little over a third of all missed lessons.

Teacher unavailability resulted partly from other work-related commitments. It is important to remember that these teachers had other job commitments while taking part in the project.

As well, the need to travel from school to school, and delays in finding children, or finding teaching space, interfered with the pattern of daily lessons.

Some children missed lessons because they were ill. This is a high-risk age group for childhood illnesses. School activities also contributed to the disturbing feature of missed lessons.

We recommend that the system needs to look very closely indeed at any activities or demands on the teacher or child which prevent such lessons taking place.

When children are regularly missing lessons, it is important that the school be persistent in searching for a unique way to get each child to school. A solution that suits one child and family might not work in another situation.

In the interests of each child's developing literacy, it is very important that we take this issue seriously. We must not put it in the "too-hard" basket.

The Need for Training

Research has shown that teachers tend to work differently with children who are making faster progress than with children who are making slower progress.[7]

The greater the child's confusion, the more likely it is that there will be a gap between the child's and the teacher's understanding of the task. And the greater this gap, the harder it is for the teacher to interpret the child's behaviour and discover the meanings the child is making of the teacher's responses and prompts. In essence, as the child becomes confused, so does the teacher.

During the formal self-monitoring phase of the project, teachers identified and focused on those children who were making the slowest progress. At the end of the project, tapes of lessons with these children were analysed by the researchers, who asked this question:

Did these *very* hardest-to-teach children receive the instruction planned?

The results were as follows:

- The tapes showed 249 undetected errors. Teachers responded with prompts to 237 of these errors (95.2%).

- The majority of teachers did not use the responses they had planned to use, *as* they had planned to use them.

Only 27 of the prompts used (11.4%) were the planned prompts, *and* were used as designed. One teacher often used the words of the prompt, but on every occasion she herself found the undetected error for the child, instead of helping the child to find it. Another teacher frequently moved to fix errors, rather than help the child to find them.

On average, with these *very* hardest-to-teach children, 2 teachers responded as they had planned at a rate of 1 in 4 times, and the other 5 responded as planned at a rate of only 1 in 19 times. The 5 *very* hardest-to-teach children of these last 5 teachers were not transferred.

These *very* hardest-to-teach children did not in fact receive the benefits of teachers' careful planning. The full power of the skeleton of prompts was not realised. Interactions between teachers and these children did not consistently engage the children in clear, task-related opportunities to learn how to monitor their own reading behaviour. Close analysis of the tapes of lessons with these children showed that:

- The teacher's focus often appeared to be on finding the error word for the child, or moving to fix the error, rather than supporting *the child* to find it.
- The instructional interactions between the teachers and these *very* hardest-to-teach children were inconsistent, and therefore potentially confusing.
- The frequency of teacher interventions had the potential to interfere with the child's own sense-making and disrupt his or her sense of phrasing.

The main focus of the project was on helping the children, not on training the teachers. However, the project findings clearly indicate that with the *very* hardest-to-teach children, even the most experienced teachers need training to enable them to make effective use of the Operational Guide, and put their intentions into practice consistently.

How Could Classroom Teachers Help?

The aim of the project's one-to-one tuition was to find out whether or not these hardest-to-teach children could develop a "self-extending system"[8] that would enable them to benefit from classroom instruction in reading and writing. Although they had made some initial moves into literacy, their gains prior to the project were not sufficient to enable them to participate appropriately with their 7-year-old classmates. They were not used to working *successfully* in the classroom.

Therefore, if they were to get maximum benefit from the gains they had achieved through specialised teaching, they had to learn how to function effectively in a group. They had to have *daily* opportunities to use and continue to develop their newly-gained strengths. But how could this be managed in a busy classroom? When children are reading and writing within an age-appropriate range, they do not necessarily receive guided reading instruction every day.

We recommended that as children approached transfer, they should work in two groups, one at their instructional level, and one receiving tuition at a lower level. This arrangement would allow the children to practice their strategies on easy material, and increase their control over processing on instructional material. It would also give the teacher a daily opportunity to observe their progress.

Based on the knowledge that reading and writing are inter-related, especially in the acquisition stages, we also recommended that the children:

- have opportunities to write *every* day.

- listen, on a daily basis, to a mature reader reading more challenging age-appropriate stories (and other texts) aloud. The benefits gained from listening to *and* engaging with the expressive responses of a mature reader are well documented.[9]

Conclusions

The philosophy which guided the research put the onus for getting children underway in literacy on us, the educators. It made educators responsible for finding ways to teach so that children can learn how to read and write. This philosophy, which gave us an unswerving stance for working, was shown to be justified.

This project demonstrated that contrary to previous research findings, expectations, and commonly held beliefs, those children who do not meet Reading Recovery discontinuing criteria can learn how to accelerate their progress and catch up to their same-age peers in a relatively short time.

It also showed that with specialist tuition, lowest-achieving children who come from a range of ethnic groups and a variety of language backgrounds can succeed.

Effective ways for specialist teachers to help these hardest-to-teach children have been developed and refined. Teacher self-monitoring underpins these teaching procedures.

Hardest-to-teach children made the fastest progress when their teachers received multiple and varied levels of support.

This research highlights the necessity for specialised training in order to get specialised teaching. Even for highly experienced teachers, formal teacher self-monitoring proves to be complex and difficult to achieve without it.

The project identifies some factors which can inhibit progress. These include teacher-dependent patterns and missed lessons. These issues need to be addressed as matters of urgency, and not avoided.

The outcomes of this project suggest that by adding this third chance to learn to our already highly effective two-pronged system, it may be possible to get at least 99.5% of all new entrants reading age-appropriate material by the age of 8.

The underlying philosophy, together with the findings of the project, point us forward and give us a vision of what is possible.

REFERENCES

1. For readers who would like more detail and further explanations, a full account of the project can be found in:

Phillips, G.E., and Smith, P.E. (1997). *A third chance to learn. The development and evaluation of specialist interventions for young children experiencing the greatest difficulty in learning to read.* Report on the J.R. McKenzie Senior Research Fellowship 1993–1994. Wellington: New Zealand Council for Educational Research.

2. The coverage of Reading Recovery in New Zealand is collated from annual returns to the Ministry of Education. See:

Kerslake, J. (1994). A summary of the 1993 data on reading recovery. *The Research Bulletin,* 3 (May), 68–72. Wellington: Ministry of Education.

Clay, M.M. (1990). The reading recovery programme, 1984–88: Coverage, outcomes and education board district figures. *New Zealand Journal of Educational Studies, 25*(1), 61–70.

3. Some studies reporting the effectiveness of Reading Recovery are found in:

Clay, M.M. (1993). *Reading recovery: A guidebook for teachers in training.* Auckland: Heinemann Education.

Clay, M.M. (1990). The reading recovery programme, 1984–88: Coverage, outcomes and education board district figures. *New Zealand Journal of Educational Studies, 25*(1), 61–70.

4. Outcomes for children who are referred for special help from Reading Recovery are reported in:

Clay, M.M., and Tuck, B. (1991). *A study of reading recovery subgroups: Including outcomes for children who did not satisfy discontinuing criteria.* Auckland: University of Auckland.

Dewar, S. (1994). Children taught by resource teachers of reading: A summary of the 1993 data. *The Research Bulletin,* 4 (Nov), 59–64.

5. Further information relating to successful outcomes for young non-English speaking children and those from non-Pakeha backgrounds experiencing difficulties in learning to read and write can be found in:

Clay, M.M., and Watson, B. (1982). *The success of Maori children in the reading recovery programme.* Report to the Director of Research. Wellington: Department of Education.

Smith, P.E. (1994). Reading recovery and children with English as a second language. *New Zealand Journal of Educational Studies, 29*(2), 141–159.

6. Discussion of research which shows the inter-relatedness of reading and writing occurs in:

Clay, M.M. (1993). *An observation survey of early literacy achievement.* Auckland: Heinemann Education.

7. Research which shows that teacher respond differently to high and low progress children can be found in:

Allington, R.L. (1980). Teacher interruption behaviors during primary-grade oral reading. *Journal of Educational Psychology,* 72 (Jun), 371–77.

8. For discussion of a self-extending system, see:

Clay, M.M. (1991). *Becoming literate: The construction of inner control.* Auckland: Heinemann Education.

Clay, M.M. (1993). *Reading recovery: A guidebook for teachers in training.* Auckland: Heinemann Education.

9. The benefits of listening to stories read aloud are discussed in:

Elley, W. (1996). The phonic debated revisited. *set 1,* Item 7. Wellington: New Zealand Council for Educational Research. (This provides a list of references.)

McNaughton, S.S. (1995). *Patterns of emergent literacy: Processes of development and transition.* Oxford: Oxford University Press.

Phillips, G.E. (1986). Storyreading to preschool children in their home environment: A descriptive analysis. Unpublished M.A. thesis, University of Auckland. (In chapter 1 the range of benefits is reviewed.).

Professional Development and Teacher Expertise

IDEA insists on "highly qualified teachers." This is based on the relatively unsurprising fact that teacher expertise is the most important factor in improving students' learning (e.g., Darling-Hammond & McLaughlin, 1999). One aspect of teacher expertise is the ability to notice and respond to what students can and cannot do. A teacher who fails to notice that a student is not yet able to analyze speech into phonemes will not know to teach that skill. A teacher who does not recognize that a student already has that skill might teach it anyway, particularly if using a scripted program, wasting precious learning time. Similarly, a lack of expertise can lead to inappropriate instructional conclusions. For example, two teachers might both notice that a student makes many reading errors. The less expert teacher is likely to attribute it to the student's inability rather than to the text difficulty. The more expert teacher's conclusion would lead to helping the student find more productive reading material so that the student could become more in control of his or her learning.

This is the heart of assessment—what teachers notice and respond to during the literate engagements in the classroom. What teachers notice and the sense they make of it influence the instruction they provide, unless their interactions are scripted and thus uninfluenced by students' current learning and behavior. Mary K. Lose provides a strong logic for teacher expertise in this section's opening chapter, Chapter 13, "A Child's Response to Intervention Requires a Responsive Teacher of Reading." She views teachers as adaptive experts, a theme that is consistent throughout the research in this section (indeed, throughout the book).

The significance of teacher expertise and its development for RTI is evident in a number of ways. For example, teachers whose descriptions of their students' literacy development are brief and lack detail are more likely to refer students for learning disability evaluation than are teachers whose descriptions are more detailed (Broikou, 1992). In other words, teachers who do not understand the children they are teaching are more likely to decide that a child is learning disabled (LD). Furthermore, research consistently shows that different teachers are more or less effective at accelerating students' literacy. The students who are not successfully accelerated in interventions are clustered with particular teachers (Phillips & Smith, 1997; Scanlon, in press).

On the positive side, as we see with Donna M. Scanlon, Lynn M. Gelzheiser, Frank R. Vellutino, Christopher Schatschneider, and Joan M. Sweeney's work in Chapter 14, "Reducing the Incidence of Early Reading Difficulties: Professional Development for Classroom Teachers Versus Direct Interventions for Children," effective interventions can be provided by specially trained research personnel— or, equally effectively, by providing classroom teachers with similar professional development. In other words, evidence suggests that teacher expertise and institutional structures that support the development of that expertise are central to reducing the number of children who become LD. The research presented in this chapter emphasizes the significance of teacher expertise and the tools and structures for developing it.

A well-trained coach also helps to constantly improve teaching expertise. A productive coach needs to teach students part of the time to maintain skill and respect. In this context, teacher and coach not only discuss data but actually take turns doing the teaching to explore alternative practices. "Consulting" is a very different process from the coaching that happens in successful instructional interventions for students experiencing the most difficulty learning to become literate (Phillips & Smith, 1997; see also Dorn & Schubert's Chapter 17 in this volume). Coaching is not simply monitoring for "fidelity," which results in the teacher adapting less to individual students and ultimately becoming less of an adaptive expert. It requires skill beyond, and including, that of the most skilled classroom teacher, as Debra S. Peterson, Barbara M. Taylor, Bobbie Burnham, and Rynell Schock show us in Chapter 15, "Reflective Coaching Conversations: A Missing Piece."

Constant improvement of classroom instruction requires ongoing professional development, data on teaching and learning, and a process that makes it possible to use the data productively. We see the importance of learning communities and of relevant, valued data for informing those communities in Chapter 16, "The Learning Schools Model of School Change to Raise Achievement in Reading Comprehension for Culturally and Linguistically Diverse Students in New Zealand" by Stuart McNaughton and Mei Kuin Lai.

The research shows that the expertise required for accelerating learners' literacy development is specifically related to *literacy* teaching and learning. It is not to do with psychometrics, or neurology, or disabilities in general. Instruction for the students experiencing the most difficulty must be the most closely responsive to the student's literacy learning. The following chapters explore the nature of that expertise and how it is developed. One thing is certain: The instruction at the heart of RTI does not come in a can.

REFERENCES

Broikou, K.A. (1992). *Understanding primary grade classroom teachers' special education referral practices.* Unpublished doctoral dissertation, State University of New York at Albany.

Darling-Hammond, L., & McLaughlin, M.W. (1999). Investing in teaching as a learning profession: Policy problems and prospects. In L. Darling-Hammond & G. Sykes (Eds.), *Teaching as the learning profession: Handbook of policy and practice* (pp. 376–411). San Francisco: Jossey-Bass.

Phillips, G., & Smith, P. (1997). *A third chance to learn: The development and evaluation of specialized interventions for young children experiencing difficulty with learning to read* (No. 13227). Wellington: New Zealand Council for Educational Research.

Scanlon, D.M. (in press). Response to Intervention as an assessment approach. In A. McGill-Franzen & R.L. Allington (Eds.), *Handbook of reading disability research.* London: Routledge.

CHAPTER 13

A Child's Response
to Intervention Requires
a Responsive Teacher of Reading

Mary K. Lose

T he revised Individuals with Disabilities Education Act (IDEA) offers U.S. schools confronting rising enrollments of students with learning disabilities (LD) two options for managing this increasing population. The first option is that local education agencies can use as much as 15% of their special education funds to pay for early intervening services (EIS) and to support professional development and literacy instruction. The second option offered by IDEA is Response to Intervention (RTI) that can be used to provide early interventions without labeling students at risk for school failure as learning disabled. RTI encourages early identification and prereferral intervention to determine if a child responds to the intervening instruction. The goal is to limit referrals based on inadequate instruction or limited English proficiency and to reduce the number of children identified for LD services. In order to do this, the lowest performing children must be identified early so that appropriately intensive interventions and tiers of support can be provided within a comprehensive approach to literacy instruction at the first indication of the child's difficulty.

Fundamental Principles

The U.S. Department of Education does not require or endorse any particular model of RTI. State education agencies may establish the criteria for identifying children with specific learning disabilities, but the state criteria must permit local agencies to choose an RTI model. In this column, I will present the

RTI in Literacy—Responsive and Comprehensive, edited by Peter H. Johnston, published by the International Reading Association. This chapter reprinted from Lose, M.K. (2007). A Child's Response to Intervention Requires a Responsive Teacher of Reading. *The Reading Teacher, 61*(3), 276–279.

fundamental principles of an appropriate RTI approach and review the evidence on early literacy interventions as provided by the U.S. Department of Education. The following points that are central to the provision of RTI and EIS within the IDEA are based on those identified by Lose et al. (2007) and are elaborated upon here:

Ensure Early Identification and Early Intervention for All Children Struggling With Literacy Learning. Research has shown that signs of a child's literacy learning difficulties usually surface after one year in school. If schools expect children to meet literacy achievement benchmarks, a child must be identified and intensive interventions provided at the first indication of a difficulty.

Provide a Way to Appropriately Identify Children With LD. Assessments must explore a child's multiple knowledge sources and literacy experiences. Assessments should examine all aspects of a child's control over literacy, including oral language skill; knowledge of letters, words, and sound–letter correspondences; concepts of print; and text reading and writing.

Provide Effective, Intensive, Evidence-Based Early Intervening Services. An intervention must show accelerative learning and steady progress over time on the part of the child or else it has failed. The U.S. Department of Education Institute for Education Sciences identified one-to-one tutoring by qualified tutors in grades 1–3 as meeting the gold standard for effectiveness for the most at-risk learners. Other researchers have documented the importance of individual lessons for the lowest-performing students at the onset of their literacy learning difficulties (Pinnell, Lyons, DeFord, Bryk, & Seltzer, 1994; Snow, Burns, & Griffin, 1998; Vellutino et al., 1996; Wasik & Slavin, 1993).

Ensure Monitoring of Student Progress and Data-Based Documentation for Each Student. Student progress is best monitored by a teacher who is a skilled diagnostician and who also designs and delivers the intervention in response to the child. Assessment information and sensitive observation on the part of the teacher are used to refine teaching decisions in response to changes in the child's control over literacy processing.

Report Annual Yearly Progress, Which Depends on Accelerated Growth of Struggling Readers. Yearly reports of progress ensure that struggling readers will receive interventions that support their accelerative progress regardless of their economic status, race, or ethnicity. Annual reporting also helps schools, systems, and the community monitor the quality of their intervention services for children and advocate for equity in appropriately and responsively serving all their low-performing students.

Provide the Highest Quality of Professional Development for Teachers of Low Achievers. Research has shown that every dollar spent on teachers' professional development yields greater student achievement outcomes than any other expenditure of school dollars (Darling-Hammond, 1996). Because they are the learners most vulnerable to instruction, regardless of the approach to instruction in our schools, the lowest-performing learners need the most skilled teachers (McEneaney, Lose, & Schwartz, 2006).

Create a Multitiered Problem-Solving Team to Support Comprehensive Literacy Efforts. For optimum child learning, all members of the school team—administrators, teachers, and intervention specialists—must acknowledge the range of students' learning abilities and assume responsibility for children's success. Intervention effectiveness may be seriously compromised by fractured approaches to children's learning. Collegial communication within a comprehensive approach to literacy and shared accountability for children by members of the school team can ensure that students' needs are quickly identified and strategies formulated to meet those needs.

Fundamental Principles of a Successful RTI Approach

What principles do we, as teachers of reading, need to keep in mind to ensure that struggling literacy learners will achieve success within the provisions of the IDEA for RTI? Unfortunately, many RTI approaches place emphasis on prescriptive instruction delivered by teachers-as-technicians who focus on what children don't know as the starting point for instruction. Such approaches lack the necessary decision making on the part of teachers to respond effectively to differing challenges posed by individual children (Clay, 2005a). In contrast, I now highlight several fundamental principles that I consider foundational to any successful RTI approach.

A Child, Not a Group, Learns to Read. Anecdotal and research evidence supports the notion that children come "by different paths to common outcomes" in literacy (Clay, 1998). A skilled responsive teacher will observe the different paths taken by individual children and will design instruction that supports their literacy learning progress.

The Only Valid RTI Approach Is One in Which the Child Responds Successfully. The intervention must be appropriately intensive, delivered without delay, and tailored precisely to the individual child. A child who has been provided with the intervention he or she needs will respond successfully, making progress daily and learning how to lift his or her own literacy performance with skilled support from a knowledgeable teacher (Clay, 2001, 2005b). While many children respond quite well to whole-class and small-group instruction, the most struggling literacy learner needs the most intensive instruction delivered individually and tailored precisely to his or her needs.

To Be Successful, the Most Struggling Child Requires the Most Expert Teacher. Teachers, not programs, teach children to read. The child who is challenged by literacy learning requires a knowledgeable teacher who can make moment-by-moment teaching decisions in response to his or her idiosyncratic literacy competencies. The struggling child is likely to be harmed by a one-size-fits-all, prescriptive intervention that fails to acknowledge his or her abilities as a starting point for instruction.

Teacher Expertise Requires High-Quality, Sustained Professional Development. Teaching the lowest-performing learners is difficult. Because no two children ever respond quite the same, teachers of the lowest-performing children must be the most tentative, skilled, and responsive in their interactions with children. Sustained continual professional development is required to continuously develop highly expert teachers (Darling-Hammond, 1996; Darling-Hammond & McLaughlin, 1995).

Given the federal requirement for evidence-based interventions, the most reliable source for teachers, administrators, researchers, and policymakers seeking effective reading interventions is the What Works Clearinghouse (WWC; www.whatworks.ed.gov). Established in 2002 by the U.S. Department of Education's Institute for Education Sciences, the WWC's mission is to provide "a central and trusted source of scientific evidence of what works in education." The WWC provides information on the relative effectiveness of a variety of beginning reading programs in four key domains: alphabetics (phonemic awareness, phonological awareness, letter identification, print awareness, and phonics), reading fluency, comprehension (vocabulary development and reading comprehension), and general reading achievement (a combination of two or more of the previous domains). Ratings are based on the statistical significance of the empirical effect estimate and the quality of the research design generating the effect estimate. They are reported at the following six levels of effects from highest to lowest: "positive effects" (+), "potentially positive effects" (+?), "mixed effects" (±), "no discernable effects" (?), "potentially negative effects" (-?), and "negative effects" (-).

Of the 20 interventions reviewed by the WWC, only one intervention, Reading Recovery, an early intervention and prevention for the lowest-performing, first-grade students, has qualifying research evidence in all four domains. Reading Recovery received the highest ratings of any of the 20 programs with two "positive effects" (+) ratings for alphabetics and general reading achievement and two "potentially positive effects" (+?) ratings for reading fluency and comprehension. Reading Recovery, developed by researcher and developmental psychologist Marie Clay, is implemented as a not-for-profit collaborative among schools and universities (Clay, 2005a, 2005b). Reading Recovery students participate in 30-minute daily lessons in reading and writing activities tailored to their individual needs and delivered one-to-one by a certified Reading Recovery teacher. Reading Recovery teachers initially receive one year of graduate-level coursework and are required to participate in continual professional development each year thereafter to remain certified.

Of the 19 remaining beginning reading programs, only 3 are rated as providing evidence for either "positive effects" (+) or "potentially positive effects" (+?) in, at most, three of the four domains. Out of those programs, only one, Kaplan SpellRead, exhibited a positive (+) rating. The program has one rating of "positive effects" (+) in alphabetics and two ratings of "potentially positive effects" (+?) in fluency and comprehension. According to the developers, Kaplan SpellRead is a literacy program for struggling students in grades 2 and above who are two or more years below grade level in reading, are receiving special education, or are English-language learners. The program is delivered in small groups of five students with one instructor; takes five to nine months to complete; and "consists of 140 lessons implemented in three distinct phases that interweave phonemics, phonetics, and instruction in language-based reading and writing" (www.what works.ed.gov/InterventionReportLinks.asp?iid=373&tid=01&pg=IntRating

.asp). Teachers who implement the program receive five days of instruction, two follow-up workshops, and regular on-site coaching visits from Kaplan K12 staff and a Web-based instructor support system to monitor student progress. The next highest rated programs with potentially positive effects (+?) in alphabetics, fluency, and comprehension are Peer-Assisted Learning Strategies (PALS) and Start Making a Reader Today (SMART).

It is clear that the emphasis today is (as it should be) on evidence-based approaches to early literacy intervention, and we, as teachers, administrators, and policymakers, have a responsibility to children to implement highly rated evidence-based approaches. We all agree that children are the focus of our work, and children who struggle with literacy learning do not deserve unproven programs when we already know what works. As indicated in the title of this column, a child's response to intervention requires a skilled, responsive teacher, and reading professionals already have enough information to make an appropriate, informed, and timely response to the challenges of RTI.

REFERENCES

Clay, M.M. (1998). *By different paths to common outcomes*. York, ME: Stenhouse.

Clay, M.M. (2001). *Change over time in children's literacy development*. Portsmouth, NH: Heinemann.

Clay, M.M. (2005a). *Literacy lessons designed for individuals: Part one: Why? when? and how?* Portsmouth, NH: Heinemann.

Clay, M.M. (2005b). *Literacy lessons designed for individuals: Part two: Teaching procedures*. Portsmouth, NH: Heinemann.

Darling-Hammond, L. (1996). What matters most: A competent teacher for every child. *Phi Delta Kappan, 78*, 193–200.

Darling-Hammond, L., & McLaughlin, M.W. (1995). Policies that support professional development in an era of reform. *Phi Delta Kappan, 76*, 597–604.

Lose, M.K., Schmitt, M.C., Gomez-Bellenge, F.X., Jones, N., Honchell, B., & Askew, B.J. (2007). Reading Recovery and IDEA legislation: Early intervening services (EIS) and response to intervention (RTI). *The Journal of Reading Recovery, 6*(2), 42–47.

McEneaney, J.E., Lose, M.K., & Schwartz, R.M. (2006). A transactional perspective on reading difficulties and Response to Intervention. *Reading Research Quarterly, 41*, 117–128.

Pinnell, G.S., Lyons, C.A., DeFord, D.E., Bryk, A.S., & Seltzer, M. (1994). Comparing instructional models for the literacy education of high-risk first graders. *Reading Research Quarterly, 29*, 8–39.

Snow, C.E., Burns, S., & Griffin, P. (1998). *Preventing reading difficulties in young children*. Washington: DC, National Academy Press.

Vellutino, F.R., Scanlon, D.M., Sipay, E.R., Small, S.G., Pratt, A., Chen, R., et al. (1996). Cognitive profiles of difficult-to-remediate and readily remediated poor readers: Early intervention as a vehicle for distinguishing between cognitive and experiential deficits as basic causes of specific reading disability. *Journal of Educational Psychology, 88*, 601–638.

Wasik, B.A., & Slavin, R.E. (1993). Preventing early reading failure with one-to-one tutoring: A review of five programs. *Reading Research Quarterly, 28*, 178–200.

Reducing the Incidence of Early Reading Difficulties: Professional Development for Classroom Teachers Versus Direct Interventions for Children

Donna M. Scanlon, Lynn M. Gelzheiser, Frank R. Vellutino, Christopher Schatschneider, and Joan M. Sweeney

1. Introduction

The increasing use of Response to Intervention (RTI) for determining whether children qualify as learning disabled is due in large measure to the recognition that instruction plays a major role in determining the learning trajectory of individual children. In fact, it is now widely acknowledged that many students currently identified as learning disabled would not have been identified if instruction had been appropriately targeted and responsive (Clay, 1987; Denton & Mathes, 2003; Lyon, Fletcher, Fuchs, & Chhabra, 2006; Scanlon, Vellutino, Small, Fanuele, & Sweeney, 2005; Vellutino et al., 1996). Further, at least one study has documented a decline in special education classification rate after a tiered approach to interventions, a common RTI model, was implemented (O'Connor, Fulmer, Harty, & Bell, 2005).

Much of the research on RTI focuses heavily on evaluating children's response to instruction while focusing little, if at all, on the instruction itself. Indeed, a major concern in many RTI studies is the incidence of False Positives

RTI in Literacy—Responsive and Comprehensive, edited by Peter H. Johnston, published by the International Reading Association. This chapter reprinted from Scanlon, D.M., Gelzheiser, L.M., Vellutino, F.R., Schatschneider, C., & Sweeney, J.M. (2008). Reducing the Incidence of Early Reading Difficulties: Professional Development for Classroom Teachers Versus Direct Interventions for Children. *Learning and Individual Differences, 18*(3), 346–359.

(i.e., cases where the assessments inaccurately identify a child as potentially learning disabled) and False Negatives (i.e., cases where the assessments inaccurately identify a child as non-learning disabled), both of which raise the important question of what kinds of additional measures can be added to the prediction equations to reduce prediction errors. However, it is widely accepted that student achievement is determined in large part by the characteristics and qualities of instruction. Indeed, a central premise of RTI approaches is the need to insure that learning difficulties are not the result of inadequate instruction (Fuchs & Fuchs, 1998; Fuchs, Fuchs, & Speece, 2002; Vaughn, Linan-Thompson, & Hickman, 2003). Therefore, in this paper, we more fully explore the influence of instruction on children's risk status. We focus, in particular, on classroom instruction as this is the critical first tier in most RTI models. Very little research has addressed either the characteristics of classroom instruction that serve to reduce the incidence of early reading difficulties or the potential effectiveness of Professional Development (PD) for classroom teachers in helping to reduce the incidence of early reading difficulties.

Thus, in this study, we analyzed the effects of PD for classroom teachers on the literacy skills of children who were deemed to be at risk of experiencing difficulties in early reading acquisition and we carefully investigated the characteristics of the instruction they offered both before and after participating in PD. Our design allowed us to investigate major premises of RTI models that are not often evaluated: 1) that the quality of the first tier of intervention (the classroom level) is a major determinant of children's ongoing risk status; and 2) that PD for classroom teachers can effectively reduce the number of at risk children who continue to be at risk at the end of the school year. We also compared the effects of PD alone to the effects of small group intervention provided directly to at risk children and to the combination of both small group intervention and PD for classroom teachers.

Despite the relative lack of attention to the characteristics of classroom instruction in the RTI literature, in the broader education literature there has been growing interest in documenting instructional characteristics and their relationship to student achievement. There is now substantial documentation that variability in student outcomes is more closely associated with "natural" variability among classroom teachers than it is with variability between and among instructional programs (e.g., Bond & Dykstra, 1967; Tivnan & Hemphill, 2005). Moreover, several studies have documented substantial variability in the effectiveness of the early literacy instruction provided by classroom teachers

(Foorman & Schatschneider, 2003; Pressley et al., 2001; Scanlon & Vellutino, 1996; Taylor, Pearson, Clark, & Walpole, 2000). Thus, although it has been well documented that certain characteristics of the child place him or her at risk for experiencing early reading difficulties (e.g., Fletcher et al., 1994; Stanovich & Siegel, 1994; Vellutino et al., 1996), it is also clear that characteristics of classroom instruction are powerful determinants of whether a child will experience such difficulties (Scanlon & Vellutino, 1996, 1997; Snow & Juel, 2005).

If RTI is to realize its promise, it is critical that more emphasis be placed on understanding the nature and characteristics of instruction that are effective in reducing the incidence of early reading difficulties and on how to help teachers become more effective in this regard. It is widely acknowledged that teachers' professional knowledge is not complete upon certification (Snow, Griffin, & Burns, 2005) and, therefore, ongoing professional education is likely to be critical to the development of a highly effective teaching force. However, the National Reading Panel (2000) found it difficult to make specific recommendations about PD because of the paucity of research showing that PD changed both teachers' practices and their students' achievement. Studies of the effects of PD on classroom instruction are particularly important, because classroom instruction has the potential to affect the largest number of students. Moreover, if changes at the classroom level reduce the number of children who need more intensive interventions, the schools' capacity to provide subsequent tiers of intervention will be enhanced because fewer students will need to be served.

Thus, the current study was conceived, in part, in response to the need for research on the contribution of PD to teachers' instruction and students' reading achievement. The study was also partly motivated by an earlier study (Scanlon et al., 2005; Vellutino, Scanlon, Small, & Fanuele, 2006) which showed that the number of children who experienced early reading difficulties could be substantially reduced through the provision of a rather limited kindergarten intervention program (30 min twice per week for 25 weeks) that supplemented the classroom program. That study also demonstrated that children who experienced reading difficulties, despite having the supplemental intervention in kindergarten, were much less likely to demonstrate severe reading difficulties at the end of first grade than were children who did not participate in kindergarten intervention. We reasoned that PD for classroom teachers, based on the intervention approach, could be equally or perhaps more effective in reducing the incidence of early reading difficulties.

1.1. Research Purposes

We used a longitudinal study that compared three approaches to reducing the incidence of early reading difficulties: 1) Professional Development Only (PDO), 2) Intervention Only (IO), and 3) Both PD for teachers and intervention for their students who were at increased risk of experiencing early reading difficulties (PD+I). The PD provided to the classroom teachers was similar to the PD program provided to intervention teachers in the Scanlon et al. (2005) study. The small group intervention provided to the at risk kindergartners in the IO and PD+I conditions was the same as the intervention provided in the Scanlon et al. study. This was, essentially, a Tier 2 intervention.

Outcomes included both measures of student achievement and documentation of the characteristics of kindergarten classroom language arts instruction. Data were gathered as the teachers taught three consecutive cohorts of students in the years before (Baseline Cohort), during (Implementation Cohort) and after (Maintenance Cohort) the various treatments were instituted. Because personnel from the research team were actively involved in guiding and supporting classroom instruction for the Implementation Cohort, the major analyses are focused primarily on contrasts between the Baseline and Maintenance cohorts.

With regard to student achievement, we anticipated improved outcomes for at risk children in the Maintenance Cohort as compared to the Baseline Cohort in all three treatment conditions. Further, it was predicted that the PDO condition would be at least as effective as direct interventions for children (IO condition) in improving the early literacy skills. However, it was also anticipated that the strongest outcomes would occur in the PD+I condition, since the children would have the benefit of both enhanced classroom instruction and additional small group intervention.

With regard to classroom observations, it was anticipated that, for teachers in the PD and PD+I conditions, comparisons of Baseline versus the Maintenance year data would reveal a shift toward instruction that was aligned with the content of the PD program and more responsive to the needs of individual children. Thus, in comparisons of instruction provided for the two cohorts by the same teachers, it was expected that for the Maintenance Cohort:

1) more time would be allocated to language arts instruction;
2) more instruction would be focused on content related to the literacy goals of the PD program;

3) greater use would be made of literacy materials that allowed students to practice and apply skills and strategies related to the literacy goals; and

4) greater support would be provided for at risk students through differentiated instructional groupings and greater use of responsive modeling and scaffolding.

2. Method

2.1. Design

This study assessed the effects of three approaches to intervention provided for kindergarten children who were in the at risk range on a measure of early literacy skill: Professional Development Only for classroom teachers (PDO); supplemental, small group Intervention Only (IO); or both PD and supplemental intervention (PD+I). All approaches utilized the Interactive Strategies Approach (ISA) to preventing reading difficulties (described below). Both longitudinal and experimental contrasts were included. To assess longitudinal effects, three consecutive cohorts of kindergartners were followed from the beginning of kindergarten to the beginning of first grade. For the Baseline Cohort, no research treatment occurred. All treatments were initiated with the Implementation Cohort. For the Maintenance Cohort, the PD activities for the teachers were discontinued however the direct interventions for children who were at risk continued in the IO and PD+I conditions.

A randomized block design was used to assign schools to the three treatment conditions. Toward the end of the Baseline Cohort's kindergarten year, schools were assigned to one of the three groups with the groups being matched as closely as possible for SES, risk status for entering kindergarten students, and grade 4 achievement on the New York State English Language Arts assessment. Schools from within the same district were assigned to different groups in order to distribute the effects of curricula.

2.2. Participants

2.2.1. Teachers. Schools were eligible to participate in the study if they 1) served a relatively high number of low income students, 2) offered full day kindergarten; and 3) were within 50 miles of our research center in Albany, New York. In schools that met the criteria and expressed an interest in participating, teachers completed consent forms independently and submitted them to the researchers in sealed envelopes. To qualify for the study 80% of the kindergarten teachers needed to agree. Schools were provided with funds for the purchase of language arts materials for each participating classroom after the year of baseline data collection.

Fifteen schools (from ten districts, six urban and four rural) and 43 kindergarten teachers elected to participate in the study. All of the teachers were Caucasian women, a circumstance that is quite typical in the Albany, NY area. Because of the substantial demands of the study and because a fairly high number of schools had half-day kindergarten programs at the outset of the study, it was not possible to limit enrollment to schools that had full day kindergarten. Therefore, two schools that had half-day kindergarten during the Baseline Cohort's kindergarten year, but full day kindergarten for the subsequent cohorts, were included in the study but excluded from the current report. Another school was excluded because it was closed at the end of the Baseline Cohort's kindergarten year. The elimination of schools reduced the teacher sample to 38 teachers.

During the three years of data collection, teacher attrition occurred as a result of teachers retiring, taking leave, moving, or taking nonteaching positions. After attrition, the sample consisted of 28 teachers for whom 3 consecutive years of data were available.[1] Four schools were included in each condition, with 1–4 teachers per school. The final sample included 9 teachers in IO schools, 10 teachers in PDO schools, and 9 teachers from PD+I schools.

2.2.2. Students. Students taught by the 28 teachers in this study were also participants in the research. Kindergarten students were recruited at the school's kindergarten registration or through letters sent home with the child. In all but one school, over 90% of parents agreed to involve their children. Only children who were available for assessment at all measurement points are included in this report. Table 1 provides demographic data for each cohort and condition.

2.2.3. Early Literacy Leaders. Each school nominated one individual to serve as an (Early) Literacy Leader (LL). In schools assigned to the PD conditions, the LLs were expected to provide ongoing support to teachers in their school once active engagement in the PD component concluded. In schools in the IO and PD+I conditions, the LLs, in most cases, provided the intervention to one group of kindergartners in the Implementation Cohort. The LLs in the IO condition

Table 1. Percentages of Children in Each Subgroup in Each Cohort and Condition Falling in Each Condition

	Intervention Only			Professional Development Only			Professional Development+ Intervention		
	Base	Imp	Main	Base	Imp	Main	Base	Imp	Main
Racial/ethnic group									
Asian	5.5	5.1	3.2	0.6	1.8	1.4	1.4	1.4	0.7
African American	12.3	17.1	15.2	10.8	6.1	9.7	7.9	11.3	6.3
Hispanic	2.5	4.2	5.6	1.3	3.7	2.1	1.4	7.0	1.4
White	77.9	71.8	75.2	84.1	87.1	80.0	77.9	69.0	88.9
Other and missing	1.8	1.7	0.8	3.2	1.2	6.9	11.4	11.3	2.8
Male	55.8	59.0	48.8	44.0	47.9	49.0	44.3	52.1	51.4
Free and reduced lunch[a]	34.4	27.5	40.0	24.8	31.9	50.3	40.7	34.5	51.4

Note. Base = Baseline, Imp = Implementation, Main = Maintenance.
[a]There is a fair amount of missing data (3% to 15%) for each group owing to reluctance on the part of the schools to release data on the children's free and reduce lunch status.

were expected to provide PD for teachers in their schools once the teachers had finished working with the Maintenance Cohort.

The LLs were all Caucasian women. Many LLs were teachers including three classroom teachers, three reading teachers, and three who taught both special education and reading. The group also included one speech and language pathologist, and three building administrators who held reading certification. All had at least 10 years teaching experience. LLs participated in the same PD as the classroom teachers. They also had ongoing monthly contact with project staff to enhance their professional knowledge.

2.3. Measures

The same data collection procedures were used for all three cohorts (Baseline, Implementation, and Maintenance). The children were assessed in the early fall and late spring of kindergarten and at the beginning of grade one.

2.3.1. Student Measures. *2.3.1.1. PALS.* The kindergarten version of the Phonological Awareness and Literacy Screening Battery (PALS-K, Invernizzi, Meir, Swank & Juel, 1999–2000) was administered to kindergartners at the beginning and end of the school year. This is a standardized measure that provides benchmarks for the identification of children who are at risk for literacy learning difficulties. The Rhyme Awareness, Beginning Sound Awareness, Alphabet Knowledge, Letter-Sound Knowledge and Spelling components were administered. The maximum score summing these subtests is 92 points. Risk status at each measurement point was based on the published benchmark (28 in the Fall and 74 in the Spring). Internal consistency reliability coefficients based on the subtests range from .79 to .85 for various subsamples (Invernizzi et al., 1999-2000).

The PALS 1–3 (Invernizzi & Meir, 2000–2001) was administered at the beginning of first grade. The outcome measure utilized for this study was the Entry Level Summed score which is the sum of the Spelling and Word Recognition components. The maximum possible score for this index is 77. The test manual reports reliability and validity indices within acceptable ranges (.73–.90).

2.3.1.2. Basic Reading Skills Cluster. At the beginning of grade 1, all students were administered subtests from the Woodcock–Johnson III Tests of Achievement (WJIII, Woodcock, McGrew, & Mather, 2001). Scores from the Letter–Word Identification and Word Attack subtests were used to derive a Basic Reading Skills Cluster (BSC) score. For four to seven year olds, the age-corrected test–retest reliability coefficient for a one year interval is .92. For the current sample, the beginning of first grade PALS Summed Score correlated .88 with the BSC.

2.4. Classroom Observations

The Classroom Language Arts Systematic Sampling and Instructional Coding (CLASSIC) system was used to gather information on instructional characteristics (Scanlon, Gelzheiser, Fanuele, Sweeney, & Newcomer, 2003). The CLASSIC is a modified time-sampling teacher observation system. The observer records both a running narrative of the instructional events involving the teacher and every 90 s records verbatim a "slice" or instructional event that is coded for seven features of instruction. The combination of the running narrative and the verbatim record provided sufficient context to allow the observer to reflect on how to best code an event, and also allowed another coder to review coding decisions.

2.4.1. Natures of Features Coded. Six of the seven coded features focus on the teacher; the seventh feature captures the students' response. Of the seven features, four tended to remain stable for periods of time and three tended to change frequently as the teacher interacted with students (see Fig. 1 for an example of a coded slice). Detailed information about the CLASSIC observation system can be obtained from the first author.

2.4.1.1. Relatively Stable Features. The codes used for the *Class Structure* feature captured whether all children were engaged in a single activity or whether multiple activities were occurring simultaneously. For the *Lesson Plan Context* feature, codes allowed the observer to document major instructional blocks of the sort typically recorded in lesson plans (e.g., read aloud, text reading, skills, calendar time, writing, non-language arts activities). Codes for *Materials Context* identified the materials the teacher was using during instruction (e.g., trade book, letters, pictures, math materials). *Instructional Group* codes identified the group with whom the teacher was interacting, allowing for an estimate of the time that the teacher provided instruction in whole class versus small group settings and also capturing whether the small groups were heterogeneous or based on instructional needs.

Fig. 1. Sample of Coded Slice Taken in the Context of a Small Group Lesson Focused on the Development of Phonemic Awareness

		Features Coded						
		Relatively Stable Features				Relatively Dynamic Features		
Slice #	Verbatim Record	Class Structure	Lesson Plan Context	Materials Context	Instructional Group	Specific Instructional Focus	Teacher Activity	Student Activity
		1	2	3	4	5	6	7
1	**T asks S: Do sail and tail rhyme?** Student says yes; teacher repeats yes, sail and tail have the same sounds at the end	LAH	FS	WO	SG-IN	QRD	PSK-SR	TR

Note. The teacher identified the group as her "middle" group prior to the observation. The segment presented in bold is coded as this is the first thing that occurred after the "observe" prompt. Translations of the codes are as follows: LAH = Language Arts instruction with students grouped Heterogeneously; FS = Foundational Skills; WO = Words presented orally; SG-IN = Small group that is identified as a group of children with intermediate level skills; QRD = Question, Request, Directive; PSK-SR = Phonemic Segmentation Skills—Sensitivity to Rime; TR = Think and Respond.

2.4.1.2. Relatively Dynamic Features. To capture the dynamic nature of instruction, we coded three characteristics of instruction. Codes for the *Specific Instructional Focus* indexed what students were expected to focus on, that is, the many objectives, sub-objectives, or tasks related to reading, writing, speaking, and listening. There were codes to indicate whether instruction was focused on such things as letter names, letter sounds, phonemic analysis, reading text, listening to text, comprehension of text read or heard, etc. *Teacher Activity* codes were used to indicate the instructional activity that the teacher used, for example, activity specifically focused on text (e.g., transcribing students' dictation), activity to promote acquisition of information or skills (e.g., scaffolding), or activity that did not involve instruction (e.g., managing behaviors). *Student Activity* codes were used to indicate what students were doing during the coded event (e.g., oral reading, shared reading, thinking about and/or providing a response, listening, art).

2.4.2. Variables Used in Analysis. For purposes of analysis, we consolidated codes to make composite variables that aligned with the research purposes. These composite variables were based primarily on the literacy goals of the Interactive Strategies Approach and the PD program. For example, the PD stressed active engagement of students; we captured student engagement in the coding system with codes such as Every Student Response and thinking and responding. Codes that occurred infrequently were often collapsed with conceptually related codes to form meaningful and interpretable instructional constructs.[2] For example, the Specific Instructional Focus feature includes 13 phonemic analysis codes which were combined to form one variable. Each of the variables used in this analysis is defined in Fig. 2a (relatively stable features) and b (relatively dynamic features).

2.4.3. Reliability. Guided by a coding manual, observers were trained through coding written examples and videos. Once an observer demonstrated acceptable reliability in coding the videos, she/he accompanied the "standard" observer on live classroom observations and coded using the same time sample. To qualify to do independent observations, new observers needed to demonstrate that they had attained the requisite reliability level in two consecutive observations. Thereafter, reliability checks were conducted every 6 to 8 weeks. Reliability was calculated for each instructional feature as well as overall. The criterion set for acceptable reliability was 85% agreement for each feature and

90% agreement across the 7 features coded. Average feature reliabilities ranged from 99% for Classroom Structure to 93% for Specific Instructional Focus.

2.5. Procedures

2.5.1. Data Collection. Similar procedures were followed for data collection during the Baseline, Implementation, and Maintenance years of the study. All participating children were assessed within the first 3–4 weeks of kindergarten

Fig. 2a. Derived Variables for the Relatively Stable Features Used in the Analysis of Observation Data

Variable	Description
Active language arts teaching	Slices where the teacher is engaged with students and the specific instructional focus is language arts.
Lesson Plan Context	
Active reading, writing and skills	Blocks of time devoted to students reading text, writing compositions, or skills such as phonemic awareness, letter names, letter sounds, letter formation, or spelling.
Comprehension	Blocks of time devoted to comprehension of a text, either before or after reading. The text may have been read by the teacher or students.
Oral language	Blocks of time devoted to development of students' oral vocabulary or oral communication, such as student sharing or vocabulary activities.
Instructional Group	
Teacher-led ability groups	Time in which the teacher is interacting with small group which has been constituted based on the students' early literacy skills.
Instructional Materials	
Written sentences, words, letters	The teacher and students are using written materials that are not complete texts and not written by students: written sentences, words, word parts or letters.
Emergent level books	The teacher and students are using books written and leveled for reading instruction at the early primary level.
Other texts	The teacher and students are using other forms of text not written by students, including tradebooks, big books, basals, or other written, structured text (poems, teacher compositions, the calendar, a graphic organizer).
Student compositions	Students are writing lists or compositions (which may include drawings that represent ideas) that record student ideas on paper, or compositions that are jointly created by the teacher and students.

Fig. 2b. Derived Variables for the Relatively Dynamic Features Used in the Analysis of Observation Data

Variable	Description
Teacher Activity	
Scaffolding and modeling	The teacher provides connections, hints or supports to facilitate students' response, or performs a task she expects students to replicate.
Questioning, response and feedback	The teacher asks a question or gives a directive, listens to students, or gives students feedback on their work.
Specific Instructional Focus	
Phonemic analysis	The teacher and students are focused on similarities or differences in the sounds of spoken words, generating spoken words with similar beginning or ending sounds, substituting sounds within spoken words, segmenting spoken words into parts, or blending auditorily presented segments to form words.
Letter names/ sounds	The teacher and students are focused on a letter's name, sound, graphic features, or matching letters.
Larger orthographic units	The teacher and students are focused on phonics patterns (word families, digraphs, blends, vowel rules) or structural analysis to identify words.
Sound spelling	The teacher and students are focused on deriving the spelling of words using sounds; with or without resources like a letter chart, word family chart, or teacher assistance.
Word ID strategies	The teacher and students are focused on strategies that facilitate identification of unfamiliar words in continuous text. Some strategies emphasize decoding, e.g., attending to the first letter, looking through the word, trying different vowel sounds, looking for word families or little words, or using structural analysis. Others are meaning-based, e.g., reading past the word, re-reading, or using the pictures or sentence to support word identification. Word identification strategies may emphasize self-regulation or integrate code-based and meaning-based clues.
Sight words	The teacher and students are focused on identification of words without the use of strategies.
Comprehension	The teacher and students are focused on strategies to support comprehension and/or composition of text, such as self-questioning, predicting, visualizing, making a personal connection, and using prior knowledge or text structure. Or, the focus is on students comprehending text or oral language.
Vocabulary and language	The teacher and student are focused on word meanings, or are using extended oral language in discussion or presentation formats.
Student Activity	
Read	Students read orally or silently, including individual, choral, shared, and buddy reading. This variable also includes tasks that demand both reading and writing.
Think and respond	Students are processing something with cognitive, academic content and are expected to prepare a response.
Listen to read alouds	Students are listening while the teacher reads text aloud.

and again during the last month of kindergarten using the PALS-K. Students who were not lost through attrition were assessed again at the beginning of first grade using both the PALS 1–3 and the Woodcock–Johnson III measures.

Observations of teachers' language arts instruction were conducted five times per year. Teachers identified a 2-hour (approximate) time period when they conducted language arts instruction. To maximize representativeness, observations were distributed across the school year, days of the week, and observers. During the Implementation year, three of the five observations of teachers in the PD conditions were conducted by a literacy coach who was supporting the teacher's ISA related PD. Because of the potential for bias, we do not present observation data collected during the course of the Implementation year.

2.5.2. Treatments—Implementation Cohort. *2.5.2.1. Professional Development.* Teachers in schools assigned to the PDO or PD+ I conditions participated in a 3 day workshop concerned with the Interactive Strategies Approach (ISA, Scanlon & Sweeney, 2004; Vellutino & Scanlon, 2002) during the summer prior to teaching children in the Implementation Cohort. They were provided with a handbook and access to the ISA PD website, which included additional teaching ideas.

2.5.2.1.1. The Interactive Strategies Approach. The ISA is an approach to early literacy instruction that we have been developing and testing for over 15 years (Scanlon & Sweeney, 2004; Scanlon et al. 2005; Vellutino & Scanlon, 2002; Vellutino et al., 1996). It is based on the premise that reading is a complex process that involves the orchestration of multiple cognitive processes, types of knowledge, and reading subskills and that most early reading difficulties can be prevented if literacy instruction is comprehensive, responsive to individual student need, and fosters the development of a Self Teaching Mechanism (Share, 1995). In the earlier studies, the ISA was implemented in small group and one-to-one instructional situations by teachers who were members of our research staff. The current study represents our first attempt to implement the ISA at the classroom level.

The ISA is not a "program." Rather, it is an approach that is designed to be useful in the context of a variety of language arts programs. In order to plan and organize instruction, teachers need the requisite knowledge and skills to identify what the children are ready to learn and to identify which children would be most appropriately grouped for instruction. Thus the PD program focused on developing teachers' knowledge in order to enable them to more fully understand their students' needs. It also provided tools, in the form of techniques and activities, which teachers could select, as appropriate, to help their at risk students make the accelerated progress needed in order to meet grade level expectations. Major emphasis was placed on the need to include small group, differentiated instruction.

For purposes of the PD program, we organized the approach around ten related instructional goals for emergent readers (see Fig. 3). Taken together, the pursuit of these goals was intended to prepare the children to become active and strategic readers who enjoyed and responded to texts read or heard and who applied their knowledge of the alphabetic code in conjunction with contextual

Fig. 3. Instructional Goals of ISA at the Kindergarten Level

1) **Motivation to Read and Write**—the child will develop the belief that reading and writing are enjoyable and informative activities which are not beyond his/her capabilities.
2) **Phoneme Awareness**—the child will have a conceptual grasp of the fact that words are made up of somewhat separable sound segments. Further, the child will be able to say individual sounds in simple words spoken by the teacher and to blend separate sounds to form whole words.
3) **Letter Identification**—the child will be able to name, rapidly and accurately, all 26 letters of the alphabet, both upper and lower case versions.
4) **Letter-Sound Association**—the child will be able to associate the sounds of the majority of consonants with their printed representations.
5) **Alphabetic Principle**—the child will understand that the letters in printed words represent the sounds in spoken words. Further, the child will be able to change single consonants at the beginning or end of one-syllable words in accord with requests made by the tutor (e.g., "change mat to bat").
6) **Print Awareness**—the child will understand that the purpose of print is to communicate.
7) **Print Conventions**—the child will understand some of the most basic print conventions, such as the left to right and top to bottom sequencing of print, where to begin reading a book, the concepts of letter and word, etc.
8) **Whole Word Identification**—the child will learn to recognize, at sight, a small set of high frequency words.
9) **Comprehension**—the child will develop comprehension skills and strategies that will enhance his/her ability to construct the meaning of texts heard or read.
10) **Vocabulary and Oral Language Development**—the child will learn the meanings of new words encountered in instructional interactions and be able to use those words conversationally. Further, the child's ability to understand and use more complex grammatical structures will improve.

cues provided by the text in mutually supportive ways to facilitate the learning of unfamiliar printed words. The goal-oriented structure of the PD program was intended to help teachers focus on these instructional purposes.

2.5.2.1.2. Coaching. During the Implementation year, each teacher in the PDO and PD+I conditions was supported by an Early Literacy Collaborator (ELC). The two ELCs were experienced teachers who were certified in reading and who had experience as ISA intervention teachers. The ELCs were considered to be collaborators rather than coaches because their primary purpose was to help teachers identify the ways in which the ISA could be incorporated into the curriculum that was in place. Teachers worked individually with their ELC on at least five occasions. The sessions typically involved observation of the teacher's 2 to 2.5 h language arts block followed by 30 to 60 min reflection session. Suggestions and modeling were also provided by the ELCs. In addition, the ELCs met once a month with all of the kindergarten teachers at a school. These meetings lasted approximately 1 h and allowed the opportunity to review the goals of the ISA and to respond to teacher questions and concerns. The school's Literacy Leader (LL) frequently attended these meetings.

2.5.2.2. Intervention. Teachers in schools in the IO condition did not participate in the PD program. At risk kindergartners in IO and PD+I schools were provided with small group instruction (3 students or fewer) by research staff teachers twice a week. The small group instruction used the Interactive Strategy Approach and followed a lesson format that included reading books (read by the children or the teacher), learning about letters and letter sounds, phonemic awareness, and writing. Research staff teachers participated in an ISA workshop similar to that used in the PD conditions. Lesson logs and audio recordings were kept for each intervention session and were used to assess (and encourage) fidelity to the instructional principles of the ISA; however, since the intent of the ISA is that teachers will modify instruction to effectively address the needs of their students, traditional indices of fidelity cannot be applied. The intervention teachers were provided with group (biweekly) and individual (every six weeks) supervision.

2.5.3. Treatments: Maintenance Cohort. At risk kindergartners in the Maintenance Cohort in schools assigned to the IO or PD+I conditions received ISA instruction in small groups as was provided for the Implementation Cohort. The research project did not provide additional PD for teachers in the PD conditions. However, the LLs were expected to provide support to teachers in these conditions. The amount and type of support provided by LLs was not documented and varied across schools.

3. Results

Below we present a classification analysis to evaluate the effectiveness of the three treatment conditions in reducing the number of children who qualified as at risk at the end of kindergarten. Because analysis of classification accuracy uses arbitrary cutoff scores, we also analyze the performance levels on the measures administered at the beginning and end of kindergarten and at the beginning of first grade. Thereafter, we analyze the effects of the PD program on the classroom instruction. Finally, we consider the instruction provided by teachers in each of the treatment conditions during the year in which they taught the Baseline Cohort, in an effort to explain unanticipated differences in end of kindergarten performance.

3.1. Reductions in the Proportion of Children Who Qualified as at Risk for Reading Difficulties

Table 2 presents the percentages of children who were classified as at risk at the beginning and end of kindergarten for the various treatment conditions and cohorts. These data indicate that, in general, at kindergarten entry, the schools

Table 2. Percentages of Children Qualifying as at Risk for Reading Difficulties at the Beginning and End of Kindergarten

			Percentage at Risk	
		n	Beginning of Kindergarten	End of Kindergarten
Intervention Only (IO)	Baseline	156	50.6	52.6
	Implementation	124	52.4	31.5
	Maintenance	125	53.6	27.2
Professional Development Only (PDO)	Baseline	154	50.6	35.1
	Implementation	164	47.0	19.5
	Maintenance	147	51.7	17.0
Professional Development + Intervention (PD+I)	Baseline	137	59.9	24.8
	Implementation	145	57.2	17.2
	Maintenance	144	61.8	17.4

assigned to the IO and PDO conditions enrolled comparable proportions of children who were at risk for reading difficulties. The schools assigned to the PD+I condition, on the other hand, enrolled students who were somewhat more likely to score in the at risk range of the PALS-K. This general pattern was evident across all three cohorts. However, the proportion of children who scored in the at risk range at the end of kindergarten varied by both condition and cohort. Considering the Baseline Cohort first, it is clear that, in the IO condition, there was no reduction in the percentage of children who qualified as at risk from the beginning to the end of the kindergarten year. However, in the PDO and PD+I conditions, there was a substantial reduction in the percentage qualifying as at risk from the beginning to the end of kindergarten. This finding suggests that the effectiveness of the instruction provided in kindergarten varied considerably by condition before any of the treatments were implemented. These differences will be more fully explored in a later section.

Comparisons of the percentages of children who qualified as at risk across cohorts within each condition provide an indication of the effectiveness of each treatment. At the end of kindergarten, for all conditions, there was a reduction in the percentage of children who qualified as at risk in the Implementation and Maintenance Cohorts relative to the Baseline Cohort.

To evaluate the significance of the patterns described, a three-level HLM model was fit to the data. Specifically, children's risk status on the PALS-K at the beginning and end of kindergarten was treated as a repeated measure and nested within classrooms and schools, which were both treated as random effects. Treatment condition, cohort, and time of test were treated as fixed effects. This analysis yielded a main effect for time ($F(1, 9) = 217.03$, p < .0001) which reflects the general trend for fewer children to score in the at risk range at the end of kindergarten than at the beginning, and a main effect for cohort ($F(2, 18) = 7.71$, p < .01) which reflects the tendency for fewer children in the Implementation and Maintenance Cohorts to qualify as at risk as compared to the Baseline Cohort. The main effect for condition was not significant. There was, however, a significant interaction effect for time by condition ($F(2, 9) = 14.95$, p < .01), reflecting the fact that, in general, there were larger differences across conditions at the end of kindergarten in the percentages of children qualifying as at risk than there were at the beginning of kindergarten. The final significant effect for this analysis was an interaction between cohort and time of test ($F(2, 18) = 10.09$, p < .01). This interaction reflects the greater reduction in the number of children who qualified as at risk at the end of kindergarten in the Implementation and

Maintenance Cohorts as compared with the Baseline Cohort. Finally, with regard to the analysis of risk status, neither the interaction between condition and time nor the three three-way interaction between condition, cohort, and time was significant, suggesting that the conditions were not differentially effective in reducing the incidence of risk status at the kindergarten level.

To further explore the impact of the different treatment conditions on the risk status of children in each of the cohorts, we analyzed the stability of the students' risk status on the PALS-K from the beginning to the end of kindergarten. Children were classified as follows: True Positives are children who qualified as at risk at both the beginning and end of kindergarten, False Positives are children who qualified as at risk at the beginning of kindergarten but not at the end, True Negatives are children who did not qualify as at risk at either the beginning or end of kindergarten and False Negatives are children who did not qualify as at risk at the beginning of kindergarten but did qualify as at risk at the end of kindergarten. We also explored the sensitivity and the specificity of identifying children who were at risk at the beginning of kindergarten and who remained at risk at the end of kindergarten. These data are presented in Table 3.

The classification data reveal substantial differences in classification accuracy across conditions and cohorts. For example, for the Baseline groups, it is clear that the highest percentage of accurate classifications overall occurred in

Table 3. Indices of Classification Accuracy for Each Cohort Within Each Treatment Condition

	TP	FP	TN	FN	Sensitivity[a]	Specificity[b]	Overall Accuracy Rate[c]
IO Baseline	40.4	10.3	37.2	12.2	76.8	78.3	77.6
IO Implementation	23.4	29.0	39.5	8.1	74.3	57.7	62.9
IO Maintenance	22.4	31.2	41.6	4.8	82.4	57.1	64.0
PDO Baseline	27.3	22.1	42.9	7.8	77.8	68.1	70.2
PDO Implementation	17.1	29.9	50.6	2.4	87.7	62.9	67.7
PDO Maintenance	16.3	35.4	47.6	0.7	95.9	56.7	63.9
PD+I Baseline	24.1	35.8	39.4	0.8	96.8	52.4	63.5
PD+I Implementation	16.6	40.7	42.1	0.7	96.0	50.8	58.1
PD+I Maintenance	16.0	45.8	36.8	1.4	92.0	44.6	52.8

[a]Sensitivity = True Positive/True Positives + False Negatives. [b]Specificity = True Negatives/True Negatives + False Positives. [c]Total Accuracy = True Positives + True Negatives.

the IO condition with approximately equal sensitivity and specificity indices. In contrast, the classification accuracy rate for the PD+I Baseline group is substantially lower but the sensitivity index is much higher than the sensitivity index for the IO group while the specificity index for the PD+I group is much lower than the same index for the IO group. Since the two Baseline groups started kindergarten with similar performance levels on the PALS-K, these data suggest differential effectiveness in language arts instruction with the PD+I Baseline group receiving instruction that was much more effective. Note also that the Baseline group in the PDO condition fell between the IO and PD+I group on all three of these indices and the combined results provide strong evidence of variability in the effectiveness of classroom instruction and of the potential effectiveness of Tier 1 interventions.

Comparisons of classification accuracy within treatment conditions across cohorts reveal a clear trend for overall classification accuracy to be reduced for the Implementation and Maintenance Cohorts as compared to the Baseline Cohort. Further, in all conditions, the sensitivity index improved for the Implementation and Maintenance Cohorts as compared to the Baseline Cohort while the specificity index became worse. In other words, with the changes in instructional experiences that (presumably) occurred as a result of the implementation of the various treatments, it became quite unlikely that a child who did not appear to be at risk at the beginning of kindergarten would perform in the at risk range at the end of kindergarten. Moreover, within each condition, the False Positive rate increased substantially for the Implementation and Maintenance Cohorts. In fact, in all three treatment conditions, there were substantially more False Positives than True Positives in the Maintenance Cohort. These data suggest that, as the quality of instruction improves, assessments designed to identify students who are at risk increase in their sensitivity but decrease in their specificity. These data provide a strong argument for the value of an RTI approach in that risk status was clearly related to instructional experiences. Further, the data also provide strong evidence for the efficacy of PD in enhancing the effectiveness of instruction at Tier 1.

3.2. Performance on Kindergarten Measures of Student Achievement

Table 4 provides means and standard deviations for PALS-K assessment administered at the beginning and end of kindergarten for the children grouped by

Table 4. Means and Standard Deviations on the Phonological Awareness Literacy Screening (PALS-K) for Each Treatment Group and Cohort at the Beginning and End of Kindergarten[a]

		% at Risk[c]		At Risk[b]		Not at Risk[b]	
				Pre	Post	Pre	Post
IO	Baseline	50.6	Mean	16.41	58.28	48.66	79.14
	(n = 156)		(SD)	6.99	18.24	16.20	9.13
	Implementation	52.4	Mean	18.05	72.12	52.85	81.86
	(n = 124)		(SD)	6.73	17.43	15.66	7.71
	Maintenance	53.6	Mean	16.46	73.60	53.98	82.64
	(n = 125)		(SD)	6.86	12.49	15.51	9.14
PDO	Baseline	50.6	Mean	16.33	66.17	49.13	83.09
	(n = 154)		(SD)	7.16	18.65	15.10	8.14
	Implementation	47.0	Mean	17.71	74.23	52.62	85.18
	(n = 164)		(SD)	6.74	16.80	15.71	5.33
	Maintenance	51.7	Mean	16.61	77.11	51.24	86.70
	(n = 147)		(SD)	6.92	14.31	15.56	4.73
PD+I	Baseline	59.9	Mean	15.29	72.72	44.35	85.38
	(n = 137)		(SD)	6.82	15.33	13.10	5.10
	Implementation	57.2	Mean	15.88	77.71	49.44	88.24
	(n = 145)		(SD)	6.94	13.59	14.67	4.40
	Maintenance	61.8	Mean	16.62	78.87	50.33	87.75
	(n = 144)		(SD)	6.35	13.45	14.27	5.32

[a]Maximum score on the PALS = 92. [b]Students are grouped by risk status at kindergarten entry. [c]Percent at risk at kindergarten entry.

PALS-K risk status at kindergarten entry. For the children in the at risk range, the data reveal that, across cohorts and treatment conditions, the children performed at similar levels on the PALS-K pretest. However, the PALS-K posttest data reveal substantial differences by treatment condition even for the Baseline Cohort. In general, consistent with the risk reduction data described above, at the end of kindergarten, students in the IO condition performed below the level of the children in the PDO and PD+I conditions. The combined results suggest that Tier 1 instruction at the kindergarten level can be at least as effective in reducing the number of kindergarten children at risk for early reading difficulties as Tier 2 supplemental intervention.

The students who did not qualify as at risk at kindergarten entry scored substantially higher than the at risk children at both the beginning and end of kindergarten. Another general trend evident in Table 4 is that, at the end of kindergarten, the children in all of the Implementation and Maintenance Cohorts consistently performed at higher levels on the PALS-K than did children in the Baseline Cohort. This pattern suggests that all three treatment conditions were effective in improving outcomes for children in both the at risk and the not at risk groups. It should be noted that smaller cohort differences emerged for the children who were not at risk. As the PALS-K has a maximum score of 92, this may be attributable to ceiling effects.

To test the effects of the various factors that might influence performance, a three-level HLM model was fit to the data. Student performances on the PALS-K total score at the beginning and end of kindergarten were treated as a repeated measure and nested within classroom and school, which were treated as random effects. Fixed effects in the model were treatment condition, cohort, subjects' risk status at kindergarten entry, and time of test for the PALS. This analysis yielded a main effect for cohort ($F(2, 18) = 41.00$, $p < .0001$), risk status ($F(1, 9) = 2299.60$, $p < .0001$), and time of test ($F(1, 9) = 9181.57$, $p < .00001$) but no main effect for treatment condition ($F(2, 9) = 1.51$, $p = .27$). There was also a significant time by condition interaction ($F(2, 9) = 33.39$, $p < .0001$) which reflects that fact that, in the Fall of kindergarten, all performance levels in each of the conditions were comparable but, at the end of kindergarten, the performance levels were substantially different with the PD+I condition performing better than the PDO condition which performed better than the IO condition.

Analysis of beginning and end of year PALS-K performances also yielded a significant three-way interaction for cohort by risk status by time of test ($F(2, 28) = 14.57$, $p < .001$). To follow-up the significant three-way interaction, we constructed a series of post-hoc interaction contrasts to compare the means on the PALS-K total score within treatment group across cohorts, risk status, and time of test. We also evaluated the magnitude of change separately for at risk and not at risk groups. For the at risk groups, the change from the beginning to the end of kindergarten for the Implementation Cohort was significantly greater than the change for the Baseline Cohort ($t(18) = -4.98$, $p < .0001$). Change in the Maintenance Cohort was also significantly greater than change in the Baseline Cohort among the at risk children ($t(18) = -6.62$, $p < .0001$). Similar contrasts comparing change from the beginning to the end of kindergarten for the children who were not at risk did not yield statistically significant differences between cohorts. However, these outcomes may have been due to ceiling effects (note that 92 is the PALS-K's maximum score and that standard deviations are reduced in Table 4). Taken together, these analyses make it clear that all three approaches to enhancing the development of early literacy skills had a positive impact on student performance, especially for students in the at risk group

3.3. Performance on Beginning of First Grade Measures of Student Achievement

To evaluate the stability of the effects observed at the end of kindergarten, parallel analyses were conducted on the PALS 1–3 and for the Basic Skills Cluster administered at the beginning of first grade (Table 5).[3]

Table 5. Means and Standard Deviations for Each Treatment Group and Cohort on Measures Administered at the Beginning of First Grade

			PALS 1–3[a] Grade 1		WJBSC[b] Grade 1	
			At Risk	Not at Risk	At Risk	Not at Risk
IO	Baseline	Mean	27.66	50.03	93.68	111.28
	(n = 129)	(SD)	13.78	16.32	13.09	15.09
	Implementation	Mean	37.98	52.61	100.73	113.88
	(n = 107)	(SD)	15.34	14.38	11.46	15.53
	Maintenance	Mean	38.45	57.04	99.54	116.24
	(n = 110)	(SD)	15.16	14.09	11.01	15.34
PDO	Baseline	Mean	38.12	57.01	100.03	113.70
	(n = 131)	(SD)	16.60	16.18	11.99	13.80
	Implementation	Mean	43.25	57.62	102.82	116.29
	(n = 151)	(SD)	15.01	13.74	10.56	13.57
	Maintenance	Mean	45.69	60.57	104.79	117.71
	(n = 129)	(SD)	16.15	14.13	10.87	13.38
PD+I	Baseline	Mean	43.66	59.78	101.95	115.56
	(n = 109)	(SD)	15.47	13.72	11.96	12.72
	Implementation	Mean	47.97	65.74	105.17	120.09
	(n = 119)	(SD)	16.12	9.64	13.85	10.57
	Maintenance	Mean	48.64	63.16	104.99	118.21
	(n = 120)	(SD)	16.00	12.56	13.03	12.01

[a]Phonological Awareness Literacy Screening, first through third grade version. [b]Woodcock–Johnson Basic Skills Cluster.

The three-level HLM analysis of the PALS 1–3 at the beginning of first grade revealed a main effect for cohort ($F(2, 18) = 18.05$, p < .0001), initial risk status ($F(1, 9) = 386.30$, p < .0001), and condition ($F(2, 9) = 4.60$, p = .042). None of the interaction effects were significant. Contrasts for the effect of condition indicated that the children in the PD+I condition performed significantly better than those in the IO condition ($t(9) = -3.03$, p = .014). The performance level for the PDO condition was intermediate between the IO and the PD+I conditions and did not differ significantly from either condition. With regard to the cohort effect, the Baseline Cohort performed substantially below the Implementation ($t(18) = -4.50$, p < .001) and Maintenance Cohorts ($t(18) = -5.69$, p < .001) while the Implementation and Maintenance Cohorts did not differ significantly.

Analyses of the BSC revealed a similar pattern with significant main effects for cohort ($F(2, 18) = 11.44$, p < .001) and initial risk status ($F(1, 9) = 349.61$, p < .001) but only a marginal effect for condition ($F(2, 9) = 2.71$, p = .119). Follow-up tests of the cohort effect demonstrated statistically significant mean differences between the Baseline Cohort and Implementation Cohort, $t(18) = 3.97$, p = .0009, and between the Baseline Cohort and the Maintenance Cohort, $t(18) = 4.28$, p = .0004, with the Baseline Cohort performing worse than the other two cohorts. The initial risk main effect revealed that students at risk performed more poorly than students not at risk. There was no evidence that the gap between the two groups narrowed; the difference in performance between the at risk and not at risk groups was essentially the same for the Baseline and Maintenance Cohorts. In the IO condition we expected that such a narrowing would occur since no treatment was provided that would influence the reading skills of not at risk children. It is not a surprise, of course, that PD for classroom teachers provided in the PDO and PD+I conditions would have influenced the performance of both the at risk and the not at risk children.

3.4. Teacher Observation Data

From the CLASSIC, we derived variables that captured specific teacher activities and practices that were the focus of the PD program and that early literacy research suggests should be related to success in early literacy development. The observation data were then analyzed to determine whether and how the kindergarten teachers who participated in the PD program (PDO and PD+I conditions) changed their instruction from the Baseline to the Maintenance year. We also conducted an exploratory analysis using CLASSIC data collected when the teachers taught the Baseline Cohort in an effort to explain the substantial end of kindergarten performance differences across the three treatment conditions.

The observation data that were ultimately analyzed included only those periods of time that were coded as language arts time. Further, because teachers' schedules varied we included only the blocks of time that were devoted to language arts instruction and, within those blocks, only those slices in which the teacher was actively engaged in instruction.[4]

3.4.1. The Effects of PD on Instruction. As teachers from the PDO and PD+I conditions participated in the same PD program and since the sample of teachers for whom we had three consecutive years of data was limited, we opted to combine the PDO and PD+I groups to increase sample size and power. Before the decision was made, we examined the teaching activities of the two groups, and found few differences. To evaluate the effects of the PD program on instruction, we compared observation data for the Baseline Cohort and the Maintenance Cohort. Data gathered while the teachers taught the Implementation Cohort are presented but not specifically analyzed because they were collected while the teachers were being actively coached and because the lasting effects of PD were of more interest than the potentially temporary effects that were observed during the period of active PD.

Data included calculation of effect sizes (Glass' d) comparing observations during Baseline and Maintenance years. In addition, HLM analyses, with teachers nested within schools, were conducted to determine whether there were statistically significant differences between the Baseline and Maintenance years. Tables 6a and b present the means and standard deviations across the five observations for the number of slices that were coded as Active Language Arts instruction and for the number of times each (derived) observation code[5] was assigned. It is important to note that the means are computed on raw counts. Note that for the relatively stable features (Table 6a) the amount of time allocated to particular instructional activities can be estimated by multiplying the number of times a particular code was assigned by 1.5 min (representing the time interval for each observational slice). Such time estimates are not possible for the relatively dynamic features of instruction (Table 6b).

Using Cohen's (1988) guidelines for interpreting effect sizes (0.2, 0.5, and 0.8 suggesting small, moderate and large effects, respectively), the data in Table 6a suggest that PD had a significant, moderate effect on the total amount of time that teachers devoted to language arts instruction, and a significant, large effect on the time allocated to having students actively reading, writing, or engaged in skill activities. However, PD did not change the time that teachers' allocated to comprehension and produced a small decrease in the time explicitly allocated to oral language, effects that were disappointing, since comprehension and oral language development were important features of the PD program.

Table 6a. Means, Standard Deviations, and Effect Sizes for the Relatively Stable Features of Instruction Coded (PDO and PD+I Teachers Combined)

	Base Mean (SD)	Imp Mean (SD)	Main Mean (SD)	Base Versus Main Effect Size	Base Versus Main p Value
Average number of slices per observation	85.2 (19.3)	101.6 (24.5)	99.7 (22.5)	.65	< .001
Active language arts teaching	41.8 (13.0)	52.2 (18.1)	51.5 (13.7)	0.75	< .0001
Lesson Plan Context					
Active reading, writing and skills	23.8 (10.5)	28.9 (10.8)	32.5 (11.9)	0.83	< .0001
Comprehension	3.1 (3.0)	4.1 (4.2)	3.3 (3.1)	0.05	Ns
Oral language	1.7 (1.4)	2.3 (2.8)	1.4 (1.4)	−0.21	Ns
Class Structure					
Teacher-led ability groups	8.1 (7.9)	12.0 (10.9)	15.7 (9.7)	0.96	< .0001
Instructional Materials					
Written sentences, words, letters	10.4 (7.0)	9.2 (5.2)	15.1 (9.6)	0.68	.001
Emergent level books	5.1 (5.7)	8.6 (7.4)	7.7 (7.8)	0.45	.03
Other texts	11.8 (4.5)	15.3 (8.7)	13.7 (6.7)	0.41	Ns
Student compositions	9.0 (4.5)	11.1 (6.4)	8.3 (5.8)	−0.15	Ns

Note. Codes were assigned to the verbatim record that was recorded at the beginning of each 90 s observational slice. For relatively stable features, such as Class Structure and Lesson Plan Context, multiplying the number of times the code was assigned by 1.5 (one and one half minutes) provides an estimate of the amount of time that particular instructional characteristics were observed. Base = Baseline, Imp = Implementation, Main = Maintenance.

Table 6b. Means, Standard Deviations, and Effect Sizes for the Relatively Dynamic Features of Instruction Coded (PDO and PD+I Teachers Combined)

	Base Mean (SD)	Imp Mean (SD)	Main Mean (SD)	Base Versus Main Effect Size	Base Versus Main p Value
Teacher Activity					
Scaffolding and modeling	4.7 (2.3)	4.5 (1.9)	4.5 (2.2)	−0.09	Ns
Question, response, feedback	24.6 (8.7)	32.2 (12.1)	31.1 (8.4)	0.75	.0003
Specific Instructional Focus					
Phonemic analysis	1.4 (1.0)	2.6 (2.7)	3.0 (2.0)	0.83	.004
Letter names and sounds	6.1 (4.3)	5.3 (3.3)	9.7 (7.6)	0.83	.009
Larger orthographic units	1.2 (1.1)	1.2 (0.9)	1.5 1.3	0.26	Ns
Sound spelling	1.9 (1.5)	2.2 (2.3)	1.7 (1.2)	−0.14	Ns
Word ID strategies	0.6 (0.9)	1.0 (0.8)	0.8 (0.9)	0.23	Ns
Sight words	2.8 (1.6)	3.3 (2.1)	3.6 (1.8)	0.52	.09
Comprehension	6.5 (3.0)	9.2 (5.0)	6.4 (3.7)	−0.01	Ns
Vocabulary and language	3.2 (1.6)	4.7 (2.9)	3.2 (1.8)	0.02	Ns
Student Activity					
Read	6.0 (3.9)	8.8 (5.8)	8.3 (4.8)	0.59	.01
Think and respond	13.6 (5.4)	16.2 (6.2)	16.0 (4.5)	0.45	.01
Listen to read alouds	2.2 (1.0)	3.4 (2.7)	3.2 (2.3)	1.001	.04

Note. Base = Baseline, Imp = Implementation, Main = Maintenance.

Following the PD program, teachers demonstrated substantial increases in the time devoted to teacher-led instruction provided to small, ability-based groups. This was consistent with the PD program, which stressed the need to match instruction to the children's current capabilities. Also, during the maintenance year, we observed significant increases in the amount of time teachers used printed materials highlighted in the PD such as emergent level books, sentences, words, and letters in isolation. There was no change in the time spent using other texts or student compositions as materials.

Data on the more dynamic features of instruction (Table 6b) indicate that following PD, teachers were coded as engaging with students by questioning, listening, and providing feedback significantly more often than in the Baseline year. This change is consistent with the increase in time devoted to small group instruction. Surprisingly, PD did not yield an observable change in the use of modeling and scaffolding, although these were stressed in the PD.

With regard to Specific Instructional Focus, there were large, significant effects on the number of times that teachers were coded as focusing on phonemic analysis and on letter names, sounds, and graphic features. However, it is noteworthy that phonemic analysis was the focus of instruction only infrequently during our observations. PD also resulted in a moderate increase in the number of times teachers were coded as focusing on developing sight word knowledge; this effect approached significance. Although also a focus of PD, only small, non-significant effects were observed on teachers' tendency to focus instruction on word identification strategies and on larger orthographic units such as word families, or on the use of instruction focused on sound spelling, comprehension, or vocabulary and oral language.

With regard to student responses during instruction, Maintenance Cohort children were coded as being engaged in listening to read alouds, in reading, and in thinking and responding significantly more often than Baseline Cohort children. All of these effects were consistent with the PD and statistically significant.

In general, the effects of the PD program seem to have had a positive and lasting effect on the kindergarten instruction. During the Maintenance year, as compared with the Baseline year, teachers were observed to spend more time on Active Language Arts instruction, to focus more on the differential needs of the children in their classes, and to focus more on the development of the foundational skills that tend to be associated with early reading difficulties. Following involvement in the PD program, teachers were also observed to more frequently engage the children in reading and in actively thinking and responding.

3.4.2. Comparison Across Conditions for the Baseline Cohort. As noted previously, there were unanticipated differences across the three conditions for the Baseline Cohort in end of year performance levels on the PALS-K. In an effort to explain these differences, we compared the CLASSIC data for the teachers in the three conditions during the year in which they taught the Baseline Cohort. Tables 7a and b provide these data. Note that the effect sizes compare the PD+I condition with the IO condition since these are the two conditions that tended to yield the largest differences in student performance for the Baseline

Table 7a. Means, Standard Deviations, and Effect Sizes for CLASSIC Codes for Relatively Stable Features of Instruction Used in Observation of Teachers in Three Conditions During the Baseline Year

		IO (n = 9)	PDO (n = 10)	PD+I (n = 9)	IO Versus PD+I Effect Size	p Value
Mean slices per	Mean	96.4	85.8	84.5	−.60	Ns
observation	SD	(18.9)	(19.1)	(20.8)		
Active language arts	Mean	40.1	40.8	42.9	0.24	Ns
teaching	SD	(8.2)	(11.3)	(15.3)		
Lesson Plan Context						
Active reading, writing	Mean	17.7	23.6	24.1	0.78	Ns
and skills	SD	(5.2)	(10.4)	(11.2)		
Comprehension	Mean	1.7	2.6	3.6	0.77	Ns
	SD	(1.4)	(2.2)	(3.7)		
Oral language	Mean	1.8	1.9	1.4	−0.24	Ns
	SD	(2.3)	(1.7)	(1.1)		
Class Structure						
Teacher-led ability groups	Mean	1.9	6.6	9.8	1.12	< .001
	SD	(4.3)	(5.8)	(9.8)		
Instructional Materials						
Written sentences, words,	Mean	6.6	10.9	9.8	0.60	Ns
letters	SD	(4.7)	(8.1)	(6.0)		
Emergent level books	Mean	1.9	4.1	6.1	0.81	Ns
	SD	(2.6)	(2.9)	(7.9)		
Other texts	Mean	14.9	11.2	12.6	−0.54	Ns
	SD	(3.9)	(4.6)	(4.5)		
Student compositions	Mean	7.9	9.3	8.6	0.18	Ns
	SD	(3.0)	(4.3)	(4.9)		

Note. Codes were assigned to the verbatim record that was recorded at the beginning of each 90 s observational slice.

Table 7b. Means, Standard Deviations, and Effect Sizes for CLASSIC Codes for Relatively Dynamic Features of Instruction Used in Observation of Teachers in Three Conditions During the Baseline Year

		IO (n = 9)	PDO (n = 10)	PD+I (n = 9)	IO Versus PD+I Effect Size	IO Versus PD+I p Value
Teacher Activity						
Scaffolding and modeling	Mean	3.5	4.7	4.7	0.66	Ns
	SD	(1.1)	(2.2)	(2.6)		
Questioning and explanation	Mean	20.1	24.0	25.3	0.58	Ns
	SD	(8.8)	(8.6)	(9.2)		
Specific Instructional Focus						
Phonemic analysis	Mean	0.8	1.2	1.8	0.59	Ns
	SD	(0.7)	(0.7)	(2.7)		
Letter names/sounds	Mean	5.5	6.4	5.8	0.09	Ns
	SD	(2.8)	(4.6)	(4.2)		
Larger orthographic units	Mean	0.3	1.3	1.0	1.22	Ns
	SD	(0.4)	(1.4)	(0.8)		
Sound spelling	Mean	0.8	2.3	1.4	0.77	Ns
	SD	(0.7)	(1.9)	(0.8)		
Word ID strategies	Mean	0.1	0.4	0.9	1.19	.03
	SD	(0.1)	(0.4)	(1.3)		
Sight words	Mean	2.6	2.9	2.7	0.06	Ns
	SD	(2.2)	(1.9)	(1.2)		
Comprehension	Mean	6.3	6.3	6.7	0.12	Ns
	SD	(3.1)	(2.3)	(3.8)		
Vocabulary and language	Mean	3.5	3.3	3.0	−0.30	Ns
	SD	(1.5)	(1.6)	(1.6)		
Student Activity						
Read	Mean	6.1	5.5	6.6	0.12	Ns
	SD	(3.3)	(2.4)	(5.2)		
Think and respond	Mean	9.9	13.3	13.9	0.75	Ns
	SD	(4.7)	(5.2)	(5.9)		
Every student response	Mean	0.0	0.1	0.0	NA	Ns
	SD	(0)	0.2	0.0		
Listen to read alouds	Mean	3.4	2.5	1.9	−1.03	Ns
	SD	(1.8)	1.0	1.2		

Note. Codes were assigned to the verbatim record that was recorded at the beginning of each 90 s observational slice.

Cohort. The data for the PDO condition are presented for purposes of comparison. Because the number of teachers in each condition is quite small, few of the comparisons are statistically significant and caution must be used in interpreting these contrasts. However, several of the effect sizes are substantial and thus may help to inform our understanding of what constitutes effective instruction.

Table 7a reveals that, while there were more observational slices for the teachers in the IO condition compared to the teachers in the other two conditions, the total time allocated to language arts instruction was similar across conditions. The three groups did differ (albeit not significantly) in time allocated to active reading, writing, and skills instruction with the teachers in the PD+I condition devoting nearly 50% more time to this topic than did the teachers in the IO condition. Differences across conditions were striking with regard to teachers attending to understanding and responding to students needs. PD+I teachers spent approximately five times more time in working with small ability-based groups than did the IO teachers. PD+I teachers made substantially greater use of emergent level books and other printed materials that would provide the children with the opportunity to attend to and analyze written text. Teachers in the IO condition made greater use of "other texts" which were typically texts that were read aloud to the children.

PD+I teachers were observed to provide more scaffolding and modeling and to engage in questioning and explanation more often (Table 7b). With the Baseline Cohort, classroom teachers in the PD+I condition focused more often on phonemic analysis, teaching about larger orthographic units, sound spelling, and word identification strategies, that is, topics that would enable the children to effectively use the alphabetic code. However, it is important to note that these foci were coded infrequently. It is also important to note similarities among the PD+I and IO teachers in most frequent topics for instruction: comprehension, letter names and sounds, and vocabulary and oral language.

With regard to what the students were engaged in during language arts instruction, the data in Table 7b reveal that children in the PD+I condition were more often coded as being engaged in thinking and responding than children in the IO condition. On the other hand, children in the IO condition were more often coded as listening to read alouds than the children in the PD+I condition. Children in both conditions were coded as being engaged in reading about equally often.

Taken together, at Baseline, the observation data suggest that the teachers in the PD+I condition differed from the teachers in the IO condition in ways that allowed their students to actively learn early literacy skills. The most striking difference between groups was in the use of small ability-based groupings. In the context of RTI models, teachers are frequently encouraged to attend to the varying instructional needs of the children in their classroom with particular attention to the needs of the children who are not meeting grade level expectations. This recommendation is consistent with the finding that teachers who were most successful in improving the outcomes for their at risk students devoted more time to working with small ability-based groups.

4. Discussion

The main purpose of this study was to investigate the reading growth of at risk kindergarten children in Response to Intervention under one of three conditions: Professional Development for classroom teachers only (PDO), supplemental small group Intervention Only (IO), or the two treatments combined (PD+I). The Interactive Strategies Approach to reading instruction was used in all three conditions. As previous intervention research had demonstrated that both supplemental small group and one-to-one intervention was effective in reducing the incidence of early reading difficulties (Scanlon et al., 2005; Vellutino et al., 1996), a major question addressed in the current study was whether classroom teachers would also be able to reduce the incidence of early reading difficulties after participating in a PD program designed to improve early literacy instruction. This is an important question given that RTI models view classroom instruction as the first tier of intervention for at risk children.

The findings suggest that all three intervention conditions (IO, PDO, and PD+I) were effective in helping to substantially reduce the incidence of early reading difficulties. Comparisons of performance levels in the Baseline and Maintenance Cohorts in each condition showed that the number of children who qualified as at risk from the beginning to the end of kindergarten was reduced and that the performance levels of at risk children were substantially increased at the end of kindergarten and beginning of first grade. Moreover, the classification analyses suggested that the instructional modifications provided in all conditions were an important determinant of classification accuracy. In general, as instruction became more effective, assessment-based classification accuracy declined. With improvements in instruction, more children made more progress that resulted in both an increase in the incidence of False Positives and a decrease in the incidence of False Negatives. To an extent, the inclusion of growth parameters of the types typically used in RTI classification studies (Compton, Fuchs, Fuchs, & Bryant, 2006; Vellutino, Scanlon, Zhang, & Schatschneider, 2008), indexes the quality of instruction—the more effective the instruction, the greater the growth demonstrated by students receiving the instruction.

The design of this study was intended to allow us to evaluate the relative effectiveness of the three treatment conditions compared. However, comparisons within the Baseline Cohort revealed that, although groups assigned to the three conditions were similar at kindergarten entry, there were marked performance differences after kindergarten instruction. That is, there were substantial differences in classroom teacher effectiveness for the three conditions before the experimental treatments were instituted. These pre-existing differences limit our ability to confidently make direct comparisons related to the relative effectiveness of the three intervention conditions. Thus, given the current data, it is not possible to determine which of the three conditions was more or less effective in improving outcomes for students who qualified as at risk. Therefore, in what follows, we discuss the effects of each condition separately.

The PDO condition served as a Tier 1 intervention. The results for this condition demonstrate that when provided with ISA-based PD, classroom teachers reduced by half (35% Baseline to 17% Maintenance) the number of children who qualified as at risk at the end of the year. Further evidence for the effectiveness of the PDO condition is provided by the improved performance levels of the Maintenance Cohort children who entered kindergarten at risk. As a group, they performed at a substantially higher level on the end of kindergarten and beginning of first grade assessments than did the Baseline Cohort.

The IO condition could be considered a form of Tier 2 intervention. The Baseline versus Maintenance group differences at the end of kindergarten were larger in this condition than in the other two conditions. However, because the end of kindergarten and beginning of first grade performance levels for the Baseline Cohort in this condition were much lower than for the Baseline Cohorts in the other two conditions, it seems likely that the large differences are at least partially attributable to substantial weaknesses in the instruction offered by classroom teachers in the IO Baseline Cohort.

We had anticipated that the provision of both Professional Development for classroom teachers and supplemental instruction for at risk students (PD+I) would have a stronger positive impact on early literacy skills for the at risk children than either of the treatments alone. However, the data do not support this hypothesis. Indeed, considering just the end of kindergarten PALS-K scores, it is evident that the smallest Baseline versus Maintenance differences occurred in the PD+I condition while the largest differences occurred in the IO condition (see Table 4). While this finding could be taken as evidence that the PD+I condition was the least effective, it is important to note that the performance level of the Maintenance group for the IO condition equaled the performance level for the Baseline Cohort in the PD+I condition. Thus, before involvement in any of the interventions instituted by the research project, the teachers in the PD+I condition were already highly effective in promoting growth in literacy skills among their students who were at risk. While the implementation of enhancements to the classroom program through PD and the addition of supplemental small group instruction did result both in reductions in the number of children who qualified as at risk and in overall improvement in performance levels among children in the at risk group, it may be that further improvements would have required the implementation of more intensive intervention (Tier 3) for the children who continued to struggle despite high quality interventions at both Tier 1 and Tier 2. It should be recalled that the Tier 2 intervention offered was rather limited (30 min of small group instruction twice per week). On the other hand, it is possible that, as suggested by the LLs when presented with these outcomes, the teachers in the PD+I condition may have felt less of a press to address the needs of their at risk students since those children were receiving supplemental instruction outside of the classroom. Nevertheless, overall, it seems safe to infer that PD for classroom teachers (which supports Tier 1 intervention) was at least as effective as supplemental small group remediation (Tier 2 intervention) in reducing the number of kindergartners who continued to be at risk for reading difficulties over the course of the school year.

Were we to make recommendations for implementing a tiered approach to intervention based on the results of the current study, we would argue strongly for beginning with PD for kindergarten classroom teachers. The current study clearly demonstrates that teachers provided with the type of PD utilized in this project can substantially reduce the number of children who are at risk for reading difficulties at the end of kindergarten. In light of the cost effectiveness of improving the quality of classroom instruction versus providing direct, supplemental interventions to children (which requires additional staffing), the argument in favor of PD for classroom teachers as a critical component of early intervention and Tier 1 intervention in particular seems strong.

This argument is buttressed by observed differences in the effectiveness of classroom instruction among teachers in the different treatment conditions. In order to better understand characteristics of kindergarten language arts instruction that were associated with better child outcomes, we conducted periodic observations of instruction. In the current paper we focused on comparisons of instructional characteristics in the year before and the year after teachers participated in a PD program. We also compared the instructional characteristics of teachers who were found to be particularly effective in promoting early literacy skills among their at risk students in the Baseline Cohort (the teachers in the PD+I condition) and those who were found to be substantially less effective (the teachers in the IO condition). With regard to the effects of PD, the analyses revealed that involvement in the program led teachers to devote more time to language arts instruction. However, that additional time was not evenly distributed across all areas of language arts. Rather, the Baseline–Maintenance group comparisons revealed that, following PD, teachers devoted significantly more time to engaging children in reading text, writing, and learning foundational skills, but no more time to comprehension or oral language development. Further, almost all of the additional time devoted to Active Language Arts instruction could be accounted for by increases in the amount of time devoted to teaching small groups of children with the groups being organized by instructional need. Increases were also noted in the amount of time teachers devoted to actively engaging the children, as evidenced by significant increases in the frequency with which teachers used questioning and provided feedback and the children were observed to be reading or thinking and/or providing responses. During the Maintenance year, teachers were observed to focus more often on developing foundational literacy skills such as teaching about letters and their sounds and developing phonemic awareness. However, although we articulated the need to attend to comprehension and oral language development during the PD program, we apparently did not emphasize this enough since changes in these aspects of instruction tended to be small and transitory (i.e., they were apparent during the Implementation year but not during the Maintenance year).

Comparisons of the two treatment groups that differed in the effectiveness of the classroom teachers during the Baseline year (IO versus PD+I) yielded results that were largely consistent with the findings derived from the analysis of the effects of PD. Thus, for example, comparisons of the more effective group (PD+I) with the comparatively ineffective group (IO) indicated that the more effective group spent significantly more time during language arts instruction working with small ability-based groups. And, while none of the other comparisons yielded statistically significant differences, the directions of several of the differences were consistent with the findings from the PD comparisons.

Before concluding this paper it is important to discuss some of the limitations of the design and procedures utilized. In designing school-based research it is almost always necessary to deviate from the generally preferred randomized control trial design that can be so powerful in allowing researchers to attribute causality to the experimental treatments. In this study we utilized a quasi-experimental design with assignment to conditions being done at the level of the school in order to avoid the multiple objections that would be raised by parents, teachers, and school administrators when children in the same school are treated in distinctly different ways. An additional limitation was the use of the Baseline Cohort as our primary control group for each treatment. While several interpretational problems can arise with the use of historical control groups, given the goal of explicitly studying the effects of PD for teachers on student achievement and the widely documented variability in teacher effectiveness, having each teacher serve as her own control seemed justified. An additional limitation that must be considered is that all of the teachers in this study volunteered to participate. While this is, of course, the only way such a study could be conducted, it has important implications for generalization of the outcomes. Teachers who were willing to participate in a university-based study that involved classroom observations across a three-year period no doubt differ in multiple ways from teachers who declined to participate.

5. Summary

Taken together the results of this investigation provide clear evidence of the role of instruction in reducing the incidence of early reading difficulties. Particularly important is the evidence related to the role of classroom instruction as it clearly supports the role of Tier 1 interventions in an RTI approach. The analyses of the child outcomes and classroom observation data for the Baseline groups provided evidence of rather dramatic "natural" variability in the effectiveness and focus of kindergarten language arts instruction. The longitudinal study of teachers before, during, and after they participated in a PD program demonstrates that kindergarten classroom instruction can become substantially more effective in improving early literacy outcomes for students who are at risk. Importantly, instructional improvements were not accomplished via the implementation of a highly prescriptive program nor by the adoption of entirely new curricula but rather by encouraging teachers to analyze and respond to the instructional needs of their lower achieving students.

NOTES

This project was supported by an IERI grant funded by the National Institute of Child Health and Human Development (NICHHD grant number 1R01HD42350). The authors express their sincere gratitude to the teachers, students, and secretarial and administrative staff in participating schools. We are also grateful to the intervention teachers and data collection personnel who participated in these projects. Finally, special thanks and gratitude go to Sheila Small and Diane Fanuele for seeing to it that the ambitious aims of this project were accomplished on schedule. We also wish to thank Danielle Snyder who served as an Early Literacy Collaborator on this project.

[1] A comparison of the 28 participating teachers for whom three years of data were available with the 14 teachers who left the study at some point after the first year revealed very similar profiles in terms of years of teaching experience (14.1 years versus 16.8 years respectively for those who remained and those who did not) and in terms of years of experience teaching kindergarten (7.0 years versus 9.9 years respectively for those who remained in the study and those who did not).

[2] For this paper, we do not report all of the codes that were used for each feature of the coding system either because they did not occur with sufficient frequency to warrant interpretation and/or because they occurred relatively infrequently and did not differentiate the groups of interest.

[3] A reviewer of an earlier version of this manuscript questioned whether the children identified as at risk at kindergarten entry were really at risk given that in the PDO and PD+I conditions the at risk group attained BSC scores in the average range at the beginning of first grade. However, it should be noted that this occurred after a full year in kindergarten and, consistent with the logic of RTI, there is every reason to expect that classroom instruction should be effective in accelerating children's progress.

[4] We removed slices that would not be considered teacher-provided Language Arts instruction as indicated by Lesson Plan Context codes. These included slices that occurred during blocks of time when another teacher (e.g., the speech and language teacher), taught the lesson, and blocks devoted to non-language

arts topics. However, we did retain from these non-language arts blocks individual slices where the Specific Instructional Focus indicated that the classroom teacher was engaged in language arts activities. Thus, the analyzed data included activities such as the teacher going over one student's composition during snack, shared reading of the directions on a math work sheet, or instances where language arts activities were incorporated into management routines such as students being dismissed by the first letter of their name. We also removed slices in which the teacher was not attending to students during a language arts block, based on Teacher Activity codes. These included situations where the teacher was called to the phone or was doing paper work while students were engaged in a language arts task. Non-instructional slices during language arts blocks were also removed. These included instances where the Specific Instructional Focus was coded as instructional management, student behavior or socialization, informal (non-instructional) interaction between the teacher and students, or where the teacher stopped teaching her group because of an interruption. Finally, we removed slices within language arts blocks where the Specific Instructional Focus was on a content area other than language arts (i.e., math, science, social studies, the arts). The remaining slices were considered to be Active Language Arts Teaching time. The analyses used these slices.

[5]It will be recalled that using the codes originally assigned by observers we collapsed related codes to form variables that characterized language arts instruction in a more comprehensive way. By doing so, we also reduced the number of variables analyzed.

REFERENCES

Bond, G.L., & Dykstra, R. (1967). The cooperative research program in first-grade reading instruction. *Reading Research Quarterly, 2,* 5–142.

Clay, M. (1987). Learning to be learning disabled. *New Zealand Journal of Educational Studies, 22,* 155–173.

Cohen, J. (1988). *Statistical power analysis for the behavioral sciences.* Hillsdale, NJ: Erlbaum.

Compton, D.L., Fuchs, D., Fuchs, L.S., & Bryant, J.D. (2006). Selecting at-risk readers in first grade for early intervention: A two-year longitudinal study of decision rules and procedures. *Journal of Educational Psychology, 98*(2), 394–409.

Denton, C.A., & Mathes, P.G. (2003). Intervention for struggling readers: Possibilities and challenges. In Foorman, B.R. (Ed.), *Preventing and remediating reading difficulties: Bringing science to scale* (pp. 229–251). Timonium, MD: York Press.

Fletcher, J.M., Shaywitz, S.E., Shankweiler, D.P., Katz, L., Liberman, I.Y., Stuebing, K.K., et al. (1994). Cognitive profiles of reading disability: Comparisons of discrepancy and low achievement definitions. *Journal of Educational Psychology, 86,* 6–23.

Foorman, B.R., & Schatschneider, C. (2003). Measurement of teaching practices during reading/language arts instruction and its relationship to student achievement. In S. Vaughn & K.L. Briggs (Eds.), *Reading in the classroom: Systems for the observation of teaching and learning* (pp. 1–30). Baltimore, MD: Paul H. Brookes.

Fuchs, L.S., & Fuchs, D. (1998). Treatment validity: A unifying concept for reconceptualizing the identification of learning disabilities. *Learning Disabilities Research & Practice, 13*, 204–219.

Fuchs, L.S., Fuchs, D., & Speece, D.L. (2002). Treatment validity as a unifying construct for identifying learning disabilities. *Learning Disability Quarterly, 25*, 33–45.

Invernizzi, M., & Meier, J. (2000–2001). PALS 1–3: Phonological Awareness Literacy Screening. Charlottsville, VA: University of Virginia.

Invernizzi, M., Meier, J., Swank, L., & Juel, C. (1999–2000). PALS K: Phonological Awareness Literacy Screening. Charlottsville, VA: University of Virginia.

Lyon, G.R., Fletcher, J.M., Fuchs, L., & Chhabra, V. (2006). Learning disabilities. In E. Mash & R. Barkley (Eds.), *Treatment of childhood disorders* (3rd ed., pp. 512–591). New York: Guilford.

National Reading Panel. (2000). *Report of the National Reading Panel: Teaching children to read: An evidence-based assessment of the scientific research literature on reading and its implications for reading instruction.* Washington, DC: National Institute of Child Health and Human Development.

O'Connor, R.E., Fulmer, D., Harty, K.R., & Bell, K.M. (2005). Layers of reading intervention in kindergarten through third grade: Changes in teaching and student outcomes. *Journal of Learning Disabilities, 38*(5), 440–455.

Pressley, M., Wharton-McDonald, R., Allington, R., Block, C.C., Morrow, L., Tracey, D., et al. (2001). A study of effective first-grade literacy instruction. *Scientific Studies of Reading, 5*, 35–58.

Scanlon, D.M., Gelzheiser, L., Fanuele, D., Sweeney, J., & Newcomer, L. (2003).

Classroom Language Arts Systematic Sampling and Instructional Coding (CLASSIC). Unpublished manuscript, Child Research and Study Center, The University at Albany.

Scanlon, D.M., & Sweeney, J.M. (2004). Supporting children's literacy development in the primary grades. Unpublished manuscript.

Scanlon, D.M., & Vellutino, F.R. (1996). Prerequisite skills, early instruction, and success in first grade reading: Selected results from a longitudinal study. *Mental Retardation and Developmental Disabilities Research Reviews, 2*, 54–63.

Scanlon, D.M., & Vellutino, F.R. (1997). A comparison of the instructional backgrounds and cognitive profiles of poor, average and good readers who were initially identified as at risk for reading failure. *Scientific Studies of Reading, 1*, 191–216.

Scanlon, D.M., Vellutino, F.R., Small, S.G., Fanuele, D.P., & Sweeney, J. (2005). Severe reading difficulties: Can they be prevented? A comparison of prevention and intervention approaches. *Exceptionality, 13*, 209–227.

Share, D.L. (1995). Phonological recoding and self teaching: sin qua non of reading acquisition. *Cognition, 55*, 151–218.

Snow, C.E., Griffin, P., & Burns, M.S. (2005). *Knowledge to support the teaching of reading.* San Francisco, CA: Jossey-Bass.

Snow, C.E., & Juel, C. (2005). Teaching children to read: What do we know about how to do it? In *The Science of teaching reading: A handbook.* Malden, MA: Blackwell.

Stanovich, K.E., & Siegel, L.S. (1994). Phenotypic performance profiles of children with reading disabilities: A regression-based test of the phonological-core variable difference model. *Journal of Educational Psychology, 86*, 24–53.

Taylor, B.M., Pearson, P.D., Clark, K., & Walpole, S. (2000). Effective schools and accomplished teachers: Lessons about primary-grade reading instruction in low income schools. *The Elementary School Journal, 101*, 121–166.

Tivnan, T., & Hemphill, L. (2005). Comparing four literacy reform models in high poverty schools: Patterns of first-grade achievement. *The Elementary School Journal, 105*(5), 419–441.

Vaughn, S., Linan-Thompson, S., & Hickman, P. (2003). Response to treatment as a means of identifying students with reading/learning disabilities. *Exceptional Children, 69*(4), 391–409.

Vellutino, F.R., & Scanlon, D.M. (2002). The Interactive Strategies approach to reading intervention. *Contemporary Educational Psychology, 27*, 573–635.

Vellutino, F.R., Scanlon, D.M., Sipay, E.R., Small, S.G., Pratt, A., Chen, R.S., et al. (1996). Cognitive profiles of difficult to remediate and readily remediated poor readers: Early intervention as a vehicle for distinguishing between cognitive and experiential deficits as basic causes of specific reading disability. *Journal of Educational Psychology, 88*, 601–638.

Vellutino, F.R., Scanlon, D.M., Small, S., & Fanuele, D.P. (2006). Response to intervention as a vehicle for distinguishing between reading disabled and non-reading disabled children: Evidence for the role of kindergarten and first grade intervention. *Journal of Learning Disabilities, 38*(6), 157–169.

Vellutino, F.R., Scanlon, D.M., Zhang, H., & Schatschneider, C. (2008). Using Response to kindergarten and first grade intervention to identify children at-risk for long-term reading difficulties. *Reading and Writing, 21*, 437–480.

Woodcock, R.W., McGrew, K.S., & Mather, N. (2001). *Woodcock–Johnson III: Tests of Achievement*. Circle Pines, MN: American Guidance Services.

CHAPTER 15

Reflective Coaching Conversations: A Missing Piece

Debra S. Peterson, Barbara M. Taylor, Bobbie Burnham, and Rynell Schock

L iteracy coaching is a critical component of many major schoolwide reading improvement efforts in our nation today. Under Reading First alone, more than 5,600 schools have hired full-time literacy coaches as a way to provide job-embedded learning for teachers (Moss, Jacob, Boulay, Horst, & Poulos, 2006). Many authors and current publications promote the use of literacy coaches for professional development and reading reform. Neufeld and Roper (2003) wrote, "When coaching is integral to a larger instructional improvement plan that targets and aligns professional development resources toward the district's goals, it has potential to become a powerful vehicle for improving instruction and, thereby, student achievement" (p. 26). Joyce and Showers (1995) stated that teachers need to have opportunities to learn about new strategies and techniques, to observe demonstration of strategies, and to practice and receive feedback on the strategies in their own classroom setting. Uzat (1998) considered coaching a practical and systematic approach to ongoing teacher improvement by engaging teachers in focused reflection on teaching methods.

As compelling as these recommendations may seem, there is little empirical evidence that having literacy coaches in schools leads to growth and achievement in students' reading. Some of the reasons for this are that the use of literacy coaches for schoolwide reading improvement and professional development is a fairly new phenomenon, there is little uniformity in the role of coaches from site to site, there is a lack of data linking coaching directly to changes in teacher practice and student achievement, and there is limited documentation of what actually occurs during coaching interactions. Deussen, Coskie, Robinson, and Autio (2007)

RTI in Literacy—Responsive and Comprehensive, edited by Peter H. Johnston, published by the International Reading Association. This chapter reprinted from Peterson, D.S., Taylor, B.M., Burnham, B., & Schock, R. (2009). Reflective Coaching Conversations: A Missing Piece. *The Reading Teacher*, 62(6), 500–509.

found that the role of the literacy coach looked very different from school to school and covered a variety of responsibilities other than coaching. They stated, "Simply knowing that literacy coaches are in schools does not imply anything about how those individuals are spending their time—there is a difference between being a coach and doing coaching" (p. iii). When surveyed, coaches reported that many non-instructional tasks overshadowed their work with teachers and students.

For example, in a study by Bean and Zigmond (2006), 100 coaches in 161 Reading First schools documented how they used their time by completing a weekly log three times during the year. Coaches reported that they spent less than 3 hours a week in each of the following: observations (1.8 hours), coaching conferences with teachers (1.8 hours), modeling (1.5 hours), and coteaching (0.5 hours). The coaches also documented more than 4 hours a week devoted to each of these noninstructional activities: attending meetings (4.4 hours), planning (4.1 hours), and attending professional development sessions (4.1 hours). Clearly, coaching activities accounted for only a fraction of time during coaches' work weeks. When literacy coaches do work with teachers in a coaching capacity, there is little documentation of what they do, how the coaching affects teacher performance, and ultimately how the coaching of teachers stimulates students' growth and achievement in reading.

The purpose of this article is to document and describe actual coaching conversations between literacy coaches and teachers in elementary schools that were seeing important gains in students' reading achievement. Examining real-life coaching interactions may provide insight on the elements of coaching conversations that are more effective in fostering teachers' reflection on the impact of their instruction on students' reading and learning. These examples may contribute to our understanding of how to help teachers modify instruction to increase its effectiveness and to sustain these practices in their daily teaching of reading. Perhaps these examples will also inspire schools that do not foster teacher reflection to consider the importance of establishing a climate of continual learning and collaboration as a means to reading reform.

With the coaching conversation model used in the Minnesota Reading First Professional Development Program, a literacy coach observed a teacher's reading lesson and collected data on the observed instruction. These data may have included a count of the number of students that were on task at various times throughout the lesson, information on teacher–student interaction patterns and the use of grouping patterns or materials, as well as concrete examples of other critical elements of instruction during a specific lesson (i.e., higher order questions, comprehension strategy instruction). The coach then used these data to ask questions to support the teacher in a process of self-reflection and conversation about her teaching practices and students' reading performance.

Coaching for self-reflection is a collaborative model in which the coach and the teacher work in partnership to make more effective decisions about classroom instruction. The ultimate goal of working with a literacy coach is to deepen the teacher's understanding of how students learn by facilitating self-reflection to bring about change in classroom instruction, which has the potential to lead to increased student achievement. Rodgers and Rodgers (2007) wrote,

> By supporting and fostering conversations about teaching...the coach has the opportunity to provoke not only deep reflection but also action regarding teaching. Through careful analysis, teachers have an opportunity to enhance practices that work, reform practices that don't work as well as they could, and abandon practices that seem to hinder what works. (p. 13)

In this model of coaching, a critical component of coaching conversations was the use of concrete data on the teacher's instruction to facilitate self-reflection and change. This critical component is often the missing piece to reading reform efforts.

Background of the Study

The 24 schools involved in the Minnesota Reading First Professional Development Program (Taylor & Peterson, 2007) were diverse in location (i.e., inner-city, suburban, small town, rural), socioeconomic status (32%–95% of their students received subsidized lunches), and percent of students who were English-language learners (ELLs; 0%–66%). As a part of their ongoing, job-embedded professional development all kindergarten to grade 3 classroom teachers and licensed resource teachers in a school participated in weekly, teacher-led, collaborative study groups to discuss scientifically based reading research, to learn new instructional techniques and to refine their current practices, to examine student data and to adjust daily instruction based on students' progress or needs.

Teachers also shared video clips of their own instruction in their study groups to gain suggestions and insights from their colleagues and to facilitate self-reflection. To assist teachers in this process of learning and reflection, each school had two literacy coaches, one full-time coach provided by the school district and one half-time coach provided by the professional development provider, the University of Minnesota. Coaches were encouraged to work as a team to support the school in its efforts to implement schoolwide instructional reading improvement in kindergarten to grade 3. Coaches had many responsibilities in their schools but were encouraged to spend 80% of their time in classrooms working with teachers on reading instruction.

The 48 Minnesota Reading First coaches were a diverse group of teachers. They ranged in experience from 5 to 30 or more years in teaching, and their educational backgrounds ranged from Bachelor to Doctorate degrees. Some of the coaches had administrative or mentoring experience but the majority of coaches had left regular education classroom teaching assignments to serve as literacy coaches in the Reading First schools. During 2006–2007, all but one of the coaches were female.

Training for Coaches

Literacy coaches met approximately every five weeks to engage in professional learning on scientifically based reading research on the five main areas of reading as described by the National Reading Panel Report (National Institute of Child Health and Human Development [NICHD], 2000) including phonemic awareness, phonics and the application of word recognition strategies, fluency, vocabulary, and comprehension. The professional development also provided time for coaches to reflect on and refine their ability to facilitate coaching conversations with teachers at their sites. Included in these professional development sessions were opportunities to view video clips of each other's teaching and then initiate coaching conversations with one another. A third coach was encouraged to observe the coaching conversation so that he or she could provide feedback to the coach.

Coaches also learned to use several protocols designed to collect data on instruction as the basis for their subsequent coaching conversations with teachers. All of the protocols were based on current research on effective reading instruction and a model of reading instruction that maximizes students' cognitive engagement (Taylor et al., 2003, 2005). The Cognitive Engagement Model encourages teachers to consider *how* they teach as well as *what* they teach by asking them to reflect on the following questions:

- To what extent were my students engaged in higher level thinking during talk or writing about text (i.e., connections between the text and their lives, character interpretation, author's message or theme)?

- To what extent am I teaching reading strategies (i.e., word recognition strategies, comprehension strategies) in addition to reading skills?

- To what extent am I teaching reading with a student-support stance (i.e., modeling, coaching, listening/watching/giving feedback) in addition to a teacher-directed stance (i.e., telling, recitation)?

- To what extent are my students engaged in active (i.e., reading, writing, manipulating, and orally responding with a partner) versus passive responding (i.e., listening, reading turn-taking, oral turn-taking) during this reading lesson?

- To what extent did I clearly identify and explain the purpose of the lesson? How will my lesson help individual students grow in literacy abilities?

Coaches also received training on elements of effective instruction not specifically addressed in the National Reading Panel Report including motivation, culturally responsive instruction, and differentiation of instruction based on student assessment data. The emphasis of the training was to consider ways to provide challenge and rigor for all students.

Selection of Schools for Further Study

We wanted to capture and describe coaching conversations that were occurring in the Minnesota Reading First schools by observing some effective coaching teams during a normal school day. We selected coaching teams based on three criteria: overall school effectiveness rating, overall school reform effort rating, and students' growth in reading. Each of these will be described below:

1. School Effectiveness Rating—All the teachers involved in the Minnesota Reading First Professional Development program were interviewed by University of Minnesota data collectors in the fall and the spring. Interviews were 30 minutes long and consisted of open-ended questions about key components of the school's reform efforts. These components included collaboration on reading instruction, building partnerships with parents and families, instructional reflection and change, professional development, shared leadership, and schoolwide use of assessment data. All responses were read and coded using a four-point rubric for each of the key components. An example of the four-point rubric for instructional reflection and change can be found in Figure 1.

Figure 1. Sample Four-Point Rubric

A. Instructional reflection and change:

0—Little or no reflection on instructional practice is expressed by the individual classroom teachers. There is some talk between individual teachers about what is working in their reading instruction.

1—Teachers talk and share with each other about what is working in their reading instruction during formal meeting times (i.e., grade level meetings, professional learning communities).

2—Teachers talk and share ideas with each other in study groups or professional learning communities. They may examine student work, reflect on their own instructional practice by sharing videos of their instruction, and read current research on best practices, but most of their discussions focus on sharing what they do in their own classrooms.

3—Teachers indicate they are intentionally reflecting on their practice by examining data on their instruction and are seriously working with others to improve their practice (i.e., study groups with action plans and video sharing of their instruction, grade level meetings where teachers look at student data to inform their instruction, discussing observation data with a coach or peer). Discussion within groups is informed by research on best practices and student assessment data.

2. Reform Effort—School artifacts were collected throughout the school year. Artifacts included meeting notes from study groups, whole group meetings, and grade-level meetings looking at student data, calendars, newsletters, and action plans from study groups. The artifacts were read and rated on a 10-point rubric focused on the school's implementation of professional development and the reform process (i.e., meeting weekly for an hour in teacher-led study groups). Schools received 1 point for successfully implementing an element of the reform. They received no points for elements of the reform process that were not evident in their documentation.

3. Students' Growth from Fall to Spring in Comprehension—All students in grades 1–3 were given the Gates–MacGinitie Reading Test in the fall and the spring. First-grade students took different versions of the test in the fall and the spring, and one of the schools did not have any grade 3 classrooms, so we selected grade 2 results in comprehension as a common criterion across all schools.

Schools were selected for further study if they scored a standard deviation above the mean for all schools on the total School Effectiveness Rating. Schools also had to score a 10 on the Reform Effort rating, which was the maximum score for that measure. These schools also had student growth in reading comprehension that ranged from 0.46 to 1.81 NCEs higher than the mean for all Reading First schools. Results from this selection process are summarized in Table 1.

Four schools met all the criteria and still had the same coaching teams in both the 2006–2007 and 2007–2008 school years. School A was an inner-city school where 95% of the students received subsidized lunch and 62% of the students were classified as ELLs. The two coaches at School A were veteran teachers with between 20 and 30 years of teaching experience each. School B was a suburban school with 32% of the students on subsidized lunch and 14% of the students were classified as ELLs. The coaches at this school each had between 15 and 25 years of teaching experience. School C was a small town/rural school where 42% of the students received subsidized lunches and 11% were ELLs. The coaches at School C were both veteran teachers. Each of them had more than 20 years of teaching experience. School D was another small town/rural school with 52% of the students qualifying for subsidized lunch and 16% of the students designated as ELLs. The two literacy coaches at School D had between 10 and 15

Table 1. Schools Selected for Further Study

Schools	School Effectiveness Rating (Total possible score = 18)	Reform Effort (Total possible score = 10)	Grade 2 Gates-MacGinitie Comprehension: Average Growth From Fall to Spring
All Reading First schools in 2006–2007	Mean 8.19 (SD 1.80)	Mean 9.08 (SD 1.06)	+ 0.38 NCE
School A (inner city)	10.40	10	+ 1.11 NCE
School B (suburban)	11.87	10	+ 1.83 NCE
School C (small town/rural)	10.00	10	+ 2.19 NCE
School D (small town/rural)	10.82	10	+ 0.84 NCE

years of teaching experience each. All the literacy coaches at these four schools were female. Seven of them were Caucasian and one was African American.

Data Collection

To learn more about the varying strategies used and the challenges faced by literacy coaches as they facilitated teachers' reflection on their reading instruction, eight coaches (two per school) were "shadowed" for six to eight hours by one of two observers. The observers were both experienced elementary teachers and literacy coaches. The observers made appointments to visit the schools on days when the coaches had several coaching conversations scheduled with teachers. Coaches had between two and three classroom observations and coaching conversations on the days they were "shadowed."

The observers attended each session with the coaches and typed as much of the conversations as possible on laptop computers. The observers documented the coaching conversations while remaining as unobtrusive as possible. The observers did not participate in the coaching conversations, give feedback to teachers or coaches, or comment on instruction. The detailed notes of the coaching conversations were then transcribed by the observers. Transcriptions were read multiple times by three researchers who looked for patterns across the four schools and the eight coaches. Patterns that emerged included the following:

1. The eight coaches did use the protocols recommended in their professional development to collect data on instruction and to structure their coaching conversations.

2. The coaches used the data from specific lessons to give concrete examples designed to draw the teachers' attention to crucial elements of the lessons.

3. The coaches asked questions to elicit conversations with teachers instead of telling teachers what should or should not be done.

4. The coaching conversations built connections between what the teachers were learning in their weekly study groups, their knowledge of their students' assessment data, and their implementation of research-based, effective reading instruction.

The following clips from coaching conversations are representative of the conversations observed in all four schools. We have selected clips that illustrate the four patterns that emerged from the field notes.

The Use of Protocols for Data Collection and Coaching Conversations

In the first example, a first-grade teacher in School B was modeling how to make predictions during a whole group lesson using a narrative text selection from the basal reader. Her goal was to demonstrate to her students how making predictions helps readers understand a text. This example of a coaching conversation illustrates how a coach used a simple protocol to help the teacher make reflective decisions regarding the effectiveness of the lesson and to set goals for future lessons. The protocol included these questions:

- What were the children able to do in this reading lesson? What went well?
- What did you as the teacher do to help the students succeed?
- What else could have been done to make the lesson even stronger or to help students be even more successful in reading?

Coach: What were the students doing well as you were working on the strategy of predicting?

Teacher: I could not believe how well they were doing. I couldn't believe their predictions and how they went back and checked their predictions. They were actually able to do this.

Coach: What did you do to make this happen?

Teacher: I think the modeling at the beginning helped the students. They never went on a tangent. I hoped that I modeled how to use predicting throughout the story.

Coach: You were modeling at the beginning.

Teacher: I kept trying to say look at the picture and think about whether or not the prediction came true. That's why I had to go back and check.

Coach: As you stopped throughout the story and asked if they were right about the prediction, you gave them the idea that it was important to go back and check if their prediction had happened. You kept asking, "Why are you saying, 'Oh no'?" You asked students to make predictions at the right time.

Teacher: The students were not able to understand the theme of the story.

Coach: How do you want to address that?

Teacher: We could do the theme of the story on another day. I could not get the children to think about the big idea of the story.

Coach: Perhaps when the students reread the story on their own, you could model how to consider the theme.

The coach used the protocol as she was taking notes about the lesson she observed. This specific information on the teacher's instruction and the students' responses guided the conversation and the teacher's reflection. Together, the teacher and the coach identified the need to provide more support to the students in understanding the theme of the story. The coach suggested that modeling could also be used to support students in this area as well. All the coaching conversations we observed used protocols to structure their data collection and the follow-up coaching conversations.

Using Data From Specific Lessons to Focus on Crucial Elements of Instruction

In the next example, a first-grade teacher from School C met with the coach for the purpose of reviewing the data from a formal observation conducted by the University data collector during whole-group instruction using informational text. This conversation demonstrates how a teacher used the data to focus on crucial elements of effective instruction. She also used the data to reflect on personal and district goals that she had set for her instruction.

Coach: Here is your goal sheet from last fall listing your goals for this year. You said you were going to work on instruction that would have more active responding from the students and you were going to provide appropriate levels of modeling, coaching, or feedback for students. How are you coming with these goals based on your observation data?

Teacher: I think the active responding has come a long way and the coaching is appropriate from what I can see.

Coach: That is my impression as well. You definitely know when and how to coach students. As you look at higher level questioning, how are you doing with using higher level questioning in your instruction?

Teacher: I was doing a whole group lesson on informational text. We were looking for key words and summarizing the text. The informational text is tougher. How can I use more high level questioning with informational text? This needs to be a new goal for me.

Coach: I see that you have already been reflecting on this area.

Teacher: It is easier to create these questions for narrative text than for informational text.

Coach: I agree. We can always ask lower level questions, but we have to think differently to develop higher level questions.

Teacher: If I am having students do a Think, Pair, Share, is that a higher level question?

Coach: It always depends on the question that is asked and the type of response that is given by the students. You will need to consider this when you are asking questions. Now, looking at your goal sheet, we see that the school goal is to use more informational text. Have you done that?

Teacher: I do use more informational text, but I need to use more higher level questions with this type of text. I need to focus on the type of questions I want to ask as I am preparing my lessons.

Coach: I agree. Your goals for instruction have been embedded into your lessons. Now, you said you are ready to write an additional goal that matches your school goals as well? How will you accomplish this goal?

Teacher: I would like to see you model a lesson with higher level questions for informational text.

Coach: I would be happy to do that. Another way I could offer support is to help you with planning or to give you feedback on your lesson. Once you have thought about and written down the questions, it will be easier to present the lesson.

Teacher: Thank you. I always appreciate your help.

The coach was able to use the observation data to talk with the teacher about the components of the Cognitive Engagement Model. Their discussion centered on the goals the teacher had set for herself based on scientifically based reading research. These goals were tied to school and district goals as well. As the teacher saw that she was meeting her existing goals, she noted new areas of growth. The teacher's reflection demonstrated her willingness to continuously refine her instruction.

Coaches Asked Questions to Elicit Conversation

In this next example of a coaching conversation, the coach was talking with a kindergarten teacher in School C about a whole group lesson where the teacher was using a think-aloud with a narrative text. She used the think-aloud to model how to ask and answer questions while reading. The coach referred to the data from the observation and asked questions to elicit a conversation with the teacher. Together, the teacher and the coach analyzed the data and looked for opportunities to refine the instruction. Through the conversation with the coach, the teacher demonstrated her understanding of how the changes she had made to her instruction had affected the students' responses and increased their ability to learn. Also, since she had implemented practices that engaged her students more fully, the teacher felt that she was matching her instruction to the needs of the students.

Coach: You are using a lot of modeling to support your students.

Teacher: Before the professional development in Reading First, I had never done think-alouds. Now I see how students respond to the modeling that happens in think-alouds. I see that my students are able to use the strategies that I have modeled.

Coach: Your data shows a lot of coaching, modeling, listening, and giving feedback in your student-supported stance of teaching. Are your students engaged in active as opposed to passive responding?

Teacher: This is an active group of students. I try to keep them actively involved by doing more reading and writing. The students are successful and making gains because these ideas are helping students.

Coach: Did you clearly state the purpose?

Teacher: With everything I've learned in Reading First, stating the purpose is so important to student learning. I am remembering to state the purpose in my lessons and it is helpful to the students.

As the coach guided the teacher through an analysis of the observation, the teacher identified the elements of her instruction that caused the students to be actively engaged. Thus, the teacher recognized the components of effective instruction that she would incorporate into future lessons. The coach did not tell the teacher what to do. She used the data to guide the teacher toward her own evaluation of the lesson.

Building Connections Between Professional Development and Instruction

A third-grade teacher from School A taught a lesson to the whole group, and her focus was on stating the purpose of the lesson as a part of explicit, cognitively engaging instruction. The conversation caused the teacher to reflect on how she was using what she had learned in study groups in her daily instruction.

Coach: Looking at my notes, I noticed how explicit you were in restating the purpose...[cites specific examples]. I also noticed that you had the students actively responding by orally sharing responses in pairs. Which part of this lesson do you think went well?

Teacher: This group needs to be actively engaged. Since this was an introductory lesson to build on the rest of the week, my goal was getting them to think about the text.

Coach: What will you do tomorrow with this group?

Teacher: I plan to have them write about the story. Also, since my students have such differing abilities, I want to remember to differentiate how I work with students who need more help.

Coach: Now that you have been in study groups and have had reflective conversations with your colleagues, do you feel that you are making changes in not only what you teach, but how you teach?

Teacher: Yes. We have really focused on being explicit in our teaching. That has made a big difference in my teaching.

In this conversation, there was evidence that the teacher's instructional practices were being impacted by reflection. The coach prompted the teacher to consider if there was a connection between the reflections in study group conversations with colleagues and the changes in her teaching. The teacher noted how the professional conversations with her colleagues in the study group setting had caused them to include more explicit instruction into their reading lessons.

Findings across several years have shown that teachers in the Minnesota Reading First Project changed their teaching practices in the directions suggested by research (Taylor & Peterson, 2007; 2008). Similar findings were reported in earlier studies as well (Taylor et al., 2005; 2007). For example, when looking at all grade 2 and grade 3 classroom teachers and specialists (e.g., Title 1, special education and ELL teachers) from years 2005–2008, we found that the mean percent of higher order talk and writing about text went from 17% to 21% of the time observed (as measured by percent of five-minute segments in which a practice was observed) in grade 2, and 22% to 26% of the time observed in grade 3. The mean percent of time for comprehension strategy instruction went from 4% to 16% in grade 2, and 11% to 18% in grade 3 (Taylor & Peterson, 2008).

Throughout the coaching conversations, concrete data served as a critical tool for guiding the questioning that led to self-reflective thinking and modification of future instructional practices. Each example demonstrated the importance of teachers having conversations about their practice with a coach who served as a facilitator and a peer.

Reflection for Coaches

As a part of the professional development for coaches, one literacy coach would watch another coach have a conversation with a teacher. The purpose of this observation of coaching was to provide feedback to the coach. Together, the coaches would reflect on what had been effective in the coaching conversation and how the coach could improve his or her questions to guide the teacher to deeper reflection in the future. The last example shows how the coaches from School A reflected on their effectiveness as coaches.

Coach 1: You had thoughts about the conversation you wanted to have with the teacher. Did you feel like you were able to accomplish those goals with this teacher?

Coach 2: The teacher is interested in learning to use new approaches in her teaching. I will need to continue to encourage her to use real-life connections in her teaching to better the students' understanding.

Coach 1: What do you think was most effective in your coaching conversation?

Coach 2: I see how you need to keep asking good questions to keep the teacher thinking about her instruction. The questions made the teacher think about the lesson and the importance of asking questions that make her students think about higher level responses.

Coach 1: Was there anything in this lesson that you learned from the teacher that you would share with other teachers?

Coach 2: Yes. I need to remember the importance of effective transitioning from small-group to whole-group instruction. I was reminded of the power of active engagement for student learning and staying on task in the whole-group time.

Coach 1: I see these conversations with your peers as a time for you to be learning along with your peer. These conversations engage us in a process that makes us think about what we did and whether or not to do it differently.

The opportunity for a coach to reflect with another coach on what was effective was an important part of the professional development for coaches. This helped them to have more robust conversations with teachers leading them to deeper reflection about instruction.

Implications for Coaches

One of the key elements of the Minnesota Reading First Professional Development Program was the intentional way teachers reflected on their own instruction. While we cannot say that the coaching conversations caused the growth in students' reading scores, we can state that teachers made changes to their instruction as demonstrated through the teacher observation data, and students made accelerated progress in reading as seen in their comprehension scores. These reflections were stimulated through collaborative conversations with colleagues. Collaborative reflection occurred when teachers shared videos of their own instruction with their peers in study groups, when they examined student assessment scores with their grade-level teams, and when they talked with their literacy coach about their instruction following an observation. Through coaching conversations, teachers focused on the elements of effective instruction and set goals for themselves for the next week's lessons. Data on their own instructional practices were critical to this process.

A third-grade teacher at School D stated,

These coaching conversations have given me more background in teaching. This is a whole new world for me. I always want to improve on and do what is best for kids. This has helped me to work with my struggling readers and get them to be more independent.

A second-grade teacher at School C said,

Every reform that has come along has told us what to do. This reform is different. We learned what was effective, but we had to work together to implement it into our teaching. We have learned about our teaching and learned about each other. We have learned how to work together to make everyone more effective. This is different than anything we have ever done. It is the best work I have done in my teaching.

These testimonials suggest that in addition to reading research and increasing their knowledge of scientifically based reading practices, or systematically analyzing the assessment data from their students, teachers can benefit from concrete data on their own instruction as they reflect and change their practice. This is a critical component to incorporate into ongoing professional development and reading reform efforts and is often the missing piece. Schools that have implemented reading reform that does not foster teacher reflection are encouraged to consider the importance of this element. Literacy coaches can help to provide these data for teachers and assist them in reflection through coaching conversations.

Schools that do not have literacy coaches can encourage teacher reflection by implementing peer observations or video sharing within teacher-led professional learning communities or grade-level teams. Following the peer observation or the video sharing, teachers can conduct coaching conversations with each other in pairs or as small groups. Simple protocols based on research, like the ones described here, can help to facilitate data collection and discussion among teacher colleagues. Reflection, collaboration, and conversations focused on instruction can empower us all to be even more effective in teaching our students to read.

REFERENCES

Bean, R.M., & Zigmond, N. (2006, May). *Professional development role of reading coaches in and out of the classroom.* Paper presented at the International Reading Association Conference, Chicago, IL.

Deussen, T., Coskie, T., Robinson, L., & Autio, E. (2007). *"Coach" can mean many things: Five categories of literacy coaches in Reading First* (Issues & Answers Report, REL 2007-No. 005). Washington, DC: U.S. Department of

Education, Institute of Education Sciences, National Center for Education Evaluation and Regional Assistance, Regional Educational Laboratory Northwest. Retrieved March 7, 2008, from http://ies.ed.gov/ncee/edlabs/regions/northwest/pdf/REL_2007005.pdf

Joyce, B., & Showers, B. (1995). *Student achievement through staff development* (2nd ed.). White Plains, NY: Longman.

Moss, M., Jacob, R., Boulay, B., Horst, M., & Poulos, J. (with St. Pierre, R., et al.). (2006). *Reading First implementation evaluation: Interim report*. Washington, DC: U.S. Department of Education. Retrieved March 16, 2007, from www.ed.gov/rschstat/eval/other/readingfirst-interim/readingfirst.pdf

National Institute of Child Health and Human Development (NICHD). (2000). *Report of the National Reading Panel. Teaching students to read: An evidence-based assessment of the scientific research literature on reading and its implications for reading instruction* (NIH Publication No. 00-4769). Washington, DC: U.S. Government Printing Office.

Neufeld, B., & Roper, D. (2003). *Coaching: A strategy for developing instructional capacity—Promises and practicalities*. Washington, DC: Aspen Institute.

Rodgers, A., & Rodgers, E.M. (2007). *The effective literacy coach: Using inquiry to support teaching & learning*. New York: Teachers College Press.

Taylor, B.M., Pearson, P.D., Peterson, D.S., & Rodriguez, M.C. (2003). Reading growth in high-poverty classrooms: The influence of teacher practices that encourage cognitive engagement in literacy learning. *The Elementary School Journal*, *104*(1), 3–28. doi:10.1086/499740

Taylor, B.M., Pearson, P.D., Peterson, D.S., & Rodriguez, M.C. (2005). The CIERA School Change Framework: An evidence-based approach to professional development and school reading improvement. *Reading Research Quarterly*, *40*(1), 40–69. doi:10.1598/RRQ.40.1.3

Taylor, B.M., & Peterson, D.S. (2007). *Year two report of the Minnesota Reading First cohort two School Change Project*. St. Paul, MN: University of Minnesota.

Taylor, B.M., & Peterson, D.S. (2008). *Year three report of the Minnesota Reading First cohort two School Change Project*. St. Paul, MN: University of Minnesota.

Taylor, B.M., Peterson, D.S., Marx, M., & Chein, M. (2007). Scaling up a reading reform in high-poverty elementary schools. In B.M. Taylor & J.E. Ysseldyke (Eds.), *Effective instruction for struggling readers K–6* (pp. 216–234). New York: Teachers College Press.

Uzat, S.L. (1998, November). *Cognitive coaching and self-reflection: Looking in the mirror while looking through the window*. Paper presented at the annual meeting of the Mid-South Educational Research Association, New Orleans, LA. (ERIC document Reproduction Service No. ED427064)

CHAPTER 16

The Learning Schools Model of School Change to Raise Achievement in Reading Comprehension for Culturally and Linguistically Diverse Students in New Zealand

Stuart McNaughton and Mei Kuin Lai

New Zealand has a deservedly high international reputation for literacy teaching, and the levels of achievement of its students are high by international standards. But New Zealand also faces a significant challenge in its literacy teaching. There is a long "tail" in the levels of achievement—an achievement gap—and differences between the lowest and highest students are very large in international terms. Moreover, two groups of students are overrepresented in this tail; they are Māori (from the indigenous community) and Pasifika students (from recent immigrant and second- and third-generation Pacific Island families). These students are most often found in schools in communities with the lowest levels of income and employment.

New Zealand's researchers and policymakers have known for some time that we have not served these school communities as well as others. With a few exceptions, schooling has not been equitable for indigenous students. Following waves of immigration of Pasifika families from the 1960s, there is now a new set of communities for whom teaching is less than effective. South Auckland schools that have a high percentage of Māori and Pasifika students from communities

RTI in Literacy—Responsive and Comprehensive, edited by Peter H. Johnston, published by the International Reading Association. This chapter adapted from McNaughton, S., & Lai, M.K. (2009). A Model of School Change for Culturally and Linguistically Diverse Students in New Zealand: A Summary and Evidence From Systematic Replication. *Teaching Education, 20*(1), 55–75.

with the lowest levels of income and employment have been identified as sites of low achievement and as in crisis. More than 20 years ago, the title of a report by Ramsay, Sneddon, Grenfell, and Ford (1981) proclaimed the crisis was such that "tomorrow may be too late" and international comparisons made through the 1990s further highlighted this failure to deliver.

Starting in 1998, an increase in research, changes in policy, new resources, and retuned practices have contributed to a reduction in the disparities in achievement levels in early reading between Māori and Pasifika students and other students. The evidence comes from national monitoring at Year 4 (9-year-olds) in four yearly cycles of assessments. From 1996 to 2006, the percentage of Year 4 students reading below their age levels dropped from 19% to 12% and then to 7% over four yearly cycles. Despite this decrease, the evidence also suggests that at Year 4 and Year 9, the differences in reading comprehension have continued, if not increased (Crooks & Flockton, 2005).

In a series of studies, researchers from the Woolf Fisher Research Centre have developed a research and development model called the Learning Schools model to help schools meet this educational challenge in reading comprehension (Lai, McNaughton, Amituanai-Toloa, Turner, & Hsiao, 2009). The major assumptions behind this work have been that an increase in instructional effectiveness in the schools would lead to acceleration in achievement levels in reading comprehension for Māori and Pasifika students in Years 4 through 8. This would require a model of improvement that built on the expertise of the teachers and solved the challenges of effectiveness. This would need, in turn, a long-term partnership among researchers, policymakers, and school professionals.

The criteria we have set for these changes being effective include accelerated rates of achievement in the schools and changes in the distribution of achievement to match the national distribution of achievement. In addition, we have set up the goal of changes being sustainable (Lai, McNaughton, Timperley, & Hsiao, 2009), which means maintaining rates of change as well as maintaining effective problem solving of local challenges to being effective for Māori and Pasifika students.

The International Context of "Schooling Improvement"

The evidence base for schooling improvement generally does not suggest we could be very optimistic about substantial and long-lasting changes. New Zealand's and other countries' response to this issue has included programs of schooling improvement and school reform with only varying degrees of effectiveness.

In the United States by early 2000, more than 100 different comprehensive school reform models aimed at improving instruction and student achievement had been developed and implemented in 10%–20% of elementary schools (Rowan, Correnti, Miller, & Camburn, 2009). Fewer than a third of these models (Borman, 2005) have been replicated to enable reliable analyses of effects. Borman reviewed the evidence for scaled-up projects of school reform in high-poverty schools in the United States. His review shows that they produce widespread, but generally modest, initial effects (effect sizes between 0.1 and 0.3); however, the evidence also suggests stronger effects appearing after five years. In addition, in a series of studies, Rowan and colleagues have reported on the effects of three types of the most widely used programs, comparing them with one another and with schools that had no specific programs for change. Their analyses included more than 100 high-poverty schools and their students.

Two of the three intervention programs, those that are specified and targeted in reading and writing were more effective than either a generic level intervention program or no special program. There were differences, however, between the two specified programs. One is a highly scripted and externally designed program focused on explicit skills instruction and, the evidence suggests, very effective in terms of beginning reading outcomes as measured at the word level or below. The other program is designed collaboratively with external advisors and leaders within the school and has a more literature-based focus on higher level reading and writing and their interconnections and, the evidence suggests, very effective at the later stages of reading and writing at school.

From these analyses general principles of effectiveness are being derived, such as the need for specificity in programs, planning for both the level and quality of implementation, and the need to design models to fit the developmental needs of students given local circumstances.

The Model of Change and Evidence

The Learning Schools model is based on several key principles. These are reviewed in the sections that follow, accompanied by a description of how these principles have operated with schools. The evidence for the effectiveness of this model is summarized in the final section. The Learning Schools model has been implemented and then replicated across three clusters of schools, involving more than five years, 10,000 students, and 250 teachers. It is important to note that we assume that to optimize schools' effectiveness there needs to be a focus on the home and school relationships and that these linkages would contribute a substantial amount to schools' effectiveness. Members of our research team continue to examine community literacy and language practices and relationships with schools; however, the strategic decision for the program of research has been to focus almost exclusively on schools' and teachers' instruction to understand and design the most effective form of in-school instruction.

This model of change is drawn from theory and research literature in several areas. These areas comprise the nature of teachers and teaching, of schools and their professional communities, of instruction for literacy, of research and development partnerships, and of sustainability and scalability. From these we have extracted several key principles.

Teachers Need to Act as Adaptive Experts

The conclusion drawn from recent policy work in New Zealand (and in other countries), based on analyses of such variables as student background, the nature and types of schools, and classrooms, is that the key to school change is more effective teaching (Alton-Lee, 2004). In our model, teachers are seen and treated as professional experts, with deep knowledge about what they do, how they do it, and why they do it. This expertise has three components. The first is a knowledge base of teaching, students' learning, and how to teach particular content effectively. The second is strategic practices that have versatility and adaptability. The third is a metacognitive component involving awareness of the effectiveness of practice through monitoring, reflection, and inquiry.

General models of expertise identify how experts are goal focused and intentional, strategic, and adaptable; they are aware of their effectiveness by being able to monitor, check, and modify (McNaughton, 2002). Teachers need extensive knowledge about the content area, how and what to teach (pedagogical content knowledge), and their students and communities. In the context of diverse students, the latter entails an understanding of their students' language and literacy practices, as these reflect students' local and global cultural identities. This means knowing how these practices relate (or do not relate) to classroom practices (New London Group, 1996).

These general attributes give experts the twin features of being technically skilled as well as innovative and adaptable. These are the features

Darling-Hammond and Bransford (2005) identify in their descriptions of new forms of teaching for a changing world. They distinguish between teachers who as "routine experts" employ scripted lessons and those who as "adaptive experts" apply known instructional procedures but are constantly refining and changing to be more effective. The former develop a core set of competencies that they repeatedly apply, while the latter continually add to their knowledge and skills. These latter experts are those that are now needed, as they are innovators who expand their expertise. This description is consistent with our view of teachers who are needed to be more effective with diverse students. It is also consistent with the findings of Rowan et al. (2009) noted previously, in that adaptable and flexible forms of teaching are needed to develop high-level reading comprehension and writing skills.

Local Evidence Is Necessary to Inform Instructional Design

Unlike other approaches, the Learning Schools model assumes the need to examine local evidence at two levels. One is to base instructional practices on evidence about teaching and learning drawn from locally observed patterns. The second is the requirement that an individual teacher is able to use a range of formal and informal assessments to broaden his or her knowledge of individual students and to better personalize instruction.

Generally there is considerable consensus on what students need to learn to be effective comprehenders, such as fast and accurate decoding, an extensive vocabulary, appropriate topic and world knowledge, and a range of comprehension strategies and fix-up strategies (Block & Pressley, 2002). It follows that students with low progress may have difficulties in one or more of these areas. Similarly, the consensus on effective teaching identifies attributes of both content (curriculum) and process (Taylor, Pearson, Peterson, & Rodriguez, 2005). In the middle grades, these attributes include instruction in which goals are made clear and students are engaged in higher level thinking skills. Effective teaching also provides direct instruction of skills and strategies for comprehension and actively engages students in a great deal of actual reading and writing where students can learn to self-regulate independently.

In addition, researchers have also identified the teacher's role in incorporating students' cultural resources such as event knowledge (McNaughton, 2002) and in building students' motivation and engagement (Guthrie & Wigfield, 2000). The latter are particularly important because quantitative and qualitative aspects of teaching convey expectations about students' ability that affect their levels of engagement and sense of being in control, and culturally and linguistically diverse students seem to be especially likely to encounter teaching that conveys low expectations (Dyson, 1999). In general, to be effective school reform must include changes to beliefs about students and more evidence-based decisions about instruction (Phillips, McNaughton, & MacDonald, 2004).

It follows that low progress could be associated with a variety of teaching and learning needs in these areas. Out of this array of needs, those for students and teachers in any particular instructional context may therefore have a context-specific profile. Although our research-based knowledge means there are well-established relationships, the patterns of these relationships are likely to vary across contexts. An example comes from Buly and Valencia (2002), who provide a case study from a policy perspective of the importance of not making assumptions about what students need. In that study, mandating phonics instruction for all students in the state of Washington who fell below literacy proficiency levels missed the needs of the majority of students, whose decoding was strong but who struggled with comprehension or language requirements for the tests. Information that accurately profiles student learning and achievement and also provides insight on teaching and instruction is needed to avoid making mistakes such as those described by Buly and Valencia. In our own research we have shown how effective changes in instructional design were dependent on having evidence about current forms of instruction and potential mistakes in fine tuning were avoided (Lai, McNaughton, Amituanai-Toloa, et al., 2009).

School Professional Learning Communities Are Vehicles to Enhance Effectiveness

Our model locates not only teachers, leaders, and other school professionals, but also researchers and local district managers (in New Zealand's case, the national Ministry of Education personnel) in the process of change. Each of these are members of the professional learning community and need to learn to act and practice effectively within the school communities.

The significance of professional learning communities has been recognized and is linked to improvements in teaching, student achievement, and learning (e.g., Louis, Marks, & Kruse, 1996; Robinson & Lai, 2006). Where communities focus on collective problem solving around agreed evidence, sustainable improvement in student achievement can also occur—particularly in the area of reading comprehension. For example, when Cawelti and Protheroe (2001) examined the factors responsible for student-achievement gains in six formerly underperforming districts in the United States with successful school-improvement efforts, one of the attributes of a successful district was teacher analysis and use of achievement data. Over eight years, districtwide pass rates in the state reading, writing, and mathematics tests rose (from 65% and 70% to 95%) with reductions in disparities among ethnic minorities in low socioeconomic groups. Similarly, a follow-up of a New Zealand schooling improvement intervention showed that school communities that maintained achievement gains or built on them after the program had a twin focus: they promoted raising achievement and a collective analysis and discussion of student achievement data to change teacher practice (Timperley, Phillips, & Wiseman, 2003).

The features of professional learning communities that can effectively analyze evidence to improve teaching practices and raise student achievement have been identified (Coburn, 2003; Robinson & Lai, 2006). One is collective inquiry (Seashore-Louis, 2006; Timperley, Wilson, Barrar, & Fung, 2008), requiring teachers to examine student learning, reflect on the teaching and learning, develop appropriate practices to address the identified needs, and monitor student progress. To do this requires the deep knowledge associated with teacher expertise noted previously. Rich inquiry requires consideration of theories in the professional community as well as the engagement of teachers' theories (Robinson & Lai, 2006; Timperley et al., 2008). Engaging in these theories means uncovering the reasons and conditions that have formed their current practices, and this process is strongly linked to improved achievement (Timperley et al., 2008).

The process of effective inquiry requires adjudication between differing theories for the patterns in achievement by carefully examining profiles of students' needs to test theories. In one study, two possible causes for low achievement in reading comprehension were compared by examining students' needs using standardized tests (Lai & McNaughton, 2008). The tests showed that students were high decoders but weak in other aspects of reading comprehension, discounting one theory (that students needed more support in decoding) and confirming the other (that students' decoding was adequate, but they needed support in comprehending what they were decoding). This highlights the need for descriptions of student learning as well as patterns of teaching to be collected and analyzed together within the community to clarify and test hypotheses about how to develop effective and sustainable practices (Phillips et al., 2004).

An analytic stance to the collection and use of evidence is required to examine how interventions affect teaching and learning and whether goals are being met. This is by no means simple, especially when considering recent debates about what counts as appropriate research evidence (McCall & Green, 2004). Our model assumes that research designs are needed that are appropriate to the "messy" conditions of schools in which change is a constant, and in which the communities' members hold values, beliefs, and ideas, and engage in practices that reflect these. Our approach to the replication of the Learning Schools model uses both quantitative and qualitative methods employed within a robust quasi-experimental design (Lai, McNaughton, Amituanai-Toloa, et al., 2009).

Various forms and degrees of expertise can be brought to these communities with the involvement of school personnel, researchers, and policymakers. Their respective expertise means that they can contribute different forms of knowledge, strategies, and reflection, thereby adding value to and extending one another's practices (Wells, 1999). Collective inquiry is also important to developing a collective as well as a personal sense of efficacy (Bandura, 1995). Self-efficacy is the belief in one's own ability to produce the desired outcome, and collective efficacy is the collective's belief in its ability to produce the desired outcome. Bandura describes a depressing cycle in which a sense of unsolvable problems lowers beliefs in personal effectiveness, which in turn decreases commitments to teaching. A high sense of collective efficacy occurs where teachers collectively share a sense of solving difficulties and of making a difference and have the evidence to support these beliefs. Higher levels predict a school's effectiveness over a school year even when different characteristics of students, their prior levels of achievement, and staffs' levels of experience are controlled. What is important to note is that this finding applies to schools serving culturally and linguistically diverse students (Bandura, 1995). Our own studies of the model support the significance of collective inquiry through professional learning conversations in which a strong collective sense of solving problems is present in practice (Lai & McNaughton, 2008; Lai, McNaughton, Amituanai-Toloa, et al., 2009).

Effective Research–Practice–Policy Partnerships Are Responsive

The features of school-based professional learning communities noted earlier require partnerships among researchers, practitioners, and policymakers who are focused on learning how to improve teaching and learning (Annan, 2007). There are risks in doing this. For example, an early evaluation of a schooling improvement initiative in New Zealand found that these partnerships were problematic, as blame could be attributed to another partner for the educational "failures," rather than attempting to learn together how best to raise achievement (Robinson & Timperley, 1999). We have avoided this in our work by using the approach outlined in Robinson and Lai (2006), where each party is able to critique each other's emerging theories of how to address students' learning needs. Therefore, no one theory is privileged, allowing each partner equal power in decision making. This raises two important considerations. The first is that the policy environment must be responsive enough to learn from partners. Annan's (2007) analysis of the policy environment of the United States, United Kingdom, and New Zealand suggests that a flat policy structure like New Zealand's allows for opportunities for engagement with policymakers. A second consideration is the engagement of the wider community of families as a major partner. In the school clusters in which the Learning Schools model has been implemented there is sustained community involvement, as the governance of New Zealand schools is via local communities (Annan, 2007). However, we have not directly focused on this element and are planning more direct research and development work with communities in the future to extend the Learning Schools model.

Implementation Requires Instructional Leadership

The importance of teacher leadership in raising achievement has been highlighted in recent studies (Robinson, Hohepa, & Lloyd, 2009). However, it is not leadership in general but rather particular dimensions of leadership that lead to greater impact on student outcomes. The Robinson et al. (2009) review of the impact of leadership highlights five dimensions associated with higher achievement—establishing goals and expectations, communicating and monitoring of learning goals; strategic resourcing and allocation to priority teaching goals; planning, coordinating, and evaluating teaching and the curriculum; promoting and participating in teacher learning and development; and ensuring an orderly and supportive environment.

Our model is based on lead teachers working effectively with the principal and other senior managers to implement the intervention in the school. Although principals may not be directly involved in leading instructional change, they have considerable influence on the shape of the intervention through their management and influence on how teacher leaders understand and enact their roles.

The function of effective leadership can be illustrated by three examples from our studies. First, schools, which in New Zealand are self-governing, had to provide funds for about half of the intervention themselves, so principals and lead teachers had to plan their budgets, particularly to include every teacher in workshops every two weeks. This also meant careful scheduling during this time, which the schools all managed to coordinate. Second, each lead teacher collaborated with the researchers and one another to plan, coordinate, evaluate, and continually monitor the impact of their practice on student achievement. Third, all lead teachers were required to participate in professional development to be able to implement it in their schools. Principals were also involved, albeit indirectly through principals' clusters and other such mechanisms to maintain focus.

In our model, the professional community at school or cluster level has to contribute to the development of these attributes of the leaders. We cannot assume that lead teachers will automatically have such attributes and knowledge and have found mixed capabilities for self-review using evidence (e.g., Timperley et al., 2008). Similarly, the model is vulnerable to changes in leadership unless it enables communities to build effective induction systems for new members.

Existing Approaches Must Be Modified to Design More Effective Instruction

Our model is built on a general proposition that rather than importing a new program for reading comprehension instruction, the existing program in schools could be made more effective. This belief comes partly from evidence based on the view of teachers as adaptive experts. Also, New Zealand's literacy instruction is relatively effective, based on measures such as the proportion of students who are in the highest achievement bands and overall performance in different areas of literacy (e.g., PISA and PIRLS). There are known features of current practices that can be used effectively, including the range and types of texts provided for instruction and the ways in which narrative texts, even in early instructional texts, deliberately use more familiar language forms (McNaughton, 2002), creating a lever for more effective practice for diverse students.

A second reason is that in analyzing our evidence we have been able to show that considerable variability in effectiveness exists across teachers and schools. As some teachers and schools are more or less effective, it is in the variability that exists that one can use exemplars to identify useful new knowledge and effective practices and leverage off existing practices. A third reason derives from a basic idea in effective change, in that we start from the existing repertoire and from that build greater expertise. The final reason is that designing whole-scale change in an existing, nationally set program runs the risk of being counterproductive to the need to treat teachers as, and move them toward being, adaptive experts.

High Treatment Integrity or Treatment Scalability and Sustainability Are Possible

Researchers on schooling improvement are currently grappling with the issue of sustainability and the closely linked ideas of treatment integrity or fidelity and scaling up. Treatment fidelity and integrity refer to the degree to which a defined treatment is actually applied as designed. Scaling up is taking a defined program of change and applying it across new contexts. The usual meaning of sustainability is akin to generalization across time (the effects of the intervention keep going to some defined level). Sustainability, however, can also mean sustaining the treatment with new cohorts of learners and also with new cohorts of teachers. The latter meanings are closer to the idea of integrity and fidelity.

There is an issue here for schooling improvement. Integrity has been associated with the degree to which the program is specified for a school or sets of schools. This specificity has been seen as very significant because changing teachers' practices requires clarity on the part of the design team (Cohen & Ball, 2007), and there is a need to guarantee effects: the core requirement of treatment integrity (Coburn, 2003). Thus in schooling improvement, the aim has been to scale up through guaranteeing high fidelity. However, adaptation on the ground is an inherent property of teachers' responses to new ideas (Datnow & Stringfield, 2000; Lefstein, 2007). This mixed implementation through local adaptation is usually seen as problematic (Davis & Sumara, 2003) because often the mixed implementation occurs through the intervention ideas not being adequately articulated (Cohen & Ball, 2007). However, it is also because teachers reconstruct and reframe their practices in idiosyncratic ways. These observations introduce a tension associated with teacher learning within schooling improvement (Coburn, 2003). It is between importing a set of procedures in a way that risks undermining local autonomy and efficacy and a more collaborative development of common procedures that risks losing instructional specificity. The research literature on schooling improvement has become ambivalent about these issues. Reviewers point out that a high degree of program specificity is important (Borman, 2005). However, reviewers also argue that approaches that employ joint problem solving on the ground are more likely to result in sustainable improvements in student achievement.

We solve these tensions by distinguishing between the degrees of prescription of the content of what to teach and the process of change. The important point is that the process of change (through features such as inquiry and analysis of evidence) can still be very specific in what is taught and how it is taught. This specificity in the content comes from a more open-ended starting point. This means we can distinguish between two sorts of fidelity. One is fidelity of a program (i.e., content) and the other is fidelity of a process that can still deliver a high degree of program specificity. Our expectation in the model is that by having a highly specified process for change that identifies what needs to change we can build fidelity to the content of the program across classrooms and schools.

Components of the Change Process Need to Be Introduced and Developed Over Time

The change model has a three-phase design in which the phases add components within an applied research (i.e., quasi-experimental) design. The first phase involves the collection and analysis of student learning (achievement and progress data) and classroom observational data. Together these provide profiles of teaching and learning from which a number of activities are possible. The evidence can provide an analysis of the strengths and weaknesses of learning and development of literacy for students at various levels, including individual classrooms, year levels, ethnic groups, and schools. Instructional approaches and students' profiles can be matched to make judgments of where the teaching appears to be less than effective and where there are strengths. In each case, sources of "positive deviance" (i.e., outlier classrooms, teachers, and perhaps schools) where the patterns of low achievement are not present can be identified for further shared analysis. This phase also builds up the communities' shared beliefs and expectations about the role of teachers, researchers, leaders, policymakers, and the shared practices around inquiring into and sharing and using evidence. The phase also is important in research design terms to give a baseline against which changes can be compared.

The second phase continues the evidence collection but adds targeted professional development. The third phase continues the evidence collection and use and shifts from the development mode to one of sustaining the change and further problem solving. For example, we design systems for teacher groups to plan together, observe, and reflect on one another's implementations. Inquiry projects are developed and the results reported.

It could be argued that if the needs for teaching and learning are clear (that is, we know what the patterns should be from existing research), then there may be reductions in these phases and a move to concentrating on the professional development part. However, an ongoing well-structured process, even if replicating a well-designed program, is still needed. The most telling researched example for this comes from the attempt to replicate the program of reform carried out in the urban schools of New York City's Community School District #2. The District #2 reform had been highly successful. In 1998, the San Diego City Schools attempted to reform their schools using the New York model. However, Hubbard, Mehan, and Stein (2006) argue the replication did not deliver what was expected when analyzed at the levels of policy, organization, schools, classrooms, and teacher–student interactions. The picture they paint is that the change objectives were undermined by the adoption of a reform template without adopting the developmental process.

Summary of Research Evidence

Our first research and development project with the model focused on reading comprehension was conducted as a collaborative partnership among researchers, schools, and the New Zealand Ministry of Education. It was designed to develop and test the model in a cluster of Decile 1 schools in South Auckland (Lai, McNaughton, Amituanai-Toloa, et al., 2009). A school's decile indicates the extent to which the school draws its students from low socioeconomic communities. Decile 1 schools are the 10% of schools with the highest proportion of students from low socioeconomic communities and often with the highest proportions of Māori and Pasifika students.

The research and development program was conducted over three years with up to 70 teachers and, in different years, between 1,200 and 1,900 students, more than 90% of whom were Māori or Pasifika. Included were six Samoan bilingual classes from two schools with between 140 and 169 students across different years. A quasi-experimental design was employed to examine relationships between the program and the outcomes over three years. The robustness of the design was enhanced by a comparison with an untreated cluster of similar schools and checks on subject attrition. Repeated measures of student achievement form the basis of the design which, among other things, examines rates of gain against predicted patterns of growth generated from a baseline.

As noted earlier, the initial step in the first phase of the program involved collecting baseline profiles of achievement, using two standardized assessments of reading comprehension, and collecting baseline profiles of classroom instruction, through observations in classrooms. Together these baselines provided detailed evidence about strengths and weaknesses in the students' reading comprehension, which were able to be mapped onto patterns of instruction in the classroom. For example, they showed that low decoding levels were generally not a problem. Rather there were other areas posing difficulties, including patterns of checking and detecting threats to meaning when reading strategically, and size and knowledge of vocabulary. The assessment data suggested that students needed more strategy instruction, but classroom observations revealed that high rates of explicit strategy instruction occurred. However, students were focused on the strategies as ends in themselves and often resorted to guessing. Classroom observations also showed a low incidence of teachers or students monitoring and checking strategies and low rates of identifying and elaborating meanings of low-frequency words, unusual uses of common words, or idiomatic uses. Detailed information on the findings from the baseline is contained in Lai, McNaughton, MacDonald, and Farry (2004) and Lai, McNaughton, Amituanai-Toloa, et al. (2009).

The first phase included systematic feedback, analysis, and problem solving at all levels, using the profiles as evidence. This process involved two key steps: close examination of students' strengths and weaknesses and of current instruction, and raising competing theories of the "problem" and evaluating the evidence for these theories. This process ensured that the collaboration was a critical examination of practice and that valid inferences were drawn from the information. The feedback procedures are described fully in Lai and McNaughton (2008) and Robinson and Lai (2006). A second phase added targeted professional development, based on the evidence in the first phase. This was designed using the profiles and known dimensions of effective teaching, using a mixture of theoretical and research-based ideas as well as teacher investigation and examples from classrooms. The third phase involved planned sustainability of teacher-designed projects and a cluster-led conference.

At baseline, students were on average at stanine 3.1, approximately two years below expected levels, with some variation across year levels and across schools. To test the impact of the program, a number of different analyses were made.

Analysis of achievement showed substantial acceleration had occurred, and that by the end of the project 71% of students were now in middle to upper bands of reading comprehension for their age level compared with only 40% at the start. National expectations are 77% in this band, indicating a significant achievement given the nature of the challenge to effective instruction. The average student now scored in the average band of achievement (mean stanine 4.21). The level of gains overall were in the order of one year's gain in addition to nationally expected progress over three years. The overall effect size for gains in stanines was 0.62. Effect sizes reported internationally are between 0.1 and 0.3 for interventions running under six years (Borman, 2005). Māori students' achievement accelerated at similar rates to those of the other ethnic groups, with the average Māori student scoring within the average band (mean = 4.73) and one cohort of Māori students (Year 4) scoring above the national expected average at stanine 5.29. Males and females made similar rates of progress over the three years in the intervention, but female students, on average, started with higher levels of achievement than male students. On average, students in each school made accelerated gains in achievement from the beginning to the end of the project.

Analyses showed that after two years and after three years, students had higher achievement than baseline comparison groups (effect sizes ranged between 0.31 and 0.59) and were achieving higher than a comparison cluster of schools (effect sizes ranged between 0.33 and 0.61).

The analyses of students in Samoan bilingual classrooms showed that the program was effective in those classes, too. Gains in English reading comprehension by students in the bilingual classrooms were at least as high as the gains by other Samoan students in the mainstream classrooms, and in three of the year levels, they were noticeably higher. Students in bilingual classrooms were significantly lower in English reading achievement in Year 4 and Year 5, but from Year 6 onward, their achievement levels in English were similar. Overall, cohorts made 0.8 stanine gain in two years; for four cohorts, this was a higher rate of gain than for Samoan students in mainstream classes. Gains in these classrooms could also be linked with the degree of participation by schools and teachers.

The improvements are even more significant considering that nationally, scores in reading comprehension have remained relatively stable for many years (Elley, 2005). A recent national review of all government-funded schooling improvement initiatives further indicates that this was the only initiative that has been able to improve achievement of culturally and linguistically diverse communities (Annan, 2007).

Our analyses suggest that thinking about and critically discussing the evidence at a classroom, school, and cluster level was a significant contributor to the overall gains in achievement (Lai, McNaughton, Amituanai-Toloa, et al., 2009). This is consistent with the research linking similar processes to improving achievement (e.g., Cawelti & Protheroe, 2001) and recent reviews identifying problem solving around evidence gathered from one's own school as an effective form of professional development (Timperley et al., 2008). What this suggests is that in general the teachers had the capacity to change practices but needed support to identify the sources of change and test their theories about raising achievement. The findings also confirm the importance of external support, in particular research–practice–policy collaborations (e.g., Annan, 2007).

Significant changes occurred in types of teacher–student exchanges relating to the focus of the intervention, including the focus on checking and detecting threats to gaining meaning in texts and boosting vocabulary acquisition, and these were linked to the pattern of the gains in the component tests (McNaughton, MacDonald, Amituanai-Toloa, Lai, & Farry, 2006). Decoding levels also increased to about the same degree as gains in other areas, despite not being a direct target of the intervention. Further case studies of teachers showed that the most effective teachers more often articulated the requirements of activities, clarified high expectations, set complex tasks, introduced more complex and less familiar language including idiomatic uses, created a classroom community that enjoyed the use and study of oral and written language, used rich and varied texts, and incorporated student cultural and linguistic resources, as well as clarified areas of confusion.

Replication Across Clusters

The first study showed that acceleration was possible and significant changes in the distribution of achievement could occur, although to fully match the nationally expected distribution continued acceleration was needed. Further research had confirmed that sustained inquiry and problem-solving process is important to maintaining gains (Lai, McNaughton, Timperley, et al., 2009).

This initial study of the process of change has been replicated twice, each time with similar results: first in a "like" cluster of schools and then in an "unlike" cluster of schools. The like set of schools were from an adjacent neighborhood to the first and whose students were from the same Māori and Pasifika communities with the lowest income levels and starting achievement about two years below national expectations. The unlike set of schools involved a range of decile levels, were from a small town and rural area of New Zealand, and involved mainly NZ European and Māori students in communities with higher income levels and starting achievement levels around national expectations (i.e., around stanine 5.0 on achievement tests).

Initial modeling of the gains for each year of the intervention in the three clusters shows that the implementation in all three settings raised achievement in every phase of the intervention. The average rate of gain in each phase of the intervention was around three months per school year in addition to nationally expected progress over the one-year period.

The results also indicate that in all three interventions there was evidence for a drop over summer—a summer learning effect (Cooper, Charlton, Valentine, & Muhlenbruck, 2000). Intervention in the unlike schools was most affected by the summer holidays, in that there was an estimated average of 0.25 stanine drop over every summer holiday during the three-year program. This means that although students in the unlike schools overall were at higher levels, they were less likely to retain their learning over the summer holidays and their results went down from the end of the academic year to the beginning of the following one. Conversely, in the original and like clusters their scores did not go down as much from the end of the academic year to the beginning of the following year.

Overall, the effects of the Learning Schools model were replicated and the process of change could be scaled up across different settings, different schools, and different cohorts of students with a variety of starting achievement levels. The replication series shows that the low-achievement levels in the poorest schools serving culturally and linguistically diverse students can be changed to meet rigorous national criteria for greater effectiveness. The evidence is that it requires considerable commitment by researchers, educational professionals, and policymakers over time, within a concerted focus on using evidence to solve the challenges—and this process is needed to sustain changes at the end of the intervention (Lai, McNaughton, Timperley, et al., 2009).

REFERENCES

Alton-Lee, A. (2004, April). *Improving educational policy and practice through an iterative best evidence synthesis program*. Paper presented at the Organisation for Economic Cooperation and Development-United States seminar, Evidence-Based Policy Research, Washington, DC.

Annan, B. (2007). *A theory for schooling improvement: Consistency and connectivity to improve instructional practice*. Unpublished doctoral dissertation, University of Auckland, New Zealand.

Bandura, A. (1995). Exercise of personal and collective efficacy in changing societies. In

A. Bandura (Ed.), *Self efficacy in changing societies* (pp. 1–45). Cambridge: Cambridge University Press.

Block, C.C., & Pressley, M. (Eds.). (2002). *Comprehension instruction: Research-based best practices*. New York: Guilford.

Borman, G.D. (2005). National efforts to bring reform to scale in high-poverty schools: Outcomes and implications. In L. Parker (Ed.), *Review of research in education* (Vol. 29, pp. 1–28). Washington, DC: American Educational Research Association.

Buly, M.R., & Valencia, S.W. (2002). Below the bar: Profiles of students who fail state reading assessments. *Educational Evaluation and Policy Analysis*, 24(3), 219–239. doi:10.3102/01623737024003219

Cawelti, G., & Protheroe, N. (2001). *High student achievement: How six school districts changed into high-performance systems*. Arlington, VA: Educational Research Service.

Coburn, C.E. (2003). Rethinking scale: Moving beyond numbers to deep and lasting change. *Educational Researcher*, 32(6), 3–12. doi:10.3102/0013189X032006003

Cohen, D.K., & Ball, D.L. (2007). Educational innovation and the problem of scale. In B. Schneider & S.-K. McDonald (Eds.), *Scale up in education: Ideas in principle* (Vol. 1, pp. 19–36). Lanham, MD: Rowman & Littlefield.

Cooper, H., Charlton, K., Valentine, J.C., & Muhlenbruck, L. (2000). Making the most of summer school: A meta analytic and narrative review. *Monographs of the Society for Research in Child Development*, 65(1), 1–17. doi:10.1111/1540-5834.00059

Crooks, T., & Flockton, L. (2005). *Reading and speaking assessment results 2004: National education monitoring project report 34*. Dunedin, New Zealand: Educational Assessment Research Unit.

Darling-Hammond, L., & Bransford, J. (Eds.). (2005). *Preparing teachers for a changing world: What teachers should learn and be able to do*. San Francisco: John Wiley.

Datnow, A., & Stringfield, S. (2000). Working together for reliable school reform. *Journal of Education for Students Placed at Risk*, 5(1–2), 183–204.

Davis, B., & Sumara, D. (2003). Why aren't they getting this? Working through the regressive myths of constructivist pedagogy. *Teaching Education*, 14(2), 123–140. doi:10.1080/1047621032000092922

Dyson, A.H. (1999). Transforming transfer: Unruly children, contrary texts and the persistence of the pedagogical order, *Review of research in education*, 24(1), 141–171.

Elley, W. (2005). On the remarkable stability of student achievement standards over time. *New Zealand Journal of Educational Studies*, 40(1–2), 3–23.

Guthrie, J.T., & Wigfield, A. (2000). Engagement and motivation in reading. In M.L. Kamil, P.B. Mosenthal, P.D. Pearson, & R. Barr (Eds.), *Handbook of reading research* (Vol. 3, pp. 403–422). Mahwah, NJ: Erlbaum.

Hubbard, L., Mehan, H., & Stein, M.K. (2006). *Reform as learning: School reform, organizational culture, and community politics in San Diego*. New York: Routledge.

Lai, M.K., & McNaughton, S. (2008). Raising student achievement in poor communities through evidence-based conversations. In L.M. Earl & H. Timperley (Eds.), *Professional learning conversations: Challenges in using evidence for improvement* (pp. 13–27). Netherlands: Kluwer/Springer.

Lai, M.K., McNaughton, S., Amituanai-Toloa, M., Turner, R., & Hsiao, S. (2009). Sustained acceleration of achievement in reading comprehension: The New Zealand experience. *Reading Research Quarterly*, 44(1), 30–56. doi:10.1598/RRQ.44.1.2

Lai, M.K., McNaughton, S., MacDonald, S., & Farry, S. (2004). Profiling reading comprehension in Mangere schools: A research and development collaboration. *New Zealand Journal of Educational Studies*, 39(2), 223–240.

Lai, M.K., McNaughton, S., Timperley, H., & Hsiao, S. (2009). Sustaining continued acceleration in reading comprehension achievement following an intervention. *Educational Assessment, Evaluation and*

Accountability, 21(1), 81–100. doi:10.1007/s11092-009-9071-5

Lefstein, A. (2007). *Changing teacher practice through the National Literacy Strategy: A micro-interactional perspective.* Unpublished manuscript, Department of Educational Studies, Oxford University.

Louis, K.S., Marks, H., & Kruse, S. (1996). Teachers' professional community in restructuring schools. *American Educational Research Journal, 33*(4), 757–798.

McCall, R.B., & Green, B.L. (2004). Beyond the methodological gold standards of behavioral research: Considerations for practice and policy. In L. Sherod (Ed.), *Social policy report: Giving child and youth development knowledge away* (Vol. 18, No. 2). Ann Arbor, MI: Society for Research in Child Development.

McNaughton, S. (2002). *Meeting of minds.* Wellington, New Zealand: Learning Media.

McNaughton, S., & Lai, M.K. (2009). A model of school change for culturally and linguistically diverse students in New Zealand: A summary and evidence from systematic replication. *Teaching Education, 20*(1), 55–75. doi:10.1080/10476210802681733

McNaughton, S., MacDonald, S., Amituanai-Toloa, M., Lai, M., & Farry, S. (2006). *Enhanced teaching and learning of comprehension in Years 4–9 in seven Mangere schools: Final report.* Wellington, New Zealand: Teaching & Learning Research Initiative. Retrieved June 30, 2006, from www.tlri.org.nz/pdfs/9206_finalreport.pdf

New London Group. (1996). A pedagogy of multiliteracies: Designing social futures. *Harvard Educational Review, 66*(1), 60–92.

Phillips, G., McNaughton, S., & MacDonald, S. (2004). Managing the mismatch: Enhancing early literacy progress for children with diverse language and cultural identities in mainstream urban schools in New Zealand. *Journal of Educational Psychology, 96*(2), 309–323.

Ramsay, P.D.K., Sneddon, D.G., Grenfell, J., & Ford, I. (1981). *Tomorrow may be too late: Schools with special needs in Mangere and Otara:* Final report of the Schools With Special Needs Project. Hamilton, New Zealand: Education Department, University of Waikato.

Robinson, V.M., Hohepa, M.K., & Lloyd, C. (2009). *School leadership and student outcomes: Identifying what works and why. Best evidence synthesis iteration.* Wellington, New Zealand: Ministry of Education.

Robinson, V.M., & Lai, M.K. (2006). *Practitioner research for educators: A guide to improving classrooms and schools.* Thousand Oaks, CA: Corwin.

Robinson, V.M., & Timperley, H., (1999). *Strengthening education in Mangere and Otara evaluation: Final evaluation report.* Wellington, New Zealand: Ministry of Education.

Rowan, B., Correnti, R., Miller, R., & Camburn, E. (2009). School improvement by design: Lessons from a study of comprehensive school reform programs. In G. Sykes, B. Schnieder, & D.N. Plank (Eds.), *Handbook of education policy research* (pp. 637–651). Washington, DC: American Educational Research Association/Routledge.

Seashore-Louis, K. (2006). Changing the culture of schools: Professional community, organizational learning, and trust. *Journal of School Leadership, 16*(5), 477–489.

Taylor, B.M., Pearson, P.D., Peterson, D.S., & Rodriguez, M.C. (2005). The CIERA school change framework: An evidence-based approach to professional development and school reading improvement. *Reading Research Quarterly, 40*(1), 40–69. doi:10.1598/RRQ.40.1.3

Timperley, H., Phillips, G., & Wiseman, J. (2003). *The sustainability of professional development in literacy: Parts one and two.* Wellington, New Zealand: Ministry of Education.

Timperley, H., Wilson, A., Barrar, H., & Fung, I. (2008). *Teacher professional learning and development: Best evidence synthesis iteration (BES).* Wellington, New Zealand: Ministry of Education.

Wells, C.G. (1999). *Dialogic inquiry: Towards a sociocultural practice and theory of education.* Cambridge: Cambridge University Press.

SECTION VI

Systemic Intervention

Many approaches to intervention are piecemeal in that they try to set up a separate RTI program as an add-on, with little relation to other parts of the school system. This final section of the book is intended to move our attention away from such quick fixes to address the larger problems within which RTI is embedded. It is common, for example, for students needing the most careful and focused instruction to travel among several teachers and specialists each with their own instructional predilections, leaving the student to figure out how to get it all to make sense (Johnston, Allington, & Afflerbach, 1985). In such systems, not only do students have difficulty learning, but also teachers are not engaged in learning in a way that helps them learn together. This amounts to an institutional learning disability (Senge, 1994). Stuart McNaughton and Mei Kuin Lai's chapter in Section V shows us the benefits of thinking not just in terms of individual teacher expertise but also in terms of whole schools and systems. Their emphasis is on developing conditions that build learning communities and on gathering data and structuring contracts such that teachers use one another to develop their expertise and to solve instructional problems. Their goal is to prevent students from becoming unsuccessful and to raise the accomplishments of all students.

Part of McNaughton and Lai's strategy is to remove institutional learning disabilities. They expect that each school is different and operates in a different context, so they focus on helping the collective institutional mind to learn and adaptively problem solve. They are sensitive to Wiliam's (2006) concern about canned programs. He observes that

> researchers have underestimated the complexity of what it is that teachers do, and in particular, have failed to understand how great an impact context has on teachers' practice. That is why "what works?" is not the right question, because everything works somewhere, and nothing works everywhere. (p. 4)

Rather than rely solely on the fact that a particular kind of instruction was demonstrated to be effective in a research study somewhere, McNaughton and Lai emphasize the need for local evidence of teaching and learning to ensure that it is effective here with these teachers and these students in this place. To limit the number of students who find themselves on a slippery learning slope and to ensure that students who do are able to find the necessary footholds to climb up, we have to consider the school as a learning institution not just for students but also for teachers, administrators, and parents. McNaughton and Lai's chapter shows us the power of an institutional learning community. For the students' sake, we cannot afford institutional learning disabilities. The fact is that in many schools, the students are somewhat transient. Although an early intervention program might be very effective, some students will arrive in the school after that program and need support. Others will not respond well to the changing nature of literacy and will need support later in their school careers.

Therefore, we begin this section with Chapter 17, "A Comprehensive Intervention Model for Preventing Reading Failure: A Response to Intervention Process" by Linda J. Dorn and Barbara Schubert, which describes an integrated, systemic approach to RTI. Dorn and Schubert's highly effective approach is based on Reading Recovery as an intensive early intervention, but the institution is structured so that there is consistency across programs, with considerable emphasis on professional development, assessment, and small-group work and, as with McNaughton and Lai, a commitment to instructional integrity and sustainability.

Sometimes, interventions require changing our way of thinking. Many children who become classified as learning disabled (LD) come from poorer communities. Richard L. Allington and Anne McGill-Franzen in Chapter 18, "Use Students' Summer-Setback Months to Raise Minority Achievement," pick up a thread described by McNaughton and Lai, the learning plateau, and even regression, shown by some students during the summer break from school. Differences in summer learning trajectory are predictably related to income, which is also related to race and which results in many minority children becoming less successful in school and disproportionately becoming classified as LD. Allington and McGill-Franzen make it clear that this is a systemic design flaw that can be altered and that doing so would both reduce the number of children going into special education and reduce the racial disparities in classification.

The final chapter, Chapter 19, "Whole-School Detracking: A Strategy for Equity and Excellence" by Doris Alvarez and Hugh Mehan, also takes a systemic approach. Rather than setting up intervention programs for students who are less successful in the high school, their intervention is to restructure the high school. Their approach might seem a bit radical because it goes against most of our institutional intuitions. Their strategy is to ensure that grouping is heterogeneous and to alter the curriculum, organizing instruction that will engage all students. The ultimate effect is that virtually all of their minority students end up attending college. Alvarez and Mehan invite us to take up a challenge. Instead of tinkering with the status quo, perhaps we should start with what we know is important—an engaging curriculum and a future of hope.

REFERENCES

Johnston, P., Allington, R., & Afflerbach, P. (1985). The congruence of classroom and remedial reading instruction. *The Elementary School Journal*, 85(4), 465–478. doi:10.1086/461414

Senge, P.M. (1994). *The fifth discipline: The art and practice of the learning organization*. New York: Doubleday.

Wiliam, D. (2006, July 11). *Does assessment hinder learning?* Presentation at the ETS Europe Breakfast Salon, London. Retrieved from www.mission-21.com/ec/images/williams_speech.pdf

A Comprehensive Intervention Model for Preventing Reading Failure: A Response to Intervention Process

Linda J. Dorn and Barbara Schubert

Why do some children have difficulty in reading and others do not? We know that good readers use more effective strategies than poor readers. We also know that many problems can arise in the strategic processing of texts. Some students might not possess the necessary background or strategies for solving problems. Or, if they do, they might not understand when to employ the strategy that leads to the most efficient solution. With poor readers, their planning actions might be disorganized, a result of unthinking reactions to the text that could be camouflaged by accurate responses. Some struggling readers might achieve the reading goal by luck or circumstance yet lack the problem-solving strategies to accomplish the goal with efficiency. This is in contrast to strategic readers who make deliberate and intentional choices that are spontaneously monitored by their desire to comprehend the message. Strategic-based interventions, such as Reading Recovery, have shown that struggling readers can acquire efficient strategies for monitoring their comprehension, thus reversing their reading failure (Clay, 1998, 2005).

The current view of learning disabilities, as described by Gersten, Fuchs, Williams, and Baker (2001), states, "inefficiency rather than deficiency most accurately characterizes the problems experienced by students with learning disabilities" (p. 2). These researchers describe how "the breakdown occurs in

RTI in Literacy—Responsive and Comprehensive, edited by Peter H. Johnston, published by
the International Reading Association. This chapter reprinted from Dorn, L.J., & Schubert, B. (2008).
A Comprehensive Intervention Model for Preventing Reading Failure: A Response to Intervention
Process. *Journal of Reading Recovery, 7*(2), 29–41.

the domain of strategic processing and metacognition," in other words, the "students' ability to control and manage their cognitive activities in a reflective, purposeful fashion" (p. 2).

For decades, school districts have used a discrepancy model to evaluate students who may have a learning disability. This model assumes that the problem lies within the child, and not in the curriculum or instruction the child is receiving. As a result, many children are overidentified as learning disabled, either because they never received intervention or because of poor classroom instruction (Gersten & Dimino, 2006).

This viewpoint is supported in the Individuals With Disabilities Education Improvement Act of 2004 (IDEA, 2004), which advocates for intervention prior to identification. Under IDEA, a response to intervention (RTI) method is designed to provide struggling readers with appropriate interventions to meet their unique needs. The RTI method is considered a preventive approach for the earlier identification of students with reading difficulties, thus resulting in a decrease in the number of students referred for special education (Lose, 2007).

The purpose of this article is to discuss the Comprehensive Intervention Model (CIM) as an effective RTI method. First, we will present information on early intervening services (EIS) and response to intervention with details on the RTI framework and core components. Then, we will describe how the Comprehensive Intervention Model is an RTI approach, including details for how layers fit within a four-tiered design, followed by a description of the intervention components and research on the model (Center for Literacy, 2007). Finally, we will present a framework for implementing the Comprehensive Intervention Model in a school.

What Is Response to Intervention (RTI)?

This section introduces the legislation on EIS and RTI as defined in revisions to the IDEA law (see http://idea.ed.gov). The intention of the law is that all children should receive a research-based intervention prior to referral for special education. The law is the result of congressional concerns that children from particular racial or ethnic backgrounds were being overidentified as children with disabilities or overrepresented in particular educational settings.

The final regulations of the reauthorized IDEA legislation were signed into law on Aug. 14, 2006. The revisions include EIS, which allow a school to use up to 15 percent of the amount received to develop and implement coordinated EIS for children who are not currently identified as learning disabled. An emphasis is placed on K–3 students, although funds can be used for 4–12 students as well. The funding can also be used to provide professional development in intervention techniques for teachers and other school personnel. However, schools can only use these funds for research-based intervention models that comply with the regulations of the law.

Response to intervention is a comprehensive assessment and intervention process that identifies students at risk and monitors the academic progress of students in the general education curriculum. Therefore, if a school district has more than 20 percent of students in a subgroup who are not successful in reading, the school or district may need to assess the classroom curriculum. This acknowledges that general education is the first line of defense against reading failure. The bottom line is to improve academic achievement of all students through high-quality classroom instruction and research-based interventions.

The law requires that states adopt criteria for determining if a child has a specific learning disability. The criteria must permit the use of a process based on the child's response to intervention. The critical components of RTI are (a) universal screening of students, (b) defining in measurable terms the problem area, (c) collecting baseline data prior to the intervention, and (d) preparing a written plan of intervention, including measures for progress monitoring.

The most common structure for implementing an RTI is a tiered framework. This provides a process for delivering interventions according to degrees of intensity and teacher expertise. The intensity of each intervention will depend on the individual needs of the student as determined by an intervention team. The typical framework is the three-tiered approach, although some districts use four or more tiers. However, regardless of the number of tiers, the concept is that the student will move to successively more-intense levels if the child fails to show progress at each level (Fuchs & Fuchs, 2006).

We believe that the tiered approach is a positive step for an RTI. Yet, we are concerned that it may present a problem for the most-tangled readers, if they have to wait too long to receive the most-intensive Tier 3 intervention. To illustrate, let's take a look at the typical structure, followed by our version of layers within tiers, which we believe leads to greater acceleration.

- Tier 1 is the universal or core literacy curriculum and whatever intervention a student would receive within the classroom framework. This tier acknowledges the importance of high-quality classroom literacy programs in meeting the needs of all students. In terms of intensity, all students are typically spending at least 90 minutes a day on the core curriculum, with some built-in interventions and benchmark screenings at beginning, middle, and end of the year. The core instruction should enable 80% of the class to perform at proficiency; if this is not happening, the classroom literacy program should be assessed and redesigned.

- Tier 2 focuses on providing intensive supplemental interventions to small groups of students who are lagging behind their peers in Tier 1. If screening assessments reveal that some students are not responding to Tier 1 classroom interventions, these students are then provided with more-intensive Tier 2 interventions. These interventions are designed to supplement and support classroom instruction, thus providing another level of support for students who need more assistance.

- Tier 3 is the most-intensive intervention, which is specifically targeted to meet the needs of students who have not responded appropriately to Tier 1 and Tier 2 interventions. Tier 3 intervention is typically one-to-one or no more than 1:3 teacher/student ratio. The intensity is also represented in the expertise of the Tier 3 staff, generally an intervention specialist. The essential elements of this level relate to intensity and expertise.

A Closer Look at the Tiered Approach

Since the tiered model is the most common approach for RTI, it seems wise to take a closer look at the underlying concepts within the framework. The dictionary definition of tiered instruction is an 'ordering system.' From an educational point of view, this implies that a reader would need to wait until he had received one intervention tier before moving to the next tier. Our caution with this concept is that it could lead to a remediation mindset, in contrast to an accelerated theory. We believe that interventions should be grounded in a sense of urgency, simply because poor readers have three challenges to overcome, and time can be their enemy:

1. Poor readers must unlearn inefficient and inappropriate responses that are preventing them from making literacy progress. Unfortunately, many of these responses have become habituated reactions to problems, thus, interfering with the new learning. The situation can be further exacerbated by inappropriate interventions delivered by unqualified staff.

2. Poor readers must make giant leaps in their learning in order to catch up with their average peers. This can be an upward struggle for low readers.

As classroom instruction improves in quality, the reading levels of average readers may also increase; and the achievement gap between the poor and average reader could actually widen.

3. Poor readers must maintain their gains after the intervention has ceased, often in spite of other social issues that can impact literacy. This implies that struggling readers need sensitive observation and flexible support for at least 1 year beyond the intervention period.

We believe these challenges are realities for most at-risk children. Therefore, an RTI plan would include multiple layers of intervention to promote and sustain reading progress over time. This plan would provide the most intense intervention up front to the hardest-to-teach students and less intensive small-group interventions for other struggling readers, while also ensuring ongoing support, with progress monitoring, for a minimum of 1 year beyond any intervention. Figure 1 illustrates how interventions are positioned within a layered four-tiered framework. It is important to emphasize that Tiers 2 and 3 are not linear or static interventions; rather, they provide a problem-solving framework for selecting the most appropriate intervention to meet the immediate needs

Figure 1. Dynamic Interventions in a Layered Four-Tiered Framework

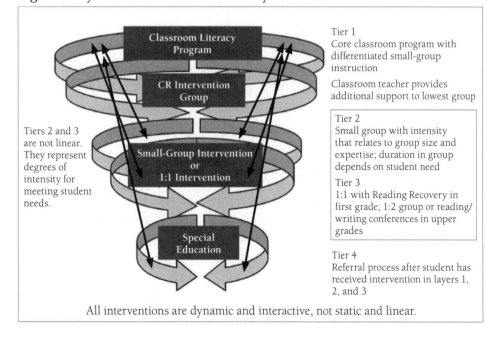

Classroom Literacy Program

CR Intervention Group

Tiers 2 and 3 are not linear. They represent degrees of intensity for meeting student needs.

Small-Group Intervention or 1:1 Intervention

Special Education

Tier 1
Core classroom program with differentiated small-group instruction

Classroom teacher provides additional support to lowest group

Tier 2
Small group with intensity that relates to group size and expertise; duration in group depends on student need

Tier 3
1:1 with Reading Recovery in first grade; 1:2 group or reading/writing conferences in upper grades

Tier 4
Referral process after student has received intervention in layers 1, 2, and 3

All interventions are dynamic and interactive, not static and linear.

Figure 2. Response to Intervention Plan for Comprehensive Intervention Model

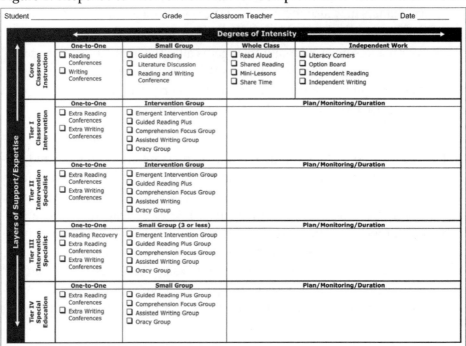

Note. From Reindl, B., & Meyer, K. (2007). *Degrees of intensity in a comprehensive intervention model.* Washington Comprehensive Literacy Charter School, Sheboygan, Wisconsin.

of struggling readers. Figure 2 provides an example of how interventions are aligned across classroom, small group, and one-to-one to ensure a seamless RTI approach. In the next section, we'll describe how these interventions are configured to provide simultaneous support for struggling readers.

Two Waves of Literacy Intervention

Schoolwide intervention designs require unique and well-developed approaches that meet the diverse needs of struggling students, including primary, intermediate, middle, and secondary students. Our RTI model is represented as "Two Waves of Literacy Defense," with the first wave taking a preventive stance with K–3 interventions. The premises of early intervention are logical.

1. Intervene as early as possible before confusions become habituated and unthinking reactions.

2. Provide intensive, short-term services that focus on problem-solving strategies in continuous texts.

3. Make data-driven decisions about the intensity of interventions, the duration period, and the need for follow-up support.

The second wave of literacy defense occurs at the fourth- to twelfth-grade levels. With appropriate interventions, struggling readers in upper grades can become successful readers. However, there are two major challenges to overcome: (a) years of unproductive reading practices can create resistance, passivity, and lack of motivation; and (b) interventions may take longer to yield positive results. These challenges may require schools to redesign their literacy programs in three significant ways.

1. Create a classroom model of differentiated instruction.

2. Place an emphasis on reading strategies in the content areas.

3. Provide interventions, including small group and one-to-one, for the students who are lagging behind.

Let's take a closer look at each wave, beginning with the elementary grades.

The purpose of wave 1 is to increase the overall literacy achievement by the end of third grade and to reduce the number of children identified with learning disabilities within 1.5% or less of the general population. Toward this goal, struggling readers are provided with multiple layers of intervention. To illustrate, at Tier 1, the classroom teacher provides the entire class with a 90-minute literacy core of differentiated instruction: whole group (shared reading, interactive read-aloud, strategy-based mini-lesson); small group (guided reading, literature discussion, assisted writing); one-to-one (reading and writing conferences); and independent (easy or familiar reading, word study). For struggling readers, the teacher provides an additional classroom intervention, for example, a reading conference or a word study lesson.

Concurrent with Tier 1, the lowest students could also receive a Tier 2 small-group intervention or a Tier 3 one-to-one intervention. In some cases, a student might receive three interventions at the same time. If a student is not progressing at the expected rate, the classroom teacher, in collaboration with the school's intervention team, initiates the referral process for special education. In Tier 4, the special education students continue to receive Tier 1 classroom instruction to meet their literacy needs, and the classroom teacher and special education teacher collaborate on a seamless approach across the two contexts. The expectation is that the special education students will continue to make good progress with the potential to reach literacy proficiency over time.

On the following pages are tables depicting the two waves of literacy defense. In Table 1, we provide a framework for layering interventions in the

Table 1. Two Waves of Literacy Defense: K–3 Represents Intervention Wave 1

Literacy Goal: To increase literacy achievement by the end of third grade and to reduce the number of children identified with learning disabilities within 1.5% or less of the general population.

Therefore, to promote accelerated learning (in contrast to remediation), students receive multiple layers of interventions at the same time. Tier 1 classroom instruction is provided alongside any supplemental intervention. Supplemental interventions are not linear, but rather are based on intensity, expertise, and student needs. Referrals to special education are based on students' responses to intervention in Tiers 1, 2, and 3.

	Tier 1 (classroom intervention beyond core program)	Tier 2 (supplemental group)	Tier 3 (supplemental instruction)	Tier 4 (special education in literacy processes)
Levels of Intensity	Classroom Teacher (differentiated instruction)	Intervention Specialist (small group)	Intervention Specialist (individual or 1:2)	Special Education Teacher (small groups or 1:1)
Layered Configurations	Tier 1 only	Tier 2 plus Tiers 1 & 3 Tier 2 plus Tier 1	Tier 3 plus Tier 1 Tier 3 plus Tiers 1 & 2	Tier 1 plus Tier 4
Kindergarten Interventions	Provides small-group intervention in emergent literacy foundations to students who are lagging behind classmates.	Provides additional layer in small-group intervention in emergent literacy group.		
First-Grade Interventions	Provides small-group intervention in assisted writing, guided reading plus, or writing conferences for students who are lagging behind classmates.	Provides additional layer in small-group intervention in assisted writing, guided reading plus, or writing process.	Provides Reading Recovery for most-needy students at beginning of school year; second-round students receive small group (Tier 2) prior to Reading Recovery.	For students who received Tiers 1 & 2 in kindergarten and Tiers 1, 2, and 3 in first grade, the classroom teacher might start the referral process for special children who are not responding to interventions.

(continued)

Table 1. Two Waves of Literacy Defense: K–3 Represents Intervention Wave 1 (*continued*)

	Tier 1 (classroom intervention beyond core program)	Tier 2 (supplemental group)	Tier 3 (supplemental instruction)	Tier 4 (special education in literacy processes)
Second-Grade Interventions	Provides small-group intervention in assisted writing, guided reading plus, writing conference, or comprehension focus groups.	Provides additional layer in small-group intervention in assisted writing, guided reading plus, writing process, or comprehension focus group.	Provides reading and/or writing conferences in 1:1 or 1:2 tailored interventions. Intervention conferences align with classroom instruction.	If student does not respond to Tiers 1, 2, and 3, classroom teacher starts referral process for special education.
Third-Grade Interventions	Provides small-group intervention in assisted writing, guided reading plus, writing conference, or comprehension focus groups.	Provides additional layer in small-group intervention in assisted writing, guided reading plus, writing process, or comprehension focus group.	Provides reading and/or writing conferences in 1:1 or 1:2 tailored interventions.	If student does not respond to Tiers 1, 2, and 3, student is placed in special education.

Literacy Goal: In the first wave of literacy defense, 98–99% of struggling learners who received Tiers 1, 2, and 3 interventions will have achieved literacy proficiency by the end of third grade. This goal recognizes that 1.5% or less of the general population may be diagnosed with a literacy disability. In Tier 4, the special education students will continue to receive Tier 1 classroom instruction to meet their literacy needs, and the classroom teacher and special education teacher will collaborate on a seamless approach across the two contexts. The expectation is the special education group will continue to make good progress with the potential to reach literacy proficiency over time.

As students move into the upper grades, a second wave of intervention is designed to ensure that struggling readers receive Tier 1 classroom support in small-group or individual interventions, plus supplemental support as needed by literacy specialists. Tier 3 intervention is provided to students who are reading at below basic levels. This intervention can be provided by literacy coaches, ELL teachers, and reading specialists.

Note. From Dorn, L. (2007). *Layers of literacy defense in a comprehensive intervention model: A response to intervention approach.* Center for Literacy, University of Arkansas at Little Rock, Little Rock, AR.

kindergarten to third-grade levels. In the second wave of literacy defense (Table 2), Tier 1 instruction uses a workshop framework for differentiating instruction, including small groups and one-to-one conferences. Interventions focus on strategy-based instruction in the content areas. In Tier 2, struggling readers receive supplemental small-group instruction from intervention specialists. Tier

Table 2. Two Waves of Literacy Defense: 4–12 Represents Intervention Wave 2

Literacy Goal: To increase literacy achievement for all students with simultaneous interventions that focus on research-based, problem-solving strategies for reading and writing in the content areas.

Therefore, classroom teachers in the content areas acquire knowledge of reading strategies, as well as management techniques for differentiating instruction to meet the needs of struggling readers. In Tier 1 classroom instruction, struggling readers receive small-group and one-to-one conferences within a workshop framework. In Tier 2 interventions, struggling readers receive supplemental instruction provided by literacy specialists, literacy coaches, and ELL teachers. In Tier 3 intervention, students who are reading below the basic level receive personalized instruction during 1:1 or 1:2 tutoring sessions. Special education teachers provide Tier 4 support in collaboration with Tier 1 classroom intervention to ensure a seamless transition for learning disabled students.

Tier 1 (classroom intervention beyond core program)	Tier 2 (supplemental group)	Tier 3 (supplemental instruction)	Tier 4 (special education in literacy processes)
Classroom Teacher (differentiated instruction)	Intervention Specialist (small group)	Intervention Specialist (individual or 1:2)	Special Education Teacher (small groups or 1:1)
Tier 1 only	Tier 2 plus Tier 1	Tier 3 plus Tier 1	Tier 1 plus Tier 4
Provides differentiated instruction in a workshop framework, including whole-group, small-group, and one-to-one conferences. Struggling readers receive classroom intervention in small-group or individual reading/writing conferences.	Provides small-group supplemental intervention for students who are reading below grade level.	Provides most-intensive intervention for students who are reading at below basic level in reading and need highly tailored tutoring in 1:1 or 1:2 conferences.	Provides small-group intervention that aligns with classroom support for students with learning disabilities.

Note. From Dorn, L. (2007). *Layers of literacy defense in a comprehensive intervention model: A response to intervention approach.* Center for Literacy, University of Arkansas at Little Rock, Little Rock, AR.

3 interventions include individual or small groups of 1:3 or less, and are provided to students who are reading below average levels. In schools with literacy coaches, the coaches spend up to 40% of their time providing Tier 2 and Tier 3 interventions to the most-needy students. Special education teachers provide Tier 4 support in collaboration with Tier 1 classroom intervention to provide a seamless transition for learning disabled students.

The Comprehensive Intervention Model as a Response to Intervention Approach

In this section, we'll examine the Comprehensive Intervention Model as a response to intervention method. A critical element of RTI is that the approach must be research-based; furthermore, the design must be solid enough to ensure integrity and consistency in implementation. Yet, at the same time, the design must be flexible enough to respect the decision-making knowledge of teachers and to accommodate the variability in students' learning. In the CIM, the intervention components have been replicated across multiple sites with consistent results and in collaboration with teachers, who have provided valuable insights on students' learning.

Development and Research on the CIM

In 1991, Dorn implemented the small-group model to support Reading Recovery teachers who worked with small groups of struggling readers in kindergarten and first grade. In the pilot year, 15 experienced Reading Recovery teachers were trained in the small-group intervention. This group was actively involved in the development and research on the small-group model, including video analysis of lesson components, record keeping, cluster visits, and data collection. In 1993, Dorn conducted a study that examined the complementary effects of Reading Recovery and the small-group intervention. The study of 187 first graders produced five positive outcomes:

1. Reading Recovery was the most effective intervention for the most-tangled readers in first grade.
2. Some needy students served in kindergarten groups did not need Reading Recovery in first grade.
3. Some first-grade students benefited from small groups and did not require Reading Recovery.
4. Some Reading Recovery students who received small-group instruction prior to Reading Recovery required fewer lessons in Reading Recovery.
5. Some nondiscontinued Reading Recovery students who received small-group instruction after Reading Recovery achieved average levels by the end of the year.

These preliminary results suggested that a comprehensive approach to early intervention was an effective design for meeting the needs of diverse learners.

During the next 13 years, additional research to examine and refine the CIM was conducted. In 1994, Dorn replicated the 1993 study with 231 students from nine schools and found similar results. In 1995, the study was published in the *Journal of School Research and Information* and was reprinted in 1996 in *Literacy, Teaching and Learning,* a publication of the Reading Recovery Council of North America. In 2002, Paige compared the achievement data of 117 Reading Recovery and small-group students over 3 consecutive years. Paige concluded that the Reading Recovery children scored significantly higher on the Stanford 9 Achievement examination than the students in the small-group intervention. Harrison (2003) studied the complementary effects of the Reading Recovery and small group interventions on 307 first graders. Her study concluded the following:

- Reading Recovery was the most effective intervention for the most-needy readers.

- A small percentage of children who needed protracted periods of intervention (beyond 20 weeks) benefited from small-group instruction and reached average reading levels at the end of the school year.

- For some children, participation in the small group prior to Reading Recovery influenced their length of time in the Reading Recovery program.

- Small-group instruction was most beneficial for children who needed supplemental help of a lesser nature. The average text level gain from fall to year-end for the lowest-achieving children who received small-group instruction was very small, indicating that small-group instruction for the most-tangled children was not enough.

- Children served in small-group instruction remained in the intervention for longer periods than the Reading Recovery children.

- The Reading Recovery and small-group programs are complementary interventions that recognize the diversity of student needs and enable more struggling readers to achieve proficiency in reading and writing.

In 2005, James replicated the work of Dorn (1994) and Harrison (2003) in a large-scale study of 12,000 first graders across six states. James was interested in a deeper exploration of the complementary effects of the two interventions, specifically, the progress of the students in the small-group intervention who were not making adequate progress. She found that of the 6,421 students originally assigned to small group, 2,423 (or 39.1%) were not making adequate progress at midyear. These small-group students were reassigned to Reading Recovery and their literacy learning was profoundly influenced. Using regression analysis, a comparison was made between the actual year-end results following Reading Recovery and projected results using small group alone. The findings revealed that Reading Recovery was the intervening factor that allowed these students to respond to intervention in an accelerated manner. In support of the CIM, over 70% of the small-group students made adequate progress, while the remaining 30% required Reading Recovery.

In 2005, Rahi examined the impact of Reading Recovery and small-group interventions on the reading acceleration of 631 first graders in the Fort Smith (Arkansas) School District. Rahi concluded that the majority of students served in both interventions made progress. Like James, she examined the progress of the group of students for whom the small-group intervention was inadequate. Rahi sought to determine if a change would occur in the learning trajectory for this sample after receiving Reading Recovery. Her findings, in support of James (2005), concluded that a statistically significant change occurred in the students' learning trajectory after they completed Reading Recovery. These studies support the importance of the CIM, indicating that small groups, although effective for a large population of struggling learners, are insufficient for the most-tangled readers. Furthermore, the studies documented that 25–30% of students within the lowest band of the low cohort required individual instruction.

In 2007, Platt investigated the influence of layered interventions (simultaneous interventions) on the writing acceleration of Reading Recovery students. Platt's research was in response to the refinements of the CIM, one of which focused on layered interventions in contrast to tiered interventions. Platt was interested in examining whether a layered, push-in writing intervention, along with Reading Recovery, would impact the writing performance of Reading Recovery students during writers' workshop. She compared three groups: Reading Recovery plus push-in writing group; Reading Recovery plus pull-out writing group; and Reading Recovery and no other intervention group. Each group was assessed on standardized end-of-year writing rubrics and teacher surveys. Platt concluded that the highest-achieving students received Reading Recovery and a push-in writing intervention during the writing workshop in the classroom. Additionally, comparable increases in reading occurred for students who received the push-in writing group.

The ability of the CIM to replicate and sustain itself in varied contexts and with diverse populations, without changing the basic design, is essential to the model's success. Toward this goal, all CIM sites are required to conduct annual evaluations that include studies of student achievement over time, including performance of subgroups on district and state assessments. A district evaluation (Zuniga, Thomas, & Weisenberg, 2007) from a California site examined the reading achievement of English language acquisition (ELA) learners who had participated in supportive (comprehensive literacy) classrooms versus a random sample of students from other classrooms. First-grade students who had the benefit of instruction over 2 years in supportive classrooms with supplemental small-group interventions made the largest reading gains within a 1-year time frame. This was related to the daily implementation of research-based instructional practices, including explicit ELA instruction, and small-group intervention. The researchers concluded that the CIM had a significant influence on the reading achievement of ELA students. Similar results were found in Wisconsin (Fraley & Landwehr, 2007; Meyer & Reindl, 2007) and Michigan (Lower, 2007) sites.

These studies, which span a period of 15 years, document the importance of a comprehensive intervention approach. In a 2007 report entitled *Implications for Reading Teachers in Response to Intervention*, the International Reading Association recognized the comprehensive literacy model in the Walled Lake School District in Michigan as an effective RTI approach. In 2007, Reading Recovery received the highest rating by the U.S. Department of Education's What Works Clearinghouse for positive effects on general reading achievement and alphabetics and for potentially positive effects on reading comprehension and fluency. In *Learning Disabilities: A Contemporary Journal*, Dunn (2007) described Reading Recovery as one component of an RTI approach. In *Reading Research Quarterly*, McEneaney, Lose, and Schwartz (2006) stressed that the RTI professional development component should focus on contingent teaching and decision making, as in the Reading Recovery design.

In summary, the CIM acknowledges Reading Recovery as the best intervention for the most-needy first-grade readers, with the small-group interventions reserved for children of lesser need. The success of the CIM is grounded in three critical areas: (a) the specialized knowledge and expertise of reading teachers, (b) the training and ongoing professional development that focus on sensitive observation and flexible decision making, and (c) the collaborative relationship between university trainers and reading teachers in the refinement of the literacy components.

Components of the Comprehensive Intervention Model

The CIM includes individual and small-group interventions that align with the classroom curriculum. Table 3 presents a grid of all components, including Reading Recovery. In this section, we'll focus on six small-group components

Table 3. Intervention Components of the Comprehensive Intervention Model

Group	Role of Reading	Role of Writing	Entry and Exit Assessments	Progress Monitoring	Materials
Reading Recovery	Reading strategies, fluency, comprehension	Writing strategies, early composing strategies	Observation Survey, text reading level	Running record, book graph, writing vocabulary chart	Leveled texts, writing journal
Emergent Language and Literacy	Emergent literacy foundations, language development	Knowledge of print, phonemic awareness, language development	Observation Survey, dictated story, record of oral language	Writing sample, observation notes and running record, if applicable	ABC chart, nursery rhymes, writing journal, interactive writing, big books, easy texts
Guided Reading Plus	Reading strategies, fluency, comprehension	Reading and writing links, writing about reading	Text reading, retelling, word test, fluency measure, writing prompt	Text reading, retelling, fluency measure, reading behavior checklist	Leveled texts, writing journals
Writing Process	Increase reading through writing	Composing, revising, editing strategies	Writing prompt	Writing portfolio, writing checklist, writing prompt	Writing portfolios, mentor texts, writing checklists
Comprehension Focus	Comprehension strategies, knowledge of text structures, deeper understanding of content	Reciprocity of reading/ writing, writing process, text organization	Text reading (oral and silent), comprehension measure, writing prompt and scoring rubric	Benchmark book in genre/ text unit, writing sample in genre/text unit	Collection of books in focus unit, writing portfolios, text maps and writing guides
Comprehension Focus in Content Area	Comprehension strategies, knowledge of text structures, deeper understanding of content	Reciprocity of reading/ writing, writing process, text organization	Text reading (oral and silent), comprehension measure, writing prompt and scoring rubric	Unseen text in content area, writing sample in genre/text unit	Content textbooks or informational texts, writing portfolios, text maps and writing guides

Note. From Dorn, L., & Soffos, C. (2007). *Comprehensive intervention model (CIM): A response to intervention method.* Center for Literacy, University of Arkansas at Little Rock, Little Rock, AR.

of the model, which can be delivered as either pull-out or push-in interventions with the exception of the writing process group, which is always implemented during writing workshop in the classroom.

Emergent language and literacy groups *for children who are in kindergarten or first grade and are at the emergent level of reading and writing*
The intervention emphasizes oral language development, phonemic awareness and phonics, and the important concepts about print that are essential to learning to read. The components include shared reading, interactive writing, and opportunities to engage in language experiences around books that have been read aloud. The groups meet for 30 minutes daily.

Guided reading plus groups *for children in Grades 1–3 who are reading at the early to transitional levels of reading and writing, but are lagging behind their classmates*
The lesson format spans 2 days with 30 minutes of instruction per day. Day 1 includes four components: preplanned word study activity, orientation to the new book, independent reading with teacher observations, and follow-up teaching points, including discussion of the message. On Day 2, the lesson format begins with assessment: The teacher takes a running record on two children while the other students read easy or familiar texts. Then the focus shifts to the writing component, which includes four predictable parts: responding to yesterday's guided reading text, composing individual messages, writing independently, and holding one-to-one writing conferences with the teacher.

Assisted writing groups *designed to support first-grade children at the early stage of writing development who are lagging behind their classmates*
During interactive writing and, later, writing-aloud, the students learn about the writing process: composing, revising and editing strategies, and the link between reading and writing.

Writing process groups *designed for first- to fourth-grade children who are struggling with the writing process in their writing workshop classrooms*
The intervention specialist provides tailored instruction that focuses on the writing process, including drafting, revising, crafting, editing, and publishing processes.

Comprehension focus groups for children who are reading at the transitional level and beyond in Grades 2–6, and who are having difficulty comprehending the wide range of text genres as they move up the grades

The interventions are designed to help students develop reading and writing knowledge for three major text types: narrative, informational, and persuasive. The intervention includes two major components: (a) Students participate in a comprehension focus unit around a specific text type or genre for a minimum of 3 weeks; and (b) Students participate in the writing process by developing an original piece of writing within the genre of the focus unit. The lessons are 30 minutes daily.

Comprehension focus groups in content area designed for upper-grade readers who are struggling with reading their content texts

The intervention utilizes the same format as the comprehension focus group described above; however, the students use their context textbooks, as well as other informational texts in the content unit of study. The intervention occurs during the content workshop in the classroom, or as a pull-out intervention.

Designing a CIM as a System Intervention

A system intervention is a seamless comprehensive approach to student achievement. The CIM provides teachers with a framework for aligning and managing interventions across the school system. The following steps provide an example of how this might work.

1. Establish an intervention team comprised of all intervention specialists and the classroom teacher. Additional team members can include the principal, literacy coach, and Reading Recovery teacher leader. Use the team to make decisions regarding appropriate services for struggling learners and the best designs for meeting student needs.

2. Use only highly trained teachers with teaching credentials for intervention services. Provide additional training for these teachers in intervention assessments and precision teaching.

3. Identify all supplemental intervention specialists according to their expertise (e.g., Reading Recovery, English language learners, special education, intervention specialists).

4. Identify the students within the school who will need intervention services and classify their needs according to intensive and less intensive.

5. Create an intervention schedule for the classroom and identify designated periods where additional classroom interventions will occur.

6. Add supplemental interventions to the classroom schedule. Collaborate on how to layer interventions; for example, if a classroom teacher is able to only provide an additional reading group three times a week, the literacy coach (who also serves as an intervention specialist 30–45 minutes each day) can provide the intervention on alternate days.

7. Collaborate on student progress across all interventions. Design a system for progress monitoring that will allow all intervention teachers to chart student growth over time.

A systemic approach requires teachers to collaborate around common goals and to monitor student progress across programs. Intervention team meetings are an essential part of the RTI process. A team consists of intervention specialists (e.g., Reading Recovery, Title I, special education, ELL), classroom teachers, and other instructional leaders (e.g., principal, teacher leaders, literacy coaches). The team reviews the student data and makes decisions regarding the appropriate interventions. The following questions may provide schools with a framework for selecting the appropriate interventions based on overall student achievement.

1. How many students at each grade level are scoring below proficiency levels on reading and writing measures? If more than 20% in a particular grade are reading at low levels, the classroom program may be inappropriate. In this case, the intervention specialist might choose to work more closely with the classroom teacher during push-in intervention groups.

2. How many kindergartners are scoring at low language levels? If disproportionate numbers are scoring at low levels, the intervention specialist might schedule time for emergent language and literacy groups.

3. How many second graders are reading below proficiency (and how far below)? Did these students receive intervention during the first grade? The intervention specialist might provide these students with a comprehension focus group, a writing process group, or a guided reading plus group.

4. Does the school have a highly mobile subgroup? What supports are in place for transfer students who need interventions in reading? The intervention specialist might include flextime in her schedule, allowing daily time for testing new students, observing in the classroom, and working with transfer students until a more permanent opening occurs.

5. How are third and fourth graders performing on state assessments? In what areas are they scoring below their classmates? The intervention specialist might schedule time to work in the classroom in selected areas, such as comprehension focus groups in the content area.

A CIM uses a problem-solving, data-driven process for increasing literacy achievement across the school. To illustrate, at the beginning of the school year, the intervention specialist might serve kindergarten and first-grade intervention groups; and at midyear, she might shift her services to third- and fourth-grade intervention groups. A typical schedule is included in Figure 3, indicating that

Figure 3. Typical Schedule for Intervention Specialist Serving Grades 1, 2, and 3

Time	Grade	Intervention	Students
8:00–8:30	1	Reading Recovery	1
8:35–9:05	1	Reading Recovery	1
9:10–9:30	1	Guided Reading Plus Group (pull out)	5
9:35–9:55	1	Guided Reading Plus Group (push in)	5
10:00–10:30	1	Guided Reading Plus Group (pull out)	3
10:35–11:05	1	Reading Recovery	1
11:10–11:30	2	Guided Reading Plus Group (pull out)	5
11:30–12:00		Lunch	
12:00–12:30		Planning Time	
12:30–1:00	1	Writing Process Group (push in)	3
1:05–1:35	2	Writing Process Group (push in)	4
1:40–2:10	1	Reading Recovery	1
2:15–3:00	3	Content Workshop (push in)	5
3:05–3:25	3	Comprehension Focus Group (pull out)	5

the Reading Recovery teacher/intervention specialist is able to service nearly 40 low-achieving readers across the school day. In a districtwide intervention plan, all teachers are provided with intervention training and professional development for supporting struggling readers. This seamless approach emphasizes a constructivist model whereas teachers build on and extend students' knowledge across programs, grades, and schools.

Closing Thoughts

In this article, we have presented the Comprehensive Intervention Model as a research-based, decision-making design for meeting the needs of diverse learners in a response to intervention approach. The model is a conceptual framework for aligning interventions across classroom and supplemental programs, ensuring consistency for our most fragile learners. The CIM is a system intervention that is based on five core principles:

1. Intervene early.

2. Use a seamless approach.

3. Provide layered interventions.

4. Make ethical and informed decisions.

5. Employ a collaborative, problem-solving method.

The heartbeat of the CIM is the responsive teacher, one who understands change over time in literacy processing and is able to adjust instruction to accommodate student learning.

REFERENCES

Center for Literacy. (2007). *A comprehensive literacy model: A guidebook for small group interventions. University of Arkansas at Little Rock.* Little Rock, AR: Author.

Clay, M.M. (1998). *From different paths to common outcomes.* York, ME: Stenhouse.

Clay, M.M. (2005). *Literacy lessons designed for individuals part two: Teaching procedures.* Portsmouth, NH: Heinemann.

Dorn, L. (1993). *Meeting the needs of struggling readers with Reading Recovery and small group interventions.* Unpublished technical report.

University of Arkansas at Little Rock, Little Rock, AR.

Dorn, L., & Allen, A. (1995). Helping low-achieving first graders: A program combining Reading Recovery tutoring and small-group instruction. *ERS Spectrum: Journal of School Research and Information, 13*(3), 16–24.

Dunn, W. (2007). Diagnosing reading disability: Reading Recovery as a component of a response-to-intervention assessment method. *Learning Disabilities: A Contemporary Journal 5*(2), 31–47.

Fraley, M., & Landwehr, A. (2007). *Program results on the comprehensive literacy model.* Unpublished report. Sullivan Elementary School, Green Bay School District, Wisconsin.

Fuchs, D., & Fuchs, L. (2006). February, March). Introduction to response to intervention: What, why, and how valid is it? *Reading Research Quarterly, 41*(1), 93–99.

Gersten, R., & Dimino, J. (2006). February, March). RTI (response to intervention): Rethinking special education for students with reading difficulties (yet again). *Reading Research Quarterly, 41*(1), 99–108.

Gersten, R., Fuchs, L.S., Williams, J.P., & Baker, S. (2001). Teaching reading comprehension strategies to students with learning disabilities: A review of research. *Review of Educational Research, 71,* 279–320.

Harrison, L. (2003). *A study of the complementary effects of Reading Recovery and small group literacy instruction.* Unpublished educational specialist thesis, University of Arkansas at Little Rock, Little Rock, AR.

International Reading Association. (2007). *Implications for reading teachers in response to intervention.* Retrieved December 10, 2007, from IRA website: http://www.reading.org/down loads/resources/rti0707_implications.pdf

James, K. (2005). *A study of the complementary effects of Reading Recovery and small group instruction on the literacy achievement of struggling first grade readers.* Unpublished educational specialist thesis, University of Arkansas at Little Rock, Little Rock, AR.

Lose, M. (2007). A child's response to intervention requires a responsive teacher of reading. *The Reading Teacher, 61*(3), 276–279.

Lower, C. (2007). *A longitudinal study of the partnerships in comprehensive literacy model on student achievement and teacher change in the Dearborn, Michigan school district.* Unpublished educational specialist thesis, University of Arkansas at Little Rock, Little Rock, AR.

Meyer, K., & Reindl, B. (2007). *Program results on the comprehensive literacy model for school improvement.* Unpublished report, Washington Charter School for Comprehensive Literacy, Sheboyan School District, Wisconsin.

McEneaney, J., Lose, M., & Schwartz, R. (2006, January, February, March). A transactional perspective on reading difficulties and response to intervention. *Reading Research Quarterly,* 117–128.

Paige, G. (2002). *Effects of Reading Recovery and early literacy programs to teach strategies to struggling first grade readers.* Unpublished educational specialist thesis, University of Arkansas at Little Rock, Little Rock, AR.

Platt, R. (2007). *The effects of layered interventions on the writing acceleration of struggling first grade writers.* Unpublished educational specialist thesis, University of Arkansas at Little Rock, Little Rock, AR.

Rahi, K. (2005). *Research on Reading Recovery and small group interventions.* Unpublished report, Fort Smith School District, Arkansas.

What Works Clearinghouse. (2007, March 19). *Intervention: Reading Recovery.* Retrieved December 10, 2007, from U.S. Department of Education Institute of Education Sciences website: http://ies.ed.gov/ncee/wwc/reports/ beginning_reading/reading_recovery/

Zuniga, J., Thomas, C., & Weisenberg, A. (2007). *Program results on the comprehensive language and literacy model.* Unpublished report, Lodi Unified School District, California.

CHAPTER 18

Use Students' Summer-Setback Months to Raise Minority Achievement

Richard L. Allington and Anne McGill-Franzen

P oor children have never fared as well as more advantaged children in American schools. In recognition of this reality, federal funding for interventions for economically disadvantaged students was initiated through Title I of the Elementary and Secondary Education Act of 1966 (ESEA) to provide funding for supplementary educational interventions in the hope of narrowing the achievement gap between more- and less-advantaged students.

While there is some evidence that this achievement gap has narrowed over time, the most recent National Assessment of Educational Progress (NAEP) in reading provides strong evidence of the pervasive nature of this seemingly intractable rich/poor achievement gap. For instance, twice as many low-income fourth-graders (those eligible for subsidized lunches) as students who were not low income fell below the basic NAEP level (58% versus 27%), and far fewer low-income students achieved at proficient level (13% versus 40%).

There have been a variety of explanations for the rich/poor achievement gap. Most likely, there are multiple sources for it. Over the past three decades, researchers have explored a variety of school-based interventions designed to reduce or eliminate the gap. But, both researchers and policy makers have largely ignored the role of summer reading setback in creating this achievement gap.

Summer Time, When the Slidin' Is Easy

Summer reading setback occurs when students return to school after summer vacation with diminished reading skills, presumably from a lack of adequate

RTI in Literacy—Responsive and Comprehensive, edited by Peter H. Johnston, published by the International Reading Association. This chapter reprinted from Allington, R.L., & McGill-Franzen, A. (2003). Use Students' Summer-Setback Months to Raise Minority Achievement. *Education Digest*, 69(3), 19–24.

reading practice. Summer setback affects children from families of different socioeconomic groups differently. Available research indicates that the reading achievement of poor children, as a group, typically declines during the summer vacation period, while the reading achievement of children from more economically advantaged families holds steady or increases modestly.

With the most recent reauthorization of the ESEA (President George W. Bush's "No Child Left Behind" Act), the reading achievement gap has again risen on the national education agenda. Federal funding for interventions to narrow the achievement gap is flowing, though this time with restrictions such that the interventions must be informed by "scientific research."

Once again, the current preferred intervention designs seem to focus on the youngest students and on developing basic phonological skills. But we have been down this path before; federal funding for code-emphasis early interventions dominated the 1970s and 1980s, and yet the achievement gap remains large. Perhaps it is time to consider alternative directions in the campaign to close the rich/poor reading achievement gap.

Twenty years ago, researchers contrasting the reading achievement patterns in schools enrolling mostly rich students and those enrolling mostly poor students concluded: "Our whole approach to equalizing educational opportunities and achievements may be misdirected." The authors of a similar, more recent study reached the same conclusion.

In both of these large-scale research studies, the achievement gap between rich and poor children was shown to grow dramatically across the elementary school years, from less than one year's difference to almost three. Both studies were designed so that data for estimating student achievement at the beginning and end of each school year (September and June) were available, allowing researchers to estimate both the reading growth during the school year and the accumulating impact of summer reading setback.

The powerful, cumulative negative impact of summer setback on poor children's long-term reading achievement led both sets of researchers to argue that efforts targeted only at improving curriculum and instruction in high-poverty schools were unlikely to close the reading achievement gap. In their view, much of the school reform effort aimed at improving the reading achievement of poor children failed to focus on a critical factor in widening the reading achievement gap: the poor child's summer reading setback.

Evidence on the differential impact of summer vacation periods on more- and less-advantaged students' achievement has now been available in the scientific literature for some time, and much of that research (13 empirical studies on about 40,000 subjects) was subjected to meta-analysis by Harris Cooper and his colleagues. They also provided narrative analysis of another two dozen studies that failed to provide adequate data for the meta-analytic procedures.

Their findings confirm the differential impact of summer vacation periods reported in the large-scale longitudinal studies reviewed above: During summer vacation, the reading proficiency of students from lower-income families declined, while that of middle-class students improved modestly. Summer vacations created, on average, an annual achievement gap of about three months between rich and poor students.

Suddenly Last Summers

This three-month annual gap can accumulate to a year and a half between the end of kindergarten and the end of grade 5—just five summers. When this accumulating reading achievement gap is combined with an achievement gap at the beginning of schooling, students from lower-income families are often two or three years behind their more-advantaged peers as they head to middle school.

There have been a variety of explanations of the rich/poor achievement gap. Generally, though, the focus of recent reform efforts has been on the nature of the reading instruction offered in schools. Nonetheless, a substantive scientific literature locates much of the source of the achievement gap outside the school, classroom, curriculum, or instructional program.

At the same time, there are good reasons to be optimistic about the potential impact of improving the curriculum and instruction in high-poverty schools, if only because so much work has demonstrated the difference it can make in student achievement. And certainly we should not ignore the prospect of improving the quality of classroom reading instruction as a way of attempting to ameliorate the rich/poor reading achievement gap.

But the scientific evidence of the accumulating impact of summer reading setback on the achievement gap is very compelling. What might be surprising is just how long that evidence has been largely ignored by educators and policy makers (though recent proposals for mandating summer school for low-achieving students could be viewed as a way of addressing the evidence regarding summer reading setback).

Summer School May Not Be the Answer

The data available consistently portray summer reading setback as the most potent explanation for the widening of the reading achievement gap between rich and poor children across the elementary years. But, mandating summer school attendance for children from low-income families may not always be the most appropriate response.

At the very least, alternatives to compulsory summer school should be explored, if only for economic and ethical reasons. Compulsory summer school attendance for students from low-income families would be an expensive response and would present a potentially discriminatory policy framework.

We should also be clear that not every poor child experiences summer reading setback. Poor children exhibit a variety of achievement patterns during the summer months. Michael Puma and his colleagues reported that higher-achieving poor students fared better than lower-achieving students. That is, lower-achieving poor children demonstrated a greater summer reading setback. While family socioeconomic status and reading achievement are highly correlated, the report's findings suggest that poor children's limited access to books in the summer is not the sole explanation of the consistent finding of substantial summer reading setback among poor children.

It seems likely that there are any number of motivational and volitional factors as well that influence reading behavior, especially voluntary summer reading activity. For instance, children's beliefs about their own efficacy are linked to past academic performance, including their experiences as more- or less-successful readers. A history of less-successful reading experiences produces a lower sense of self-efficacy in readers than a history of successful reading experiences. The lower sense of self-efficacy then predicts lower levels of engagement in reading, especially voluntary reading.

And it is the poor readers who are most likely to be assigned texts that are too hard—texts they read with little fluency, limited accuracy, and lack of comprehension. It is poor readers, then, who would seem least likely to exhibit the motivation to read voluntarily—during the school year or the summer. Greater success in school reading, then, is central to enhancing out-of-school voluntary reading. Thus, a dual focus is needed: Improve classroom instruction and, at the same time, address the problem of poor children's access to appropriately complex books for voluntary summer reading.

But providing books of appropriate complexity seems to be only the first step in encouraging voluntary reading. There is good scientific evidence that building on student interest can stimulate an interest in reading, even among lower-achieving readers.

Central to fostering enhanced interest in voluntary reading is providing a substantial degree of autonomy in the choice of texts to be read and a substantial quantity of books that vary on several dimensions, including difficulty, genre, topic, and length. In an optimal environment, self-selection of books on topics of personal interest or written by favorite authors or within a particular genre are all important features of efforts to promote greater voluntary reading, especially among lower-achieving students.

Conclusions Safe to Draw

From the available scientific research we draw several conclusions:

- There is abundant evidence that summer reading setback is one of the important factors contributing to the reading achievement gap between rich and poor children.
- There is powerful evidence indicating that children from lower-income families have more restricted access to books, both in school and out of school, than do their more-advantaged peers.
- There is consistent correlational evidence illustrating that better readers read more than poorer readers, a finding that supports theoretical models that emphasize the importance of the volume of successful reading experiences in the development of reading proficiency.
- There is a substantial body of research linking successful school reading experiences with the motivation to read voluntarily; successful school reading experiences require a curriculum framework that emphasizes matching children with books appropriate to their level of reading development.

Given these findings, what are the implications for current education reform initiatives that seek to eliminate the reading achievement gap between rich children and poor children? There are at least two broad principles to be drawn from this research that might guide education reform efforts focused on closing the reading achievement gap.

1. **Volume of reading is important in the development of reading proficiency.** Does the reform design ensure that all students engage in extensive,

high-success reading activities throughout the school day? Does it reliably enhance the volume of voluntary reading that students do in the evenings, on the weekends, and during summer vacations?

2. **Children must have easy—literally fingertip—access to books that provide engaging, successful reading experiences throughout the calendar year if we want them to read in volume.** Does the reform design provide classroom book collections so that all students, regardless of their achievement levels, have easy access to hundreds of titles of appropriately difficult books? Does it provide an array of books available to students every Friday for take-home weekend reading? Does the reform design ensure that books are easily available throughout the summer months? Does it provide teachers with the skills needed to match children and books?

Having set forth these two principles, we would further note that all children also need consistent access to explicit demonstrations of the thinking that proficient readers do before, during, and after reading. In other words, they need access to expert instruction. We wish that children needed only to be given substantial blocks of time to read and easy access to appropriate books to foster reading development.

But they also need to be taught. Still, good teaching may go unrewarded if students do not practice those emerging skills and strategies successfully and extensively. It is during such successful, independent practice that students consolidate their skills and strategies and come to own them. Without extensive successful reading practice, reading proficiency inevitably lags.

If current education reform efforts are to succeed in narrowing the reading achievement gap, intervention designs must reflect the scientific research available. Children need an enormous supply of successful reading experiences, both in school and out, to become proficient, independent readers.

The potential role of voluntary summer reading in closing the reading achievement gap has been neglected too long by educators, researchers, and policy makers. Schools that serve many poor children must play a substantive role in ensuring that each and every child has year-round access to appropriate books to read, books they cannot wait to read.

CHAPTER 19

Whole-School Detracking:
A Strategy for Equity
and Excellence

Doris Alvarez and Hugh Mehan

In an unprecedented move by a major research university, the University of California, San Diego (UCSD) has established a charter middle/high school on our campus for the express purpose of preparing students from low-income backgrounds for college. Students at the Preuss School are selected by lottery; in the 2002–2003 school year, 57.3% of the student population was Latino, 14.2% African American, 19.7% Asian, 6.3% White, 2.0% Filipino, and 0.5% Pacific Islander. The curriculum from 6th to 12th grade is exclusively college prep. The school supplements instruction with a comprehensive system of academic and social supports, including a longer school day and longer school year (which provides more intense opportunities for in-depth learning), tutoring by UCSD undergraduates, Saturday Academies for students who continue to struggle, psychological counseling, mentoring by community members, and parental involvement and education.

Eighty percent of the students from the first graduating class of 55 were attending 4-year colleges as of Fall 2004; 20% are attending community colleges—with their transfer to UC campuses guaranteed in 2 years (McClure & Morales, 2004). This gives us an existence proof that detracking (i.e., presenting underserved students with a rigorous academic program, supplemented by a comprehensive system of academic and social supports), can propel students from low-income households toward college eligibility and enrollment. This article describes the Preuss School's detracking strategy, its curriculum, and the scaffolds erected to support student success. We also discuss how these

RTI in Literacy—Responsive and Comprehensive, edited by Peter H. Johnston, published by the International Reading Association. This chapter reprinted from Alvarez, D., & Mehan, H. (2006). Whole-School Detracking: A Strategy for Equity and Excellence. *Theory Into Practice, 45*(1), 82–89. Copyright © by Taylor & Francis. Reprinted by permission of the publisher (Taylor & Francis Group, www.informaworld.com).

structures provide the organizational framework for a culture of learning for teachers and students.

The Cognitive and Sociological Rationale for the Preuss School

The principles of the Preuss School are derived from current thinking about cognitive development and the social organization of schooling. Research in cognitive development supports the *universal development* thesis, which suggests that all normally functioning humans have the capacity to reason sufficiently well to finish high school and enter college when they are supported with the appropriate academic and social scaffolds (Bruner, 1986; Cicourel & Mehan, 1985; Meier, 1995; Resnick, 1995). By contrast, students segregated into low-track classes are often exposed to a limited range of cognitive tasks that do not stretch their higher order thinking and communicative skills, do not extend them to solve new and complex problems, and do not facilitate the transfer of knowledge gained in one situation to another situation. The implication of the universal development thesis is that schools should not segregate students into high and low tracks. Indeed, all students—those enrolling in college and those entering the world of work—benefit from a rigorous academic curriculum.

This modern conception of cognitive potential is supported by sociological critiques of tracking (Education Trust, 2003a, 2003b; Haycock & Navarro, 1988; Lucas, 1999; Oakes, 2003; Oakes, Gamoran, & Page, 1992). The distribution of students to high-, middle-, and low-ability groups or academic and general tracks correlates with ethnicity and socioeconomic status. Children from low-income or one-parent households, families with an unemployed worker, or linguistic and ethnic minority groups are more likely to be assigned to low-ability groups or tracks. Furthermore, African American and Latino students are consistently underrepresented in programs for the gifted and talented but overrepresented in special education programs (Mehan, Hertweck, & Meihls, 1986; Mercer, 1975).

Recognizing that tracked schools are inequitable and ineffective, educators have been exploring alternatives to these practices since the 1980s, notably replacing the tracking system (Burris & Welner, 2005; Comer, 1988; Levin, 1987; Oakes & Wells, 1998; Sizer, 2004; Wheelock, 1992; Yonezawa, Wells, & Serna, 2002). Detracking attacks the problem of students with varying educational experiences in a fundamentally different way than tracking. Whereas tracking segregates students of varying background into separate courses of study and holds instruction time constant, detracking has the potential to hold high standards constant and varies the amount of instruction time, and social and academic supports.

We are attracted to the idea of detracking students due to its commitment to rigorous academic preparation for underrepresented students. Academic rigor is a necessary ingredient, but we also need to intensify the academic and social system supporting untracked students to increase the possibilities that under-served students will become eligible for college and university enrollment.

Mission and Goals of the Preuss School

This is where the Preuss School enters the picture. The curriculum and pedagogy of the Preuss School is based on a belief in the value of a traditional liberal arts education. Every graduating student should be capable of written and spoken expression (in both English and a foreign language), mathematical reasoning, and understanding scientific procedures and results. Each should also have a broad appreciation of the diverse cultures that make up Western and non-Western civilizations. The fine and performing arts are not construed as electives but well-considered courses in the intellectual development of students. The senior year of the school is integrated with the UCSD freshman year; seniors are expected to take at least one UCSD course during their final year.[1]

Above all, the Preuss School provides an environment where students are made to feel confident and safe, and are encouraged to develop a greater sense of self-worth and a sense of pride in their academic accomplishments. Although specializing in secondary education, the school is designed to reflect UCSD's high level of achievement by continually fostering a culture of academic accomplishment. Students are taught the art of questioning and the skill of logical thinking in an environment that encourages risk-taking. The school also seeks to develop personal character, good physical health, good judgment, and ethical behavior. It is further recognized that the home and school should share dual responsibility for encouraging young people to develop as scholars and citizens.

Creating a Culture of Learning

The Preuss School at UCSD uses a lottery to select low-income sixth-grade students with high potential but underdeveloped skills, and immediately enrolls them in rigorous college-prep classes. This rigorous middle school curriculum in Grades 6 to 8 prepares them for a high school core curriculum that fulfills or exceeds the University of California and California State University entry requirements. Courses at the Preuss School include 4 years of English, 4 years of math, 4 years of science (including three lab sciences), 4 years of a foreign language, and 1 year of a visual and performing art. At the Preuss School, students' course-taking sequence mirrors that of most private or elite public schools.

Preuss students are not typical private or affluent public school students, however. Some of the students speak English as a second language, some have not been successful in elementary or middle school, and none of the students' parents has graduated from college or in some cases even high school. Therefore, the founding faculty and principal knew from their collective experience that it was important to structure academic supports and a culture of learning to assist students in meeting the challenging curriculum required for competitive eligibility for 4-year colleges and universities (Mehan et al., 1996).

A visitor noted that at the Preuss School, "a college culture is everywhere" (Brandon, 2004, p. 10). Indeed, the first step in preparing underserved students for college eligibility was creating a college-going culture. Elements of this culture include what Peterson and Deal (2002) described as shared purpose shown through rituals, traditions, values, symbols, artifacts, and relationships that characterize a school's personality. Culture is important because it "shapes the way students, teachers, and administrators think, feel, and act" (Peterson & Deal, 2002, p. 9).

The application process to the Preuss School acts as a student's first introduction to a college-going culture. The application form resembles a college application and forces students to think about college at a very early age. Students describe their reasons for wanting to attend the school, discuss their commitment to the rigorous courses they will encounter, and express their interest and desire in attending college.[2] From the first day of school, students become immersed in exploring different types of colleges and learning about requirements, costs, and potential sources of support. They tour the UCSD campus on special enrichment activities and interact with college tutors on a daily basis.

The college application process, including writing college essays, becomes a regular part of the student's advisory curriculum beginning in high school. High school students take courses at the university and intern on campus, giving them access to the library and professors, thereby increasing their cultural capital and connecting them to valuable social networks. The Preuss School requires that all students apply to at least one University of California, California State University, and private college or university. This combination of actions both fosters a college-going culture at the school and assists students' application and admission to colleges.

Parents are also educated early about college requirements, costs, and sources of aid. University outreach officers provide much of the parental information in the early middle years. In the high school years, the college counselor and advisory teachers conduct regular application and financial aid workshops for students and their parents, making the option of going to college an integral part of students' and parents' lives.

Other symbols that focus students on college are the location of the school and the daily presence of UCSD students as tutors and interns. Operating on university grounds acts to integrate students into the culture of learning associated with a university campus. UCSD students serve as role models for the students they tutor. Preuss students rotate through their eight classes on alternate days mimicking the college Monday–Wednesday–Friday and Tuesday–Thursday class schedules.

One recent interchange in a classroom highlights how clearly the students share common beliefs and attitudes about attending college. A sixth grader working on a particular math problem was approached by a visitor and asked why he thought he needed to learn fractions. Without hesitation, he answered, "Because I'll need it for college."

Rigorous Courses

Students benefit from taking rigorous courses as well as attending school on the UCSD campus, because students enrolled in higher level courses perform better than those in low-level courses. "In California, only 35% of our students successfully complete the college readiness curriculum...currently 3 out of 4 African American and nearly 4 out of 5 Latino graduates are not eligible for admission to the UC/CSU systems for lack of access to, and enrollment in an appropriate high school curriculum" (Ali, 2002, p. 6). Even those minority students who score in the top quartiles on objective tests are frequently not enrolled in a rigorous course of study.

Preuss School students have no choice in the core curriculum. They all take the same college-prep classes at each grade level (with some exceptions for higher achieving mathematics students who may take university classes).

The curriculum symbolizes the high expectations that the school has for each child, which further emphasizes the culture of learning being instantiated at the school.

A Personalized Learning Environment

A personalized learning environment is also an important part of the culture of learning at the Preuss School. The school is small in comparison to most—300 at the middle school and 400 at the high school. Small schools and small classes enable students and teachers to get to know each other well and ensure that student achievement is monitored closely (Kluver & Rosenstock, 2002; Meier, 1995).

An advisory teacher who works with the same group of students from Grades 6 to 12 serves as their advocate and counselor. Because the advisory class is a regular class in the student's schedule, its importance is not compromised. Further, to ensure that the advisory teacher has adequate time to "do advisory work," the school provides the teachers with 6.5 release days per year. A trained on-site substitute rotates through the classes and provides quality instruction. During this time the advisory teachers observe their students in classes, communicate with parents, or conduct one-on-one conferences.

Block scheduling is also intended to personalize the students' lives. Students and teachers spend longer periods of time together in classes, enabling each teacher to get to know his or her students well, cognitively and developmentally.

Academic and Social Supports

A central tenet of the school is that students must have a variety of supports to meet the challenges of the rigorous curriculum. Most notably, the school extends its year by 18 days, keeping students and teachers together longer than the traditional year. This longer time in school gives students more opportunities to meet the rigorous academic demands. In a recent testimony before the University of California Regents, a Preuss graduate in her first year at the University spoke about her experience as a freshman: "I thought I couldn't possibly compete with anyone at UCSD but after taking my first mid-terms, I realized how prepared I was. All of the time and work at the Preuss School paid off more than I could ever imagine."

In addition to scaffolds, there must also be a systematic method to identify early those students who are struggling academically. The staff determined that the following elements would guide their efforts in building these supports:

1. Teaching strategies in the classroom that use the most current research on how students learn (Bransford, Brown, & Cocking, 1999).

2. An ongoing and weekly professional development model directed at assisting teachers to teach for understanding by using research-based methodologies.

3. An advisory class that provides supports in the form of peer collaboration, study skill methodologies, and information and dissemination of college information.

4. A method to help students remember the key skills needed for better understanding of concepts. The acronym I CLEAR (inquiry, collaboration, linking, evidence, application, and research) was developed by the initial founding staff and has become the school-wide organizational format around which to demonstrate student learning. Portfolios, for example, could be organized into the six areas, with student work inserted into the categories as an example of the skill used.

5. An early warning system that sets in motion a number of interventions to help students who are not meeting standards.

6. A system of tutoring—after-school, Saturdays, and in advisory classes—that serves to reinforce and remediate subject material.

Each of the supports is understood by the students to be an aid in their preparation for college. I CLEAR is used by all faculty members and is part of the school's culture. The number of students who are at risk decreases as they move through the grades, suggesting that these scaffolds are instrumental.

Establishing a Culture of Professional Learning to Improve Student Learning

Just as a culture of learning for students is a clear focus for the school, so is professional learning for teachers. To foster professional learning activities, the school has carved out staff development time for 2 hours each week. In that time, the teacher staff developer, who is a senior member of the faculty, provides teachers with opportunities to share strategies, learn new teaching techniques, meet as departments or grade levels, and collaborate for improved student learning. The weekly meetings are rich in content and give teachers an opportunity to learn by doing. For example, they might try out a new teaching strategy one week and bring it back for discussion the next week. Using the model found in *The Teaching Gap* (Stigler & Hiebert, 1999) as a guide, the staff engages in lesson study, where teachers plan a lesson together and then observe one another teaching it. After the lesson is taught once, it is critiqued and changed and taught again by one of the other teachers in the group.

The type of instruction that engages students and provides the background knowledge needed for deep understanding takes planning and preparation time. Teachers cannot develop projects, plan activities with the needs of learners in mind, or analyze materials without time. That is why the time that has been set out for teacher collaborative planning and sharing is so important. Respecting teachers' time is a part of the culture of learning at the school.

As a result of the ongoing and school-based professional development, teachers are made more aware of what it means to be a learner and how they must plan activities that take into account how students will better understand the material. Teachers dialogue frequently about professional development activities. If teachers request a change, the staff developer is responsive, because like students, teachers must have ownership in their own learning.

Preliminary Results

The first class graduated from the Preuss School in June 2004; 80% of the 55 graduates were attending 4-year colleges as of Fall 2004, including UCSD, UCLA, Berkeley, MIT, Stanford, NYU, Dartmouth, and Spellman; the remaining 20% will attend community colleges—with their transfer to UC campuses guaranteed in 2 years. In addition, McClure and Morales (2004) presented some notable test score information and course-taking patterns about Preuss School students:

- Preuss School students scored above the 50th percentile in reading on the CAT/6 reading test in 2002–2003; greater than 80% of Grade 9 to 12 Latino and Asian students scored at or above the 50th percentile in reading.

- The percentage of students scoring at or above the 50th percentile on the CAT/6 Mathematics test ranged from 70% for 8th graders to 83% for 10th graders in 2002–2003.

- 90% of the Preuss School graduating class of 2004 passed both portions of the California High School Exit Exam by March 2003; 92% of the 2005 graduating class passed both portions of the California High School Exit Exam by March 2003.

- Students in the 8th through 11th grades wrote 327 AP exams during the 2002–2003 school year; 37% received a score of 3 or higher (which earns college credit).

- Every member of the Preuss School graduating class completed the UC/CSU A-G requirement; the rate for the graduating classes in San Diego County from 2000 to 2003 ranged from 35% to 39%.

- Ninety-eight percent of the class of 2004 took the SAT-I in 2002–2003; the California average was 37% and the SDCS average was 49%.

- The Preuss School average SAT combined score was 984; the California average was 1012, and the San Diego County and SDCS average was 1003.

- In 2002–2003, the Preuss School had the highest API scores in San Diego County for schools with greater than 80% of students eligible for meal assistance and ranked in the top 10 of all schools, regardless of meal assistance eligibility.

Summary and Conclusions

Detracking is often associated with the removal of courses with differentiated curriculum. In addition to making that structural change at the Preuss School, the faculty and founding principal have made cultural changes to foster instruction and learning. The structures that have been developed to ensure that all students at the Preuss School UCSD are prepared for college also define the culture of the school. From the location on the college campus, to the extension of time in school, Preuss students are immersed in a culture of learning. The academic supports such as tutoring, mentoring, advisory classes, and the structure of the school day are also symbolic of the importance of time and effort to meet the goal of academic preparation.

A considerable body of research (e.g., Bowles & Gintis, 1976; Coleman et al., 1966; Jencks et al., 1978; Jencks & Phillips, 1998; Jencks et al., 1972) suggests that the socioeconomic conditions that students bring with them to school are more influential on their academic outcomes than what happens inside schools. The Preuss School at UCSD counters that assertion and provides an existence proof that students from low-income backgrounds can succeed in a rigorous course of study when provided the appropriate academic and social supports.

The question of replicability is often raised in discussions about the Preuss School. Critics ask: "The circumstances surrounding the school are so unique—how could they ever be duplicated anywhere else?" We have two answers to the question of replicability. First, UCSD is already serving as a model for university–school partnerships; most notably, we are adapting the principles learned at the Preuss School to Gompers Charter Middle School, a No Child Left Behind program improvement school. In addition, other universities are asking us about how to establish college-prep charter schools on or near their campuses. Of course, these would not be exact replicas of the Preuss School at UCSD; any university would develop an appropriate school to meet the needs of its local contexts.

Second, the school has developed a combination of components that contributes to accelerated student achievement and college eligibility. Those educators committed to improving the opportunities of underserved students to learn may be able to adopt these practices in the context of their own school improvement efforts.

NOTES

[1] For information about the formation of the Preuss School, see Rosen and Mehan (2003).

[2] Even if students are not selected for the school, at least they will have begun thinking about college. The application process influences more than Preuss's own students to imagine college as a future possibility (parent interview, 2002).

REFERENCES

Ali, R. (2002). *The high school diploma: Making it more than an empty promise.* Testimony before the California Senate Standing Committee on Education, Hearing on Senate Bill 1731, Sacramento, CA.

Bowles, S., & Gintis, H. (1976). *Schooling in capitalist America.* New York: Basic Books.

Brandon, K. (2004, May 4). Poor kids thrive in charter school. *Chicago Tribune*, p. 10.

Bransford, J., Brown, A., & Cocking, R. (Eds.). (1999). *How people learn: Brain, mind, experience and school.* Washington, DC: National Academy Press.

Bruner, J. (1986). *Actual minds, possible worlds.* Cambridge, MA: Harvard University Press.

Burris, C., & Welner, K. (2005). Closing the achievement gap by detracking. *Phi Delta Kappan*, 594–598.

Cicourel, A., & Mehan, H. (1985). Universal development, stratifying practices and status attainment. *Social Stratification and Mobility, 4,* 3–27.

Coleman, J., Campbell, E., Hobson, C., McPartland, J., Mood, A., Weinfeld, F., et al. (1966). *Equality of educational opportunity.* Washington, DC: U.S. Office of Education.

Comer, J. (1988). Educating poor minority children. *Scientific American, 259*(5), 42–48.

Education Trust. (2003a). *African American achievement in America.* Washington, DC. Retrieved November 4, 2005, from http://www.edtrust.org

Education Trust. (2003b). *Latino achievement in America.* Washington, DC. Retrieved November 4, 2005, from http://www.edtrust.org

Haycock, K., & Navarro, S. (1988). *Unfinished business.* Oakland, CA: Achievement Council.

Jencks, C., Bartlett, S., Corcoran, M., Crouse, J., Eaglesfield, D., Jackson, G., et al. (1978). *Who gets ahead? The determinants of economic success in America.* New York: Basic Books.

Jencks, C., & Phillips, M. (Eds.). (1998). *The Black–White test score gap.* Washington, DC: The Brookings Institution.

Jencks, C., Smith, M., Acland, H., Bane, M., Cohen, D., Gintis, H., et al. (1972). *Inequality: A reassessment of the effect of family and schooling in America.* New York: Basic Books.

Kluver, J., & Rosenstock, L. (2002). *Choice and diversity: Irreconcilable differences?* San Diego, CA: High Tech High.

Levin, H. (1987). Accelerated schools for disadvantaged students. *Educational Leadership, 44*(6), 19–21.

Lucas, S. (1999). *Tracking inequality: Stratification and mobility in American high schools.* New York: Teachers College Press.

McClure, L., & Morales, J. (2004). *The Preuss School at UCSD: School characteristics and students' achievement.* San Diego: University of California, San Diego. Retrieved November 4, 2005, from http://create.ucsd.edu/Research_Evaluaton/

Mehan, H., Habbard, L., Villanueva, I., & Lintz, A. (1996). *Constructing school success: The consequences of untracking low-achieving students.* Cambridge: Cambridge University Press.

Mehan, H., Hertweck, A., & Meihls, L. (1986). *Handicapping the handicapped: Decision making in students' educational careers.* Stanford, CA: Stanford University Press.

Meier, D. (1995). *The power of their ideas: Lessons from a small school in Harlem.* Boston: Beacon Press.

Mercer, J. (1975). *Labeling the mentally retarded.* Berkeley: University of California Press.

Oakes, J. (2003). *Critical conditions for equity and diversity in college access: Informing policy and monitoring results.* Los Angeles: UC ACCORD.

Oakes, J., Gamoran, A., & Page, R. (1992). Curriculum differentiation: Opportunities, outcomes and meanings. In P. Jackson (Ed.), *Handbook of research on curriculum* (pp. 570–608). New York: Macmillan.

Oakes, J., & Wells, A. (1998). Detracking for high school achievement. *Educational Leadership, 56,* 38–41.

Peterson, K., & Deal, T. (2002). *The shaping school culture field book.* San Francisco: Jossey-Bass.

Resnick, L. (1995). From aptitude to effort: A new foundation for our schools. *Daedalus, 12*(4), 55–62.

Rosen, L., & Mehan, H. (2003). Reconstructing equality on new political ground: The politics of representation in the charter school debate at UCSD. *American Educational Research Journal, 40,* 655–682.

Sizer, T. (2004). *The red pencil.* New Haven, CT: Yale University Press.

Stigler, J., & Hiebert, J. (1999). *The teaching gap: Best ideas from the worlds' teachers for improving education in the classroom.* New York: Summit Books.

Wheelock, A. (1992). *Crossing the tracks: How "untracking" can save America's schools.* New York: The New Press.

Yonezawa, S., Wells, A., & Serna, I. (2002). Choosing tracks: Freedom of choice in detracking schools. *American Educational Research Journal, 39,* 37–67.

Discussion Guide: Reading This Book

Peter H. Johnston

RTI is literally about leaving no child behind in literacy learning. This book is intended to generate new ways of thinking about how best to accomplish that, now and for the future, and to help educators reflect on their current efforts in ways that might lead to change. The book is designed so that it does not have to be read cover to cover; although individuals will read the book, it will also be read by groups of educators, for example, in schools, school districts, and university classes. Each group will have different immediate goals and will be starting from different places, so even though reading the first couple of chapters will help provide a framework for thinking about RTI, from there on it will depend on your needs and interests.

Some people prefer to have questions and activities to help them think through what they have read. In this Discussion Guide, I have provided some of these for each section. Before using any of these questions, people should bring their questions, confusions, wonderings, and discoveries to the table. Everyone should realize, too, that the people reading the chapters will have diverse experiences and expertise with respect to literacy and the chapters will not all be equally accessible to all readers, so it is important to be able to think, I didn't get this part.

If you are using this book as a vehicle for change or for developing an RTI stance or program in your school, there are some important considerations. RTI in literacy brings up some long-standing conflicts in beliefs and values that can easily divide people based on their educational histories. Working for change and building new programs in the face of conflicting views require attending to the social conditions that allow productive disagreement, learning, and change.

RTI in Literacy—Responsive and Comprehensive, edited by Peter H. Johnston.
© 2010 by the International Reading Association.

Changing beliefs and values is not as simple as changing socks and underwear, although some dirty linen might be aired along the way. It is important to make clear from the start that you expect opinions to differ. Ask questions like, "What other views do people have?" and when you are more comfortable, "Can someone push back against that perspective?"

Talk in ways that do not push people into a corner. For example, "Can you help me understand this part of your thinking?" Let them know that you are listening to them and taking them seriously by reflecting back to them your paraphrasings and summaries: "Let me see if I have this right...." Inviting critique of your own thinking helps set a productive tone: "Are there places where you think my logic breaks down or I've missed something?" "Have I overgeneralized anywhere?" "Can anyone add to or clarify my thinking?" Making your logic concrete with specific examples makes it easier for people to see—and critically examine—your proposals. It also makes it easier to ask others to do the same: "Could you give me an example of that, so I can fully grasp what you're saying?" There are, of course, no-no's. Under no circumstances should you use fixed categories or personalized critique, such as, "Your literacy specialists always...."

RTI discussions are complicated further, because they can raise questions about work responsibilities, power, and change. Although disagreement can be very productive, dividing people is not. Consequently, if we are to use book discussions to think and act productively as a learning community, there are some principles that we have to commit to in our discussions. If the discussion group is diverse in any way, we can expect disagreement, which is good, because it makes everyone articulate the logic and assumptions of their position. In order for this to lead to learning, we have to assume that each person engaged in the discussion has positive intentions. Articulating the logic and assumptions of our ideas helps maintain the assumption of positive intentions. We can't just say, "I think..." without saying "because...." Once a logic has been laid out, it can be inquired into, expanded, or respectfully disagreed with.

Moving forward requires getting new ideas on the table, often well before they are ready for prime time. You have to have many half-baked ideas before the group can bake one or more into a productive plan of action. Consequently, group members need to commit to listening actively to others and to themselves and to assuming that an idea put on the table is not in its final form. Active listening requires waiting, asking questions, and paraphrasing to reflect ideas back for clarification. These principles are, of course, no different from what we should use to guide classroom discussions.

Similarly, when you are setting up a discussion group, be sure to avoid overload. Take manageable bites, keep a record of your discussions, and always close a session with a concrete plan of action. If you are an administrator, it is important that you help make time available to teachers and arrange for conditions that make it safe for participants to deprivatize their teaching to learn from one another and confront conflicting beliefs and values.

Section I—The Logic of RTI in Literacy

Chapter 1—Response to Intervention: An Overview: New Hope for Struggling Learners
Donna M. Scanlon and Joan M. Sweeney

RTI is not fundamentally new in many ways. However, in many locations, it provides a very different framework for thinking about learning disabilities. In your situation (e.g., school, district, community), consider the following questions:

- What new opportunities does RTI open?
- What percentage of students in your school are classified as learning disabled in literacy?
- Which concepts or beliefs in RTI go against the grain of current school thinking, and which are likely to be hardest for people to agree with or adjust to?
- What obstacles do you see to implementing a focus on prevention and instruction?

Section II—High-Quality Classroom Literacy Instruction (Tier 1)

Chapter 2—What I've Learned About Effective Reading Instruction From a Decade of Studying Exemplary Elementary Classroom Teachers
Richard L. Allington

Chapter 3—Reading Growth in High-Poverty Classrooms: The Influence of Teacher Practices That Encourage Cognitive Engagement in Literacy Learning
Barbara M. Taylor, P. David Pearson, Debra S. Peterson, and Michael C. Rodriguez

Chapter 4—Decisions, Decisions: Responding to Primary Students During Guided Reading
Robert M. Schwartz

High-quality classroom instruction is the most important component of the overall RTI plan, because any intervention beyond that is likely to disrupt learning communities and create complexities and communication gaps that can be difficult to address.

- A good topic of conversation to begin with is what would make the RTI plan more (and less) likely that you would make your teaching public, particularly the parts that are not going as well as you would like?

- Use Allington's six T's of effective elementary literacy instruction—time, texts, teaching, talk, tasks, and testing—to analyze your classroom. Do only two dimensions at once. Bring data to the group for discussion.

- In what ways does your instruction and curriculum privilege this student's engagement in literate activities?

- What percentage of your prompts for book discussions are open (have no predetermined answer)? How often do the students respond directly to one another's comments about books rather than to or through the teacher?

- How often do the students and teacher make the *process* of their thinking and problem solving publicly available?

- How does the decision making described by Robert M. Schwartz fit with your daily decision making? What questions does it raise?

- One way to examine the qualities of your instruction is to shadow a student for whom your instruction is less successful than you would like. Focusing on data for one student is one way to find leaks in your overall program. Gather the following data to share in your problem-solving group:

  o How many words did the student read and write during the course of the day (or period)? Compare this with the experience of students for whom instruction seems to be going well. Multiplying the data by the number of days in a school year will give an important comparison.

  o How many words did the student offer in genuine discussion of a text?

  o What percentage of the time was the student reading material with an error rate of no more than one word in 15?

  o In what ways are reading and writing set up to be engaging for this student?

Before you begin to collect the data, make a prediction for each category. After you have collected and presented the data, consider what you will change and make plans to effect those changes.

Section III—Literacy Assessment

Chapter 5—Thinking Straight About Measures of Early Reading Development
Scott G. Paris

Chapter 6—Responsive Intervention: What Is the Role of Appropriate Assessment?
Anne McGill-Franzen, Rebecca L. Payne, and Danielle V. Dennis

Chapter 7—A Comprehensive Assessment System as a Response to Intervention Process
Linda J. Dorn and Shannon Coman Henderson

Chapter 8—Helping a Learning-Disabled Child Enter the Literate World
Carol A. Lyons

Assessment has to do with the gathering and use of data for a purpose, and there are two crucial sides to assessment. One side is construct validity, which is the extent to which data provide a good reflection of the characteristic, or construct, of interest—in this case, literacy. The other side is consequential validity, which is the consequence of the assessment practice. Because literacy is complex, a single kind of data will not give a good picture of a student's literacy development or a teacher's teaching. It is important, then, to use multiple data sources to inform decisions, plus each data source is limited by particular kinds of error. For the following discussion questions, the important thing is to focus on evidence to decide what should be done as a consequence.

- In what ways do your assessments reflect the complexity of literacy?

- Discuss as a group which qualities in students' literacy development you particularly value. Bring to the discussion group all of the assessment data you have on a student you have difficulty teaching. Talk about what each piece of data tells you and how it relates to the qualities you value. Which data might shore up the difference?

- After Chapters 6, 7, and 8, ask, How could we do that here? What are the obstacles? How could we overcome them? Remember, you don't have to have everyone do something at once. It is perfectly reasonable to pilot changes.

- After reading Chapter 5 by Scott G. Paris, make a list of your data sources (assessments) and check to what extent they are dependent on constrained skills.

- Is your RTI approach more oriented toward *identifying* students with learning disabilities or *preventing* students from acquiring or being handicapped by them? You might construct a table with columns of evidence for each. Alternatively, you might construct a two-column table with assessments on one side and the questions that the assessments answer on the other side, so you can examine those questions that your assessments are answering.

- How can you ensure that your assessments draw attention to the reading and writing *processes*—the strategies students use and where they are in control of literate processes?

- How do your assessment practices expand teachers' (and other school community members') teaching expertise?

- How do your assessment practices ensure that the students most in need of support get the support they need?

- How does the data you gather inform teaching strategies for particular students?

- How does your learning community use data to improve instruction? How might you maximize this use?

- What data do you use to improve your teaching interactions with students with whom you are unsuccessful?

  o Arrange to spend 15 minutes working with a student who you think is benefiting least from your instruction and record the session. Repeat with a student who is benefiting appropriately from classroom instruction.

  o Listen to the recording and tally (a) the wait times for each of your interactions and (b) the focus of your response (i.e., print detail vs. meaning, correct vs. partially correct vs. error, correction vs. setting up self-correction, process vs. accuracy).

  o Compare your interactions with these two different students and share with your group.

- How are you gathering and using data that help you refine your interactions with the students with whom you are least successful?

- Describe the learning of a student you are having the most difficulty teaching. Examine each other's descriptions for instances where you have focused on what the student cannot do or doesn't know rather than what he or she knows and can do. Look for instances in which you have used fixed-characteristic language, such as *treatment resister* or *poor reader*. Rewrite the description focusing centrally on what the student knows and can do and what he or she is beginning to do or sometimes does.

Section IV—High-Quality Interventions in Literacy

Chapter 9—Reading Recovery: A Major Component of Many RTI Models
Salli Forbes, Beth Swenson, Tonya Person, and Jolene Reed

Chapter 10—Kindergarten Intervention: Teaching to Prevent Reading Difficulties
Donna M. Scanlon and Joan M. Sweeney

Chapter 11—An Adapted Interactive Writing Intervention for the Kindergarten Classroom: Creating a Framework for Responsive Teaching
Sharon A. Craig

Chapter 12—Closing the Gaps: Literacy for the Hardest-to-Teach
Gwenneth Phillips and Pauline Smith

When we decide that we cannot adequately accelerate a student's growth in the classroom, we often decide to take other steps to accelerate learning using interventions either inside or outside the classroom. The interventions must be research based, and we need to monitor and expand their effectiveness. Even if we decide that a student has a specific learning disability, we must continue to gather data that will help us improve our instruction for that student.

- What is the *specific* research that supports the intervention you are using or considering using? Which measures were used to show effectiveness in that research?

- How can you use these research-based models to focus your intervention measures?

- How does your intervention address students' literacy learning at and beyond the word level, both in writing and in reading?

- How are you helping students to understand from the beginning that reading and writing are related and are about making meaning and doing meaningful things? What does it sound like?

- Where is writing in your interventions?

- How can you mount an intervention focused on a third chance?

- What would make it possible for people to deprivatize their teaching, sharing data on their interactions for problem solving? What are the obstacles?

Section V—Professional Development and Teacher Expertise

Chapter 13—A Child's Response to Intervention Requires a Responsive Teacher of Reading
Mary K. Lose

Chapter 14—Reducing the Incidence of Early Reading Difficulties: Professional Development for Classroom Teachers Versus Direct Interventions for Children
Donna M. Scanlon, Lynn M. Gelzheiser, Frank R. Vellutino, Christopher Schatschneider, and Joan M. Sweeney

Chapter 15—Reflective Coaching Conversations: A Missing Piece
Debra S. Peterson, Barbara M. Taylor, Bobbie Burnham, and Rynell Schock

Chapter 16—The Learning Schools Model of School Change to Raise Achievement in Reading Comprehension for Culturally and Linguistically Diverse Students in New Zealand
Stuart McNaughton and Mei Kuin Lai

This section of the book assumes that the heart of effective interventions lies in adaptive, responsive teaching and that the development of teacher expertise and teacher learning communities is at the heart of preventing students from becoming learning disabled. These chapters show evidence, in fact, that one form of productive intervention is professional development. One important source for developing professional expertise is the detailed knowledge of one student allowing more detailed observations of another.

- List the similarities among the expertise-expanding strategies used in Chapters 1, 6, 9, 10, 12, 14, and 16 through 19. How could these common practices be implemented in your school?

- How can you make the productive practices of some teachers in the school available to other teachers for learning?
- How can you expand the ability to notice and respond to what students can and cannot do, know and do not know?
- In what ways does the school or district support teachers' learning communities?
- Which school organizational structures support the expansion of expertise at the individual and learning community levels?
- What does it require to be a coach in this school? What qualifications and experiences do coaches need before and during coaching? Do the coaches have ongoing experience teaching students who are experiencing the most difficulties and groups of students? How could coaching be improved in this school, and how can you maximize the coaches' expertise?
- Bring to your teacher-learning group all of the data you have on a student who is not profiting from your teaching. Use it to describe what you know about the student's literacy development. Invite discussion of your data with the goal of creating a plan for further data gathering and instructional strategies.

Section VI—Systemic Intervention

Chapter 17—A Comprehensive Intervention Model for Preventing Reading Failure: A Response to Intervention Process
Linda J. Dorn and Barbara Schubert

Chapter 18—Use Students' Summer-Setback Months to Raise Minority Achievement
Richard L. Allington and Anne McGill-Franzen

Chapter 19—Whole-School Detracking: A Strategy for Equity and Excellence
Doris Alvarez and Hugh Mehan

Keeping the bigger picture in mind as we try to help all students become capable literacy learners is important so that we don't get stuck with a bunch of unconnected interventions and don't lose sight of our overall goals. Keeping the bigger picture in mind can also help us monitor the opportunity costs of particular strategies. For example, focusing our attention centrally on phonic analysis in the early grades can lead to a reduction in vocabulary and comprehension development. Reminding ourselves that a school culture of inquiry and procedures that constantly expand teachers' and administrators' professional knowledge will help reduce the number of students who encounter difficulties. Thinking big, like Alvarez and Mehan, requires boldness and a clear understanding of the larger goals of schooling and the central principles for learning in schools and classrooms, particularly an engaging curriculum linked to a future of hope.

- How is your learning community set up to be sustained in its learning? What are the institutional obstacles to professional learning? Which personnel are not part of the learning community?

- Which institutional structures, such as summer breaks, are not well set up to optimize student development? How might these be changed?

- Gather data on the persistent effects of summer on students' learning in your school. Contemplate the cost of the summer drop-off.

- For one day, follow, or have someone follow, a student who is not benefiting well from instruction and is receiving either special education services or some sort of literacy support. Consider differences in the curriculum he or she encounters and the time spent on noninstructional activities.

- How are local data used to detect and solve problems with instruction in a timely manner and to build professional expertise?

- How are local data used to detect and solve institutional problems?

- How do we bring transfer students into the learning community, particularly those who have been unsuccessful in other contexts?

- Which school structures and procedures keep the various professionals in the school (e.g., teachers, administrators, special education teachers, speech therapists, school psychologists, teacher aides) in a productive, common conversation?